EDI DEVELOPMENT STUDIES

Unemployment, Restructuring, and the Labor Market in Eastern Europe and Russia

Edited by
Simon Commander
Fabrizio Coricelli

The World Bank
Washington, D. C.

The Economic Development Institute (EDI) was established by the World Bank in 1955 to train officials concerned with development planning, policymaking, investment analysis, and project implementation in member developing countries. At present the substance of the EDI's work emphasizes macroeconomic and sectoral economic policy analysis. Through a variety of courses, seminars, and workshops, most of which are given overseas in cooperation with local institutions, the EDI seeks to sharpen analytical skills used in policy analysis and to broaden understanding of the experience of individual countries with economic development. Although the EDI's publications are designed to support its training activities, many are of interest to a much broader audience. EDI materials, including any findings, interpretations, and conclusions, are entirely those of the authors and should not be attributed in any manner to the World Bank, to its affiliated organizations, or to members of its Board of Executive Directors or the countries they represent.

Because of the informality of this series and to make the publication available with the least possible delay, the manuscript has not been edited as fully as would be the case with a more formal document, and the World Bank accepts no responsibility for errors. Some sources cited in this book may be informal documents that are not readily available.

The material in this publication is copyrighted. Requests for permission to reproduce portions of it should be sent to the Office of the Publisher at the address shown in the copyright notice above. The World Bank encourages dissemination of its work and will normally give permission promptly and, when the reproduction is for noncommercial purposes, without asking a fee. Permission to copy portions for classroom use is granted through the Copyright Clearance Center Inc., Suite 910, 222 Rosewood Drive, Danvers, Massachusetts 01923, U. S. A.

The backlist of publications by the World Bank is shown in the annual *Index of Publications*, which is available from Distribution Unit, Office of the Publisher, The World Bank, 1818 H Street, N.W., Washington, D.C. 20433, U.S.A., or from Publications, Banque mondiale, 66, avenue d'Iéna, 75116 Paris, France.

Simon Commander is principal economist in the National Economic Management Division of the World Bank's Economic Development Institute, and Fabrizio Coricelli is associate professor of economics at the University of Siena, Italy.

Library of Congress Cataloging-in-Publication Data

Unemployment, restructuring, and the labor market in Eastern Europe
  and Russia / edited by Simon Commander, Fabrizio Coricelli.
      p.   cm.—(EDI development studies, ISSN 1020-105X)
    Includes bibliographical references and index.
    ISBN 0-8213-2988-X
    1. Labor market—Europe, Eastern. 2. Europe, Eastern—Economic
  conditions—1989–   3. Unemployment—Europe, Eastern. 4. Labor
  market—Russia (Federation) 5. Russia (Federation)—Economic
  conditions—1991–   6. Unemployment—Russia (Federation)
  I. Commander, Simon.   II. Coricelli, Fabrizio.   III. Series.
  HD5764.7.A6U54   1994
  331.12'0947—dc20   94-29583
                                                               CIP

Contents

Foreword

When transition started in Eastern Europe and in Russia, it was clear that unemployment would emerge and that, at least initially, job losses were likely to be large given the size of the shocks and the disruption to systems of production and trade. How large that unemployment would be and for how long it would persist was, and to some extent remains, an unknown. This book is a first attempt at examining this phenomenon and provides a coherent framework for thinking about changes to employment in the countries that are undergoing substantial transition.

Several important and general findings emerge. First, state and privatized firms have actively sought to adapt to new relative prices and markets, even if they have commonly faced major constraints, including the inadequacy of capital for restructuring. State firms in almost all countries reduced employment and sought to rationalize production. Governments signaled, and to a significant extent imposed, hard budget constraints on state firms. In some countries, a reformed commercial banking system has begun to impose market rationality to credit allocation, exposing the failures of many enterprises but also inducing adjustment and rewarding improved performance. Incomes policies and fears of unemployment similarly translated into wage restraint by workers.

Second, while there has been impressive growth in the private sector in most of the countries, many of those who have lost their former state sector jobs are either unemployed or have left the labor force. Most new employment has been generated by private firms engaged in trade and services, for which the skills acquired in the state-owned sector are not appropriate.

While the effects of privatization are still difficult to identify, the large-scale voucher privatization in the Czech Republic has successfully drawn in outside investors and the local population as shareholders, while allowing the government to withdraw. Although with more hesitancy, a similar picture seems to be emerging in Russia. Over time, we can expect the appropriate discipline on firm behavior to emerge. By contrast, more piecemeal or inconsistent privatization strategies have generally failed to stop financing from the budget to state firms and have sent the wrong signal to workers and managers. In limbo, state firms, as the Bulgarian example highlights all too well, will not only remain claimants on public finances but will tend to be a source of wage pressure in the economy. Further, the absence of restructuring has a powerful negative impact on the private sector, crowding out resources and sending the wrong signals. The result is likely to be low aggregate levels of employment.

A final and critical lesson that emerges from this book is that steps to a more efficient allocation of labor resources in the transitional economies and to a well-functioning labor market depend very powerfully on a sound macroeconomic policy. This confirms results from elsewhere and would argue against tradeoffs between structural adjustment and stabilization, even where privatization has preceded stabilization (as in Russia).

As is well known, in Eastern Europe and in Russia, the costs of these shifts have been large. For workers who find themselves unemployed, the chances of getting back into paid employment are low. Long-run unemployment has emerged as a major phenomenon. This share already exceeds 50 percent on a rising trend in Eastern Europe, as against a West European average of under 40 percent, at unemployment rates on average at least 3 to 4 percentage points above Western European averages.

Aside from the large social costs, which will clearly play back into the political arena and future decisions on reform, long-run unemployment will weaken the more desirable effects that unemployment might create in the labor market. The presence of some unemployment is critical, at least initially, if private sector growth is to occur in the transitional economy. Slack in the labor market will tend to reduce pressures for wage growth in the economy, and a low wage is a major factor motivating the creation of jobs in the private sector. But if long-run unemployment in Eastern Europe exhibits the same duration effects that have been observed in OECD countries, this may result in a relatively weak effect of unemployment on wage behavior. In this case the clear danger is that equilibrium unemployment will tend to be high, and we should not expect major improvements to the unemployment rates currently observed.

Some of the lessons from OECD experience are clearly relevant here and may be used to help reduce labor market rigidities. There are still many impediments to mobility across labor markets, most noticeably in access to housing and infrastructure. Large dispersion in regional unemployment rates appears to be common to all countries. One clear option is to allocate over time more resources to infrastructural investments designed to reduce mobility constraints. Although there have been some isolated successes, across the region the problems of divestiture of social assets remain as a thorny and politically sensitive issue to be resolved. While the gradual development of a housing and rental market will be an important factor promoting mobility, regional inequalities in unemployment will likely be reduced by projects that facilitate commuting to and contact with areas of higher labor demand. A second, complementary option is the use of active labor market programs, such as training and other skill-forming programs, and the selective use of marginal wage subsidies targeted at the long-run unemployed that hold more promise than simply providing unemployment benefits or social assistance. The Czech Republic, which continues to have a very low aggregate unemployment rate and a low share of long-run unemployed, is the one case in the East where active programs have been an important policy choice.

Michael Bruno
Vice President, Development Economics
and Chief Economist
The World Bank

Acknowledgments

The research on which this book is based has been generously supported by the World Bank's Research Committee and by the Economic Development Institute of the World Bank. The editors would particularly like to thank Amnon Golan, Peter Knight, and Alan Gelb for their consistent support. Vittorio Corbo was very helpful at the start of the project. Nancy Birdsall and Michael Bruno have also helped us significantly.

During the course of the research, two workshops were organized at Dobris and Stirin Castles in the Czech Republic, as well as a larger conference at the World Bank in Washington, D.C., in October 1993. These occasions were most ably put together by Helena Bambassova, Helena Ott, Dulce Afzal, and Jane Madden.

In preparing this volume, John Didier of the Economic Development Institute's Studies and Training Design Division was essential in ensuring a rapid and high-quality publication, Caroline McEuen was responsible for copy-editing, and Alicia Etchebarne-Bourdin did an excellent job of giving form to the manuscript. The mechanics of the research project were superbly handled by Olga del Cid, as were all budgetary matters by Crummella Medley.

We would like to thank the Organization for Economic Cooperation and Development (OECD) in Paris and the Center for Economic Research and Graduate Education and the Economics Institute (CERGE/EI) in Prague for their collaboration.

Contributors

Iskra Beleva	Institute of Economics, Bulgarian Academy of Sciences, Sofia
Olivier Blanchard	Massachusetts Institute of Technology, Cambridge
Tito Boeri	OECD, Paris
Michael C. Burda	Humboldt University of Berlin
Simon Commander	The World Bank, Washington, D.C.
Fabrizio Coricelli	University of Siena
John S. Earle	Central European University, Prague
Krzysztof Hagemejer	Warsaw University and the International Labour Organization, Geneva
John Ham	University of Pittsburgh
Richard Jackman	London School of Economics
Janos Köllô	Institute of Economics, Hungarian Academy of Sciences, Budapest
John McHale	Harvard University, Cambridge
Mariela Nenova-Amar	Agency for Economic Coordination and Development, Sofia
Gheorghe Oprescu	Polytechnic University of Bucharest
Krzysztof Rybinski	Warsaw University and Stefan Batory Foundation
Jan Svejnar	University of Pittsburgh and CERGE-EI, Prague
Katherine Terrell	University of Pittsburgh and CERGE-EI, Prague
Cecilia Ugaz	The World Bank, Washington, D.C.
Balacs Vilagi	Institute of Economics, Hungarian Academy of Sciences, Budapest
Ruslan Yemtsov	Moscow State University and the World Bank, Washington, D.C.

Introduction

Simon Commander and Fabrizio Coricelli

In only a few years, unemployment has become one of the most critical issues facing the transitional economies in Eastern Europe, and increasingly in the countries of the former Soviet Union (FSU). As of early 1994, in Eastern Europe 10-15 percent of the region's labor force lacked work and over 40 percent had been jobless for more than a year. Even in Russia, where registered unemployment barely exceeded 2 percent, household and labor force surveys indicate unemployment already in excess of 6 percent. The significance of this change cannot be underestimated. Under central planning, workers in these economies virtually had been guaranteed full employment, creating a network of bloated and unproductive state enterprises. With the collapse of the centrally planned economy, governments abandoned the objective of maintaining full employment. For the first time in decades, large numbers of workers found themselves out of work.

It has been widely accepted that unemployment was a necessary result of the resource reallocation that would occur as former state-owned enterprises privatized, restructured, and shed labor. The earlier regime of full employment was unsustainable. Yet contrary to some expectations, private sector growth has only partially offset the decline in state employment. As a result, unemployment has expanded rapidly, with little downward pressure yet discernible. For those in unemployment, exit probabilities to jobs have remained low. Moreover, the bulk of jobs that have been lost have been lost because of macroeconomic or aggregate shocks to output, rather than the hypothesized reallocation of resources across firms and sectors. One consequence is that high unemployment has emerged as an obstacle to restructuring of the economy and for the privatization of state firms. Indeed, the economic and political costs of high unemployment levels have affected the overall reform process, slowing restructuring and discrediting reform governments. Today, some of the most pressing issues facing the economies in transition revolve around slowing the growth of unemployment and bringing the long-term jobless back into the active labor force.

This volume is a first attempt at understanding the nature and dynamics of the transition in Eastern Europe and Russia from the perspective of the labor market. It is mainly organized around a set of country chapters (Chapters 1-6) that provide a detailed analysis of the changes since the start of the respective transitions. The objective of these country chapters is to take a close look, using both official and survey data, at the evolutions of output, employment, wages, and unemployment, distinguishing over sector, region, and other key variables. They also explicitly focus on the effects of macroeconomic policy and institutional changes—particularly with respect to ownership and title change—on the labor market.

The simple framework underlying the country studies is one in which the transition is characterized by the decline of the state sector and the rise of a private sector, with their asymmetric evolution yielding unemployment. The country chapters focus in detail on the interaction of these three labor market states. In particular, these chapters focus on the behavior of the large state firm sector, looking at the influence of macroeconomic, sector, and firm-specific variables on the decisions made with respect to employment levels and wages, and also with regard to the impact of ownership change on these decisions. The evolution of the private sector and its capacity for labor absorption is strongly conditioned by the nature and rate of decline in the state sector. The country studies give us a feel for the different evolutions arising from different paths of ownership reform and policy toward state firms.

While the simple distinction over state and private firms obviously camouflages some of the important nuances, it provides a sufficiently general and analytically convenient way of organizing our results. This framework is made explicit in Chapter 7, which also provides an overview of the country experiences. Chapter 8 discusses the role of labor market institutions and the consequences of different labor market policies across the region, emphasizing the likely gains to a greater reliance on active as opposed to passive labor market policies. Finally, Chapter 9 takes a comparative view of unemployment dynamics and policy and emphasizes the need to address the problem of a stagnant pool of unemployed and the associated long-run unemployment that has emerged.

Although considerable local color remains in these transition experiences—particularly in the Russian case—certain common themes emerge from the work reported in this volume. In addition, the chapters raise a host of puzzles or ambiguities that, for both empirical and analytical reasons, have as yet few answers. What follows is thus an attempt at summarizing the main results and indicating the areas for further work.

Firm Behavior: Employment and Wages

The country chapters verify that while employment changes have generally lagged those to output, declines in state employment have indeed been large, with most of that decline until recently *not* accounted for by privatization and title change. At the start of the transitions, state firms moved slowly, cutting employment by attrition, early retirements, and other voluntary means. This was associated with quite large movements out of the labor force, in part the result of a decline in high inherited participation rates. Only where shocks were sufficiently large, as in Bulgaria, did involuntary separations figure in a major way early in the transition. A second phase followed in which layoffs and involuntary separations increased, raising the inflow rate to unemployment. The timing appears to be explained by a combination of changes in the financing environment for state firms, by announced changes to ownership, and by some rearrangement in the internal bargaining powers of workers and managers. Although it is far too early to assert that hard budget constraints have been imposed on state firms inducing profit-maximizing behavior, it is generally evident that there has been significant tightening in their access to subsidies, credits, and other forms of financial support, whether through the budget or the banking system. Even when this tightening has been weak or episodic—as in Romania and Russia—it has nevertheless translated into nontrivial employment declines, whether explicit or through resort to short time and involuntary leave. In short, state firms have commonly induced significant reductions in employment even prior to privatization. What is less easy to interpret is the apparent size of gross flows in and out of state firms, as discussed in Chapter 7. These seem to be capturing a diversity of responses, some of which are consistent with a restructuring story, but others—such as that indicated in Chapter 4 on Russia—have to be related to bargaining over subsidies and technological considerations.

This may partly be explained by a shift in bargaining powers within firms as managers have gained greater autonomy and decisionmaking rights in relation to workers. Yet the cross-country differences in the allocation of the impact of negative shocks between employment and wages between settings in which workers appear to have more bargaining power, such as Poland, Bulgaria, and Romania, as against Hungary and the Czech Republic, where workers seem more passive, is far from obvious. For example, Chapter 5 indicates that at least initially the shock was absorbed principally in employment in Bulgaria, whereas in the former Czechoslovakia the shock was taken by wages. While there is no obviously strict or predictable association between the extent of worker bargaining power and the employment-wage choice, the general impression is that a larger worker voice has translated into more gradual employment adjustment. Avoidance or limitation of involuntary separations and layoffs has remained an important objective for both managers and workers in state firms. Chapter 6, for instance, clearly shows that Romanian industries that receive subsidies and preferential government assistance have adjusted employment least, controlling for output and energy price shocks. Further, these protected industries have experienced relative wage increases. And even when unions or other labor organizations have exercised little direct say in firm decisions, their implicit voice may not have been small.

Evidence from a number of countries—Bulgaria, Poland, Romania, and Slovakia—suggests that the process of employment reduction is by no means linear. Phases of accelerated involuntary separations have been followed by clear slowing down, with firms continuing to hoard labor. This appears to be explained primarily by political economy factors, as governments, sensitive to the aggregate unemployment rate, have partially sanctioned labor hoarding by relaxing financial constraints. And a satisfactory measure of the extent and channels that allow the budget constraint facing firms to remain soft is still elusive. Although subsidies through the budget have declined, credits to heavily indebted firms from the banking system continue. In some cases, as in Hungary, this has led to large and repeated bail-outs of the financial system by government. In addition, tax relief, nonpayment of social security contributions, and other mechanisms have been used to support state firms.

The offset provided by growth in private sector employment has been far from trivial. In almost all cases, a new private sector has emerged rapidly, for the most part concentrated in services. This has led to a clear shift in the structure of output and employment, with more movement toward Western European ratios, in part correcting for inherited sectoral imbalances. Nevertheless, the share of manufacturing remains high in all cases. The overall impression is that the first flush of private sector growth has been complementary to inherited production and has occurred mostly among small firms, often with high failure rates. The rate of expansion of such private jobs has obviously not only been a function of the size of the gap to be filled. Although the Czech Republic and Bulgaria, for example, had quite similar initial conditions, the former has experienced very substantial growth in services employment, the latter surprisingly little. Combinations of the size of the initial shocks and the resulting aggregate demand effects, locational good fortune, and government policy have been critical factors explaining these differences.

But the obvious question that arises is whether having completed the stock adjustment, can further growth be expected from such initiatives? The answer is unclear. At the same time, the likely employment path for privatized firms, the bulk of which are not in services, is yet to be understood. In the immediate aftermath of title change, we might expect that additional restructuring and further job losses are likely. The limited evidence that is currently available indicates that, for example, in the Czech Republic the conclusion of the first round of voucher privatization at end-1993 was not immediately associated with a notable increase in bankruptcy filings or accelerated employment losses. But given lags, such adjustments may be in the pipeline. In short, the future ability of this enlarged private sector to create jobs remains a crucial question. And hard evidence concerning restructuring and employment decisions in privatized entities is still missing. This is a clear area for further research.

The path of wages betrays considerable similarities across countries. In the wake of price liberalization, declines to consumption wages were often large, but over time we observe a clear recovery toward pretransition levels. But with the exchange rate used as a nominal anchor in a number of stabilizations, alongside the increase in relative prices of services, a wedge between changes in consumer and producer prices opened up. One implication was that product wages—save initially in Romania and Russia—rapidly recovered and often surpassed earlier levels. The data on unit labor costs, which incorporate the wedge effect, show strong increases, except in the Czech Republic (see Chapters 6 and 7). It is clear from the country studies that profits in the state firm sector have generally evaporated over the same period, and this would seem to imply rent appropriation by incumbents, with wages closer to average rather than marginal product. But if this were to hold, then we would likely observe far greater dispersion in wage changes across firms and sectors. The data available point to small cross-sectional variation. Part of this may be attributed to the application of incomes policies to state firms. But this is not completely convincing because such policies have often been flouted or have been of a form—targeted on the wage bill—that would in principle allow for greater variation in wages, both at the firm level and in relative skill wages. In short, wage setting in both the remaining state firms and the emerging transformed firm sector is an area requiring further research.

Private-state wage relativities are another area in which both the data and our analysis need sharpening. As discussed in Chapter 7, what data are available indicate that private wages are generally lower than those in state firms. Nevertheless, the private sector appears to have several constituent parts: a larger low-skill, low-wage end, primarily in services, and a much smaller high-wage component. But in general, the absence of a private wage premium implies weak or absent wage pull, and hence low incentives for workers to quit the state sector. Quite striking is the evidence reported for almost all countries that workers, including those unemployed, generally express a preference for state employment. In the case of the unemployed, this may be a result of their attaching a low probability to finding a private sector job, but more generally this reflects the perception that job conditions, including wages and benefits, are superior in the state sector. And, of course, there is the legacy of values and expectations from the planned economy.

A crucial question that is raised in several of the country papers concerns the effect of the timing and method of privatization on wage and employment decisions, given that privatization is likely to have an impact on the horizons of insiders. Here, the picture is quite diverse: some countries have barely started (Bulgaria and Romania), while others have already completed large-scale privatizations (the Czech Republic, Slovakia, and, in a rather different way, Russia, are cases in point). In general, privatization has largely occurred from below, respecting in large measure the interests of incumbents. Even when large-scale privatization from above has dominated, the restructuring and associated employment consequences have yet to wash through. One apparent result of the cooption of insiders has been the lengthening of their horizons, a point emphasized in the chapter on Poland. An implication of this is that predatory wage behavior has abated, at least in the short run. But given what is now known about the distribution of profits, the share of loss-makers, and the continuing absence of effective bankruptcy laws (save in Hungary and the Czech Republic), significant parts of the state sector continue to survive largely through external financial support. Hard choices on closure and restructuring remain to be taken in all countries.

Unemployment

The convergence in unemployment rates through our sample is evident. By early 1994 most countries had registered unemployment in the range of 10-15 percent. The obvious exceptions—but for different reasons—are the Czech Republic and Russia, with unemployment rates below 4 and 2 percent respectively. In the Russian case, this is in part a measurement problem, as indicated in Chapter 4, but also points to the slow pace of reform and structural change and the widespread prevalence of labor hoarding in state firms. Chapters 3, 7, and 9 indicate some of the reasons for the divergence of the Czech Republic, including larger flows out of the labor force alongside stronger job creation in the private sector and, possibly, greater reliance on active labor market policies, a point emphasized in Chapter 8.

It appears that, in contrast to most OECD countries, the pool of unemployed remains stagnant (see Chapter 9), with lower inflows and outflows than in OECD comparators. The inflow rate has been kept down by large flows out of the labor force, and the exit rate to jobs from unemployment remains low. Job-to-job transitions, rather than transitions through unemployment, appear to dominate. One implication is that average durations of unemployment are increasing, and a significant body of long-term unemployed—over 40 percent of the current unemployed— has already emerged. The evident challenge is to try and raise the exit rate to jobs and to avoid undesirable duration effects. The country studies already find rather weak evidence of unemployment, whether regional or aggregate, feeding back into wage setting, and the de facto departure from the labor force of large numbers of long-run unemployed can only further weaken the emergence of any more conventional equilibrating role for unemployment.

The available evidence on the impact of labor market policies on job search behavior by the unemployed is still very partial. While Chapter 8 suggests that initially generous benefits programs and high replacement rates had adverse effects, more recent evidence on benefits levels and durations gives a rather different picture. As Chapter 9 indicates, the duration for receipt of unemployment benefits has been severely curtailed. In the Czech Republic and Slovakia, benefits are currently paid for no longer than six months; in most other cases, for a year. Further, the replacement ratio is by no means generous, ranging between 40 and 60 percent. In the most extreme case—Russia—benefits are derisory and access difficult, one result of which has been a low level of registrations. Finally, it should be noted that on expiration of benefits eligibility, the unemployed in principle have continued rights to social assistance. Access has been by no means automatic, however, and the levels of assistance are clearly very low. In short, generally it is difficult to attribute persistence in unemployment to the set of passive labor market policies that have been pursued.

The country chapters also enable us to see the importance of regional or spatial mismatch. For example, Chapter 2 provides some measure of such mismatch for Poland, suggesting that over 20 percent of current unemployment could be eliminated by raising labor mobility. Part of the difficulty can be attributed to housing shortages that impede labor mobility, as well as information failures in the job matching process. The most extreme case is probably Russia, where labor mobility is very restricted—often by institutional features, as well as housing. Given concentration in output and small diversity in many regional production bases in Russia, shocks to regional employment will tend to be long-lasting. Even in the Czech Republic, the dispersion in regional unemployment rates is quite large. This suggests not only that policies addressing infrastructural constraints will be needed, but also that a larger menu of programs than is currently in place, including public works and retraining, will be required if significant numbers of persons in long-run unemployment—often in disadvantaged regions—are to be reinserted in the labor force. The evidence on the effectiveness of the Czech Republic's active labor market policies is by no means unambiguously positive (Chapter 3). Nevertheless, the reliance on low benefits and income support programs, with little attention to active programs, that remains characteristic of the other countries runs the obvious danger of promoting social unrest, with concomitant political feedback, as well as the risk of sustaining large shares of long run in total unemployment.

There is further scope for thinking more systematically about a possible role for employment subsidies, an issue not really dealt with in this volume. It is evident that governments offer employment subsidies to significant numbers of state firms throughout the region. But these are often given on an ad hoc basis, dependent on the relative bargaining power of the firm or sector. There may be a role for temporary employment subsidies through payroll tax relief that reflects explicit policy decisions rather than episodic responses to negative shocks. But aside from the danger that such subsidies will not be credibly temporary, by also reducing the flow into unemployment they may result in less downward pressure on wages, and hence yield lower incentives for private job creation.

Concluding Remarks

This volume begins to provide a coherent picture of the various evolutions in transitional labor markets. But there remain many partially answered or unanswered questions, some of which have been mentioned above. In particular, further research will be required to understand more satisfactorily the options facing state and privatized firms and their subsequent choices over employment and wages. While in general it seems that such firms operate as if under hard budget constraints, the outside financing environment may not be adequately summarized by subsidies from the budget. It is clear that a variety of channels exist by which firms can, at least temporarily, secure preferential financing. A channel of growing importance appears to be tax and other arrears to government and the banking system.

While the simple distinction over state and private firms has been a useful organizing device, it is obvious that there are many components to both the private and state sector firms, including those that have been privatized. These differences can be measured across a number of dimensions, including sectoral, regional, and control characteristics. For privatized firms, the main outstanding questions relate to the extent of future employment losses and recomposition of the structure of labor demand that will accompany restructuring or, in some cases, outright closure. As reallocation effects come to dominate aggregate effects in driving the adjustment, we can presume that this will have major implications for the privatized concerns. But the way in which these factors will play out remains elusive, in part because of uncertainties over the control mechanisms within and outside these firms and the implications of any likely changes for decisions over wages and employment. For instance, it seems probable that within both the state and privatized firms, current members should not be viewed as strictly homogenous, and this lack of homogeneity will be emphasized in a context where choices over restructuring become paramount. At that point, we can easily imagine that decisions will need to be taken over which parts of the firm can be salvaged and which will need to be closed down. And such decisions will not simply be a function of management's relative bargaining power. Both managers' and workers' incentives to restructure need better understanding.

Finally, this volume begins to provide some of the necessary information for understanding the nature of the unemployment that has so far been generated. The picture is, of course, mixed. But there are already signs that unemployment may stay high if duration effects set in. While the regional component warrants further research, it is clear that mobility and infrastructural constraints pose a major barrier to a well-functioning labor market. These features will tend to weaken any desired play-back from unemployment to wages and may result, in the absence of corrective policies, in low aggregate employment. While a simple application of active labor market policies that have yielded positive results in Western Europe, such as training programs, may be difficult to generalize, given institutional shortcomings and the structural changes at the heart of transition, reliance on passive programs is unlikely to be sufficient to lower equilibrium unemployment. Reintegrating a larger share of the long-run unemployed in work—a high priority in Western Europe—is similarly a major policy challenge in the East.

1

Hungary

Simon Commander, Janos Köllô, Cecilia Ugaz, and Balacs Vilagi

At one time, the view was that in Hungary reforms are done gradually and have lower costs. But the rapid rise in unemployment since 1990 and the depth of the recession suggest otherwise. By mid-1993 the unemployment rate was around 13 percent, while gross domestic product (GDP) was down over 20 percent from its 1989 level. Over the same period industrial output fell by nearly 35 percent. Table 1-1 provides some basic indicators.

These are depressing numbers; they are also misleading, for two reasons. First, they obviously camouflage significant structural changes occurring within the economy that result, among other things, in large underestimations of growth outside the state sector. For example, end-1993 estimates of unreported economic activity outside of the tax system range as high as 25 percent of GDP. Second, they cover up major changes over time in the nature of the output drop and unemployment. Significant private sector job creation, alongside restructuring and productivity improvements in the state sector, are signs that a dynamic adjustment is occurring.

This paper is an attempt to put together the various strands and to understand the nature of that dynamic adjustment. This is not so easy.

We thank Saul Estrin for very helpful comments on an earlier draft and Richard Jackman for help with the appendix.

Table 1-1. Hungary, Basic Indicators, 1990-93

Indicator	1990	1991	1992	1993
Real growth (percent change)[a]				
GDP	–4.0	–10.7	–4.5	–1.5
Industrial output	–9.2	–19.1	–9.8	3.9
Price (percent change)[b]				
Consumer	28.9	34.8	22.8	22.5
Producer	22.0	32.6	12.3	11.1
Employment (percent change)[c]				
Total	–0.5	–4.1	–7.3	–3.3
Industry	—	–5.2	–11.6	–7.4
Productivity (percent change)				
Industry	–4.0	–9.7	–6.6	
Unemployment rate[d]				
(end of year)	1.5	7.5	12.3	12.1
Fiscal balance[e]				
(percent of GDP)	0.4	–4.8	–8.0	–6.0/–7.0
Shares of GDP [f,g]				
Industry	41.9	—	37.5	—
Agriculture	16.2	—	14.0	—
Services, etc.	41.9	—	49.5	—
Shares of employment				
Industry	36.1	35.1	33.6	26.7
Agriculture	15.0	13.7	11.7	8.1
Services	49.0	51.4	54.7	55.9

— Not available.
a. Central Statistical Office, Monthly Bulletin, November 1993. World Bank estimates.
b. National Bank of Hungary, Monthly Report, January 1994.
c. Employment Observatory, December 1993 (1993 is mid-year).
d. Central Statistical Office, Monthly Bulletin.
e. National Bank of Hungary, Monthly Report, January 1994. World Bank estimates.
f. World Bank estimates.
g. OECD and World Bank estimates.

National statistics have not kept pace with the changes and we need rely on more fragmentary pieces of information, including household and firm surveys, particularly for the private sector and the transition routes in the labor market. Nevertheless, we feel that the picture that emerges is coherent and, in large measure, encouraging.

Output losses in the state sector have indeed been very large, as has been the scale of labor shedding. Flows into unemployment were initially large; flows out, particularly to jobs, were low. Private sector expansion, primarily in trade and services, was able to mop up some of the slack, but by no means all of it. The regional dimensions of unemployment have proven particularly intractable, as areas with low diversity in production emerged with high local unemployment, compounded by low labor mobility. But by 1993, the picture appears to have changed. There are signs that much of the restructuring in state industry has been done, aided by a functioning bankruptcy law. Industrial output rose by almost 4 percent in 1993 and private sector expansion continues, including growth through title transformation. The country remains the largest recipient of foreign direct investment in the region. Even so, fiscal pressures are strong. The economy and state sector tax base have shrunk, while revenues from taxing the private sector remain very low. High levels of interenterprise debt and mounting bad debts of the firm sector to the banking system brought about a third and large injection of resources by government into the financial system at end-1993, further compromising the fiscal position. Consumer price inflation refuses to fall below 20 percent a year. There are also signs of real wage resistance and pressure on unit labor costs, possibly accentuated by the abandonment of the incomes policy in 1993. Exports have declined significantly—by over 30 percent in the first half of 1993—provoking depreciation of the exchange rate. And regional unemployment problems continue; the northeast region has unemployment rates over double the national average.

This chapter is an attempt to monitor and evaluate these changes. First, we account for recent changes in employment. The second section focuses on the still dominant state sector and partially attempts to explain the response of state firms to the output and policy shocks after 1990. The most appropriate analytical setting is of an efficient bargain setup in which managers and workers can determine all dimensions of the labor contract. We develop this setup more fully in the appendix but, given data and other restrictions, at this stage empirical work is limited to simpler wage and employment estimations. This is done using panel data covering the branches of state industry, complemented by a look at the impact of title transformation on firm employment decisions. The third section turns to the private sector, which, although large, is also statistically elusive. Using household and firm survey data we attempt to get a handle on employment in the sector and on the ways in which it attracts and rewards labor. The fourth section looks at flows and concludes that the dominant source of employment growth in the private sector is hiring directly from state firms rather than from unemployment. The changing nature of unemployment is examined in more detail in the fifth section, and the last section discusses our conclusions.

Employment, Participation, and Unemployment, 1990-93

Between 1990 and 1993, employment fell by 1.03 million; a decline of nearly 20 percent (see table 1-2). The gap between the number of available jobs and potential job seekers was further widened by some growth in the working-age population. The gap led to growth of unemployment (0.6 million), although nonparticipation and a drop in employment of workers above retirement age were also noted.

Job losses in both absolute and relative terms were most severe in agriculture, but they were also large in industry, construction, and in the nonmaterial (education and health) branches.

Table 1-2. Labor Force Participation and Employment, 1990-93
(January 1, in thousands)

Category	1990	1992	1993	Net change
Employed (above working age)	488	334	300	−188
Working-age population	5,957	6,031	6,061	+104
Employed	4,984	4,462	4,143	−841
Employed abroad	4	30	45	+41
Unemployed	24	406	680	+656
Early retired	251	346	374	+123
Other inactive	211	239	268	+57
Student	483	548	551	+68

Source: A nemzetgazdaság munkaerômérlegei, KSH (labor force accounts, CSO, Budapest, 1993).

Table 1-3. The Employment Gap

Item	Number (thousands)
Drop in state employment	1,661
Increase in working-age population	74
Sum	1,735
Factors closing the gap	
Increase in	
Private employment	985
Employment abroad	26
Unemployment	382
Early retirement (stock)	95
Nonparticipation of working-age adults	28
Students of working age	65
Drop of	
Employment above the retirement age	154
Sum	1,735

Note: The gap is the difference between employment, on the one hand, and the working-age population plus the elderly in employment in 1990, on the other. The difference roughly equals the number of nonemployed workers eligible for paid employment. The gap between supply and demand is most probably narrower, and surely more difficult to calculate.

We can partially account for the change in state and private employment over this period. The change in private employment was indeed large, jumping from under 9 percent at the start of 1990 to over 30 percent at the start of 1992.[1] A reasonably full account of the net shifts between various labor market states is given in table 1-3.

Several features stand out from these tables. First, nonparticipation seems to be a remarkable feature of the early period of reforms. In 1992, by contrast, a further flow out of employment was mostly absorbed by the growth of unemployment.[2]

1. The numbers for the private sector for 1990 are taken from Laky 1993 and for 1992 from Nagy and Sík 1993, although there may be some underestimation at both ends.
2. Clearly, nonparticipation is an important feature. The unemployment measure will be biased given options such as early retirement, as also eligibility effects.

Second, the shift from state to private employment seems to be a striking feature of the transition, but a net flow from the state to the private sector may coincide with massive job destruction and job creation on both sides. A more reliable account of the role of the two sectors requires more detailed information on transition routes. We shall come back to this question later in the chapter.

In order to get an integrated view of the respective evolutions behind these numbers, we now turn in more detail to analyzing the behavior of the state sector. Although declining, state firms still dominate and the bulk of employment is still in the sector. It is clearly essential to get a handle on the factors driving the wage and employment decisions of state firms.

The Behavior of the State Sector

Output

The large shocks to industrial output, indicated in figure 1-1, have had both aggregate and structural components, with weight that has changed over time. Separating out these effects is difficult. Nevertheless, sectoral or relocation effects can be identified by 1990; the coefficient of variation of changes at industry branch level is actually larger than in subsequent years. Introducing a relative price term in panel estimations of industrial branch output—on the assumption that relative demand changes are an important component in determining output and hence on the expectation that there will be a positive correlation between sectoral price and output changes—we find that the relative price term becomes positive and significant from 1990 onward (Commander and Ugaz 1993). But the Council for Mutual Economic Assistance (CMEA) shock that hit Hungary in 1991 not only accelerated the rate of output decline, but also gives the impression of an aggregate shock generating relatively common sectoral outcomes. The variation of output changes in state industry declines over 1991 and 1992. This may camouflage major changes within branches. Although aggregate output fell nearly 10 percent in 1992, the output of firms with less than fifty employees doubled, even if their contribution to total industrial output remains quite small. While the CMEA shock was felt on both supply and demand sides, the primary effects were through the latter and were most strongly felt in branches, such as engineering,

Figure 1-1. Hungary, Total Industry Indicators

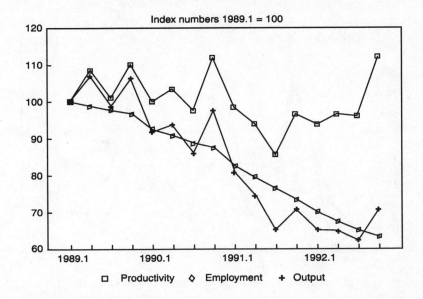

where foreign sales to CMEA partners were large and not easily substituted. But declining domestic demand, led by falling public expenditures and investment, played a major role, particularly after 1992, with firms increasingly citing insufficient demand as the major barrier to production.[3] Initially employment changes lagged output—in common with other Eastern European experience—but by 1990 we observe a sharp acceleration in the rate of job decline in the state sector (figure 1-1), which led to increases to labor productivity. Over this period, consumption wages remained constant, but product wages and unit labor costs drifted upward (figure 1-2).

Wages and Employment

The industrial sector is still dominated by state firms, but the environment has changed drastically. Subsidies have declined, and firms have been allowed to close—a harder budget constraint appears to have been

---

3. Kornai 1993. The large decline in agriculture, through drought, explains possibly as much as 3 percent of the output decline in 1992; OECD 1993.

Figure 1-2. Hungary, Wages and Unit Labor Costs

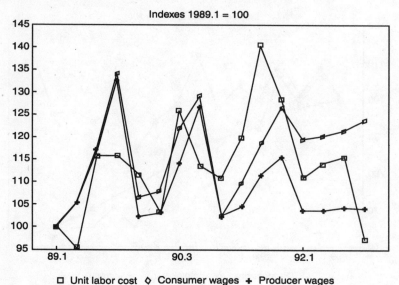

☐ Unit labor cost   ◇ Consumer wages   + Producer wages

imposed. At the same time, workers perceive high unemployment, which we would expect to feed back to wage claims.[4]

In the appendix we lay out a model of wages and employment that attempts to capture the essentials. The setting is with an efficient bargain (cooperative game) where managers and workers can determine simultaneously all dimensions of the labor contract, subject to the usual constraints. Managers' utility is associated to profits; workers' utility depends on the real consumption wage and effort. With a standard Nash bargain, the main difference in a transitional economy might be that the workers' bargaining power parameter would be larger than in a "true" capitalistic setting.

The model provides a general framework for thinking about the transitional firm, but it has obvious problems when turning to the reduced form. These arise, in part, from the joint determination of wages and employment in the game. Further, we lack an appropriately rich data set with which to implement the model empirically. In particular, we lack financial data at the same level of disaggregation. As a result, we have to

---

4.   Note that a standard Phillips curve estimation does not work; variables are either incorrectly signed or insignificant.

rest content at this stage with a less ambitious attempt at pinning down with the available data the factors affecting the wage and employment decisions of state firms.

Panel Estimations

We work with a data set comprising quarterly observations for the period 1989.I to 1992.IV, covering sixty-eight subbranches of the industrial sector and including firms with more than fifty employees. We apply a fixed-effects procedure to estimate a system of equations recursively. We also know a priori that there is a high degree of heterogeneity across branches, including size differences and associated returns to scale. By using a fixed-effects procedure we are assuming that the differences among individual branches are fixed over time and can be captured by introducing different intercepts. The estimated slopes are supposed to be common to all branches after correction for individual effects, and for that reason they can be interpreted as aggregate values for the industry as a whole. Variables are in indexes based to the first quarter of 1989 and are in logs and first differences. We thus estimate wage and labor demand equations in rate-of-change form and implicitly impose a sequence on the way in which decisions are made within the firm. We assume that wages are used as inputs in the labor demand equation, and hence choose a recursive form with the wage equation nested in the employment estimation. The estimated equation for wage setting has the following form:

$$\text{RWAGE}_t = \beta_1 \frac{\text{RPROD}}{\text{EMP}_{t-1}} + \beta_2 \frac{\text{PPI}}{\text{CPI}_{t-1}} + \beta_3 \frac{\text{PPI}^i}{\text{PPI}^T_{t-1}} + \beta_4 \text{SDUMMY}_t$$
$$+ \beta_5 \text{TIME} + \text{FIXEDEFFECTS} + \mu_t$$

The estimated equation for employment follows.

$$\text{EMP} = \gamma_1 \text{RWAGE}^*_t + \gamma_2 \text{RFSALES}_t + \gamma_5 \text{RDSALES}_t + \text{FIXEDEFFECTS} + \mu_t$$

In which:[5]

RWAGE: Average product wage by branch deflated by the PPI of total industry, 1989.I

RFSALES: Foreign sales in real terms, Forints 1989.I

RDSALES: Domestic sales in real terms, Forints 1989.I

RPROD: Real industrial output, Forints 1989.I

---

5. Central Statistical Office (CSO).

EMP: Number of employees (manual and professionals)
CPI: Consumer price index, 1989.I=100
PPI^i: Producer price index of branch i, 1989.I=100
PPI^T: Producer price index of total industry, 1989.I=100
SDUMMY: Seasonal dummy. Equals 1 in the fourth quarter of
              the year.
TIME: Time trend.

Wage Setting

We estimate a real wage equation where wages are related to productivity, measured in terms of output per worker, an inverse wedge term (introduced to proxy profits), a relative price term, time, and a dummy for 1989. The latter was introduced as structural reforms and largely proceeded from 1990 onward.

As we see from table 1-4, all the right-hand-side variables, save the productivity term, are significant at a 5 percent and more level. Wage changes are positively related to branch productivity change. Similarly, the inverse wedge, or quasi-profits, term is positively associated with wages. We presume that a firm's ability to pay is likely to be heavily influenced by its own cash flow. The sign on the inverse wedge term hints at some underlying positive association between wages and profits. Predictably, relative branch prices—branch-specific product prices in relation to total industry prices—have a positive sign with a similar size coefficient to that for the wedge term. In short, branch price effects appear to have a clear link to branch wage setting. The 1989 dummy picks up expected structural effects and is highly significant.

Employment

The labor demand equation is conventional. We nest the wage equation, which then has both the right sign and is very significant. We also try and explore in more detail the demand-side effects on employment. Accordingly, we introduce in a disaggregated form the variables for both domestic and foreign sales. The motivation for that disaggregation is to evaluate the effects of the CMEA shocks. The term for foreign sales is positive but very insignificant, a result that can probably be attributed to the large variation in external trade exposure across branches. Domestic sales are

Table 1-4. Wage Setting
(Two-stages least-squares with group dummy variables)

Item	Variable	Coefficient	Standard error	t-ratio
Dependent variable, RWAGE				
	Productivity	0.0065	0.0049	1.335
	PPI^i/CPI	0.1850	0.0680	2.720
	PPI^i/PPI^T	0.1749	0.0679	2.576
	Time	0.0060	0.0006	10.418
	Dummy 1989	−0.0568	0.0056	−10.113
	Number of observations	952		
	R-squared	0.1452		
	Log-likelihood	1,550.5582		
Labor demand				
Dependent variable, EMP				
	RWAGE*	−0.3270	0.1475	−2.1840
	RDSALES	0.0415	0.0089	4.6430
	RFSALES	0.0145	0.0151	0.9620
	Dummy 1989	−0.0221	0.0068	−3.2310
	Number of observations	952		
	R-squared	0.1626		
	Log-likelihood	1,062.8661		

not only positive but highly significant. The size of the coefficient, however, is not that large. Finally, the 1989 dummy proves significant.

The necessarily preliminary conclusions that we can draw from the panel estimations are that state firm behavior appears consistent at the least with cost minimization. The richer characteristics of the budget constraint effectively facing firms cannot be dealt with using the data currently available. The wage and employment equations that we have estimated have broadly conventional properties, suggesting that Hungarian state firms have in some measure adapted their behavior, leaving behind most vestiges of the earlier controlled regime.

Employment Setting in State and Transforming Firms: Survey Evidence

The panel work can now be complemented, using a different data set, to answer the question of whether ownership changes have any measurable bearing on employment.[6] The question's importance is obvious, given the large changes in title that have been occurring, but also difficult given problems of causality. However, the Labor Market Forecast Survey (LMF) allows us to control employment changes for some simple variables measuring the market position and other characteristics of the firm. We estimate an OLS equation relating the change in employment for 1992/1991 to a set of right-hand-side variables summarizing firm characteristics. These are listed below. Table 1-5 gives the results with all the variables entered simultaneously.

The estimation drives home the point that employment was indeed sensitive to both market indicators and to anticipated or announced title changes. The outcome is similar if orders and the price dummy are replaced for revenues. The coefficients for LTD (limited and other, mostly private, firms) and the impact of privatization are significant after controlling for size, industry, and some market indicators. The negative coefficient on the commercializing and privatizing variables points to the rationalization in state firms *prior* to privatization that raised job losses in 1992.[7] Further, these coefficients are mostly stable (the coefficient for LTD falls somewhat) when industry dummies are included. The size effect is insignificant in any specification and so are the sector effects, apart from LTD. Because engineering—the most severely affected branch—is the reference, industry effects are all positive but not always significant; the unexplained variation is large. Estimation of similar functions distinguishing over state firms and LTDs does not reveal any major differences in the elasticity of employment with respect to orders, but the latter seem

---

6.   We use the National Labor Market Center's Labor Market Forecast Survey (LMF) based on a bi-annual 4,000 firm survey. See Székely 1993a, b, c.

7.   The coefficient on the bankruptcy variable picks up the two waves of bankruptcy in 1992 that affected over 4,000 firms with around 27 percent of the labor force outside budget institutions; Laky 1993.

more responsive to prices. State firms undergoing privatization and commercialization tend to reduce employment at a higher rate (Köllô 1993).

Table 1-5. Staff Change in 1991 (OLS)

Item	Parameters	T
L1	−9.38806E-04	−1.452
ORDERMAX	8.479262	6.475
ORDERMIN	−4.517446	−3.785
PSQUEZE	−13.451166	−12.528
COMM	−2.515670	−1.719
PRIVAT	−5.993501	−3.981
CLOSE	−37.342503	−18.031
COOP	0.625411	0.374
RT	1.619424	0.998
LTD	6.846334	4.457
Heavy	3.096129	1.094
Other industry	9.533815	6.895
Construction	3.515369	1.821
Transport	6.920739	2.815
Trade	3.268527	1.948
Services	5.061381	2.220
(constant)	87.596755	46.358

Note: Adjusted R-Square=0.27105; F=60.19086; Signif F=0.0000; N=2552.
Variables:
Size—E1 - Number of employees, end of 1991.
*Output, revenues, prices—*REVMAX1 = 1 if revenues increased in 1992, reference = revenues unchanged; REVMIN1 = 1 if revenues decreased in 1992, or alternatively; ORDERMAX = 1 if the amount of orders given to the firm at the end of 1992 was larger than at the end of 1991, reference = no change in the amount of orders; ORDERMIN = 1 if the amount of orders given to the firm at the end of 1992 was smaller than at the end of 1991; PSQUEZE = 1 if the relation of REVENUES and ORDERS suggests decreasing prices, or ORDERMIN=1 and REVMIN1=1 / and 0 otherwise.
*Changes in legal status—*COMM = 1 if the firm was to be commercialized in the 4th quarter of 1992; PRIV = 1 if the firm was to be privatized in the 4th quarter of 1992; CLOSE = 1 if the firm was to be liquidated in the 4th quarter of 1992, reference = no change in the firm's status in the 4th quarter of 1992.
*Sector dummies—*reference - state companies; COOP - co-ops
RT - joint stock companies; LTD - limited and other companies (mostly private).
Industry dummies: reference - engineering.

The Behavior of the Private Sector

Employment

As we have already indicated, measuring the size of the private sector is complicated by the degree of title transformation and the lags with which the statistical system has adapted. Nevertheless, several features stand out. The first is that Hungary started the reforms with a reasonably well-established second economy. This implied that the extent of gap-filling—the provision of services neglected by the previous order—was less than in most Eastern European settings. But it was still large. The sectoral attribution of the private sector is picked up in surveys and seems to broadly conform to the picture of a large stock adjustment, concentrated in trade and services.

Given the problems with official data, we rely for the most part in this section on survey-generated information. The Hungarian Household Panel (HHP) yields the information in table 1-6, which breaks employment down in more detail for March 1992, allowing us to discriminate over private and privatizing firms. Between 1990 and 1993 private sector employment jumped from around 9 percent of total employment to over 40 percent. We can also see that the self-employed, partnerships, and fully private firms account for nearly 75 percent of private employment.

To get a more detailed view of the employment behavior of private firms, we now draw upon the results of an eighty-three-firm survey that we organized in January 1992 that covered a mix of state, privatized, and new private entities in four regions. The regions—Budapest, its environs, Gyor, and Miskolc—were selected in an attempt (of course, unrepresentative) to capture the clear regional diversity. Simply put, the Budapest area

Table 1-6. Private and State Employment, March 1992

Category	Percentage
Private sector	35.8
Part private	9.3
Full private	14.1
Self-employed or partnership	12.4
State sector	64.2

Source: HHP; Nagy and Sík 1993.

and Gyor in the west represent the more dynamic sections of the economy; by contrast, Miskolc in the east has a concentration of heavy industrial firms—particularly in metallurgy—that are in clear decline. The unemployment rate range is indicative; by mid-1993 unemployment in Miskolc exceeded 24 percent, as against a range of 4-8 percent in the west and Budapest.

Table 1-7 provides some information on the sectoral affiliations of firms in the sample. The most striking feature is that once we exclude privatized entities, over 60 percent of new initiatives are in trade and services, and this holds across regions. Clearly, the bulk of new private sector activity has been in the nature of a stock adjustment. This is also reflected in the firm size data, which show that the average new private firm size is between 10 and 15 percent of privatized and state firms. Although new private firms tend to have larger female shares in employment—probably reflecting the services bias—we also find larger shares of personnel with university education. The skill structure points to a feature of the new private sector, a feature that can be identified in other countries:[8] the coexistence of a high-skill, relatively high-wage end with a dominant low-skill, low-wage end largely concentrated in services.

The rapid expansion in the employment share of the private sector that we have already cited disguises a number of interesting branch and regional effects. Table 1-8 is largely predictable in that state firms had sig-

Table 1-7. Distribution by Branch of Private Sector Business
(percentage)

Sector	All private initiatives	New operations	Other private[a]	Former state firms	Total private firms
Manufacturing	19.0	14.3	42.9	54.5	26.4
Construction	21.4	20.0	28.6	0.0	17.0
Trade	26.2	31.4	0.0	27.3	26.4
Services	31.0	31.4	28.6	18.2	28.3
Health services	2.4	2.9	0.0	0.0	1.9
Total	100.0	100.0	100.0	100.0	100.0

a. Existed before 1990.

8. See chapters on Bulgaria and Poland in this volume.

nificant net reductions to employment in the preceding year. While this is also true for privatized firms in manufacturing, it is interesting to note the smaller size of the adjustment. This may indicate that by January 1992 privatized firms were generally firms in better shape than their remaining state counterparts. The employment expansion rate in new firms is predictably large, particularly in trade, but has also to be related to the common low base. The numbers for construction are hard to interpret, given possible seasonal effects, but probably reflect depressed aggregate activity. The regional changes to employment are striking for showing that behavior in the eastern part of the sample is very different from elsewhere. For a start, state firms register a significant employment decrease, but we also find a clear decline among privatized and new private firms. The survey results show that all new private firms in the east are in retail services, and its seems plausible that the decline in private employment is a direct reflection of the depth of the regional depression. The crisis of the state industrial firms has spilled over, squeezing out the space for private sector job creation.

HIRINGS AND SEPARATIONS.   Data on flows in and out of firms confirms not only the regional diversity but also allows clarification of the hiring and firing behavior of state and private firms.

The survey focused primarily on involuntary separations and ignored quits and attrition. This is not serious, because we have already seen that by 1992—the year of coverage—involuntary separations were widespread among state firms. And it is interesting to note that two-thirds of state firm respondents and over 85 percent of private respondents reported no serious constraints on dismissing workers. In the larger state firms—generally in manufacturing—union presence was cited as a factor in 6 percent of cases, with legal constraints being cited by 15 percent of all respondents. This confirms the view that unions and workers' councils have been relatively weak forces in Hungary (and incorporated in the model presented in the appendix).

Table 1-9 presents a crude distribution of involuntary separations by title. There is a higher incidence of dismissals and expected dismissals in state firms, but sectoral disaggregation points to some common branch features. Dismissals and expected separations are higher, for example, in construction. Privatized firms do not generally have higher dismissal rates than state firms, possibly suggesting that privatization is not necessarily associated with higher involuntary separations.

Table 1-8. Employment Changes

Sector and area	State	Privatized	Other private[a]	Total private
Manufacturing	−49.9	−13.2	0.0	−10.9
Construction	−53.1	—	−8.0	−8.0
Trade	−15.5	1.7	47.1	11.8
Services	29.5	133.3	14.5	38.8
Health services	55.8	—	50.0	50.0
Budapest	−33.9	−27.0	3.1	−16.0
Near Budapest	−27.5	—	10.0	10.0
Eastern towns	−60.1	−28.6	−11.4	−11.7
Western towns	−12.2	−1.1	13.8	−0.9

— Not available.
a. Existed before 1990.

Table 1-9. Dismissals during 1992
(percentage)

Category	None	1-5	6-10	11-20	>20
State firms					
Manufacturing	23.1	15.4	7.7	7.7	46.2
Construction	0.0	33.3	0.0	0.0	66.7
Trade	37.5	25.0	12.5	0.0	25.0
Services	75.0	0.0	25.0	0.0	0.0
Health services	100.0	0.0	0.0	0.0	0.0
Privatized firms					
Manufacturing	16.7	16.7	33.3	0.0	33.3
Trade	66.7	33.3	0.0	0.0	0.0
Services	100.0	0.0	0.0	0.0	0.0

The regional aspect is again important. In the western region nearly 80 percent of firms reported no dismissals in 1992 and a similar share expected no future dismissals. This was true for two-thirds of state and privatized firms. The story in the east is quite different. Nearly 50 percent of firms reported significant dismissals, with over 40 percent of the state firms and 33 percent of private firms expecting further involuntary separations in 1993. The rate of layoffs in private firms in the east was particularly high; almost half reported cuts of more than ten workers.

The motivation for separations generally highlights sector-specific features; manufacturing in particular is subject to a demand constraint, across all title classes. By contrast, trade and services turnover seems largely motivated by quality of work and other individual-specific reasons. The overall picture is predictably one in which state firms, facing demand barriers, have been forced to dismiss workers. Further, at least half of sampled state firms intended to fire more workers, with relatively small variation across sector. By contrast, privatized and private firms generally selected quality of work and disciplinary factors as the main motivation for dismissals.

Hiring behavior across the sample is revealing in a number of respects. First, as observed elsewhere in this chapter, significant numbers of state firms continue to hire, but at relatively low levels. Indeed, a quarter of all state firms report vacancies, with the great majority of those vacancies being for skilled workers. Vacancy rates are, however, notably lower in manufacturing, and roughly half the state firms expected to have no or only replacement hiring through 1993. Private and privatized firms have higher hiring rates than state firms, particularly in manufacturing, which may point to some restructuring by privatized firms, but they also have relatively restricted hirings projected over 1993. Again, vacancies of skilled workers in privatized firms are observed.

Regional divergences in hiring are again quite pronounced, with the western region sample having a clearly higher hiring rate, particularly among privatized firms. Vacancy rates, especially for privatized and private firms, are high, with the majority of vacancies being for skilled workers. Not surprisingly, hiring rates were very low for all firms in the eastern region. Branch features are again significant, particularly in accounting for the relatively common and low hiring rates in construction.

A feature that stands out—and to which we return later—is the transition routes that these hiring numbers represent. Here, the most striking aspect is the dominance of job-to-job transitions, with recruitment largely through word-of-mouth and personal contacts, and to a lesser extent by advertising vacancies. Transitions from unemployment to a job, whether state or private, remain of marginal significance. Hiring from unemployment occurred in only 7 percent of cases.

Private Sector Wages

Table 1-10 confirms the impression presented in other chapters that the emerging private sector in Eastern Europe generally follows a low wage regime. With the exception of the trade sector, private firms consistently pay less than their state counterparts, and privatized firms appear to pay even less than other private firms in the sample. Further, the prevalence of low wages in the private sector is confirmed by the incidence of workers on minimum wages. Table 1-11 shows that new private firms, particularly in services, have very high shares of workers on minimum wage; the clear impression is that private sector earnings for the most part provide little wage pull. This result is amplified by inclusion of benefits. Outside of Budapest, the majority of state firms—particularly in manufacturing—provide a significant range of benefits, including housing, transport, and paid holidays. In general, size of firm and trade union presence were strongly and positively correlated with density of benefits' availability. In contrast, private firms provide far fewer benefits and none provide housing or rental assistance. Factoring in these nonmonetary components of income would imply that private wages are even lower in relation to state wages, with the exception of firms in the trade sector. We should note, however, that benefits are generally offered by larger firms, and the gap is much less distinct outside this category.

Wage setting likewise differs in a number of strategic ways. Respondents were asked about the wage bargain over three skill groups: professionals, skilled workers, and unskilled workers and with regard to the

Table 1-10. Average Wage
(forints)

Sector	State	Privatized	Other private[a]	Total private
Manufacturing	40,232	28,106	31,200	30,010
Construction	38,165	—	27,233	27,233
Trade	33,385	26,771	43,938	41,077
Services	55,172	21,429	51,671	49,345
Health services	18,270	—	33,333	33,333

— Not available.
a. Existed before 1990.

Table 1-11. Minimum Wage
(percentage of workers)

Sector	State	Privatized	Total private
Manufacturing	4.5	0.0	7.3
Construction	2.1	0.0	11.9
Trade	18.8	40.0	53.3
Services	0.0	0.0	100.0
Health services	0.0	0.0	0.0

primary reference criterion. These included individual bargaining, trade-union-negotiated wages, state or private sector comparable wage, fairness, local labor market rates, and incomes-policy-determined rates. While individual negotiation was important across all skill groups, comparable same-sector wages were important reference points for state firms. Regressions with factor scores—using relative wages and local labor market conditions as the dependent variables and ownership type, size of firm (by employment), and trade union presence as explanatory variables—confirm the importance for state firms of ownership type wage relativities and local labor market conditions. Similarly, same-sector wages were significant references for private firms in trade and services, but in general private firms did not base their wage offer on comparable state sector wages. Yet we should also note that fairness was an important factor across all title groups, branches, and skill categories, a likely inheritance from the previous system. Trade union influence in the wage bargain appears to have no strong branch determinants, but regional factors are more relevant. In both the western and eastern components of the sample, union participation in both state and privatized firm wage setting was important. New private firms generally have little union presence and influence on wages.

We are able to complement these results with information from the HHP. These data relate only to March 1992, and they document respondents' wages and earnings, including cash payments. Aside from the larger sample size, we are also able to control wages and hourly earnings for some personal characteristics as well as industry and sector of the employer. The estimation results are given in table 1-12.

The effects of personal characteristics appear to be robust in either linear or log specifications, but the parameters for the two industry dum-

Table 1-12. Estimation of Log Earnings (OLS)

Item	Log wage	Log earnings	Log income	Log hourly earnings
		Dependent		
Female	−.278	−.282	−.299	−.174
	(−13.5)	(−13.4)	(−14.9)	(−8.1)
Age	.043	.043	.027	.024
	(8.1)	(8.0)	(5.3)	(4.2)
Age squared	−.005	−.005	−.002	−.002
	(−7.3)	(−7.4)	(−3.8)	(−3.4)
Years in school	.075	.076	.077	.082
	(19.2)	(19.1)	(20.3)	(19.9)
Industry, construction, and agriculture	−.027	−.011	−.057	−.024
	(−1.0)	(−0.4)	(−2.1)	(−0.8)
Services	.048	.049	.047	.009
	(1.7)	(1.7)	(1.7)	(0.3)
Partly private	.080	.099	.088	.075
	(2.4)	(2.7)	(2.8)	(2.1)
Private	.053	.063	.088	.004
	(2.0)	(2.4)	(3.5)	(0.1)
Constant	7.830	7.891	8.124	2.951
	(69.9)	(68.9)	(74.6)	(24.2)
R^2	.2946	.2930	.3305	.2525
F	86.65	85.92	101.63	68.51

Note: Sample = HHP (working: self-employed excluded).

mies are not always significant and change in the two specifications. The industry dummies are not significant in the hourly earnings equations.

The striking conclusion that follows is that—after controlling for gender, age, education, and industry—wages, earnings, and incomes are all *higher* in private firms, but hourly earnings are not higher in the fully private sector.[9]

---

9. Private employees work on average 45.2 hours (47.4 if the self-employed are included) a week as against 41.7 in state firms and 42.8 in semiprivate firms.

The widening gap between private and state sector .workers as we move from wages to income may either reflect the more frequent use of payment by results and profit-sharing in the private sector (the return to extra hours appearing as part of the earnings above the wage) or, in some cases, could be attributed to better access to second jobs, although the latter is not generally supported by the data.

More on Flows: 1991-92

To get a better handle on the nature of the transition so far, we need to look more closely at gross flows of workers between employment, state and private, and other states. The most comprehensive view of transitions on the Hungarian labor market in 1991-92 can be drawn from the HHP. By distinguishing six states on the labor market we get table 1-13.

A shortcoming of the matrix is that it neglects shifts from the state to the private sector through privatization. Underestimated transition probabilities are indicated with (_) and the overestimated ones with (~) in table 1-13. Fortunately, the shifts between sectors *via the labor market* are all observed properly. These are shown in table 1-14.[10]

Table 1-13. Transition Probabilities (i) to (j), March 1991-March 1992

(i)	State	Private	Unem-ployment	Inactive	Student	Pension
				(j)		
State	.832~	.045_	.076~	.005~	.001~	.040~
Private	.022_	.889~	.069_	.003_	.000_	.018_
Unemployment	.112	.068	.789	.012	.012	.006
Inactive	.031	.018	.018	.903	.004	.027
Student	.071	.037	.054	.010	.828	.000
Pension	.002	.001	.000	.000	.000	.997

Note: State in 1991: In 99.6 percent of the cases the variable reflects the respondent's state on March 31, 1991. *Unemployed/inactive*: Based on the classification of the respondent. *State/private*: Private if the firm is not fully state-owned. Self-employed included. Sample: HHP (N=4,212).

10.   For the sake of simplicity, students, pensioners, and the inactive are grouped to one category (other). Shifts between the constituent groups appear as mobility within this category. The diagonal cell for the unemployed indicates the occurrence of repeated spells.

The other source where similar data are available is the International Labor Organization's (ILO) survey of cohorts entering unemployment in June 1991 in three regions of the country. The main features are presented in table 1-15.[11]

Table 1-14. Transition Probabilities of Workers Changing Employer/Status

Transition	State	Private	Unemployed	Other
State employees leaving their employer	.237	.205	.344	.214
Private employees leaving their employer	.134	.319	.420	.126
Unemployed completing their spells current in March 1991	.461	.282	.128	.128
Other	.320	.175	.206	.299

Note: Sample: HHP changing job/status/ *N*=594.

Table 1-15. The Risk That a Worker Entering Unemployment in June 1991 Moves to State or Private Employment by November 1992

	Status at the end of the period		
Status before becoming unemployed	*State employment*	*Private and other*	*Unemployment*
State employment	.107	.111	.782
Private employment	.128	.139	.733
School leaver	.241	.205	.554
Other	.142	.071	.787
All workers	.133	.130	.734

Note: Sample: ILO (*N*=650).
Source: Godfrey 1993.

---

11. Preliminary results presented in Nagy 1993 (p. 43) and verbal information provided by Stefano Scarpetta and Istvan Gy. Tóth (OECD) suggest that the patterns of flows in March 1992 were similar to those seen in table 1-13, except for an increased probability of flow from unemployment to employment (an increase from 18 to 27 percent) and of flow from U to out of the labor force (from about 4 to 20 percent). The relative position of the state and private sectors did not change.

Several conclusions can be drawn from these two sources. First, the probability of transition from employment to unemployment appears to be roughly equal in the two sectors in the HHP sample. But the high proportion of state firms among preunemployment employers (83 percent) in the ILO survey suggests a higher risk in the state sector.

Second, for unemployed workers the probability of being hired by a state firm roughly equals the likelihood of being hired by a private firm, a feature of both data sets. Given that the private sector's share is smaller, these figures indicate a higher rate of hiring in the private sector. Third, both surveys reject the assumption that the private sector plays an outstanding role in absorbing unemployment. The net flow is *from* private employment *to* unemployment rather than the other way around. The net position of the state sector is even less favorable. Fourth, these findings suggest that the dominant source of employment growth in the private sector is hiring directly from the state sector (and/or privatizing existing jobs). Hiring from the pool of the unemployed plays a minor role. As can be seen in table 1-16, no more than 10 percent of the newly hired workers came from the ranks of the unemployed. The ratio to all workers entering private employment (by virtue of being hired or through privatization) is even lower, and probably does not exceed 5 percent.

These results reinforce the findings of our survey, reported above, in which little hiring occurs from unemployment in both state and private sectors. In general, the results suggest that job destruction and creation is occurring in both state and private sectors. Further, the unemployed have a high probability (75-80 percent) of remaining unemployed or leaving the labor force, a point we will consider in the next section.

The dominance of job-to-job flows—as opposed to a flow from the state to the private sector through unemployment—raises the question of the worker's gain. Private wages provide alternative income possibilities for workers who quit or are fired from the state sector and hence are critical in driving the labor reallocation that characterizes the transition. Although we observe no apparent wage premium in the private sector, we should probably not draw strong conclusions because we lack appropriate time series. Further, for the state-private comparison, we should not ignore that workers can earn more in private firms through longer hours; this flexibility is likely absent in state firms. In addition, private employment may offer greater job security. Even though the probability of becoming unemployed is roughly equal in the two sectors, the risk of being dismissed is higher in a transforming state firm. This is significant

Table 1-16. The Composition of Newly Employed Workers by Their Former Status

	New employer		New employed	
Status in 1991	State	Private	State	Private
State employee	55.2	51.1	—	71.3
Private employee	11.0	28.1	24.6	—
Unemployed	12.4	8.1	27.7	11.3
Other	21.4	12.7	47.7	17.4

— Not available.
Note: Sample: HHP. "Newly hired workers" are employees with a different status or sectoral attachment one year before the survey *plus* workers who changed employer within a sector.

because it suggests that an important share of private sector employment is quite stable and not characterized by particularly high turnover rates, as already indicated.

Unemployment and Its Path

Unemployment raced from a negligible level to over 13 percent in two years (figure 1-3). The process was dominated by a low exit rate rather than by high (but unequal) flows on both sides (figure 1-4). As in post-Franco Spain, this change occurred with a monthly inflow rate well below 1 percent throughout the period. Table 1-17 shows how Hungary was moving toward a high rate with modest flows—a pattern characteristic of most European Community (EC) countries.

How can we explain this evolution? Although the output decline after 1990 was not followed immediately by symmetric cuts in employment, the change in hires was drastic and instantaneous. This was also reflected in a very low vacancy/unemployed ratio in 1990-91 and in the low rates of exit from unemployment.

The rough hazard rates in table 1-18 give the conditional probability of leaving the benefit register after t days of insured unemployment in July 1991. Because no distinction was made between job-finding and exhaustion of benefits, these figures considerably overestimate the job hazard rate, especially in the 330 days previous-duration category. But even these biased rates seem very low, suggesting, for a constant hazard, an

Figure 1-3. Hungary, Unemployment Rate

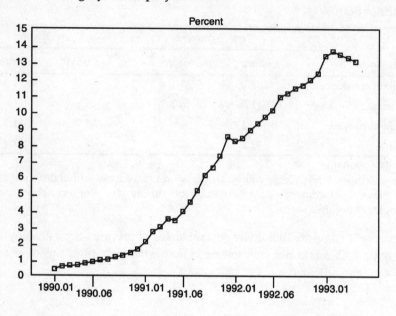

Figure 1-4. Unemployment Flows

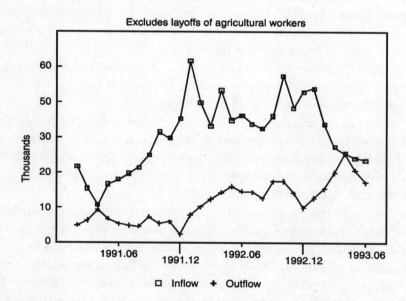

Table 1-17. Stock, Flow, and Steady-State Duration in Selected OECD Countries and in Hungary

Country	Unemployment rate (percent)	Monthly inflow (percent)	Steady-state duration (month)
Low inflow, long duration			
Spain	23.6	0.2	105
Hungary 1992, November	10.5	0.6	18
Belgium	8.3	0.2	50
Denmark	9.4	0.8	11
Hungary 1991, December	8.5	0.7	11
Germany	6.6	0.4	16
Netherlands	10.1	0.4	25
High inflow, short duration			
Canada	8.3	2.6	3
United States	5.8	2.2	3
Low inflow, short duration			
Japan	2.6	0.5	5
Hungary 1991, February	2.7	0.4	7
Sweden	1.6	0.5	3

Source: Layard, Jackman, and Nickell 1991 (p. 222) and OMK Mùnkaerôpiaci Helyzetkép 1991, December.

expected completed duration of at least 2/3 years. The outflow from unemployment to employment declined through 1991, reaching a low point in December 1991 when only 0.9 percent of the (insured) unemployed could find a job.

Why was the exit rate so very low in 1990-91? This can be traced to the changing behavior of state firms, indicated above. In effect, the rules of the game were changed in 1990 and made transparent by the government's unwillingness to bail out several bankrupt firms. The response was fairly immediate and was initially concentrated on dismissals of the least capable and strongly discriminated groups, complemented by hiring freezes. The large share of marginal workers in the pool of the unemployed magnified the latter effect. The pool of unemployment became rapidly populated with marginal workers and acquired its stagnant character.

Table 1-18. Exit from the Benefit Register, July 20-September 20, 1991

t	Exit rate
90	0.045
150	0.092
210	0.057
270	0.108
330	0.248
450	0.026
510	0.035
570	0.015

Note: The conditional probability of leaving the UI register within two months after *t* days of unemployment.
Source: OMK Munkaerôpiaci Helyzetkép, issues July-October.

This is most easily observed with Gypsies, a group historically discriminated against and concentrated in marginal jobs. The rate of unemployment among Gypsies was over four times higher than for others.[12] Calculations based on regional data (Köllô 1992) indicate that although the size of the Gypsy population was a highly significant variable in explaining regional unemployment rates (and thus the inflows) in 1990, this was not the case in 1991. The effect of a larger Gypsy population could still be traced in a higher duration of unemployment, but not in the inflow or the rate.

The important initial weight of marginal workers in unemployment can partly be captured by the changing proportion of unskilled and skilled workers. Unfortunately such statistics are only available for the stock. They therefore underestimate the degree to which the locus of job displacement changed, but the trend is clear. The proportion of unskilled workers fell from 4:1 to 3:1 between 1990 and 1991-92 as unemployment grew (Laky 1993). Finally, the high flow from employment out of the labor force in 1990-91 also suggests that dismissals affected marginal workers with poor reentry prospects the most.

But, over time, we see this picture changing. The number of firms hiring labor grew substantially in 1992-93 (table 1-19) and exit rates from

---

12. Nagy and Sík 1993. The ratio hardly changes when comparing workers with eight or fewer years of education across these brackets; 42.2 percent rate for Gypsies against a 13.9 percent rate for others.

unemployment steadily increased after January 1992. Figure 1-4 shows that both inflow and outflow subsequently followed an increasing trend.[13]

The scatter (figure 1-5) shows that not only did the outflow increase after January 1, 1991, but so did the outflow rate (despite a growing stock of benefit recipients).[14]

It is obviously interesting to know whose exit rates increased. In particular, did those who lost their jobs in 1990-91 have a higher probability of returning to employment, or is this accounted for by short-term unemployed? To provide a full answer we would need information on the behavior of hazard rates over time. These we do not have. The available data suggest that the exit rate of some of the short-term unemployed

Figure 1-5. Exit Rate and Outflows over Time

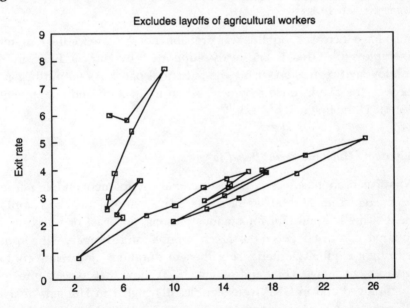

13. Figure 1-4 smooths out a jump in the outflow rate in February 1992 that was caused by the deletion from the register of 50,000 agricultural workers put on "involuntary leave." The phenomenon, incidentally, suggests that Feldstein's (1976, 1978) model of temporary layoffs might be applicable to the agricultural cooperatives.
14. Note that the series are too short to adjust for seasonality. But the drop in the inflow rate in October-December 1992 was of a seasonal nature.

Table 1-19. Firms Planning New Hires
(percent)

Period	Number of employees					
	1,000+	501-1,000	301-500	101-300	51-100	51 or fewer
1991, July-December	8.0	6.4	7.2	9.6	9.7	12.5
1992, January-June	10.0	8.0	9.2	10.0	11.5	17.9
1992, July-December	19.1	16.9	17.4	16.1	14.6	20.8
1993, January-June	20.7	19.2	18.8	23.9	23.2	36.0

Note: Data based on Waves 1-4 of LMFS.
Source: Székely 1993.

must have increased, but this was probably not the case for the long-term unemployed.[15] This is indirectly supported by our findings in the employment regressions using the industrial panel. As output began to recover, the rise in unemployment began to level off and subsequently decline in the first half of 1993.[16]

A Note on Unemployment Benefits

What has been the effect of the institutional environment and, in particular, the replacement ratio, on the choice over unemployment and employment? This is important for obvious reasons, not least of which is the apparent contrast between the Czech Republic and Hungary—the former with tight eligibility criteria, short benefit durations, and relatively low replacement ratios. Köllô and others (1993) show that expenditures per unemployed and in GDP were significantly higher in Hungary than in other Eastern European countries. Recent work by Nagy and Mickle-

---

15. This (weak) conclusion follows from using the Nagy-Micklewright survey where benefit expiration and transfers are not that important; the job hazard rate at $d=90$ in March-May 1992 was higher than the reduction rate, $r(t,90)$, through 1991; see Köllô 1993 for more details.

16. Both the registered rate and the ILO numbers show unemployment peaking in January 1993 and subsequently declining by around 1 percent by 1993.Q3.

Table 1-20. Benefit/Reference Wage Ratios along a Spell of Unemployment Starting January 1, 1992 *(percent)*

Months of continuous unemployment	Last wage (Ft)			
	7,000	11,000	15,000	22,000
At start	100	73	70	70
3	96	70	67	67
6	92	67	64	64
9	88	64	61	61
12	100	73	54	42
15	96	70	51	40
18 (social benefit)	53	33	25	18

Note: Reference wage = $(1+\_)^t w$, where _ is the rate of wage inflation (here: _=0.5 percent/month). The minimum wage is adjusted by the rate of wage inflation, annually. See Köllô and others 1993.

wright (1993) and the simulation results presented in Köllô and others (1993) show that the benefit/wage ratio is rather high in the case of low-income workers. For the 1992 benefit regime, we can derive the replacement ratios presented in table 1-20.

Low-income workers may receive 90-100 percent of their previous earnings throughout a long spell of unemployment. Nagy and Micklewright (1993) report the proportion of this lowest income group—receiving benefit at the level reported in the first column of table 1-20—at 28 percent at entry to unemployment. The high replacement ratio clearly would discourage active search behavior and may partly explain some of the duration effects that we observe. Using a small sample of the unemployed in the HHP data set, Galasi (1993) found evidence for a benefit effect with men (but not with women). An assessment of the importance of such effects awaits further research.

Conclusions

Hungary has passed through several difficult years with large, cumulative output losses and rapid growth in unemployment. Inherited regional imbalances seem likely to persist, constraining growth or at least resulting in continuing differences over the western and eastern parts of the country. But there are now signs that output is recovering, albeit slowly, while unemployment decreased in 1993. State sector firms that initiated drastic cuts in employment after 1990 have been restructuring, often as a prelude to privatization. There are, of course, significant pockets of state industry that remain uncompetitive and continue to receive, in one form or another, supports from the budget. Part of this has shown up in the high level of interenterprise debt and the de facto default by many larger state firms on ancillary obligations, including social security payments, to the fisc.[17] Further, state firms have continued to accumulate bad loans with the banking system. By mid-1993 these amounted to over 13 percent of outstanding lending and they have been concentrated primarily in the larger state banks. The size of the bad loans and their apparent concentration has deterred banks from remedial action; the banks also fear triggering a chain of bankruptcies. This has led to a large injection of resources by the government in order to recapitalize the most severely affected banks. By choosing to bail out the state banks (for the third time), and by doing so through government equity stakes, the obvious risk is that the insurance thus provided by the exchequer will send the wrong signals and fail to address the underlying problems, both by reasserting state control over these banks and by implying that further bail-outs are possible.

Despite these clear problems and the fiscal crunch that they represent, the overall picture that emerges from this chapter is of a state sector and workers that anticipated and acted upon the announcement of harder budget constraints and associated changes. State firms responded to the negative shocks to output by extensive restructuring, including large contractions in employment, and by seeking out, where feasible, non-CMEA export markets. Nevertheless, the domestic demand shock appears to have been the major factor driving changes to employment. But it is also worth emphasizing that the absence of a price shock, as in other transitional economies, meant that the wage path has been much smoother. Consumer wages have moved very little while product wages and unit labor costs have crept upward. This suggests cost-side rigidities, which the elimination of the incomes policy in 1993 risks exaggerating. There is

---

17. The complexity of these channels of support to the firm sector is worth emphasizing, in part to counteract the view that explicit subsidies alone are a proper measure of the hard budget constraint. Significant tax and other arrears have been important factors behind the deterioration in the overall fiscal position of government. See also Kornai 1993.

still an apparent absence of conventional equilibration mechanisms for wages. Further, if regional unemployment levels remain significantly different and labor mobility is not adequately eased, large shares of the unemployment generated will have little effect on current wage claims. Regional and duration effects will set in.

Private sector growth, through stock adjustment and through title transformation, has been strong and accounts in part for the increased outflow rate to jobs from unemployment that we observe in 1993. And because of unrecorded activity, the private sector's contribution to GDP is likely significantly higher than official estimates. Unemployment benefits, which have been relatively generous and an increasing fiscal burden as well as discouraging to job search, at least by low-skill categories, have been partly reformed. But the basic challenge of going beyond the stock adjustment phase remains.

A Note on Data Sources

Hungarian Household Panel

The *Hungarian Household Panel (HHP)* is a representative panel survey of 2,000 households with 4,520 adult members. The first wave took place in March 1992; the first report and the data were made available in February 1993. Retrospective data were collected for March 1991. The HHP defined unemployment both by the ILO standard and on the basis of the respondent's actual worktime in the month preceding the interview.

The results presented in the paper are based on calculations with the original data file and also rely on the chapters by Kolosi and Sík 1993 and Nagy and Sík 1993 in the first report.

Short-Term Labour Market Forecast Survey

The Labour Market Centre's *Short-Term Labour Market Forecast (LMF)* is based on a survey of 4,000 firms—employing 1.2 million workers—selected by labor offices twice a year. The data file of, and the first report on, the wave of September 1, 1992, were made available in February 1993. The sample is consciously biased toward larger firms and industry. Although theoretically the selection procedure within the prescribed quotas ought to have been random, randomness was not strictly guaranteed in practice. Furthermore, the LMF survey failed to cover a wide range of important variables and many of its existing variables are quite vaguely defined. The sample, however, worked well in forecasting the trends and composition of employment and will be used in this paper as the *single* available source on the employer side of the labor market.

See Székely (1993a, b, c) for further details and analysis.

Appendix

Modeling the Transitional Firm: A Cooperative Game between Manager and Workers

In this appendix, we present a general model that captures the bargain between managers and workers, the principal players in the SOEs. The model can be made consistent with a wide range of settings, including what we believe to be the appropriate characterization for Hungary.

As a first approximation, state firms are run by a coalition of workers and managers, who at the same time determine the basic features of the labor contract, subject to the usual constraints. The setting is of an efficient bargain.

Suppose that the utility of a representative worker employed in state industry includes effort and expected real wage. The utility function can be written as

(1-1) $$U_W = u(Z) + v(W)\dots$$

We assume that

$$u'(Z) < 0; u''(Z) < 0$$

and that

$$v'(W) > 0; v''(W) < 0.$$

The second-order condition in u follows from the fact that the disutility associated with a high effort increases with more effort. The indifference curves will be upward sloping in the "effort-wage" space.

There is a given number of workers, m, seeking employment in the state sector. Unemployment amounts to $m - n$.

The utility for an unemployed worker is

(1-2) $$U_w = u(B) + v(0).\dots$$

where B denotes exogenous unemployment benefits. Involuntary unemployment requires that

$$u(Z) + v(W) > u(B) + v(0).$$

Aggregating the utility function for the group of workers seeking employment in the state sector obtains

$$U_s = nv(W) + (m - n)v(B) + nu(Z) + (m - n)u(0).$$

The "threat point" of workers is presumably unemployment, so the payoff to the workers from working in the SOE is

(1-3) $$U - \overline{U} = n[u(Z) - u(0) + v(w) - v(b)]. \ldots$$

To derive the remuneration of the manager, however, we first have to formulate the firm's production function as

(1-4) $$Y = aZN^\beta. \ldots$$

Production is a function of labor input multiplied by a measure for the effort of workers, Z; a is a technical coefficient that can embody the effects of supply shocks. Assume that

$$f(n) > 0; \ f'(n) > 0; \ f''(n) < 0.$$

In this context, the manager is concerned with real profits. Profits, R, have the following form:

$$R = PY - WN - F$$

where P is the price index of output deflated by the consumer price index, Y is the volume of output, and F stands for fixed costs.

The fallback level of profit for the firm is net earnings if production stops; that is

$$\overline{R} = -F.$$

The manager's payoff is therefore

(1-5) $$R - \overline{R} = PY - WN. \ldots$$

Suppose that the demand curve is elastic in the relative price. The firm's output price is therefore also its price to consumers:

$$Y = hp^{-g} \ldots g > 1$$

where g is the elasticity of demand and h embodies the effects of demand shocks.

Given these conditions, the efficiency locus is found as the first-order condition to the following problem:

(1-6) $$\text{MAX}_{W,n}\{[U_S - \overline{U}_S]^\Theta [R - \overline{R}]^{1-\Theta}\}. \ldots$$

In equation 1-6, we can replace the specific utility functions (equations 1-3 and 1-5) to obtain the efficiency locus:[18]

---

18. For a more detailed derivation, see Commander and Staehr 1991.

(1-7) $\text{MAX}_{W,n}\{n[u(Z) - u(0) + v(W) - v(b)]^{\Theta}[PY - Wn]^{1-\Theta}\}. \ldots$

If we assume that the production function is linear and we replace it in the expression for the manager's revenue, the maximand becomes

$$\text{MAX}_{W,N}\{N[u(Z) - u(0) + v(W) - v(b)]^{\Theta}[h^{\alpha}(\alpha ZN^{\beta})^{1-\alpha} - WN]\}$$

where

$$\alpha = 1/g.$$

The efficiency locus is found as a first-order condition of equation 1-7, and it can be written as

(1-8)

$$[\beta(1-\alpha)h^{\alpha}(\alpha Z)^{1-\alpha}N^{\beta(1-\alpha)-1} - W]$$
$$= \frac{v(W) - v(b) + u(Z) - u(0)}{v'(W)} \ldots$$

The efficiency locus shows that the manager's marginal rate of substitution between employment and wage must equal minus the worker's marginal rate of substitution between employment and wage, since;

$$v(W) - v(B) + u(Z) - u(0) > 0; \quad h^{\alpha}(\alpha Z)^{1-\alpha}(1-\alpha)N^{-\alpha} - W < 0.$$

This expression suggests that the manager employs more labor than would be the case if he were operating in a competitive labor market.

From that specification we can derive an equation to explain the wage-setting and employment, of the form

(1-9) $W^{*} = W(h,\alpha,Z,b,g). \ldots$

(1-9′) $N^{*} = N(h,\alpha,g,Z,b). \ldots$

The multipliers give the change in bargained wages with respect to changes in the exogenous variables. Unemployment benefits have a positive sign, and all the remaining multipliers—the demand and supply shocks and the effort level—are indeterminate.

On the employment side, we find that the multipliers for the demand (h) and supply (a) shocks are positive, but that the multiplier for unemployment benefits is indeterminate.

In this setting, we can introduce the bargaining power of workers and managers into the maximization problem, but it is considered constant during the process of negotiation, and the same reasoning applies to the elasticity of demand.

The cooperative game described above gives a framework for thinking about the impact of exogenous shocks on state firms. But this setup does not yield equations that can be estimated directly, for several reasons. On the one hand, there are data and measurement constraints. On the other hand, there are problems associated with the joint determination of employment and wages.

Bibliography

Björklund, E., and Holmlund, B. 1991. "Unemployment Insurance." In A. Björklund, R. Hollister, and B. Holmlund, eds., *Labor Market Policy and Unemployment Insurance*. Oxford: Clarendon.

Commander, Simon, and Karsten Staehr. 1991. *The Determination of Wages in Socialist Economies: Some Microfoundations*. Washington, D.C.: World Bank.

Commander, Simon, and Cecilia Ugaz. 1993. *The Determinants of Output in Hungary, 1989-1992 — Panel Estimations*. Washington, D.C.: World Bank.

Fazekas, K., and J. Köllô. 1991. "The Patterns of Unemployment in Hungary—A Case Study." *Structural Change and Economic Dynamics* 1:35-51.

Feldstein, M. 1976. "Temporary Layoffs in the Theory of Unemployment." *Journal of Political Economy* 84:937-57.

_____. 1978. "The Effect of Unemployment Insurance on Temporary Layoff Unemployment." *The American Economic Review* 68:834-46.

Galasi, P. 1993. *Unemployment Benefit, Wages and Job Search Intensity*. Working Paper 8, ILO/Japan Project, November, Budapest.

Godfrey, M. 1993. *Elôzetes jelentés a munkanélküliek és a munkaerôpiaci programok résztvevôi körében 1992*. október-novemberben lebonyolított reprezentatív adatfelvétel eredményeirôl (Preliminary report on a representative survey of the unemployed and of the participants of active labor market policy programs). Országos Munkaerôpiaci Központ, Budapest: ILO.

Köllô, J. 1992. "Elôtanulmány és adattár a magyarországi munkanélküliség tanulmányozásához" (Pilot Study and Regional Database for the Study of Unemployment in Hungary). Budapest: Institute of Economics.

_____. 1993. "Flows of Labor, Employment and Wages in the Private Sector in Hungary." Budapest: Institute of Economics. (Prepared for World Bank research project.)

Köllô, J., K. Fazekas, E. Fülöp, Gy. Nagy, and B. Váradi. 1993. "Background Paper on Unemployment and Related Budget Expenditures." The Blue Ribbon Commission, May. Mimeo.

Kolosi, T., and E. Sík. 1993. "Munkaerôpiac és jövedelmek" (The Labor Market and Incomes). In *Jelentés a Magyar Háztartás Panel I*. hullámának eredményeirôl. Budapest.

Kornai, J. 1993. *Transformational Recession*. Working Paper 1, Collegium Budapest.

Laky, T. 1993. *A munkaerôpiac keresletét és kínálatát alakító folyamatok* (Processes Governing Labor Supply and Demand). Budapest: Labor Research Institute.

Layard, R., R. Jackman, and S. Nickell. 1991. *Unemployment.* New York: Oxford University Press.

Nagy, Gy. 1993. "Munkanélküliség" (Unemployment). In *Egy év után—Jelentés a MHP II. hullámának eredményeiről.* Budapest: BKE-TÁRKI.

Nagy, Gy., and E. Sík. 1993. "Munkenélküliség és munkanélküliek" (Unemployment and the Unemployed). In *Jelentés a Magyar Háztartás Panel I. hullámának eredményeiről.* Budapest.

Nagy, Gy., and J. Micklewright 1993. How does the Hungarian benefit system really work? European University, Florence. Mimeo.

OECD. 1993. *Hungary Survey.* Paris.

Székely, J. 1993a. "Rövidtávú munkaerôpiaci prognózis" (Short-Term Labor Market Forecast). Országos Munkaerôpiaci Központ, Budapest.

———. 1993b. "Gazdasági reálfolyamatok 1993. I. félévében" (Economic Trends in January-June 1993). Országos Munkaerôpiaci Központ, Budapest.

———. 1993c. "Rövid távú munkaerôpiaci prognózis" (Short Run Labor Market Forecast). June 1993. Országos Munkaerôpiaci Központ, Budapest.

Vilagi, Balacs. 1993. *The Behavior of Hungarian Firms in 1992: Evidence from a Survey.* Budapest: Institute of Economics.

2

Poland

Fabrizio Coricelli, Krzysztof Hagemejer, and Krzysztof Rybinski

The analysis of the evolution of labor market variables in the first four years of transition in Poland highlights three important facts. First, the Labor Force Survey carried out since 1992 reveals that high unemployment is not a statistical artifact. This simple fact should not be overlooked. According to an influential view, the Polish recession has been largely overstated on the basis of distorted statistics (see Berg and Sachs 1992). The growth of unemployment from zero to about 16 percent leaves little doubt that after 1990 Poland went through a deep, serious recession.

Second, unemployment has continued to grow during 1992 and 1993 despite a significant recovery of the economy. This suggests that unemployment is not a simple cyclical phenomenon. Third, unemployment has steadily increased in the context of sharply asymmetric dynamics of state and private sector employment. Thus unemployment has developed during a period of massive reallocation of labor from state to private sectors.

Against this background, this chapter addresses the issue of the characteristics of unemployment and its role during the transition to a full-fledged market economy. Is unemployment the cost of an unnecessary recession, or is it a necessary phenomenon—albeit costly in the short

We thank Annette Brown, Brian Pinto, and the participants at the World Bank Conference, "Unemployment and Restructuring in Eastern Europe," for very useful comments on an earlier version of the paper.

run—supporting an efficient reallocation of resources from state to private sectors, and with it the long-run growth of the Polish economy? As expected, the answer is mixed, and the characteristics and the role of unemployment have likely changed over time.

The evidence presented here suggests that in the first four years of transition unemployment has been, by and large, a "stagnant pool" (see Boeri 1993). Indeed, inflows into unemployment and outflows from unemployment have been very small. A large proportion of those who have entered the unemployment pool have remained unemployed. This implies that job-to-job movements, with no transit into unemployment, have accommodated a large share of new jobs filled after 1990.

By extrapolating current flows one would conclude that unemployment in Poland is likely to become a persistent phenomenon. Nevertheless, the chapter argues that aggregate flows conceal fundamental asymmetries in the underlying dynamics of job creation and destruction in state and private sectors. Current flows are unlikely to continue in the future. As the relative size of the private sector continues to increase, the growth of the private sector will outweigh the decline of the state sector, and will thus yield an aggregate increase in employment. Moreover, there are important feedbacks from unemployment to employment in the state sector, with high unemployment rates reducing the incentives for moving out of state employment.

Therefore, one could expect that as the recovery of the economy takes hold, unemployment might soon decline. This is what can be inferred by extrapolating current trends of the dynamics of state and private sector employment.

This chapter points to some possible obstacles to the reduction in unemployment, among which the lack of labor mobility across regions stands out. Indeed, we have computed measures of regional mismatch between labor demand and supply that may explain up to a quarter of total unemployment in Poland. The chapter concludes that high unemployment has been the result of the sharp recession that affected the Polish economy in 1990-91. The further increase in 1992-93, however, reflects a process of restructuring and reallocation of labor among firms, above all from state to private firms. Thus, extreme views are likely to be wrong, either those attributing unemployment to a simple Keynesian recession, or those interpreting high unemployment as an inevitable, and desirable, instrument to achieve an efficient restructuring of the economy.

While unemployment was partly an inevitable outcome of reforms launched in a country starting from zero unemployment, a large proportion of unemployment has reflected an aggregate contraction of the economy. High unemployment might have been an obstacle to the restructuring of the economy, increasing resistance to privatization either because of political pressures or fiscal pressures coming from the budgetary costs of unemployment.

The chapter is organized as follows. The first section contains an overview of the behavior of output, employment, and wages. The second section analyzes the dynamics of unemployment, focusing on labor market flows and, in particular, on the process of job destruction in the state sector and of job creation in the private sector. The third section provides a description of the characteristics of the unemployed. The appendix presents more details on the analysis of "mismatch" presented in the second section, "Labor Market Flows: Dynamics and Characteristics of Unemployment."

Overview

In mid-1992 Poland began its recovery from the deep recession that followed the reform program of 1990. In 1993 the recovery was consolidated, led by a rapid growth in industrial production (figure 2-1).

Output and Employment Changes: Aggregate and Reallocative Factors

The behavior of labor market variables has to be evaluated against this background. However, the nature of both the recession and growth may matter more than the simple rates of change in GDP. Indeed, unemployment is likely to respond quite differently, depending on the characteristics of the forces affecting the overall economic activity. In particular, it is important to assess the relative role of aggregate and structural or reallocative factors behind the movements of economic activity. In principle, the stronger the structural factors, the larger is the variability across sector and firms of output and employment changes, and thus the larger the needed reallocation of labor across different branches and firms.

Unemployment arising from the sluggishness in the reallocation of labor across activities has, of course, a completely different nature than unemployment arising from an overall contraction of economic activity.

Figure 2-1. Industrial Production and Unemployment

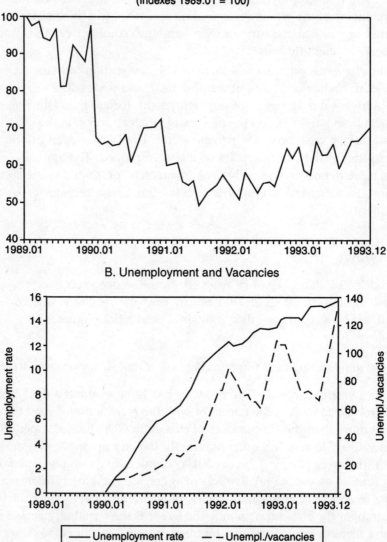

A. Industrial Production

(Indexes 1989.01 = 100)

B. Unemployment and Vacancies

Unemployment rate   − − Unempl./vacancies

Although it is beyond the scope of this chapter to discuss the causes and characteristics of output behavior in post-reform Poland, it is worth emphasizing that the characteristics of output behavior have changed significantly over time. In 1990 the recession was broad based. The low variability across sectors and the lack of an association between output changes and changes in relative prices suggests that the output decline resulted from a shift away from the production possibility frontier rather than from sectoral reallocation.[1]

Table 2-1 indicates that the variability of sectoral output sharply increased after 1990. Moreover, for 1992 one can note a positive and statistically significant relation between sectoral output changes and changes in relative prices.[2]

Contrary to expectations, changes in the employment structure across the main sectors of the economy during 1990-92 were not very significant. The share of industrial employment has fallen by only 1 percent in favor of an increase in the share of services (table 2-2). By contrast, within industry the sectoral dynamics of employment changes mirror that of output, with the variability of changes across sectors sharply increasing after 1990. Information for three-digit industries reinforces this finding. Not only does the sectoral variability increase, but the number of sectors showing employment growth increases as well.[3] Moreover, the significant improvement in labor productivity that took place in 1992-93 may be an additional signal of structural change and better allocation of resources.

Besides the increased variability of employment changes across branches, the main feature of structural change can be identified in the asymmetric behavior of state and private sectors. Table 2-3 clearly shows that after 1990 the behavior of aggregate output hides the diverging dynamics of state and private sector output. It also suggests that the generalized initial drop in output in 1990 became persistent in the state sector, while it was rapidly reversed in the private sector. By 1992 aggregate output began to increase entirely because of the growth of private sector output.

---

1. The idea would be that adjustment costs produce a temporary output decline while resources shift among sectors.
2. For 1990-91 such relation was not significant (see Borensztein, Demekas, and Ostry 1993).
3. The coefficient of variation of employment changes at the three-digit level increased from 0.07 in 1990 to 0.25 in 1992, while at the two-digit level it increased only from 0.05 to 0.08. Out of 113 industrial branches, only 11, and almost all in the energy sector, expanded employment in 1990, as opposed to 36 branches in 1991.

Table 2-1. Poland, Industrial Production and Employment by Sector

Item	Production				Employment			
	1990	1991	1992	1993	1990	1991	1992	1993
Fuel	−20.1	−14.6	11.7	4.2	−0.4	−1.7	2.4	4.0
Coal	−31.8	1.0	−8.4	−5.3	−11.4	−9.3	−4.9	−4.4
Power	−9.7	−5.7	−6.0	−0.6	1.7	1.7	0.5	2.0
Iron and steel	−17.1	−24	−3.4	1.2	−5.6	−4.2	−10.0	−7.2
Nonferrous metallurgy	−23.7	−21.1	−5.7	−2.2	−2.8	−10.3	−4.8	−15.7
Metal products	−25.6	−16	7.8	2.9	−11.4	−7.1	−6.0	0.3
Engineering	−19.6	−21.3	−7.3	−3.9	−10.3	−13.6	−15.5	−8.3
Precision instruments	−16.1	−31.2	10.0	−31.3	−8.6	−17.8	−18.4	−11.2
Transport equipment	−25.2	−38.3	23.1	5.8	−8.1	−8.5	−11.7	−3.0
Electrical engineering	−20.2	−21.1	7.4	−2.6	−7.7	−17.9	−18.7	−7.6
Chemical	−24.6	−15.2	6.8	3.7	−9	−5.8	−7.0	−1.0
Building materials	−20	−8.5	−1.8	10.4	−5.4	−4.8	−2.0	−3.7
Glass products	−27.3	−5.1	6.7	−4.0	−6.5	−6.8	−6.8	−6.1
Pottery and china	−21.6	−13.9	−2.1	12.2	−2.9	−10.2	−17.5	−1.4
Wood	−25.2	−4.1	15.6	9.3	−14.5	2.7	−1.5	2.3
Paper	−23.8	−2.8	8.4	1.6	−8.5	−9.1	−10.7	−4.3
Textile	−39.6	−19.2	4.1	2.1	−11.2	−20.2	−20.0	−6.3
Wearing apparel	−24	−13.1	13.8	−6.5	−14.5	−5.9	−1.3	7.9
Leather	−30.6	−19.7	−3.9	−16.2	−11	−14.5	−16.8	−10.8
Food	−23.7	−0.5	4.2	16.6	−2.5	2.2	3.3	1.4
Average	−23.7	−14.7	3.6	−0.4	−7.9	−8.4	−8.9	−4.1
Standard deviation	6.2	10.3	8.4	10.3	4.1	6.4	7.1	5.5
Coefficient of variation	0.3	0.7	2.3	28.6	0.5	0.8	0.8	1.3

Source: Central Statistical Office, *Monthly Statistical Bulletin,* various issues.

Table 2-2. Poland, Employment Distribution

Sectors and years	1989 (thousands)	1990 (thousands)	1991 (thousands)	1992 (thousands)	1989 (percent)	1992 (percent)
Total	12,154	11,375	10,406	9,831	100.0	100.0
Budgetary	2,390	2,418	2,378	2,323	19.7	23.6
Industry	4,443	4,182	3,798	3,502	36.6	35.6
Construction	1,155	1,069	931	902	9.5	9.2
Agriculture	758	668	514	367	6.2	3.7
Forestry	136	123	109	94	1.1	1.0
Transport	765	696	618	532	6.3	5.4
Communication	168	171	167	171	1.4	1.7
Trade	1,213	1,037	1,042	954	10.0	9.7
Communal services	325	313	285	284	2.7	2.9
Housing	208	197	168	171	1.7	1.7
Research and development	112	96	82	71	0.9	0.7
Education	1,072	1,097	1,084	1,045	8.8	10.6
Culture	115	107	91	85	0.9	0.9
Health care	869	893	863	828	7.2	8.4
Recreational services	115	88	73	62	0.9	0.6
Administration and justice	222	220	235	259	1.8	2.6
Finance and insurance services	140	149	165	187	1.1	1.9

Note: This take includes wage and salary earners, yearly average.
Source: Rocznik Statystyczny 1992; Maly Rocznik Statystyczny 1993.

Table 2-3. Poland, Industrial Production by Ownership
(percentage change over same period of previous year)

Category	1990	1991	1992	1993[a]
Total	−24.2	−11.9	4.2	6.9
Public sector	−23.7	−19.4	−4.8	−5.9
Private sector	−27.2	25.2	32.2	38.6

a. First three quarters.
Source: Central Statistical Office (GUS), *Information on Economic Situation in Poland 1992*, Warsaw 1993; and *Monthly Statistical Bulletin*, January 1994.

Financial Conditions and Wage/Employment Adjustment

While output and employment have shown an increasing sensitivity both to relative price changes and to the financial conditions of firms (figure 2-2), the behavior of wages displays a less clear-cut picture.

In the aggregate, after the sharp fall at the beginning of 1990, wages for 1990-91 grew well in excess of the amount warranted on the basis of the behavior of productivity and of producer prices. As a result, real unit labor costs (the share of wage bill in output) steadily increased after the first quarter of 1990, reaching levels by the end of 1991 even higher than those of end-1989; and the latter were considered exceptionally high. With 1992 this trend has been interrupted, as productivity growth compensated the adverse effect of the "wedge"—the difference between consumer and producer prices. Figure 2-3 illustrates the process behind the above dynamics, showing a high degree of real consumer wage rigidity, with wages clearly trying to catch up with the consumer price index, irrespective of the movement in producer prices. A simple regression analysis supports this view. Results summarized in table 2-4 confirm the high degree of de facto indexation to consumer prices and the responsiveness with respect to productivity changes. Moreover, real monetary balances of enterprises are important and statistically significant in affecting wage dynamics, supporting the relation between wage behavior and enterprise liquidity noted in cross-section analysis (see Calvo and Coricelli 1993).

The aggregate behavior conceals important differences across sectors. Separating sectors into three groups through profitability indexes, figure 2-2 illustrates three interesting points.[4] First, in line with the hypothesis of

4.   *AAA* sectors display positive profits after tax; *AA*, positive profits before tax; *A*, losses even before tax. This classification has been used by Pinto, Belka, and Krajewski (1993).

Table 2-4. Poland, Regression for Real Wages, OLS Regression,
January 1990-March 1993

Variable	Coefficient	t-statistics
Constant	0.00	(0.33)
Change in log of productivity	0.21	(1.82)
Change in the wedge	1.03	(4.45)
Change in log of real M2	0.78	(7.25)
Dummy, January	−0.08	(−3.01)
Adj. R-squared	0.90	
DW	1.73	

Note: Dependent variable: Change in log of real producer wages.

a high degree of indexation to consumer wages, changes in nominal wages display a striking homogeneity across sectors (figure 2-2b). Second, given the asymmetric behavior of producer prices—with relative prices positively associated with profitability—it turns out that real producer wages increase in the less profitable sectors. They increase even in the loss-making sectors (figure 2-2c). Finally, the real wage bill closely reflects the financial conditions of the sectors (figure 2-2d).

On the basis of this, admittedly partial, evidence one can advance the following conclusions. (1) The strict association between the real wage bill and financial conditions is a sign of hard budget constraints. For given wages, employment cannot be maintained above what the firm is able to pay. This is also confirmed by the concentration of the excess wage tax (*PPWW* in figure 2-2e) in the more profitable firms. (2) The combination of increasing real wages per worker and a declining real wage bill in the less profitable firms suggests that wage pressure was a factor contributing to the difficulties of these firms. One can conjecture that the horizon of the worker-controlled firms is an increasing function of the financial conditions of firms. In loss-making firms the horizon is short, leading to wage pressure and reduced output and employment.[5] Such a short horizon seems to be confirmed by indicators of "decapitalization" (figure 2-2f), which show loss-making firms as an outlier, at least in 1992.

---

5.   Calvo and Coricelli (1993) offer an example of this phenomenon in a model in which firms are liquidity-constrained and need real monetary balances to purchase their inputs.

Figure 2-2. Output, Employment, Producer Prices, and Average Wage Changes by Category of Firm, 1990-92

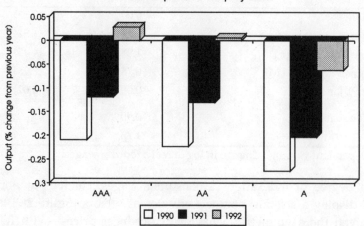

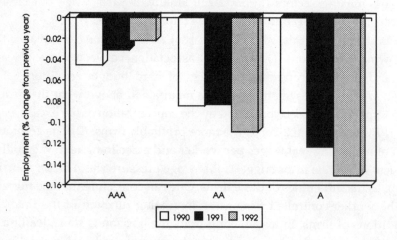

B. Producer Price and Average Wage

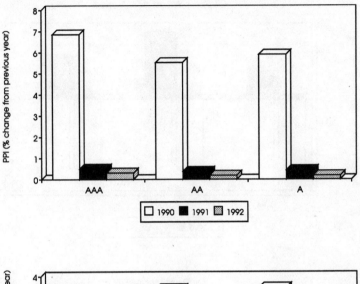

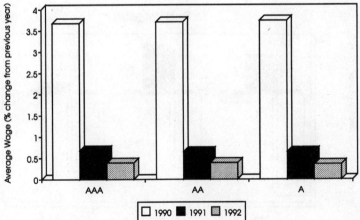

Figure 2.2   *(continued)*

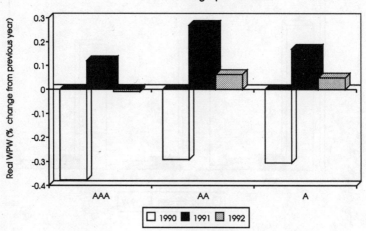

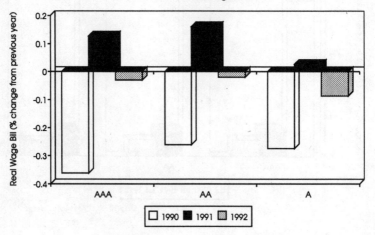

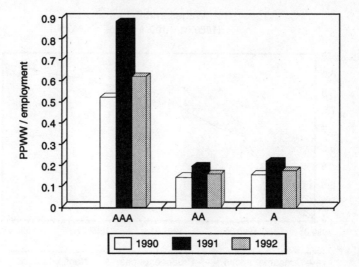

E. Popiwek/Employment by Firm Category

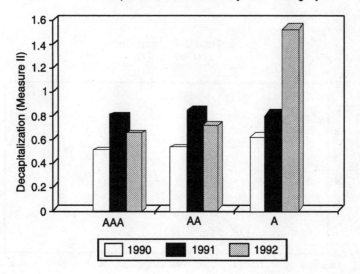

F. Decapitalization Measure by Firm Category

Figure 2-3. Wages, Prices, and Labor Costs

A. Wages and Prices
(1989.01 = 100, in logs)

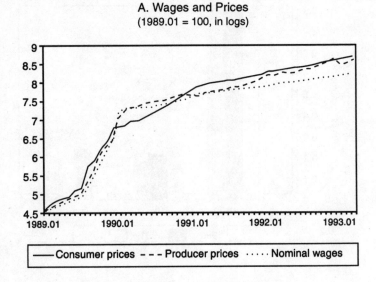

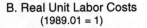

B. Real Unit Labor Costs
(1989.01 = 1)

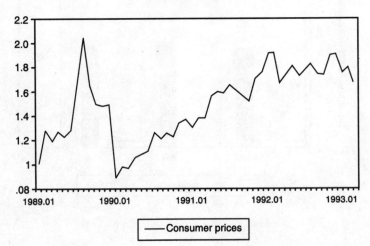

Summing up, and combining time series and sectoral information, a picture emerges in which within a broad enforcement of hard budget constraints, the horizon of worker-controlled firms has changed significantly over time and across sectors. After the initial wage moderation in the first half of 1990, the workers' horizon shortened sharply in the second half of 1990 and in 1991, raising the fear of end-game behavior on the part of the workers.[6] This fear was overcome in 1992, although we noted that the variance of the sectoral behaviors increased sharply. These data refer to industry, which is still largely dominated by state firms, and thus point to a lengthening of the horizon even in workers of state firms. It is worth noting, however, that enterprise profits steadily dropped after 1990, stabilizing in 1992 at an average level close to zero. This suggests that wages are set closer to the average than to the marginal product of labor. Although this kind of wage setting—which likely dominates state firms—is consistent with preserving the level of output and existing assets in the firm, it is nevertheless an obstacle to new investment.

There are several explanations for the above pattern of wage/employment behavior. We emphasize three channels. (1) The changed nature of the privatization process and the attendant changed perception on the future stake of the *insiders* in the firm. (2) The growth of the private sector and its large weight in the economy. (3) The increase in unemployment, with its disciplining effect on wage demands.

The next sections discuss these three channels.

WORKERS' HORIZON AND PRIVATIZATION. The actual privatization process has followed a pattern radically different from that proposed in 1990 by advisers in the process, who envisioned a mass privatization dominated by outside investors. By contrast, privatization in Poland has been so far dominated by liquidation, which in 80 percent of the cases implies the transfer (lease or sale) of assets to employees' companies. Therefore, with a few exceptions, privatization has been an *insider-dominated* process. Table 2-5 summarizes the main routes followed in the privatization of nonagricultural firms.

Table 2-5 shows a marked deceleration in the privatization process in 1992, with the number of firms involved in privatization falling almost to half that of 1991.

---

6. These fears are, for instance, reflected in the analysis of Commander and Coricelli (1993), which focused on the period 1990-91.

Table 2-5. Poland, Privatization

Category	Total	1990[a]	1991	1992
State enterprises qualifying for privatization	1,955	130	1,128	697
Capital privatization	481	58	250	173
Liquidation	1,474	72	878	524

a. For 1990, September-December.
Source: Information on social and economic situation in Poland I quarter 1993, Central Statistical Office (GUS), Warsaw, 1993.

Both the postponement of mass privatization and the evolution toward a privatization process dominated by insiders should have, in principle, increased the perceived stake of insiders, both workers and managers, in their firms. Thus, the horizon of the insiders should have lengthened.

THE GROWTH OF THE PRIVATE SECTOR.   Table 2-6 displays the rapid growth of employment in the private sector, which by 1992 accounts for about 43 percent of total nonagricultural employment. Assuming that problems of short horizons are absent in private firms, where the nature of the property rights is well defined, it follows that, loosely speaking, the average horizon in the economy lengthens with the increasing share of the private sector in the economy. Nevertheless, microeconomic evidence (Pinto, Belka, and Krajewski 1993) shows that the horizon has also lengthened in state enterprises.

Table 2-6. Poland, Share of Private Sector in Employment
(percentage)

Category	1989	1990	1991	1992
Total outside private agriculture	31.2	33.6	40.3	42.8
Industry	29.1	31.2	35.8	40.5
Construction	37.4	42.1	59.5	71.9
Transport	14.3	15.2	26.0	25.4
Trade	72.7	82.2	88.3	90.7

Note: Percentage represents total number employed at end of year.
Source: Report on socioeconomic situation in 1992, Rzeczpospolita, February 6, 1993; Report on socioeconomic situation in first half of 1993, Rzeczpospolita, August 7, 1993.

THE DISCIPLINING ROLE OF UNEMPLOYMENT.   The high levels of unemployment reached after 1990 could, in principle, explain the wage moderation that surfaced in 1992. The data, however, do not indicate the presence of a traditional Phillips curve. Indeed, inserting the rate of unemployment into the wage equation estimated in table 2-4 yields a statistically insignificant coefficient. The lack of a significant correlation at the aggregate level between wage changes and unemployment does not imply that unemployment exerts no effect on wage setting. Rather, it is likely that those effects are at work at a more disaggregated level.

First, there could be an asymmetric wage setting in state and private firms.[7] Efficiency considerations, concern with the effort provided by the workers, are likely to be more important in private than in state firms. As a result, efficiency wages may accurately describe wage setting in private firms, with unemployment exerting a disciplining role, because the premium over unemployment benefits that private owners are willing to pay is a decreasing function of unemployment.[8] If these considerations are not relevant in the state sector, it may happen that aggregate wages and unemployment are not significantly correlated. Unfortunately, lack of microeconomic data impedes a check the validity of this view.

Another important aspect relates to the possible presence of "local" or regional labor markets. With limited labor mobility across regions, what matters for regional wage setting is regional rather than aggregate unemployment. Choosing 1992 as less affected by the exceptional events of the stabilization program of 1990 and the CMEA shock of 1991, a simple regression linking regional wage changes to regional unemployment reveals a negative and statistically significant coefficient.

Summing up, factors affecting the horizon of workers and regional unemployment have exerted an important influence on wage behavior. These factors were likely more important than wage policy in shaping the pattern of wage behavior. Nevertheless, especially in 1990 wage policy was an important instrument, given that the country started the stabilization program from a position of zero unemployment and with enormous

---

7.   Such a possibility is discussed analytically by Commander, Coricelli, and Staehr 1992; Chadha, Coricelli, and Krajnyak 1993; and Aghion and Blanchard 1993.

8.   In the so-called shirking model of efficiency wages, higher unemployment implies higher costs for workers who are caught shirking. Indeed, if fired they are likely to spend a longer period unemployed, receiving unemployment benefits that are lower than wages.

uncertainty on the prospects for privatization and changes at the enterprise level.

WAGE DIFFERENTIALS.   Table 2-7 indicates that wage dispersion has not increased significantly in the aggregate. This result is mainly a product of the stability or even the decline of dispersion of wages in the state sector, particularly among manual workers. Indeed, dispersion indexes are significantly higher in the private sector and for white workers.

Table 2-7. Poland, Wage Distribution

Measure	Employed	1987	1988	1991	1992	Public	Private
Concentration							
coefficient	All	0.230	0.213	0.242	0.247	0.236	0.288
(Lorenz)	Manual	0.239	0.219	0.231	0.230	0.225	0.243
Decile	All	275.6	260.5	285.9	292.0	280.2	338.2
ratio[a]	Manual	290.4	270.9	284.8	283.1	277.8	300.1
Quartile	All	166.6	162.3	168.1	171.4	168.2	186.6
ratio[b]	Manual	170.7	165.0	169.5	170.5	168.9	178.2
Asymmetry	All	2.021	1.636	4.495	4.056	3.352	4.979
index[c]	Manual	1.765	1.440	1.660	1.731	1.529	2.485
Coefficient	All	45.0	40.9	51.9	53.1	49.0	68.0
of variation	Manual	46.4	41.3	44.0	44.0	42.8	48.4

a. Ratio of 9th decile to 1st decile.
b. Ratio of 3rd decile to 1st decile.
c. Ratio of third-order moment to the third power of standard deviation.
Source: Hagemejer 1993.

The stability of the wage distribution among skill categories, together with the low variability of wages across industrial sectors, is quite striking. One possible contributing factor could be the national wage policy, which acted as a constraint on increasing the differentiation of wages. Moreover, the larger compression of the wage distribution in state firms suggests that wage setting rules are different in the two sectors, with a larger weight for income equalization objectives in state firms.

Differentials between state and private sector wages. Data on the wage differential between state and private sectors do not strongly support the view of a largely voluntary shift from state to private jobs. According to official statistics, wages in the private sector are on average

Table 2-8. Wages in State and Private Sectors, 1992-93
(average monthly wages, thousand zlotys)

	1992		1993	
Category	State	Private	State	Private
Industry	3,171	2,551	4,221	3,564
Trade	3,295	2,425	4,421	3,256
Construction	2,921	3,069	3,627	3,852
Transport	2,779	3,070	3,776	4,223

Source: *Monthly Statistical Bulletin,* Warsaw, January 1994.

lower than in the state sector. This holds in trade and industry, while in construction and services other than trade, private sector wages are higher than those in the state sector (table 2-8).

The first qualification to be made is that the private sector includes the old cooperatives, which are in financial disarray. Even factoring in the effect of the cooperatives, however, a differential in favor of state firms remains in the industrial sector. Unfortunately, there are no data on wages for comparable skills or jobs, and thus the aggregate comparison is affected by potentially different skill composition.

The distribution of wages by decile can be used as a substitute for the missing data on wages by occupation type. Figure 2-4a shows that the lower aggregate wage in the private sector arises mainly from the concentration of private jobs in low-wage categories. In the upper end of the scale, wages tend to be higher in the private sector (figure 2-4b).

The above pattern suggests that wages in the private sector are compressed by the presence of a large share of low-paid jobs.[9] In addition, it is likely that the high rate of unemployment exerts downward pressure on private sector wages. Without consistent time-series data on private sector wages, however, this effect cannot be verified empirically.

Working conditions and benefits are less favorable in private firms. Low wages and worse working conditions may explain survey results that indicate a clear preference of workers for state-firm jobs.[10] The pro-

9. Simon Johnson (1993) calls these "bad private jobs."
10. The Hirschman's "tunnel effect" indicated by Freeman (1992), with workers in declining sectors endorsing reforms because they observe the successful stories of workers in growing firms, is unlikely to be operative.

Figure 2-4. Employment and Wages

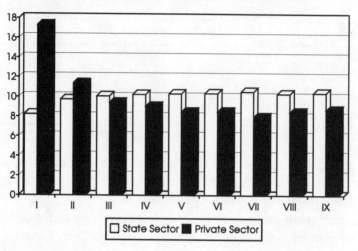

A. Employment Shares in Deciles for All Workers

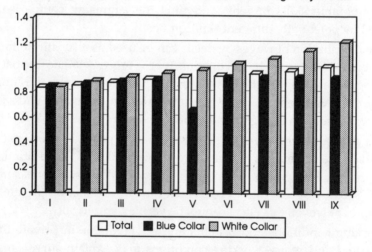

B. Wage Distribution Ratio of Private/State Wages by Decile

spective conditions in private sector jobs have created resistance both to privatization and to labor mobility out of state firms.

Reservation wage. The Labor Force Survey (LFS) contains a question that asks the unemployed for what wage would they be willing to accept a job. Table 2-9 shows the distribution of answers in the September 1992

Table 2-9. Poland, Wage Expectations of the Unemployed, 1992

Expected wage (millions zl)	Total	Men	Women	Actual wage distribution
Less than 1	1.1	0.8	1.3	0.0
1-1.5	36.8	28.1	45.1	4.5
1.5-2	38.3	37.2	39.3	14.1
2-2.5	11.6	15.3	8.1	19.9
2.5-3	8.5	12.9	4.4	17.2
More than 3	3.7	5.7	1.8	44.3
Average expected wage	1.9	2.1	1.8	
Average actual wage	3.1	3.4	2.7	
Minimum wage	1.35	1.35	1.35	

Source: Hagemejer 1993.

survey and compares them with the minimum wage in November 1992 and the average monthly wage and salary in the whole economy in the same month. The average monthly wage that the unemployed would accept was about 1.9 million zlotys. Almost 40 percent of the surveyed unemployed would have accepted a wage between 1 million and 1.5 million, close to the minimum wage. Contrasting the distribution of unemployed by wage expectations and the actual distribution of employed by wage brackets, it seems that wage aspirations of the unemployed do not constitute a serious constraint on hiring.

Labor Market Flows: Dynamics and Characteristics of Unemployment

Since the launching of the reform program in January 1990, unemployment has steadily grown from a zero starting level. By the end of 1992 unemployment reached 2.5 million people, or 13.6 percent of the labor force. With an improvement in the overall state of the economy, in the second half of 1992 the rate of unemployment stabilized—at least according to registration numbers (see box 2-1 for issues in measurement and definition of unemployment). During 1993, however, the unemployment rate increased to 15.7 percent, despite a buoyant economy.

Box 2-1. Unemployment Data Sources

Until 1992 registered unemployment was the only source of unemployment data. In 1990 data on registered unemployment were not very reliable because of very generous laws on unemployment benefit eligibility and because labor offices were not organized properly and were not able to keep registers in order and to process data. In both areas there have been improvements over time. Time series on registered unemployment, however, are affected by changes in regulations and by periodic verification of the registers. For instance, the reduction at twelve months of the duration of unemployment benefits established at the end of 1991 is likely to bias downward registered unemployment. In a situation in which labor offices are mainly engaged in registration payments procedures and the scope of active labor market activities is rather limited, there are weak incentives for the unemployed without right to benefits to be registered.

The scope of register data was very limited in 1990 and 1991. It is much wider since the beginning of 1992, when a new registration form was introduced.

In May 1992 the Central Statistical Office (GUS) started a quarterly labor force survey. Register data will remain the only source for regional patterns of unemployment, because the labor force survey sample is too small to provide representative data on voivodships. Data from registers and from the survey are not fully comparable. Not all registered unemployed are unemployed according to the definition assumed in LFS. Also, according to the Survey there is a large number of unemployed who are not registered.

According to the 1992 Labor Force Survey, 8.6 percent of the unemployed had quit their jobs for early retirement.

Unemployment, Labor Force, and Employment

Table 2-10 shows that the increase in unemployment from 1989 to 1992 arose from a decline in employment by 2 million units and an increase in the labor force by 500 thousand units.[11] If confirmed, the increase in par-

---

11.   In this regard, data are unfortunately contradictory. While Labor Force Survey data indicate a declining labor force during the first years of reform, data from the Central Statistical Office (GUS) indicate an increase in participation rates. According to the 1992 Labor Force Survey, the labor force participation rate in May 1992 was 61.4 percent (69.9 for men and 53.7 percent for women). Since 1970, participation rates have systematically decreased: from 70.6 percent in 1970, through 65.3 percent in 1988 (census data), to 61.4 percent (Labor Force Survey data) in 1992.

ticipation rates after 1990 would be remarkable. Indeed, it would imply a massive new entry or reentry into the labor force, which more than compensated the large increase in early retirements. During 1990-91 about 700 thousand people left the labor force for retirement or disability pension (table 2-11).[12] Early retirements accounted for a large proportion of the initial decline in employment that began in 1990. Recently, a significant proportion of those who had retired have tried to reenter the labor force.

The 2 million decline in employment during the period 1990-92 took place entirely outside private agriculture (table 2-10). In 1992, in conjunction with the end of the decline in GDP, the decrease in the total number of employed was smaller than during 1990-91. Employment levels fell less than output, especially during 1990-91—in these years employment fell by about 10 percent, while GDP fell by about 20 percent. This should not, however, be taken as a signal of lack of response of enterprises to the new economic conditions. Indeed, rather than shedding labor to a fuller extent, firms may have adopted other forms of adjustment. First, there was a significant decrease in hours worked, achieved by reducing the number of shifts, eliminating overtime, shortening weekly working hours, and forcing partially paid or unpaid leave. The total number of hours per worker declined by 3 percent in 1989, 5 percent in 1990, and 3 percent in 1991, while it increased in 1992.[13] *Therefore, output per hour worked fell much less than output per worker, while it increased less in 1992* (table 2-12).

Another way to adjust the level of employment was to reduce new hirings, likely limiting them to those necessary for strictly technological reasons. Gross hirings by state industry fell in 1990 by over 30 percent (24 percent in the whole state sector), while gross separations have increased only by 7 percent, an increase smaller than in 1989 (11 percent) (table 2-13).[14] In 1992 the hiring rate was 11.9 percent in the state sector, thus roughly in line with the rate in 1990, which is surprising given the differ-

12. Although the overall measured increase in labor force participation appears improbable, the Labor Force Survey indicates a significant increase in women's participation in urban areas—from an already high rate when compared with market economies. This likely reflects the income effect of tight economic conditions on Polish households.

13. The share of overtime hours in total hours worked per worker has fallen from over 8 percent in 1988 to less than 5 percent in 1991.

14. Unfortunately, there are no comparable figures for 1991, because for that year there are only figures for state and private sectors combined.

Table 2-10. Poland, Employment and Unemployment, 1988-92

| Category | Employed and unemployed in public and private sectors (end of year in millions) | | | | | | | | |
	1988 1	1989 2	1990 3	1991 4	1992[a] 5	5-1	(5-1)/1	5-2	(5-2)/2
Total employed	17.7	17.6	16.5	15.9	15.6	-2.1	-11.8%	-2.0	-11.3%
Outside private agriculture	13.6	13.5	12.4	11.8	11.5	-2.1	-15.1%	-2.0	-14.5%
Public sector ("new")	9.6	9.3	8.2	7.0	6.6	-3.0	-31.2%	-2.7	-28.8%
Public sector ("old")	12.3	11.8	10.1	8.8	7.7	-4.6	-37.3%	-4.0	-34.3%
Nonagriculture private sector ("new")	4.0	4.2	4.2	4.8	4.9	0.9	23.5%	0.7	17.3%
Nonagriculture ("old") sector	1.3	1.8	2.3	3.0	3.8	2.5	194.5%	2.0	114.9%
Private agriculture	4.1	4.1	4.1	4.1	4.1	0.0	-0.8%	0.0	0.0%
Unemployment	0.0	0.0	1.1	2.2	2.5	2.5	[a]	2.5	[a]

a. The 1992 data on number of employed differ from data previously reported by GUS.

Source: Estimates based on: Rocznik Statystyczny GUS 1989, 1990, 1991; 1992 GUS report on socioeconomic situation in 1992; Rzeczpospolita February 6, 1993; and GUS report on socioeconomic situation in first half of 1993, Rzeczpospolita, August 7, 1993.

Table 2-11. Poland, New Pensions, 1985-92

Reaching retirement age	1985	1988	1989	1990	1991	1992
Number (000's)	118	136	133	144	138	—
New pensions	382	405	437	653	912	481
Old-age	127	132	158	322	497	160
Disability	174	189	188	243	318	236

— Not available.
Note: Peasants' pensions are excluded.
Source: Rocznik Statystyczny, GUS 1990, 1992; GUS data for 1992.

Table 2-12. Poland, Hours Worked, 1988-92

Item	1988	1989	1990	1991	1992
Total (number per worker)	1,920.3	1,864.4	1,770.7	1,716.0	1,758.0
Previous year = 100	—	97.1	95.0	96.9	102.4
Overtime in percent of total time	8.4	7.9	5.5	4.6	4.3
Industry (number per worker)	1,874.2	1,818.6	1,721.3	1,655.0	—
Previous year = 100	—	97.0	94.6	94.1	—
Overtime in percent of total time	7.8	7.3	4.8	4.1	—

— Not available.
Source: Rocznik Statystyczny, GUS: 1989, 1990, 1991, 1992.

ent macroeconomic context and output behavior in the two years. Separations dropped significantly, falling below the 1989 level.

Typology of Unemployment and the Role of Unemployment

The turnover of unemployment is extremely low in Poland, if compared with market economies (table 2-14).[15] Roughly half of the exits from unemployment consist in exits to jobs. Moreover, there are no clear signs

---

15. For rates in market economies see Boeri 1993 and in this volume.

Table 2-13. Poland, Gross Hiring and Separations, 1988-92

Category	1988	1989	1990	1991[a]	1992[b]
Gross Hirings and Separations					
Total hirings	1,960	1,908	1,453	1,721	1,642
Pr. year=1	—	0.973	0.761	a	b
Total separations	2,178	2,417	2,594	2,727	2,040
Pr. year=1	—	1.110	1.073	a	b
Industry hirings	692	699	485	532	586
Pr. year=1	—	1.010	0.694	a	b
Separations	788	879	938	961	734
Pr. year=1	—	1.115	1.067	a	b
Hiring and Separation Rates (percent of number employed, end of previous year)					
Total hirings	17.3	16.2	12.2	16.1	17.9
Total separations	18.0	19.8	23.0	26.8	22.4
State					
Hirings					11.9
Separations					18.4
Private					
Hirings					38.8
Separations					36.3
Industry					
Hirings	16.1	15.8	10.7	12.9	17.1
Separations	17.2	19.3	22.0	25.2	21.6
State					
Hirings					10.8
Separations					18.6
Private					
Hirings					40.4
Separations					32.5

a. Until 1990 "socialized" sector only, 1991 public and private sector, excluding individual business units ("zaklady osob fizycznych").
b. In 1992 excluding units of less than five employees.
Source: Rocznik Statystyczny, 1990, 1991, 1992; Stan i Ruch Zatrudnionych w Gospodarce narodowej w 1992r.

Table 2-14. Poland, Unemployment Inflows and Outflows
(*percent*)

Month	Inflow rate	Outflow rate	Job exit rate
1/92	6.14	3.53	1.94
2/92	4.61	3.08	2.13
3/92	4.29	5.59	2.23
4/92	4.60	4.51	2.70
5/92	4.81	4.35	2.58
6/92	7.69	4.63	2.36
7/92	8.38	3.48	2.00
8/92	4.86	2.87	1.84
9/92	6.00	4.31	2.58
10/92	5.15	6.00	3.23
11/92	5.49	4.98	2.64
12/92	5.13	4.35	1.90
1/93	7.04	4.06	1.89
2/93	5.12	3.49	1.87
3/93	4.90	4.03	2.02
Average	5.61	4.22	2.26

Note: Flows as ratios to the stock of unemployed.

of increasing job exit probabilities even during the recovery of output in 1992. This has led observers to argue that unemployment is mainly a *stagnant pool* (Boeri 1993).

Low inflow rates were affected by large movements from employment out of the labor force, through early retirements, and by the reduction in hours worked, which has allowed firms to contain the employment reduction. Another important factor in containing inflow rates to unemployment were job-to-job movements, which have allowed significant employment reallocation without intervening unemployment spells.

The magnitude of this phenomenon, however, might have been exaggerated. Indeed, job-to-job movements are inferred by comparing the outflow from unemployment to jobs and the total number of hirings. Outflows to jobs were about 500 thousand in 1992, while gross hirings were more than 1.6 million. Thus, a rough estimate would attribute to job-to-job movements about 70 percent of gross hirings. The outflow to jobs, however, comprises only vacancies filled through the intermediation of labor offices, which is likely to grossly underestimate job finds by the unemployed.[16] A better proxy of the job-to-job movements could be given by quits, which most likely are associated to a direct movement to another job. Quit rates in 1992 were about 30 percent of total separations. If the latter were a good proxy of job-to-job movements, it would follow that most exits from unemployment were exits to employment.

We next discuss the asymmetric behavior of state and private sectors, summarized by a process of net job destruction in the state sector and of net job creation in the private sector. As discussed above, this does not imply assuming homogeneity within the state sector. From a macroeconomic point of view, however, it remains true that the dynamics of unemployment can be characterized in those two asymmetric, and complementary, dynamics. In addition to the above observation, focusing only on aggregate flows may be misleading. Indeed, inflows and outflows result from sharply different dynamics of state and private enterprises. Therefore, it is not clear what can be learned from the extrapolation of aggregate inflow and outflow rates. In particular, extrapolating exit probabilities and thus concluding that unemployment will remain a stagnant pool may not be warranted.

Inflow and outflow rates observed at present reflect an initial stock adjustment—especially in 1990—and are affected by the large difference in initial size of state and private sectors. These factors tend to compress the weight of reallocative effects that emerged over time.

If one instead extrapolates not inflows and outflows but the current trends in employment decline in the state sector and employment creation in the private sector, we would reach the conclusion that—with an unchanged labor force—unemployment is bound to decline as early as 1993 and disappear by 1996. While not very meaningful, this extrapolation is simply meant to caution against extrapolating from current exit rates from unemployment, which are conditioned by the above mentioned "level" effects.

Aggregate dynamics is bound to be crucially affected by the distribution of employment and labor market flows between state and private sectors. The asymmetric behavior of state and private sectors is reflected in

---

16.   An indirect indication of the unreliability of that figure is that it implies that in 1992 about 500 thousand people moved from unemployment out of the labor force.

the sharply different rates of both hirings and separations. The gap between the rates in the private sector and in the state sector is striking (table 2-13). Thus, the two sectors not only display different net employment changes, but they also display extremely different turnover rates. Lack of microeconomic data impede a rigorous analysis of the sources and characteristics of such different turnover rates. We can conjecture that higher worker turnover reflects (1) more dynamism in the population of private firms and (2) faster technical change with the attendant redefinition of skills. The first point suggests that higher freedom of entry and exit in the private sector leads to higher rates of birth and mortality of firms.

Job Destruction and Job Creation

During the 1980s—especially after 1987—there was already a significant process of reallocation of labor from the state to the private sector. In 1989 there was a shift from state to private nonagricultural jobs by more than 600 thousand people.[17]

Starting in 1990 the decline in employment in the public sector was not matched by the growth in jobs in the private sector. During 1990-92 the number of employed in the public sector (including cooperatives) fell by about 4 million, while the number of jobs created in the private sector rose by 2 million (table 2-10).

OUTFLOWS FROM STATE SECTOR EMPLOYMENT. Outflows from public sector employment can be divided into the following categories:

(a) employed who become employed in the private sector through privatization by staying in the same job

(b) employed who leave the labor force (retirements, and especially early retirements)

(c) employed who quit public sector employment to move to private sector employment or to self-employment

(d) laid off from the public sector.

---

17. In 1989 the increase in employment in the nonagricultural private sector (by nearly 43 percent) consisted of an increase of over 200,000 in owners and self-employed, and over 300,000 in wage and salary-earners. The expansion of the private sector in 1989 was stimulated by new liberal regulations on private economic activity introduced by the last Communist government at the end of 1988. This new policy fostered spontaneous privatization in such areas as trade, construction, and even in small industrial activities.

In 1989 the number of layoffs in the public sector was negligible, thus categories (a)-(c) dominated. Changes were dominated by people quitting the public sector and starting a private sector activity. In 1990-92 category (a) becomes more and more important. Privatization mainly affected small and medium-size units, not large state enterprises, where industrial employment is still concentrated. This phenomenon accounts partly for the observed large flows directly from jobs to jobs, without transiting unemployment (Boeri 1993).

Category (b), early retirements, was an important factor in the decline of state sector employment in 1990-91. Over time, layoffs (category (d)) increased. In 1992, 26 percent of separations arose from mass layoffs, and more than 60 percent from total layoffs. Quits, which dominated in 1989, accounted for 26 percent of separations in 1992, while 12 percent were associated with retirements. These aggregate proportions hide important differences across sectors and across ownership categories. Indeed, as regards the state sector, quits account for a much smaller share of separations in industry, 16 percent, and, overall, they account for a smaller share of separations in relation to the private sector. In the latter, quits account for 35 percent of total separations, and 40 percent for separations in industry. This points to the higher mobility of labor in private sectors.

In the state sector, employment declined by 28 percent, in addition to the 5.5 percent decline that took place in 1989. The rate of decline of employment in the state sector, however, slowed down significantly in 1992. This is apparent if one excludes cooperatives, a rather atypical group (table 2-10). The improvement in economic activity is certainly a factor behind this phenomenon. It may also, however, reflect a growing opposition on the part of workers to employment reductions proposed within restructuring plans of state enterprises, as suggested by the sharp increase in industrial conflicts. The slowdown in the pace of privatization can also be ascribed to this opposition. Workers' concern toward privatization has grown significantly.[18]

---

18. Opinion polls (September and November 1992) indicated that public employment is generally preferred because of the drawbacks of private employment in areas such as working conditions, social benefits, relations between management and workers, job security, and possibilities for trade union activity. About 48 percent of people surveyed preferred to work for state enterprises, 28 percent for private, while the remaining 20 percent were indifferent, although people perceived that wages were higher in the private sector.

TURNOVER IN THE STATE SECTOR. While the decline in state sector employment represents the main source of unemployment in Poland after 1990, data on hirings indicate that despite a sharp fall in 1990, gross flows into the state sector have remained high. In 1992 the hiring rate in the state sector was at the same level as in 1989. The factors determining this turnover are still unclear. Lack of microeconomic evidence does not allow us to determine whether the hiring rate is the result of the aggregation of heterogeneous firms, among which some are increasing and some are decreasing employment, or whether the same firms that display a net fall in employment still replace a significant part of their work force. Information on three-digit industrial branches, in which state firms still account for a large proportion of output and employment, indicates that in 1992 the increase in net employment of expanding sectors was roughly 3 percent of total industrial employment at the end of 1991. Thus, a significant proportion of gross hirings in state firms likely reflects turnover (see Chapter 7 in this volume for similar results on other transitional economies). This turnover could be related to technological factors. Certain workers—for instance, supervisors or skilled workers—have to be replaced when they leave because they are essential for the functioning of the firm.

The technological assumption finds some support in sectoral data on hirings and separations. Of course, a main caveat of these data is that they do not distinguish state and private sectors. Nevertheless, the correlation between hirings and separations within industries is striking (figure 2-5).

JOB CREATION IN THE PRIVATE SECTOR. Employment in the "old" (excluding cooperatives), nonagricultural private sector increased by over 120 percent during the period 1990-92. This increase was not sufficient to absorb people laid off from the state sector.[19] While remaining high, the rate of growth of private sector employment slowed down in 1992, despite the more favorable overall macroeconomic environment. Because we do not have data on employment changes by ownership for the different sectors of the economy, we use the difference between separations and hirings as a proxy.[20]

---

19. Employment in cooperatives—which since 1990 are classified as private sector—fell sharply in 1990, and it continued to decline in 1991-92 (table 2-1).
20. Hirings and separations are average figures for the year.

Figure 2-5. Poland, "Sectoral" Labor Markets

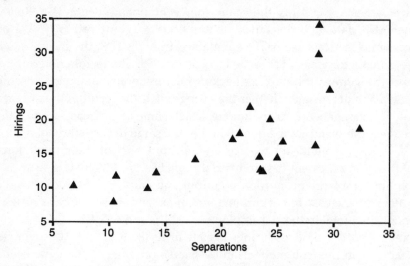

It is worth noting that in industry (plus 32,000), construction (plus 26,000), and finance (plus 7,000) hirings in the private sector were higher than separations in 1992.[21] By contrast, in private sector trade separations were in excess of hirings by more than 40,000.

These sectoral trends may indicate where the most important employment gains, led by private employment, are likely to come in the future. They also indicate that a large proportion of growth in private sector employment in sectors such as trade represented mainly a stock adjustment, with changing title from state to private activities.

Thus, it is likely that rates of growth of private sector employment will slow down in the future. Indeed, the process of growth of the more dynamic sectors, especially medium- and large-scale firms in industry, is much more complex than that of small-scale trade, because it requires large investments, and thus access to credit markets. Results from interviews indicate that the growth of medium- and large-scale industrial firms is severely constrained by limited private domestic capital, high interest rates, and uncertainty (Johnson 1993).

---

21. If one could factor out the effects of the declining cooperatives—mainly concentrated in industry—the figure on industry would give a much larger gap between hirings and separations.

If the private sector continues to remain concentrated in small-scale activities, the absorption capacity of the private sector will be limited. Even in industry, at the end of 1992, 30 percent of private employment was in firms with fewer than five employees.[22]

Unemployment, Restructuring, and Growth

This section tries to sum up the information discussed above and propose an interpretation. The main hypothesis we advance is that the dynamics of unemployment can be characterized by a nonlinear process relating the growth of the private sector and the rate of unemployment. As the private sector grows, unemployment grows as well, for restructuring and labor reallocation produce transitional unemployment. Initially the private sector is too small to absorb unemployment. Over time, the growth of the private sector will reach a point at which unemployment will decline. We use cross-section data on forty-nine voivodships to verify this hypothesis. Of course, the analysis is merely suggestive because available data do not permit a rigorous empirical test.

Figure 2-6a reports hiring rates in the private sector and unemployment rates in the forty-nine regions. The points in the scatter diagram can be roughly distributed along a bell-shaped curve. The presence of two segments, one with a positive coefficient followed by one with a negative coefficient, is verified statistically. The break occurs at a value of the hiring rate of about 34 percent.

It is worth noting that no relation can be detected between hiring rates of the state sector and unemployment (figure 2-6b). Separations from the state sector appear strongly associated with unemployment, while, as expected, this does not apply to separations from private firms (figure 2-6c and 6d). It is also interesting to note that there is no relation between net hirings (hirings-separations) in state and private firms across regions (figure 2-6e). This applies to gross hirings as well (figure 2-6f). All this information tends to confirm the asymmetric behavior of state and private sectors.

An important issue raised by this analysis is whether the country as a whole will move along the path indicated by the cross-section behavior of

---

22. Excluding cooperatives, the proportion would be higher, around 40 percent.

Figure 2-6. Poland, Regional Labor Markets

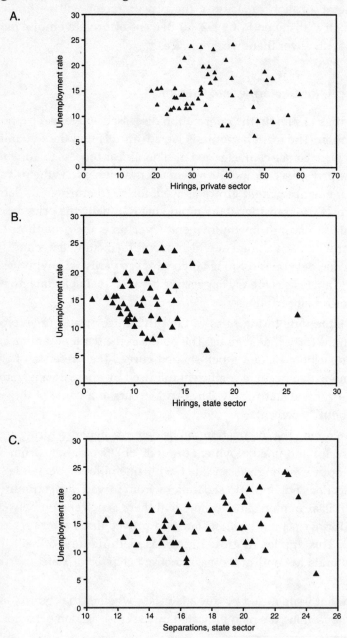

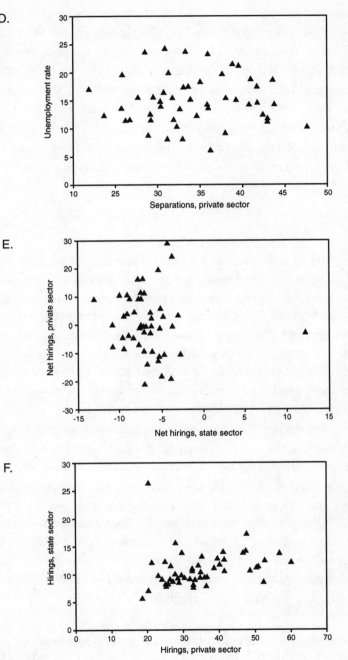

regions. The asymmetric behavior across regions could be sustained by lack of mobility and a "mismatch" between potential for job creation (thus additional labor demand) and labor supply by the unemployed. In other words, the growth of labor demand may continue to be concentrated in regions with low unemployment. In addition to the regional dimension, even within regions there could be a level of "structural" unemployment affected by discrepancies between the characteristics of job requested and the supply of labor. The next section briefly reports the results of an analysis of this mismatch (more details are given in the appendix).

Mismatch

Underlying the idea of mismatch is that dispersion of unemployment rates across regions, occupations, and the like does increase aggregate unemployment. The appendix presents two definitions of mismatch, one based only on the variation of unemployment rates across types, the other also on the regional dispersion of vacancies. The first index takes into account the structure of the population—in each category analyzed—in relation to unemployment rates of different kinds within that population.[23] The second index takes into account the discrepancies between the regional distribution of unemployment and of vacancies.

The first index suggests that there is no significant mismatch for any category. Moreover, mismatch indexes did not grow over time. In the case of regional mismatch, these indexes decreased during 1992 (see appendix).

The second index of mismatch—which we could compute only for regional mismatch—points to a much stronger importance of regional mismatch. Taken literally, the index implies that almost 25 percent of unemployment could be eliminated by improving mobility of labor across regions. Recall that results on the relation between wage changes and regional unemployment support the presence of regional labor markets, and thus low regional labor mobility.

---

23. For instance, if unemployment rates are higher for people with university degrees, and over time the share of people with university degrees grows in relation with other levels of education, this would lead *ceteris paribus* to an increase in aggregate unemployment.

Patterns of Unemployment

This section provides information on the characteristics of the unemployed.

Who Are the Unemployed?

The total number of unemployed from register data and from the Labor Force Survey are almost identical (2,229 and 2,254 thousand in May 1992). However, 743 thousands who were classified as unemployed in the LFS were not registered in labor offices. Therefore, an equal number of people registered in labor offices were not unemployed according to the ILO classification adopted in the LFS (table 2-15a).[24]

GENDER. The number of unemployed men and women surveyed are nearly equal. The unemployment rate is higher for women (14.1 percent) than for men (11.9 percent).

PLACE OF LIVING. Of the unemployed, 70 percent live in towns, and 30 percent in the country. Over 16 percent of the unemployed live in the smallest towns, with less than 20,000 inhabitants; 12.5 percent are living in towns with a population between 20,000 and 50,000. Nearly one-third of the unemployed are in the biggest cities, with populations over 100,000. The urban unemployment rate is higher than the rural unemployment rate. Within urban unemployment, the unemployment rate declines within the size of towns. In small towns with populations of less

Table 2-15A. Unemployment: Labor Force Survey, May 1992
(thousands)

	Total	Men	Women	Urban	Rural
Register data	2,229	1,057	1,172	—	—
LFS data	2,254	1,126	1,128	1,597	657
Registered	1,511	748	763	—	—
Unregistered	743	378	365	—	—

— Not available.

24. In the following quarterly survey the situation was similar: for example in February 1993 the total number of unemployed registered in labor offices was 2,626 thousand. The February Labor Force Survey reported 2,467 thousands unemployed, of which only 1,766 were registered in labor offices.

than 20,000, the unemployment rate is 17 percent, while in large towns of over 100,000 inhabitants it is 13.8 percent (tables 2-15b and 2-15c). In large cities such as Warsaw, unemployment is at the lowest level. There are several factors behind this phenomenon. First, there is the phenomenon of the "one-company towns." Indeed, in many areas there is (or there was) only one large enterprise giving employment to a large part of the population. In small towns there is insufficient local demand for small trade or service activities. In addition, lack of financial infrastructure constrains the growth of new activities. Overall, according to register data, voivodships with big cities as centers (Warsaw, Krakow, Katowice, Poznan, Wroclaw) are characterized by lower unemployment rates. It is hard to find a unique explanation, however, for the high variation of unemployment rates across regions.

Table 2-15B. Unemployment Rate by Gender and Place of Living

Place of living	Total	Men	Women
Total	12.9	11.9	14.1
Towns	15.1	13.8	16.6
20 thousand or fewer	17.0	15.8	18.4
20-50 thousand	16.3	15.1	17.5
50-100 thousand	15.5	13.8	17.7
Over 100 thousand	13.8	12.6	15.2
Country	9.6	9.1	10.2

— Not available.
Note: Figures represent percentage of labor force in each area and gender group.
Source: Labor Force and Unemployment in Poland, GUS 1992.

Table 2-15C. Unemployed by Place of Living
(percentage)

Place of living	Total	Men	Women
Total	100.0	100.0	100.0
Towns	70.9	69.3	72.4
20 thousand or fewer	16.2	16.0	16.3
20-50 thousand	12.5	12.4	12.6
50-100 thousand	9.6	9.1	10.1
Over 100 thousand	32.6	31.8	33.5
Country	29.1	30.7	27.6

Source: LF Survey.

AGE.   The average age of the unemployed is low. About 85 percent to 90 percent of the unemployed are less than 44 years old, and thus they belong to the mobile working age.[25] Youth unemployment rates are high: in the age group 18-19 the unemployment rate is 32-32 percent for men and 38 percent for women. In the next age group (20-24), the unemployment rate is also very high (27 percent). The unemployment rate falls with age and it is lowest at age 45 and older (tables 2-15d and 2-15e).

Table 2-15D. Unemployment Rate by Age
(percentage)

Age	Total	Men	Women
15-17	8.4	4.8	13.2
18-19	33.9	31.7	37.8
20-24	26.9	25.4	28.6
25-29	16.6	15.0	18.9
30-34	13.4	10.1	17.6
35-44	11.1	10.3	11.9
45 & over	7.4	7.5	7.2
Productive age	13.4	12.2	14.9

Note: In percent of labor force in each age.
Source: LF Survey.

EDUCATION.   Regarding the educational level of the unemployed, the larger group is the one with basic (and also secondary) vocational education. This points to the shortcomings of the Polish educational system. The system used to be based largely on vocational schools, tied closely with specific industrial enterprises or branches. As a result, the schools provided a very narrow range of specializations, which appear ill-suited to new activities. There is also a substantial share of unemployed (25 percent) largely without education—with primary education or even less. People with higher education account for only 4 percent of the unemployed (table 2-15f).

---

25.   There are differences in register and LFS data as to the age structure of unemployment. According to register data, over one-third of the unemployed are younger than 24, while the figure drops to 25 percent in the LFS. This difference is likely because young people registered as unemployed are at the same time engaged in some economic activities (maybe short-term) and are not unemployed according to ILO definition. They are, however, seeking more stable employment.

Table 2-15E. Unemployed by Age
(percentage)

Source	< 24	25-34	35-44	45-54	> 55
Register data					
Iq1991	31.2	29.9	26.1	10.4	2.4
IIq1991	33.4	30.3	25.3	9.1	1.9
IIIq1991	36.3	29.4	24.2	8.3	1.8
IVq1991	35.1	29.9	24.6	8.6	1.8
Iq1992	32.8	31.1	25.2	9.1	1.8
IIq1992	33.2	30.6	25.3	9.1	1.8
IIIq1992	35.5	29.5	24.2	9.0	1.7
LF Survey data (May 1992)					
Total	25.2	31.2	27.3	10.6	5.7
Men	26.0	29.6	26.7	10.5	7.2
Women	24.4	32.9	27.9	10.8	4.0

Table 2-15F. Unemployed by Education

Source	Higher	Secondary vocational	Secondary general	Basic vocational	Primary
Register data					
Iq1991	3.3	21.0	7.6	36.9	31.3
IIq1991	3.2	23.1	7.6	34.5	31.7
IIIq1991	3.0	23.0	7.3	37.0	29.7
IVq1991	3.0	22.4	7.2	37.4	30.1
Iq1992	2.6	21.2	7.3	37.7	31.1
IIq1992	2.4	22.3	7.2	36.8	31.3
IIIq1992	2.3	21.8	7.4	38.2	30.3
LF Survey data (May 1992)					
Total	3.9	25.8	7.9	37.8	24.6
Men	3.8	20.8	3.1	46.0	26.3
Women	4.0	30.7	12.6	29.7	23.0

Differences in unemployment rates across education levels are strikingly small. The only group that deviates significantly from the mean is those with higher education, for which the unemployment rate is only 5.5 percent (table 2-15g).

Table 2-15G. Unemployment Rate by Educational Attainment
(percentage)

Level	Total	Men	Women
Higher	5.5	5.2	6.0
Secondary vocational	13.2	11.0	15.5
Secondary general	16.3	12.5	17.6
Basic vocational	15.5	13.9	18.9
Primary or less	12.0	12.1	11.7

Note: In percent of labor force with each education level.
Source: LF Survey.

Why Are They Unemployed?

Layoffs are the dominant cause of unemployment. About 57 percent of the unemployed were laid off—not necessarily according to special regulations for mass layoffs (61 percent of men and 52 percent of women). Those who quit their job and found themselves unemployed account for only 8 percent of the total number of unemployed (10 percent for men and 6 percent for women). Reentrants account for 20 percent of the unemployed, with a larger share among women (26 percent) than among men (15 percent). Two-thirds of reentrants among men are those who left their jobs through early retirements (or were receiving disability pension). New entrants account for 15 percent of the unemployed: less than 14 percent of men and over 16 percent of women. Among new entrants, 6 percent of the total number of unemployed are graduates (table 2-16). Unemployed with a previous work experience account for 82-85 percent of the unemployed. But the shorter the work record in the last job, the greater the chance to be unemployed. Twenty-five percent of the unemployed with previous work experience were employed in their last job for a year or less; 22 percent for two to three years, 13 percent for four to five years, and about 13 percent for six to nine years. There is one exception to this pattern: 18 percent of unemployed were employed in their last job for a period of ten to nineteen years.

Where Do They Come From?

The largest group of unemployed with previous work experience were employed in industry, nearly 36 percent; 14 percent were working in con-

Table 2-16. Unemployment: Laid off, Quits, New Entrants, and Reentrants
(percentage)

Category	Total	Men	Women	Urban	Rural
Total	100.0	100.0	100.0	100.0	100.0
Laid off	56.6	61.1	52.1	54.7	61.1
Quits	7.9	9.9	5.8	8.8	5.7
Reentrants	20.5	15.3	25.7	23.1	14.0
Retired	8.6	10.2	6.9	10.9	2.9
New entrants	15.0	13.7	16.4	13.4	19.2
Graduates	6.2	5.0	7.3	5.6	7.7

Source: LFS, May 1992.

struction, 16 percent in trade, less than 5 percent in transport, less than 8 percent in agriculture, and 22 percent in all other sectors. Compared with the employment structure, the share of unemployed working in agriculture is of course much lower than the share of agriculture in total employment. Nevertheless, focusing on the employment structure outside individual agriculture, it seems that each sector is represented quite proportionally. This confirms the absence of a sharp structural change in employment, which was mentioned earlier. What is surprising is the high share of the unemployed coming from the private sector: about 40 percent (table 2-17). It is difficult to say if this reflects greater labor mobility and easier layoffs in the private sector, or whether a great number of unemployed tried different forms of private activities on a small scale (like street trade) and are temporarily without a job, or whether a large proportion of those unemployed were working in declining cooperatives, which have been reclassified from state to private sector activity.

Unemployment Spells, or How Long Are They Unemployed?

There are differences in unemployment duration between register data and LFS data, because register data defines the duration of being without employment, while the LFS defines the duration of job seeking.

The average duration of unemployment is about eleven months. It is worth noting that there are negligible differences in average duration between different social groups of unemployed (such as the unemployed with different education levels). It seems that gender, education, and

Table 2-17. Unemployed by Sectors of Origin
(thousands)

Category	Total	Share (percent)	Laid off	Unemployment (percent)
Total	1,742	100.0	1,033	59.3
Industry	626	35.9	372	59.4
Construction	238	13.7	154	64.7
Agriculture	132	7.6	91	68.9
Transport	84	4.8	54	64.3
Trade	279	16.0	177	63.4
Other	383	22.0	185	48.3
Public sector	1,066	61.2	615	57.7
Private sector	676	38.8	418	61.8

Source: LFS, May 1992.

previous work experience have nearly no impact on how long one is unemployed.

The figures on duration of unemployment mirror the indications coming out from the exit probabilities we discussed above. Of the unemployed, 25 percent have already been in that state for more than one year, 35 percent—the larger group—have been unemployed more than seven months but less than one year, and 20 percent for between four and six months. Only 20 percent of unemployed have been unemployed for less than three months. The worrying implication is that more than 60 percent of the unemployed would have lost unemployment benefits by the beginning of 1993. This reveals the complex tradeoffs facing the benefit policy. While incentives for an efficient search argue for a short duration, the objective of protecting the standard of living of the unemployed calls for continued income support for the unemployed.

Recipients of Unemployment Benefits

The tightening of unemployment benefit regulations in 1991 led to a sharp decline in the proportion of benefit recipients in total unemployment. This proportion dropped from 79 percent at the end of 1991 to 45.5 percent in September 1993, which is roughly the share of the long-term unemployed, people who have been unemployed for more than twelve months.[26]

Concluding Remarks

Without neglecting the role of structural factors, especially low regional labor mobility, this chapter has characterized the evolution of unemployment in the aggregate outcome of two asymmetric dynamics: (1) declining state sectors and (2) an expanding private sector. We have argued that the dynamics of the two sectors are unlikely to lead to a significant reduction in unemployment in the short run. Even during the period of positive growth in 1992-93, the outflow from unemployment to employment—an indicator of job creation—has been strikingly low, and the share of long-term unemployment in total unemployment has steadily increased. At the same time, despite its improved performance, the state sector is unlikely to generate new employment opportunities on a significant scale and a sustained basis.

The simple characterization of the dynamics of unemployment in two broad sectors was a useful organizing device. The chapter has, however, illustrated the more complex heterogeneity that characterizes both state and private sectors. Regarding the state sector, the chapter emphasized the heterogeneity of performance across sectors and, even more important, over time. The evidence suggested that in addition to sectoral issues—such as changing relative prices, different exposure to CMEA trade, and import competition—the main factors affecting the behavior of state enterprise are liquidity constraints and the horizon of the firm. The latter is crucially affected by the prospects—real or perceived—of regime change in ownership and control of firms. The evidence clearly indicates that state firms do not behave as "perverse" labor-managed firms, maximizing income per worker and disregarding the employment and output effect of such decisions. By contrast, employment seems to figure as a main component of the objective function of the firms. The response of these firms to changes in relative prices is not dissimilar to that of profit-

26. As discussed earlier, however, the Labor Force Survey, on the basis of people actively seeking jobs, reports a much lower share of long-term unemployed, about 25 percent. This indicates that a significant number of registered unemployed are not actively seeking work, while a significant number of nonregistered unemployed are actively seeking work but do not receive benefits.

maximizing firms. Therefore, the real issue does not seem to be the static objective function of the firms, but rather their horizon and the expectations on the future of the firm and the prospective role of current insiders. Evidence of changes both over time and across sectors suggested the crucial role of the horizon factor, which seems to have been even more important than government wage policy in affecting wage behavior.

Regarding the private sector, we have emphasized the variation across sectors and over time of the characteristics of private jobs. First, Poland, even outside agriculture, had a significant private sector *before* reforms were launched. Second, the initial boom in private sector employment was largely a stock adjustment in sectors such as trade and construction where setup costs, capital, and skill requirements are low. Many of these jobs were associated with low wages and bad working conditions. This explains why survey results indicate that the majority of workers prefer state sector jobs and increasingly resist privatization. Moreover, once the title change has been completed these sectors will provide little dynamism in job creation. The evidence we have presented suggests that Poland has already entered this phase. Third, despite a remarkable growth of small private firms in manufacturing, there is no significant growth of medium- and large-scale private manufacturing firms. Constraints from credit markets and lack of human capital seem to have been a major obstacle. Thus, the overall prospects for net job creation in private firms are not very bright in the near future.

The heterogeneity both within and across sectors leads to an evolving nature of the aggregate dynamics of unemployment. So far, unemployment has not been dominated by a process of "creative destruction," in which unemployment is a necessary, albeit painful, condition and supporting factor for economic growth. Indeed, a large proportion of unemployment has been generated by the deep recession of 1990-91. Creative destruction has become more relevant over time. It may explain that in 1992-93 Poland experienced simultaneously the growth of output and unemployment. It is possible that once this creative destruction takes hold, unemployment will continue to increase. Recent experience, however, suggests that the fear of this outcome, based both on political and fiscal reasons, might have been a major factor in determining the continued postponement of privatization and its changing nature, with the process increasingly dominated by the insiders. Pressures to maintain state sector employment have grown. They have been partially accommodated, giving rise to a typical phenomenon of time inconsistency. This did not imply a reversal to soft budget constraints, but rather a de facto concession of increased power to the *insiders* in state firms. Several state firms have positively reacted to these changed incentives.[27] Nevertheless, the implications of such a phenomenon are still uncertain. The aggregate performance of state firms remains disappointing. Indeed, in 1993 more than 40 percent of state firms were loss-making, and their losses were larger than profits of profit-making firms. Even after the improvements of 1992-93, state sector output has barely stabilized at a level that is 30 percent below the prereform period. In sum, the opportunity cost of postponing privatization may be large.

Appendix

Structure of Unemployment: A Mismatch Analysis

Mismatch indexes may provide an indication of the extent to which a reduction in unemployment requires increased mobility of labor across regions, sectors, and occupations. The first index, denoted *MM* (see box 2-2), simply provides a measure of the asymmetric impact of unemployment across regions, occupations, and sexes. By focusing only on the supply-side, however, the index *MM* gives little information on the mismatch between demand and supply of labor. By contrast, the index *MM'* (see box 2-2) involves both the supply and demand sides, by taking into account unemployment and vacancies. Such an indicator can be used to analyze regional mismatch, because data on vacancies do not specify the demand for particular skills, gender, and so forth. Therefore, we present both types of indexes. The values reported below could be interpreted as the proportion of unemployment that can be attributed to the various measures of mismatch.

Age Structure of the Unemployed

It is difficult to talk about the age mismatch of the unemployed, because people cannot move between different age groups. Nevertheless, table 2-18 suggests that age mismatch accounted for 11 percent of the unem-

---

27. Pinto, Belka, and Krajewski (1993) provide an excellent analysis of the adjustment in large state firms.

Box 2-2. Data Sources and Methodology

(i) Data Sources

Two data sources were used to provide data for the mismatch analysis on Poland: (1) Labor Force Survey, which is conducted every three months starting May 1992, two editions were included in this research—May 1992 and August 1992; (2) monthly data on registered unemployed and vacancies from employment offices, obtained from the Department of Employment at the Ministry of Labor and Social Policy. There are several limitations in the data collected by employment offices. Data collected by employment offices provide monthly time series on unemployed and vacancies with a regional breakdown. These data, however, are biased toward high unemployment and a low vacancies level. This is because private firms have no incentives to post a vacancy in an employment office; the law on employment and unemployment obliges every firm to report vacancies to the employment office, but this obligation is not enforceable. At the same time, the socialized sector, which is accustomed to reporting vacancies, is contracting. There is also a very high scope of unrecorded activity in the grey economy, much of which accounts for black employment of officially unemployed persons. It is estimated that about 30 percent of registered unemployed are employed in the black market, and only about 20 percent of vacancies are posted in employment offices.

(ii) Methodology: Mismatch Indexes

Two mismatch indexes are used: *MM* and *MM'* (see "Mismatch: A Framework for Thought," by R. Jackman, R. Layard, S. Savouri, in *Mismatch and Labor Mobility*, F. P Padoa-Schioppa, ed., 1991). *MM* is defined as:

$$MM = 1/2 * \text{VAR}(u_j/u)$$

MM' takes into account both unemployment and vacancies:

$$MM' = 2 * [1 - \text{SUM} \{N_j/N * (u_j/u * v_j/v)^{1/2}\}]$$

where:

u - unemployment rate (U/N)
v - vacancy rate (V/N)
u_i - unemployment rate in category i (region, occupation, etc.)
v_i - vacancy rate in the category i (region, occupation, etc.)
N - number of people in the labor force in the whole population
N_j - number of people in the labor force in region (occupation, etc.).

Table 2-18. Age Mismatch
(percentage)

Period	Total	Men	Women
May 1992	11.69	12.10	21.70
August 1992	15.58	16.33	15.58
November 1992	14.91	16.12	14.92
February 1993	15.41	16.58	14.96

Source: Labor Force Survey, editions for May 1992, August 1992, November 1992, February 1993.

Table 2-19. Mismatch in Cities
(percentage)

Period	Total	Men	Women
May 1992	0.45	0.57	0.38
August 1992	0.47	0.79	0.30
November 1992	0.31	0.13	0.23
February 1993	0.47	1.12	0.15

Source: Labor Force Survey, editions for May 1992, August 1992, November 1992, February 1993.

ployed in May 1992 and grew to 16 percent in March 1993. Moreover, the mismatch, which was higher for women in May 1992, became higher for men.

Unemployment in Urban Areas

Table 2-19 indicates that unemployment is relatively homogeneous in urban areas.

Educational Background and Occupational Mismatch

Table 2-20 suggests that a relatively small part of current employment could be reduced by reorganizing the educational system. By contrast, the occupational mismatch is high. Thus, one possible conclusion is that effort should be concentrated on vocational training rather than generic education.

Table 2-20. Occupational and Educational Mismatch
(percentage)

Period	Occupational mismatch	Educational mismatch		
		Total	Men	Women
May 1992	15.30	3.02	2.29	4.74
August 1992	14.58	2.59	2.15	3.82
November 1992	14.63	2.88	2.26	4.70
February 1993	15.46	3.93	3.76	5.47

Source: Labor Force Survey, editions for May 1992, August 1992, November 1992, February 1993.

Table 2-21. Sectoral Mismatch
(percentage)

Period	Sectoral mismatch
May 1992	11.60
August 1992	11.90
November 1992	12.40
February 1993	12.33

Source: Labor Force Survey, editions for May 1992, August 1992, November 1992, February 1993.

Sectoral Mismatch

Sectoral mismatch in Poland seems stable at a level of 11-12 percent (table 2-21).

Evolution of Regional Mismatch Indexes over Time

Table 2-22 displays the evolution over time of the regional mismatch indexes, presenting the values of both *MM* and *MM'* indexes. Interestingly, the magnitude of the *MM'* index is much higher than that of the *MM* index. Moreover, while the *MM* index steadily declines over time, the *MM'* index by November 1992, the endpoint of the sample, is roughly back to the value of January 1992. The magnitude of the *MM'* index points to an important role of the regional mismatch in affecting unemployment.

Table 2-22. Regional Mismatch Indexes, January 1991-November 1992 *(percentage)*

Month	MM	MM'
1991		
January	6.56	
February	8.02	
March	6.89	
July	7.01	
August	6.74	
September	6.61	
October	6.64	
December	6.40	
1992		
January	6.24	25.61
February	6.53	22.81
March	6.51	16.62
April	6.49	15.34
May	7.49	20.54
June	6.49	17.42
July	6.28	18.69
August	6.07	16.53
September	5.91	18.06
October	5.98	19.76
November	5.89	23.12

Bibliography

Aghion, P., and O. J. Blanchard. 1993. "On the Speed of Transition in Central Europe." Working Paper 6, European Bank for Reconstruction and Development, London.

Berg, A., and J. Sachs. 1992. "Trade Reform and Adjustment in Eastern Europe: The Case of Poland." *Economic Policy* 14: 117-73.

Berg, A., and O. J. Blanchard. 1994. "Stabilization and Transition: Poland 1990-91." In O. J. Blanchard and others, eds., *Transformation in Eastern Europe*. University of Chicago Press.

Boeri, T. 1993. *Labor Market Flows and the Persistence of Unemployment in Central-Eastern Europe*. Paris: OECD.

Borensztein E., D. Demekas, and J. Ostry. 1993. "Output Decline in the Aftermath of Reform: The Cases of Bulgaria, Czechoslovakia and Romania." In M. Blejer, G. Calvo, F. Coricelli, and A. Gelb, eds., *Eastern Europe in Transition: From Recession to Growth?* Discussion Paper 196, The World Bank, Washington, D.C.

Calvo, G., and F. Coricelli. 1993. "Output Collapse in Eastern Europe: The Role of Credit." In M. Blejer, G. Calvo, F. Coricelli, and A. Gelb, eds., *Eastern Europe in Transition: From Recession to Growth?* Discussion Paper 196, The World Bank, Washington, D.C.

Chadha, B., F. Coricelli, and K. Krajnyak. 1993. "Unemployment, Restructuring, and Growth in Economies in Transition." *IMF Staff Papers*, December: 714-80.

Commander, S., and F. Coricelli. 1993. "Output Decline in Hungary and Poland in 1990/1991: Structural Change and Aggregate Shocks." In M. Blejer, G. Calvo, F. Coricelli, and A. Gelb, eds., *Eastern Europe in Transition: From Recession to Growth?* Discussion Paper 196, The World Bank, Washington, D.C.

Commander, S., F. Coricelli, and K. Staehr. 1992. "Wage and Employment Setting in Economies in Transition." In G. Winckler, ed., *Central and Eastern Europe: Roads to Growth*. Washington D.C.: IMF and Austrian National Bank.

Freeman, R. 1992. "Labor Market Institutions and Performance in Eastern Europe." National Bureau of Economic Research, Cambridge, Massachusetts.

Johnson, S. 1993. "Private Sector in Poland: A Small-Scale Survey." The World Bank, Washington, D.C. Mimeo.

OECD. 1993. *Employment Outlook*. Paris.

Padoa-Schioppa, F., ed. 1991. *Mismatch and Labor Mobility*. Cambridge, U.K.: Cambridge University Press.

Pinto, B., M. Belka, and S. Krajewski. 1993. "Transforming State Enterprises in Poland: Evidence on Adjustment by Manufacturing Firms." *Brookings Papers on Economic Activity* 1:213-70.

Schaffer, M. 1992. "The Polish State-Owned Enterprise Sector and the Recession in 1990." Research Paper Series EE 7, The World Bank, Washington, D.C.

3

Czech Republic and Slovakia

John Ham, Jan Svejnar, and Katherine Terrell

In labor market performance, the Czech Republic (CR) is unique among the transitional economies of Central and Eastern Europe. Its unemployment rate is the third lowest in the world, wages are competitively low, and the population is peacefully accepting the trials and tribulations of the transition process from a command economy to one based on private enterprise. In contrast, the labor market of the Slovak Republic (SR), which was until 1991 virtually indistinguishable from its Czech counterpart, has diverged substantially and started to display problems similar to those of the other transitional economies. The Slovak unemployment rate dramatically rose from virtually zero to double digits, real wages and exports have declined, and the government has had to resort to populistic policies to maintain social peace.

Why is the Czech Republic, unlike Slovakia and other Central and Eastern European countries, perceived as doing well in labor market performance? Are these apparent results brought about by policies that

In preparing this chapter, the authors were in part supported by a World Bank grant on "Labor Markets in Transitional Socialist Economies," Grant No. 806-34 from the National Council for Soviet and East European Research, and NSF Grant No. SES 921-3310. They would like to thank Daniel Munich and Mario Strapec for assistance in preparing the final revisions of the chapter. The chapter draws on an earlier larger study prepared in collaboration with Michaela Erbenova, Sharon Fisher, and Martina Lubyova.

could be fruitfully used in other transitional economies? In this chapter we examine the principal changes that have taken place in the Czech and Slovak labor markets since the start of the economic transformation from a centrally planned to a market economy after the November 1989 Velvet Revolution. We identify the legal and institutional changes, transformation policies, and external shocks and examine the extent to which they have affected the functioning of the labor markets. In doing so, we focus on three principal variables—wages, employment, and unemployment.

The study is structured as follows: Stylized facts of the principal labor market as well as broader economic features are presented in the first section. The second section contains an account of the macroeconomic policies, institutional reforms, and external shocks, as well as an examination of the response of firms, unions, and individuals to these shocks. Unemployment and its dynamics are the subject of the third section, which is followed by a discussion of policy options and constraints. In view of the January 1, 1993, partition of Czechoslovakia (CSFR) into two separate countries, we present data for the Czech and Slovak republics separately whenever possible.

The Principal Labor Market Features

Before the Velvet Revolution of November 1989, Czechoslovakia had many of the labor market characteristics found in other centrally planned economies: a relatively low level and slow growth of wages, reportedly small wage differentials across most skill groups and industries, zero open unemployment and visible excess demand for labor reflected in significant quit rates, low geographic mobility of labor, and virtually 100 percent membership in the official trade unions. With the advent of the economic reform after 1989, we see the following developments: (a) a major fall in real consumer as well as producer wages, (b) rising wage differentials (between the republics and among job categories), (c) a modest rise in the unemployment rate in the Czech Republic from zero to a mere 4.4 percent in contrast to the substantial rise to 14.4 percent in the Slovak Republic by December 1993, (d) a very limited increase in geographic mobility, (e) a decrease in quits and a rise in layoffs, and (f) a major restructuring of trade unions, with successor unions dominating the scene but exerting little visible influence on wages and working conditions.

Wages

Being an integral part of the overall planning system, wages were strictly controlled in Czechoslovakia. Keeping wages low enabled the planners to maintain relatively high rates of investment, which were indispensable for maintaining economic growth in view of slow technical progress. Enforcing a low rate of growth of wages over time was in turn a means for controlling inflation. The Czechoslovaks were more successful in this respect than most of their counterparts in the other socialist countries; as can be seen from table 3-1, nominal wages in Czechoslovakia grew only about 2 percent a year in the 1985-89 period. A broader measure of nominal incomes, including transfers from abroad, grew at a faster rate (3.5-4.0 percent).

The growth of nominal wages and incomes increased in 1990, and especially 1991, 1992, and 1993, but, as can be seen from table 3-1, real wages and incomes started declining in 1990 and fell dramatically in 1991 before recovering some (but not all) of the lost ground in 1992 and 1993.

Under communism an emphasis was also placed on keeping wage dispersion low as the regime stressed equity rather than efficiency. A centralized schedule of wages that varied by sector, difficulty of work, level of education, experience, and occupation was published in the *Unified Code Book* and was used by all organizations. Although all centrally planned economies had a deliberate policy of wage equalization, the Czechoslovak system was one of the most effective. Actual earnings could deviate from the published wage rates in relation to enterprise's fulfillment of the plan, but the extent of the deviation was much smaller in Czechoslovakia than in Poland or Hungary. Czechoslovakia was reported to have one of the most equal distributions of income in the world (see, for example, Yotopoulos and Nugent 1976 and Begg 1991). In 1989, two-thirds of all wage earners received wages that fell into the narrow range of 2,000-4,000 crowns a month. The system was able to function because the authorities maintained strict control over absolute as well as relative wages, and workers tolerated the system since it seemed egalitarian and was promulgated and supervised by the trade unions.

While these widely quoted characterizations of the socialist labor market seem by-and-large correct, our examination of the underlying data suggests that the role of market-like factors and the extent of wage differentials may have been underestimated. First, note that although the wage rates set in the *Unified Code Book* reflected the priority accorded to heavy

Table 3-1. Annual Rate of Change in the Principal Macroeconomic Indicators (*percent*)

Indicator	1985-89[a]	1989	1990	1991	1992	1993
Real GDP						
CR[b]	2.3	4.5	−1.2	−14.1	−7.1	−0.9
SR[c]	2.4	1.1	−2.5	−14.0	−7.0	−4.7
Industrial production						
CR[d]	2.1	1.5	−3.5	−24.4	−13.7	−7.4
SR[e]	2.1	−1.1	−4.1	−25.4	−14.4	−18.2
Consumer price index						
CR[f]	0.6	1.5	9.6	56.7	11.1	20.8
SR[g]	0.2	1.3	10.4	61.2	10.0	25.6
Producer price index						
CR[h]	0.1	0.1	4.3	70.4	9.9	13.4
SR[i]	−0.7	−2.7	4.8	68.9	5.3	16.6
Average wage						
CR[j]	2.0	2.2	3.5	16.7	23.1	20.3
SR[k]	2.1	2.3	4.1	16.5	20.6	24.0
Money incomes						
CR[l]	3.5	4.1	8.3	17.7	17.7	28.2
SR[m]	4.0	3.3	7.0	15.2	15.1	17.3
Average employment						
CR[n]	0.6	0.1	−0.1	−5.4	−2.6	−0.1
SR[o]	0.9	−0.2	−0.8	−7.9	−5.3	—
Productivity of labor						
CR[p]	2.2	2.2	−0.3	−14.5	−2.3	−1.4
SR[q]	1.9	−0.2	−0.8	−14.1	−3.2	−11.6
Productivity of labor, hourly						
CR[r]	3.4	3.7	1.7	−10.2	−8.5	—
SR[s]	3.4	1.8	1.4	—	—	—
Unemployment rate						
CR[t]	—	—	0.8	4.1	2.6	3.5
SR[u]	—	—	1.5	11.8	10.3	14.4

— Not available.

Note: Abbreviations used in notes: CSY, *Czech Statistical Yearbook*; CSSY, *Czechoslovak Statistical Yearbook*; CSO, Czech Statistical Office.

a. Average annual rate of change.
b. GDP is calculated in constant prices January 1984. Data for 1992-93 are preliminary data. The figure for the index for 1993 is calculated as 3Q93/3Q92; Source: CSY93, p. 42. *Prehled ukazatelu ekonomickeho a socialniho rozvoje Ceske Republiky (Survey of Indicators of Economic and Social Development in Czech Republic)* 3Q93, part I.
c. GDP is calculated in constant prices January 1984. Data for 1992-93 are preliminary data. The index for 1993 is calculated as 3Q93/3Q92. The figure for 1993 is an estimate. Source: CSY93, p. 56. *Hospodarske noviny,* February 2,3/1994.
d. Indexes calculated from constant prices valid in the period concerned; 1991 for enterprises with more than 100 workers; 1992 for enterprises with 25 workers or more. Source: CSY93, p. 50. *Prehled ukazatelu ekonomickeho a socialniho rozvoje Ceske Republiky (Survey of Indicators of Economic and Social Development in Czech Republic)* 3Q93, part II.
e. The same as note d. Source: CSY93, p. 64. *Bulletin Slovenskeho Statistickeho Uradu* 9/93, p. 7.
f. Source: CSY93, p. 42. *Prehled ukazatelu ekonomickeho a socialniho rozvoje Ceske Republiky (Survey of Indicators of Economic and Social Development in Czech Republic* 3Q93, part VII. Czech Statistical Office-Indexy spotrebitelskych cen a zivotnich nakladu 1/94.
g. The figure for 1993 is an estimate. Source: CSY93, p. 56. *Hospodarske noviny,* February 2,3/1994.
h. The index for 1993 is calculated as 3Q93/3Q92. Source: CSY93, p. 56. *Statistical Bulletin of Slovak Statistical Office* 3Q93.
i. The same as the note l. Source: CSY93, p. 56. *Statistical Bulletin of Slovak Statistical Office,* 3Q93.
j. Average wage of worker in national economy (without agricultural sector). The index for 1993 is calculated as 1.Q-3.Q93/92 Source: CSY93, p. 44. *Prehled ukazatelu ekonomickeho a socialniho rozvoje Ceske Republiky (Survey of Indicators of Economic and Social Development in Czech Republic)* 3Q93, part V.
k. Average wage of worker in national economy (without agricultural sector). 1993 index 3.Q93/92. The index for 1993 is calculated excluding the estimate of the small entrepreneurs income. Source: CSY93, p. 58. *Ekonomicky monitor Slovenske Republiky,* 10Q/93, part II.
l. Money incomes of population in total. The figures for 1990, 1991, and 1992—the money incomes of population include incomes abroad in place of balance of incomes from abroad. 1992-1993 preliminary data. The 1993 index is calculated as 3Q93/3Q92. Source: CSY93, p. 44. *Prehled ukazatelu ekonomickeho a socialniho rozvoje Ceske Republiky (Survey of Indicators of Economic and Social Development in Czech Republic)* 3Q93.
m. Money incomes of population in total. The figures for 1990, 1991, and 1992—the money incomes of population include incomes abroad in place of balance of incomes from abroad. 1992-93 preliminary data. The index for 1993 is calculated as 3Q93/3Q92. Source: CSY93, p. 58. *Ekonomicky monitor of Slovak Republic,* 10/93 part II.
n. Excluding women on maternity and additional maternity leaves, trainees and including workers in secondary occupation; workers in farming cooperatives classified

(Continued on following page)

(Table 3-1, *continued*)
in industries according to activities carried out. Consistent figure for 1993 is not available yet and so the presented index is computed as 1.Q-3.Q93/92 average number of employees in firms with more than twenty-five employees, excluding agricultural coops (relevant index for 92/91 is -16.2). Source: CSY93, p. 44. *Prehled ukazatelu ekonomickeho a socialniho rozvoje Ceske Republiky (Survey of Indicators of Economic and Social Development in Czech Republic)* 3Q93/part V.

o. Excluding women on maternity and additional maternity leaves, trainees and including workers in secondary occupation; workers in farming cooperatives classified in industries according to activities carried out. Source: CSY93, p. 58.

p. Of worker in industrial enterprise; using gross production minus the production of side-line workshops and nonindustrial organizations; up to 1991 for enterprises with 101 workers or more; from 1992 for enterprises with 25 workers or more; 1993 index November 93/92. Source: CSSY91, p. 347; CSY93, p. 239. *Statisticke Informace CSO*, Prumysl 11/93, p. 1.

q. The same as note p; The index for 1993 is calculated as 1.-9.93/1.-9.92. Source: CSSY91, p. 347; CSSY92, *Bulletin of Slovak Statistical Office* 9/93, p. 12.

r. The same as note p. Source: CSSY91. p 347; CSY93, p. 239.

s. The same as note p. Source: CSSY91, p. 347.

t. Unemployment rate is measured as of December 31. Denominator is so-called Disposable Labor Force (total number of people employed in economy with only one or main job + with part-time job + registered unemployed). Source: Czech Ministry of Labor and Social Affairs.

u. The same as note t. Source: Slovak Ministry of Labor and Social Affairs.

industry, they were based on criteria such as hard physical labor, education, occupation, and experience. Apart from giving priority to heavy industry, the wage structure thus reflected standard labor market factors such as compensating wage differentials (hard labor) and human capital characteristics (education, occupation, and experience). Hence, the distinguishing feature was presumably the centralized nature of the wage setting process.

GDP, Employment, and Labor Productivity

In examining production and employment data, it must be stressed that it is difficult to derive sharp conclusions about developments over time because the statistical offices in the two republics have experienced difficulties in capturing fully the growth of the private sector. Nevertheless, the recently published data series for 1990-93 already reflects a serious effort to adjust for the growth of this sector.

The late 1980s appear to have been a period of stagnation or modest growth of GDP, because underreported inflation probably eroded some of the GDP growth reported in official data. As can be seen in table 3-1, in 1990 the real GDP figures of both republics reflect a modest decline that becomes much sharper at 14 percent in 1991 and still continues at 7 percent in both republics in 1992 as external shocks wreak havoc and the reform takes on speed. The year of 1993 appears to be the first when the decline stopped in the Czech Republic but continued at almost 5 percent in Slovakia.

The patterns of industrial production also indicate that both republics experienced a very similar (37-38 percent) decline between 1989 and 1992.[1] With the separation of the two countries, the 1993 data show a major divergence, with Czech industrial production recording a further 7.4 percent decline compared with a more precipitous 18.2 percent fall in Slovakia. In both countries one observes a much milder decline in the broader GDP measure than in industrial production, reflecting the rapid development of the service sector.

As in the case of output, during the mid-to-late 1980s Czechoslovakia experienced a modest growth in employment (approximately .7 percent a year), with the Slovak Republic showing stronger employment growth (.9 percent) than the Czech Republic (.6 percent).[2] Employment growth came to a standstill in both republics in 1989 and declined between 1990 and 1992. Because employment data are collected with a lag, we do not yet have reliable figures for 1993. An estimate for the Czech Republic suggests, however, that the employment decline stopped in 1993. The official data reported in table 3-1 indicate that employment declined at a significantly faster rate between 1990 and 1992 in Slovakia than in the Czech lands. With virtually identical GDP and industrial production profiles, the two republics thus experienced significantly different employment trajectories during the first three years of the transition.

The data on labor productivity in industry, measured on a per worker basis, indicate that both republics registered a minor (less than 1 percent)

---

1. It should be noted that the real decline between 1991 and 1992 is probably underestimated in the data because the statistical offices produce 1991 data for enterprises with 100 or more workers, while 1992 data cover firms with 25 or more workers.

2. By the end of 1990 there were 5.2 million Czechs and 2.4 million Slovaks employed in the economy.

decrease in 1990, followed by a major (14-15 percent) fall in 1991, and smaller (3 percent or less) declines in 1992. Sectoral data indicate that the major 1991 decline in productivity was broad-based, occurring in all sectors except for fuels and energy. The relative similarity in the 1990-92 data on industrial production and productivity in the two republics confirms that the dynamics of industrial employment were similar in the two countries. The more rapid decline in overall employment in the Slovak Republic hence occurred primarily in areas other than industry.

In 1993 the industrial productivity data show a major divergence between the two countries, with the Czech Republic registering a 1.4 percent decline compared with a 11.6 percent fall in Slovakia. This differential reflects almost exactly the difference in the fall of industrial production in 1993.

In order to pursue the issue of labor adjustment further, we also present in table 3-1 data on labor productivity expressed as output per hour worked by manual (blue collar) workers. As can be seen from the data, available primarily for the Czech Republic, this measure of hourly productivity rose faster than productivity per worker in the late 1980s. Moreover, its decline lagged that of productivity per worker in 1990 and 1991. In 1992, however, hourly productivity declined much more markedly than productivity per worker, so that in 1992 both indexes of productivity stood at 83 percent of their 1989 value. These data hence indicate that hours of work grew more slowly than employment in the second half of the 1980s and fell more dramatically in 1990 and 1991 than employment. In 1992 the downward adjustment in employment appears to have exceeded the fall in hours so that both productivity indexes stood 17 percent below their 1989 levels. In short, enterprises have actually increased the extent of labor hoarding during the early phase of transition and in the first two years relied significantly on reducing hours of work in order to limit the extent of layoffs.

Labor Mobility

Unlike their counterparts in some of the other former socialist countries, Czechoslovak workers enjoyed relatively free mobility (within the borders) even under the centrally planned system. Their mobility, however, was restricted by a housing shortage, which was caused by strict rent control at below market clearing prices. According to the official data (see *Statisticka rocenka Ceske a Slovenske Federativni Republiky* 1992, p. 126), each year between 1980 and 1990 one observed about 1 percent of the total population moving between villages or townships within a district, about .8 percent of the population moving between districts within a region, about .5 percent of the population in the Czech Republic moving to Slovakia, and about 1-2 percent of the population in the Slovak Republic moving to the Czech lands. Total geographic mobility in the Czech Republic was somewhat higher than in Slovakia (2.7 percent of the population in the Czech Republic vs. 2.2 percent of the population in the Slovak Republic in 1990), and the difference did not seem to increase in 1990 relative to the late 1980s.

During 1992 the migration flows between the Czech and Slovak republics escalated as the date of separation of the two republics neared. Although no official statistics are available, anecdotal evidence indicates that the net flows were clearly from Slovakia to the Czech lands.

International migration became a significant phenomenon from 1990 onward. Prior to 1990, relatively few Czechoslovaks were employed abroad. By the end of 1990, however, 35,100 Czechoslovak citizens were officially recorded as being employed abroad, 41 percent of them in Germany. By the end of 1991, this figure had risen to 65,720, with an even higher proportion (48 percent) of them working in Germany. Other sources present higher estimates of persons working abroad because many Czechoslovaks are believed to work in the neighboring countries without official work permits. While the official data reportedly allowed for this phenomenon, the estimates were probably quite crude. Since 1991 the Czech and Slovak labor ministries have not been publishing estimates of the number of Czech and Slovak citizens working abroad. There is a broad perception, however, that the number of people working abroad is significant and growing, particularly in the Czech Republic.

Unemployment

The unusual phenomenon of zero open unemployment was a primary objective of the Soviet-type system. The system required all adult individuals with the exception of housewives to work, and it promised to provide work for each member of the society. Single individuals and heads of households who were unwilling to work fell into the legal category of "social parasites" and faced the possibility of fines or imprisonment. On the labor supply side, the regime hence forced all healthy men and single women to enter the labor force. The low wages also induced many married women to work, and female labor force participation was one of the highest in the world (83.4 percent in 1989; see *Employment Observatory Central and Eastern Europe* 1992).

On the labor demand side, low wages, soft budget constraints, shortages of material inputs, and penalties for underfulfillment of plan targets made it rational for state enterprises and other organizations to hoard labor. This combination of factors resulted in full employment of labor, much of which was redundant, together with a large number of vacancies (see, for example, Svenjar 1992). The district offices of the Ministry of Labor and Social Affairs were primarily striving to recruit workers for labor-hungry enterprises. Unemployment was thus an unknown phenomenon until the Soviet-type system began to disintegrate at the start of 1990.

Czechoslovakia started to experience unemployment again in 1990. As can be seen from figure 3-1, unemployment reappeared in the first quarter of 1990 with a rate of .1 percent in both republics.[3] By January 1991 the rates for the Czech and Slovak republics had risen and diverged to 1.1 percent and 2.4 percent, respectively. One year later (January 1992), the rates peaked at 4.4 percent and 12.7 percent for the Czech and Slovak republics, respectively. From January 1992 they fell continuously until the fourth quarter of 1992, reaching 2.6 percent and 10.4 percent in the Czech and Slovak republics, respectively. Since then the rates have risen again and the increase has been steadier and more pronounced in the Slovak Republic. By the end of 1993, Slovakia's unemployment rate reached 14.4 percent, as compared with a mere 3.5 percent in the Czech Republic.

It is important to remember that the more rapid growth of unemployment in Slovakia in 1990-92 is consistent with the more rapid decline of employment there than in the Czech lands, although it occurred in the presence of similar (officially registered) declines in GDP and industrial production in the two republics. It is also interesting to note that while unemployment grew faster in Slovakia than in the Czech lands in 1990 and 1991, the rates in the two republics have followed similar paths throughout most of the 1990-93 period (figure 3-1). The factors influencing this interesting dynamic of unemployment in the two republics are examined later in this chapter.

---

3.   The information is from the registry data collected by the district labor offices. Data from the Labor Force Survey launched in 1993 suggest that the registry data somewhat underestimate the unemployment rate. The denominator in the formula used by the district labor offices for calculating the unemployment rate is the number of unemployed plus employed in the state and cooperative sector.

Figure 3-1. Czech vs Slovak Unemployment Rate

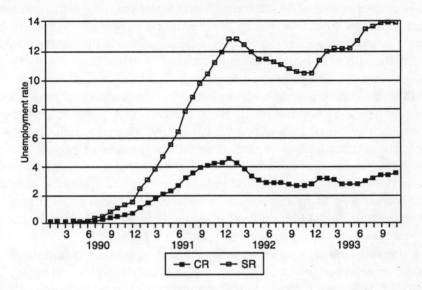

Explaining Wage and Employment Behavior

The Economic Reform Package[4]

The November 1989 revolution brought in a liberally oriented federal government, which immediately devalued the Czechoslovak crown (Kcs) in relation to the convertible currencies, revalued it relative to the ruble, and tightened budgetary policies for 1990. The start of the transformation was delayed by one year, however, because government officials at the federal, Czech, and Slovak levels could not agree on the details of an economic program, and the situation was aggravated by the need to create and pass totally new laws guiding economic activity.[5]

---

4. In this section we follow closely Dyba and Svejnar 1994. We refer the readers to these papers for a more detailed discussion of the various features of the reform package.
5. A few reform measures were naturally undertaken in the course of 1990, including the elimination of the negative turnover tax that was accompanied by a 140-crown compensation for each citizen on July 9, 1990; the gradual start of negotiations with market economies and organizations such as the EC; and further devaluations of the currency in the fall of 1990.

On January 1, 1991, the government finally launched a major set of reforms, consisting of liberalizing 85 percent of (unweighted) producer and consumer prices, devaluing the crown and pegging it to a basket of five Western currencies, introducing internal convertibility of the crown together with a 20 percent import surcharge, controlling the growth of wages, and activating a social safety net.

These radical measures were introduced in the context of a proclaimed determination to pursue restrictive macroeconomic policies, and they were supplemented by a strong push to carry out privatization of state property, attract foreign capital, promote the growth of private firms, decrease government subsidies to firms and other government expenditures (for example, on arms), and generally reduce the role of the state in the economy. In many respects, the measures introduced by the Czechoslovak authorities in January 1991 resembled those launched by the Poles a year earlier.

The measures set for 1992 were similar and represented a continuation of the original policies until the partition of Czechoslovakia on January 1, 1993. In 1993, the Czech and Slovak governments started pursuing different policies. The Czech government set itself the task of pursuing restrictive macroeconomic policies while rapidly finishing privatization of most firms. The Slovak authorities pursued less restrictive policies and temporarily slowed down privatization, while reassessing the relative merit of different privatization techniques.

In 1991 and 1992 the federal and republican governments generally persevered in pursuing the policies set for this period. Bank credit to state enterprises and households was held in check, while bank credit to private enterprises rose from almost zero in mid-1990 to 71.4 billion Kcs at the end of 1991 and 125.7 billion Kcs in mid-1992. Credit to private firms thus became equivalent to 12 percent of credit extended by banks to state enterprises at the end of 1991 and 22.3 percent by mid-1992, when large-scale privatization of state enterprises commenced.

The government also permitted the protected banking sector to establish a sizable spread between the interest rate on loans and deposits, thus allowing the undercapitalized commercial banks to build up reserves. The official, unified exchange rate, established at the start of 1991, was set near the parallel market rate, and the differential between the two has remained quite small. Czechoslovakia's modest foreign debt increased from $8.1 billion at the end of 1990 to $9.4 billion by the end of 1991 because the country borrowed $2.135 billion in 1991.[6] The increased debt, however, was fully reflected in increased foreign currency reserves, which rose from $1.2 billion in December, 1990, to $3.3 billion in December, 1991. The debt remained virtually unchanged in 1992, thus testifying to Czechoslovakia's ability to proceed with the economic transformation without incurring a major foreign debt burden.

Fiscal policy was also quite successful. After finishing 1990 with a minor surplus, the Czechoslovak government ended 1991 with a deficit equal to 10.4 billion Kcs (1.1 percent of GDP). In 1992 the country again recorded a minor total deficit of 8 billion crowns (0.8 percent of GDP). The feature that was significant for the post-partition developments, however, was that in 1992 the deficit in the Slovak budget was 7.9 billion Kcs, while that of the Czech budget was merely 1.7 billion Kcs.[7] Indeed, in 1993 the Czech Republic displayed a modest budget surplus while the Slovak Republic registered a deficit of 23.0 billion Ks (about 7 percent of GDP).

External Shocks

In assessing the effect of the Czechoslovak stabilization and transition policies, one must bear in mind that these policies were carried out in the context of disintegration of the CMEA and decline in economic activity of the traditional trading partners. The absorption of East Germany by West Germany in 1990 represented the first shock because East Germany was a major trading partner, accounting approximately for 10 percent of Czechoslovakia's foreign trade. Further shocks came from the disintegration of the Soviet economy and the reduced demand from Eastern European trading partners. The switch from CMEA trade to free trade based on world prices on January 1, 1991, also resulted in a significant shift in the terms of trade against Czechoslovakia. Official calculations point to a 26 percent worsening of Czechoslovakia's terms of trade in the first quarter, 28 percent in the second quarter, and a cumulative 22 percent decline in the first three quarters of 1991. The final set of shocks came on January 1, 1993, when Czechoslovakia separated into two republics. The inability to

---

6.   The loans were provided as follows: IMF, $1,313 million; World Bank, $205 million; the European Community, $248 million; G24, $89 million; and the financial sector, $280 million.

7.   The deficit of the federation was 7 billion Kcs and the budget of villages ended up with a 8.6 billion surplus.

maintain a single currency and the gradual erection of trade barriers reduced the flow of goods between the two countries. The introduction of a value added tax system on January 1, 1993, also generated an inflationary wave in the first quarter of 1993.

Labor Market Legislation, Policies, and Institutional Developments since 1990

During 1990, legislation and institutional provisions were drafted with the aim of allowing the labor market to function "properly" in response to market conditions. The Federal Assembly adopted the Law on Employment on December 4, 1990, and the law came into effect on January 1, 1991. In 1991 it also modified the Labor Code, Law on Social Security, and Law on Collective Bargaining. These laws, which were extended to the level of the two republics after the January 1993 split, constitute the legal framework for the functioning of the Czech and Slovak labor markets to date.

The Law on Employment created two republican ministries of labor and social affairs, in addition to the federal ministry, which was abolished on January 1, 1993. Labor offices at the federal, republic, and district level were assigned the responsibility for implementing active employment policy. Their task is to provide information, advice, and assistance in finding employment, as well as to help create jobs through subsidies to employment-generating enterprises. They are also responsible for providing retraining and administering unemployment benefits. These are described below.

EMPLOYER'S RIGHTS IN HIRING AND FIRING.   The Law on Employment gives employers full rights over hiring. It stipulates, however, that it is the employers' duty to inform the local labor offices of vacancies and inform trade unions and labor offices within specified time limits about intended structural and organizational changes or rationalization measures involving dismissals.

Termination of employment is regulated by the Labor Code. An employer can lay off workers under specified circumstances, the most frequent ones being: (a) the employer's organization is ceasing to exist, or is being physically moved; (b) a part of the employer's organization is being transferred to another organization that has no work for the employee; or

(c) there is a need for increasing efficiency. The last category is quite broad and it has by and large permitted firms to lay off workers as needed.

Layoffs may be carried out with a statutory minimum notice period of two months. This period is raised to three months in cases of labor redundancy. Some categories of employees (for example, those who care for a child under the age of three) have the right to a redundancy payment equal to their average monthly wage for five months. In the case of redundancy, the employer must also attempt to find suitable alternative work for the employee. If this is not possible, the employer is obliged to actively assist the state in finding a new job for the former employee. In practice, the assistance provided by the employer has usually been limited to notifying the local labor office about the impending layoffs.

TRADE UNIONS. Important changes of the system of industrial relations were brought about by the amendments to the 1991 Law on Collective Bargaining (Act 2/1991 on Collective Bargaining). The amendments legalized independent trade unions, set procedures for collective bargaining, accorded workers certain rights, and established a system of final settlement of disputes by courts.

In many respects, the amendments legalized practices that evolved after the 1989 revolution. The reconstruction of trade unions, for instance, had already started at the end of 1989. Professional trade unions, independent of political parties and state authorities, were established from the bottom up. The monopolistic Revolutionary Trade Union Movement controlled by the Communist Party ended its existence at a congress held in March 1990 and the new trade unions formed the Czech and Slovak Confederation of Trade Unions (CSKOS). CSKOS had sixty unions, of which nineteen were Czech, twenty Slovak, and the remaining twenty-one covered the entire country. CSKOS was reorganized into two national organizations after the partition of Czechoslovakia in January 1993.

As a result of the amendments to the 1991 Law on Collective Bargaining, individual employment contracts must include the contents of collective bargaining agreements and employers must provide the relevant trade union with a written report on all new employment contracts. The employer is also obliged to inform and consult with the trade unions on proposed measures that are likely to affect the work force. For example, trade unions must be consulted on proposed redundancies or measures for creating new jobs for workers, mothers, the disabled, and the like, on major problems of workers' welfare, on measures for improving working conditions, and so forth. As we discuss later, trade unions also participate in wage setting, although wage controls have so far imposed limits on this activity.

Finally, the Law on Collective Bargaining accorded workers various rights but also imposed constraints. The fundamental right given to workers was the right to strike, although this right is conditioned by the stipulation that a strike is illegal before the parties go through mediation and, if mediation is unsuccessful, the parties must consider arbitration. Moreover, at least one-half of workers must vote for the strike before the trade union may officially declare it.

Another important legal right (constraint) relates to the length of the work week, which must not exceed forty-three hours. Moreover, compulsory overtime is discouraged and most employees may not work more than eight hours of overtime a week. Annual leave is three weeks a year, increasing to four weeks after fifteen years of employment.

WAGE REGULATION.   Under the centrally planned system wages were subject to very strict regulation, and since then there has been a public policy debate as to the extent to which wages should be regulated. The wage setting system was modified significantly on January 1, 1990, when trade unions and employers were allowed to take active part in wage setting within a new system of industrial and labor relations. The Council of Social and Economic Agreement (CSEA), which is a tripartite assembly composed of government, employer, and trade union representatives, makes decisions at the national level, and in principle there is no lower-level bargaining over wages in excess of the nationally agreed upon norm.

The CSEA has established a new grid of base wages, which constitute the basis for wage setting in state enterprises. The base wages are meant to reflect the complexity, responsibility, and intensity of different jobs. For large enterprises there is a maximum of twelve wage levels; seven levels are distinguished for blue-collar workers. For small enterprises only six levels are allowed. Outstanding specialists may have their wages set separately outside of the grid. The wage grid is to be unified for all industries, with the exception of mining (see, for example, Nesporova 1991, pp. 18-19 for details).

Fearing an outburst of inflation during the transition, governments have maintained relatively tight regulation over the growth of wages. The main aim of the authorities has been to keep the average wage increases below expected inflation. As a result, in January 1991 the federal government (together with CSEA) established the first annual scheme to regulate wage growth by regulating the growth of a firm's wage bill.[8] In the first quarter of 1991 the maximum annual growth rate of the wage bill was set at 5 percent for state-owned enterprises and 6 percent for budget-financed organizations (public administration) with more than twenty-five employees. Employers whose wage bill growth exceeded these targets were penalized with a graduated tax, set as follows: (a) zero tax if the annual growth of the wage bill was less than 3 percent above the target rate; (b) a tax of 200 percent of the amount of the wage bill increase above the norm if growth of the wage bill was between 3 percent and 5 percent above the target; and (c) a tax of 750 percent of the wage bill increase above the norm if growth of the wage bill was more than 5 percent above the target.

In the first half of 1992, the Czechoslovak economy actually operated without any wage regulation because the CSEA could not reach an agreement until the late spring of that year. The July-December 1992 scheme changed the 1991 practice in several ways. First, it only covered enterprises with 50 percent or more state or municipal share ownership. State-owned enterprises with more than 30 percent share of foreign capital, however, were not subject to the regulation. Second, three different targets of wage growth were set according to the firm's level of efficiency. In particular, firms with higher profit-to-cost ratios were allowed a more rapid wage growth. The wage growth targets for the nonfinancial sector, set in accordance with the tripartite agreement of July-December 1992, were as follows: (a) 12 percent for firms with profit-to-cost ratios between 0 and 12 in 1992; (b) 16 percent for firms with profit-to-cost ratios higher than 12 in 1992; and (c) 6 percent for other (that is, loss-making) firms. The 1992 target wage growth for banks, savings banks, and insurance companies was set at 0 percent because wages in this sector grew at above target rates in 1991. The tax rate on excessive wages for this sector was identical to the one for 1991 described above.

During January-June 1993, wages were again left unregulated. On July 1, wage regulation was reimposed in the Czech Republic by the decree of

---

8. This was established in the Directive of the Government of CSFR on Regulatory Taxes on January 3, 1991. Further amendments can be found in Collection of Law No. 15/1991 (amendments No. 139 and No. 257) and the Directive of the Government of CSFR on July 25, 1991.

the government against the opposition of the union and employer representatives. Coverage was expanded to include all (including privately owned) enterprises with more than twenty-five employees. The average wage was allowed to grow more rapidly (up to 15 percent over the prior year), and there were no productivity requirements attached to different wage growth rates. Compared with the 1992 regulation, the penalty was reduced, as was the "margin of error": firms whose average wage grew between 15 percent and 30 percent above the previous year's rate were to pay a fine equal to 100 percent of the wage bill increase above 15 percent. Those allowing the average wage to rise above 30 percent were to face an additional penalty equal to 200 percent of the wage bill in excess of 30 percent. The penalties have been levied by the district labor offices on a quarterly basis.

Interestingly, no wage regulation was imposed in 1993 in Slovakia. The Slovak authorities prepared a wage control package for 1994, but as of February 1994 it was not legally in force.

Responses to Policies and Shocks Outside of the Labor Market

As we discussed earlier, the impact of the transformation policies and external shocks has been considerable. All aggregate measures of output show a mild decline in 1990, a major fall in 1991, and a still sizable decline in 1992. The sectoral breakdown of industrial production suggests that the most severely declining sectors were mining, manufacturing of machinery, electrical and optical tools and transportation vehicles, and textiles. Agriculture experienced a significant decline in the entire 1990-93 period. In contrast, construction staged an impressive recovery in 1992 (4.2 percent in CR and 24.1 percent in SR) after declining in both 1990 and 1991, but estimates for 1993 suggest that construction declined over 4 percent in the Czech Republic and over 20 percent in Slovakia.

Inflation, as measured by the consumer price index, averaged less than 1 percent a year in 1985-89 but rose to 10 percent in both republics in 1990. In 1991, consumer prices rose 57 percent in the Czech Republic and 61 percent in Slovakia. The respective price increases were 11 percent and 10 percent in 1992 and 21 percent and 26 percent in 1993. Most of the 1991 price jump was brought about by the sudden liberalization of 85 percent of prices on January 1, 1991. By April 1991 the inflationary surge had stopped, and inflation stayed under a 1 percent average monthly rate until the end of 1992.

Consumers' purchasing power was severely eroded during the first phase of the transformation. As can be readily calculated from the figures presented in table 3-1, real consumer wages declined by 6 percent in 1990 and 25-27 percent in 1991. In 1992 nominal wages increased over 20 percent, thus resulting in an 11 percent real wage gain in the Czech Republic and a 10 percent gain in Slovakia. In 1993, real consumer wages remained about constant in both republics. Overall, at the end of 1993 real consumer wages were 22.5 percent below their 1989 level in the Czech Republic and 27 percent in Slovakia.

Evidence from some other transitional economies suggests that the fall in real consumer wages was accompanied by a rise in real producer wages. This has not been the case in the Czech and Slovak republics. Upon deflating nominal wages by the producer price indexes in table 3-1, one finds that at the end of 1993 real producer wages were 20 percent below their 1989 level in the Czech Republic and 16.5 percent in Slovakia. What appears to have happened is that real consumer and producer wages proceeded more or less in tandem in the Czech lands, while in Slovakia real consumer wages fell much more dramatically than real producer wages. In both republics, however, the companies experienced a significant fall in real producer wages. The fact that Czech employer representatives argued in favor of not imposing wage controls in 1993 is consistent with this development.

There has also been a major decline in investment activity. Real net fixed investment rose by 6.5 percent in the Czech Republic and 5.3 percent in the Slovak Republic in 1990 but in 1991 it declined to 78 percent and 76 percent of its 1989 level, respectively. Investment activity picked up somewhat thereafter, and in 1992 the level of investment relative to 1989 was 85.5 percent and 92.2 percent, respectively. Preliminary data for the first half of 1993 indicate that in the Czech Republic investment grew by about 7 percent, while in Slovakia it declined about 16 percent. With the low product demand, restrictive macroeconomic policies, and uncertainty over the transfer of property rights, many enterprises have thus opted to cut down on investment during the 1991-93 period.

A major response of enterprises to the restrictive monetary and fiscal policies has been an increasing reliance on interenterprise debt (credit). A measure of this phenomenon is the unpaid obligations of enterprises as shown in enterprise accounts. This series shows a major rise in interenterprise debt from 45 billion crowns at the end of 1990 to 145 billion at the end of 1991. Hence, while the interenterprise debt was equal to 8.4 percent of the total bank credit to enterprises at the end of 1990, by the end of 1991 it jumped to over 28 percent. This is a significant rise, which represents an enormous potential problem for the government and the banks. It also in large part explains why virtually no state enterprises have gone bankrupt in the presence of the seemingly very restrictive macroeconomic policies and great external shocks. The government has been aware of the problem, and in the fall of 1991 it allocated 50 billion crowns from its (future) privatization income to the banks for the purpose of increasing their capitalization and partially (selectively) reducing the bank debt of promising enterprises. The data on interenterprise debt show a decline in the first half of 1992 to 123.7 billion Kcs, but it appears to have risen again in 1993. Unfortunately, since mid-1992 the accuracy of this series has been questioned. In early 1994, the size of interenterprise debt in the Czech Republic is estimated at 150-200 billion Kcs.

As far as foreign trade is concerned, the Czech and Slovak republics have carried out a major structural transformation. Trade with the (former) socialist economies, which accounted for more than 55 percent of Czech and Slovak foreign trade in 1989, dropped to less than 24 percent of foreign trade in the Czech Republic and 39 percent in the Slovak Republic by 1992.[9] Trade in nonconvertible currencies all but disappeared in 1991.

The disintegration of the CMEA resulted in a decline in the volume of trade in 1990-91. In the 1991-93 period, however, Czech exports and imports increased steadily, while in Slovakia, where 1993 data are not yet available, there was a stagnation in exports and imports from 1991 to 1992.

The split of Czechoslovakia into the Czech and Slovak republics on January 1, 1993, has resulted in a decrease in trade between the two republics. While the exact magnitude of the decline is still unclear, it was reportedly on the order of 30-40 percent in the first three months of 1993.

Privatization is one of the cornerstones of the transformation program and Czechoslovakia has arguably progressed the furthest in privatization among the transforming economies. The privatization of small and medium-size enterprises started in the fall of 1990, and by the end of 1991 the Czechoslovak government sold over 15,000 units; by the third quarter of 1992 the figure was reported to be close to 30,000. An even more important means of privatizing small and medium-size properties has been the restitution of property to previous (pre-1948) owners or their heirs. By

9.   In these calculations, Czech-Slovak trade is calculated as internal trade.

mid-1992 over 120,000 units were restituted through a process that also included housing, thus creating a precondition for the future establishment of a real estate market. The proceeds from the small-scale privatization amounted to about 15 billion crowns (about $500 million) in 1991. In comparison, the amount of foreign investment for 1991 was about $600 million.

The process of privatizing approximately 6,000 large Czechoslovak firms was divided into two waves. The first wave covered 2,930 firms (2,210 of them in the Czech Republic) and took place in 1992. In this wave, 1,491 out of the 2,930 firms allocated part of their shares for the voucher privatization scheme. In this scheme, 8.56 million adults (that is, most of the eligible individuals) purchased voucher books and used the points to bid for those shares of the 1,491 companies that were allocated for the voucher distribution. The voucher book holders voluntarily placed 72 percent of their points with 434 privately formed Investment Privatization Funds (IPFs), so that only 28 percent of the points were invested directly by individuals (for an analysis of the scheme see Svejnar and Singer 1992). With the separation of the country into the two republics, the Czech Republic launched the second wave of the privatization of the large firms in September 1993. Slovakia has so far delayed the second wave.

Overall, before separating in 1993, the Czech and Slovak economies had succeeded in extinguishing inflationary pressures brought about by the liberalization of prices and in the relatively rapid development of the private sector. The Czech Republic has also been remarkably successful in stemming the trade shock and increasing its exports and imports. On the negative side, the economies of the two republics have plunged into a more severe and prolonged recession than was officially expected. The recession has been to a significant extent caused by external shocks associated with the disintegration of the CMEA and the accompanying unfavorable shift in the terms of trade, as well as by the impact of the restrictive macroeconomic policies.

In undertaking the tough measures in 1990-92, the Czechoslovak government greatly benefited from the willingness of the population to undergo a painful transition. Unlike the other transitional economies, Czechoslovakia experienced virtually no strikes or social unrest. The January, 1993, partitioning of Czechoslovakia into independent Czech and Slovak republics in part reflected the different views that the two governments have had on how to proceed with economic policy. The Czech government has proceeded with relatively restrictive monetary and fiscal policies and moved on to complete the privatization process with the aid of the voucher system. The Slovak government appears to prefer a more expansive macroeconomic policy; use of quantitative restrictions rather than price, tax, and tariff instruments; and place priority on more traditional methods of privatization.

Responses to Policies and Shocks—Wages

WAGE LEVELS.   As can be seen from the data on nominal wages and employment in table 3-1, enterprises responded to the policies and shocks by keeping real wages down. Nominal wage bill increases in the first half of 1991 fell well below the target set by the tripartite agreement, and it was only in the second half of 1991 that the wage bills started to approach target levels.[10]

At the firm level, initial below-target increases were brought about by the desire of trade unions, management, and workers to limit layoffs in the initial period of uncertainty. Once the unions and workers realized that real wages were falling abruptly and that employment reductions could be accomplished largely through hiring freezes and termination of employees on fixed-term contracts, they pushed for higher wages. With inflation rising rapidly in 1991, pressure for wage increases naturally mounted. As we discussed earlier, however, the pressure of unions and workers was quite ineffectual as real wages fell dramatically in 1990-91, recovered part of the ground in 1992, and just kept up with inflation in 1993. Over the entire 1990-92 period, real wages therefore fell dramatically.

WAGES IN THE REPUBLICS BY SECTOR AND FIRM.   An examination of average wages across twenty-eight sectors reported by the statistical offices until 1991 indicates that the average wage differentials that existed across these sectors before the 1989 revolution were actually sizable, and that the 1989 ratio of the highest to lowest average sectoral wage amounted to 1.62 in the Czech Republic and 1.54 in the Slovak Republic. The ratio remained the same in Slovakia and actually decreased to 1.55 in

---

10. To obtain the percentage increase in the wage bill from table 3-1, sum the percentage increase in nominal average earnings and employment.

the Czech Republic in 1990. In 1991, however, the ratio rose to 1.73 in the Czech Republic and 1.77 in Slovakia. The statistical offices changed their classification of sectors in 1992, and thus strictly comparable data for 1992 and thereafter cannot be obtained. Nevertheless, the data based on the new (OKEC) classification indicate that the ratio of the highest to lowest average sectoral wage jumped to 2.41 in the Czech lands and 2.21 in Slovakia in 1992. As the transformation started to take place, one thus began observing a widening of the range of average wages.

In contrast to the sectoral wage dispersion, the Communist regime succeeded in maintaining a very small (2-3 percent) differential in the average wage across the two republics. This small differential remained virtually unchanged in the 1989-91 period, and only in 1992 does one observe the emergence of a 5 percent Czech-Slovak average wage differential. Comparisons across the two republics for each branch show that the same temporal pattern is by and large observable at a more disaggregated level.

The branch-level findings are supplemented by data from the enterprise file of the Federal Statistical Office in table 3-2. This table shows the evolution in the average wage in the two republics between the first quarter of 1989 and the second quarter of 1992. As the calculated statistics indicate, except for seasonal variations such as the second-quarter profit-sharing payout, average wages in the two republics moved very much in tandem, remaining within a 5 percent range of each other in most quarters. Table 3-2 also demonstrates that the coefficients of variation in wages remained comparable across the two republics. Enterprise-level data indicate that neither the mean nor variance of wages changed significantly across the two republics in the 1989:1-1992:2 period.

The above findings thus suggest that the transformation policies and shocks did not change relative average wages and their dispersion across the two republics until late 1992. Public discontent with the reform in Slovakia, which is reported to have contributed to the split of Czechoslovakia at the end of 1992, does not therefore seem to have been fueled by rising wage differentials within Slovakia or across the republics. Rather, it may have been brought about primarily by falling real wages and the rapidly rising unemployment rate (discussed below).

WAGES BY EDUCATION. The traditional belief among observers of labor markets in centrally planned economies has been that wages were not adequately linked to education. This conjecture is in part dispelled by

Table 3-2. Average Gross Monthly Wages in Czech and Slovak
Enterprises, 1989:1-1992: 2
(values are in thousand crowns)

Period	Czech Republic			Slovak Republic		
	Mean	*S.D.*	*S.D./mean*	*Mean*	*S.D.*	*S.D./mean*
1989: 1	2.97	0.28	0.095	2.94	0.29	0.098
1989: 2	4.33	0.31	0.071	3.77	0.31	0.081
1989: 3	3.75	0.31	0.083	3.77	0.32	0.084
1989: 4	3.34	0.30	0.091	3.32	0.31	0.094
1990: 1	3.07	0.29	0.094	3.07	0.30	0.097
1990: 2	4.41	0.31	0.071	3.86	0.31	0.081
1990: 3	3.86	0.32	0.083	3.88	0.33	0.084
1990: 4	3.72	0.21	0.056	3.62	0.21	0.057
1991: 1	3.46	0.31	0.090	3.35	0.32	0.096
1991: 2	3.93	0.34	0.087	3.69	0.36	0.096
1991: 3	4.14	0.36	0.086	4.00	0.39	0.097
1991: 4	4.76	0.22	0.047	4.56	0.22	0.048
1992: 1	3.91	0.48	0.123	3.97	0.46	0.116
1992: 2	4.72	0.24	0.050	4.61	0.23	0.051

Source: Federal Statistical Office—file of all enterprises.

the evidence that in 1988 the average wage differential between university graduates and elementary (junior high) school graduates was 58.4
percent, while that between university graduates and secondary vocational or general school graduates was 28.6 percent (table 3-3). The latter
differential is similar in magnitude to the same differential found in the
United States in the 1970s. For male workers with five years of experience
this U.S. differential was 31 percent in 1973 and 27 percent in 1979 (Bound
and Johnson 1992). It must be noted, however, that because of the tremendous change in the relative wages in the United States in the 1980s, the
same U.S. differential in 1988 was 66 percent. The picture that emerges
with respect to education and wages in prerevolutionary Czechoslovakia
is one of fairly significant education-related wage differentials.

Results from two surveys conducted by the Federal Ministry of Labor
in 1988 and 1991 indicate that education-related wage differentials may
have increased in Czechoslovakia since the 1989 revolution. As can be
seen from tables 3-3 and 3-4, in 1988 an average university graduate
earned approximately 58 percent more than an average elementary
school graduate, whereas in 1991 this differential was 63 percent. An

examination of the average earnings in each educational group reveals that university graduates seem to have been the principal gainers, earning 40 percent above the total average wage in 1991 compared with 32 percent in 1988. Vocational school graduates were the losers, earning only 97 percent of the total average wage in 1991 as compared with 102.5 percent in 1988. The latter pattern seems to be driven by a sharp decline in the relative wage of vocational stream workers in the health sector, although there were slight declines in many other industrial branches as well. The results point to an increase in the return to human capital connected with the liberalization of the economy and perhaps also an asymmetric application of the wage controls to wages compared with salaries.

WAGES BY OWNERSHIP OF FIRM.   Table 3-5 provides a glimpse at the evolution of wages across firms with different ownership characteristics as these were reported to the Federal Statistical Office. The first interesting finding is that private firms generally tend to pay slightly higher (0-10 percent) average wages than state enterprises. The breakdown within private ownership, however, indicates that private corporations pay substantially more than private entrepreneurs. Except for the first quarter of 1991, private entrepreneurs paid wages at least 10-20 percent lower than state enterprises and private corporations. Together with agricultural cooperatives and municipal organizations, private entrepreneurs were thus the lowest paying type of firm. When one takes into account the in-kind compensation in agricultural coops, the private entrepreneurs and municipal firms end up as the lowest paying units in the economy. This finding is consistent with the account given by Swanson and Webster (1992, p. 28) that "most [private] entrepreneurs set salaries by combining the minimum wage and the status quo for that industry with an assessment of workers' experience and productivity."

Wholly foreign-owned firms pay a significant premium and this pattern squares with their wage policies observed in other countries. Joint ventures with foreign partners are much more conservative, however, paying average or below-average wages.

WAGES BY GENDER.   The effort of planners to minimize the wage dispersion in the pre-1990 period was also geared toward diminishing the male-female wage differential. A survey carried out in 1988, however, indicates that women on average earned 71 percent of the men's wage

Table 3-3. Average Gross Monthly Wages of Workers in Czechoslovakia by Education and by Industrial Branch in June 1988

		In Kcs Educational level[a]			
Branch	*Total*	*1*	*2*	*3*	*4*
Total workers	3,196	2,660	3,275	3,273	4,213
Agriculture	3,162	2,882	3,320	3,214	4,075
Industry	3,265	2,706	3,413	3,450	4,439
Mining	4,689	3,833	4,924	4,915	6,180
Metallurgy	3,741	3,069	3,858	3,969	5,137
Chemicals	3,512	2,921	3,552	3,695	4,488
Machinery	3,226	2,569	3,341	3,308	4,155
Electrotechnics	3,064	2,456	3,118	3,181	4,033
Textiles	2,704	2,579	2,766	3,073	4,129
Food	2,811	2,390	2,946	3,150	4,249
Construction	3,444	3,004	3,523	3,490	4,426
Transport	3,317	3,173	3,300	3,510	4,125
Trade	2,667	2,156	2,600	3,019	4,282
Education	3,037	—	2,234	2,708	3,910
Health institutions	2,879	2,055	2,569	2,749	3,959
		Index			
Total workers	100	83.2	102.5	102.4	131.8
Agriculture	100	91.1	105.0	101.6	128.9
Industry	100	82.9	104.5	105.7	136.0
Mining	100	81.7	105.0	104.8	131.8
Metallurgy	100	82.0	103.1	106.1	137.3
Chemicals	100	83.2	101.1	105.2	127.8
Machinery	100	79.6	103.6	102.5	138.8
Electrotechnics	100	80.2	101.8	103.8	131.6
Textiles	100	95.4	102.3	113.6	152.7
Food	100	85.0	104.8	112.0	151.2
Construction	100	87.2	102.3	101.3	128.5
Transport	100	95.7	99.5	105.8	124.3
Trade	100	80.8	97.5	113.2	160.5
Education	100	—	73.6	89.2	128.7
Health institutions	100	71.4	89.2	95.5	137.5

— Not available.
a. Educational level is classified as follows:
    1 - elementary (8-9 years of) education
    2 - secondary technical/apprenticeship (2-4 years) education
    3 - secondary (4-year degree) education
    4 - university graduates.
Source: CS Statistics, 15/10 1989.

Table 3-4. Average Gross Monthly Wages of Workers in Czechoslovakia by Education and Industrial Branch in June 1991

Branch	Total	*In Kcs* *Educational level[a]*			
		1	2	3	4
Total workers	3,982	3,402	3,856	4,073	5,560
Agriculture	3,694	3,519	3,760	3,563	4,674
Machinery	4,174	3,426	4,277	4,279	5,136
Electrotechnics	3,423	2,947	3,424	3,901	4,660
Textiles	3,471	3,307	3,511	3,883	3,475
Food	4,106	3,844	4,187	4,110	5,305
Transport	4,220	4,076	4,261	4,307	4,510
Trade	3,302	2,784	3,283	3,849	5,244
Education	4,700	266	3,357	3,591	5,431
Health institutions	4,619	3,085	3,118	4,219	6,181
		Index			
Total workers	100	85.4	96.8	102.3	139.6
Agriculture	100	95.3	101.8	96.4	126.5
Machinery	100	82.1	102.5	102.5	123.7
Electrotechnics	100	86.1	100.0	114.0	136.1
Textiles	100	95.3	101.2	111.9	100.1
Food	100	93.6	102.0	100.1	129.2
Transport	100	96.6	101.0	102.1	106.9
Trade	100	84.3	99.4	116.6	158.8
Education	100	56.6	71.4	76.4	115.6
Health institutions	100	66.8	67.5	91.3	133.8

a. Educational level is classified as follows:
   1 - elementary (8-9 years of) education
   2 - secondary technical/apprenticeship (2-4 years) education
   3 - secondary (4-year degree) education
   4 - university graduates.
Source: Czech Statistical Office, 1992.

(table 3-6). This 29 percent differential actually exceeds the 24 percent female-male wage differential reported for the United States in 1988 by Bound and Johnson (1992). It must be noted, however, that the 24 percent U.S. wage differential is a relatively new development—as recently as 1980 this differential stood at 31 percent. An international survey of the ratio of female average wages to male average wages around 1988 indicates that they range from 47 percent in Chile (50 percent in Japan) to 97 percent in Paraguay. Hence, the average ratio in Czechoslovakia at that time was in the middle range for a set of thirty-two countries at various levels of development (see Terrell 1992).

As can be seen in table 3-6, the 1988 female-male wage differential in Czechoslovakia varied considerably across sectors and with education. The women's relative wage was the lowest in mining (55 percent of the men's wage) and highest in agriculture (81 percent of the men's wage). The average female-male relative wage differential was between 69 percent and 73 percent for those with secondary (senior high school) or less education. It jumped to 81 percent, however, for those with university education. This pattern of decreasing male-female wage differentials with increasing education is not uncommon (Terrell 1992).

Since the 1989 revolution there appears to have been a narrowing of the male-female wage differential. As the data in table 3-6 indicate, the 29 percent wage differential observed in 1988 diminished to 24 percent by 1991. The largest gains were made among the vocational school graduates, although women in each educational group improved their earnings position in relation to men. Since the 1988 and 1991 data come from special surveys, we are unfortunately unable to trace the evolution of the male-female differentials into 1992 and 1993.

MINIMUM WAGES.   An important effect of the transition to a market economy was the introduction of the minimum wage legislation in February 1991 (Directive of the Federal Government No. 99/Coll). The minimum wage was fixed in the tripartite General Agreement at 10.8 crowns an hour for those working a 42.5-hour week and paid on an hourly basis and 2,000 crowns a month for workers paid monthly salaries. Disabled persons eligible for "partial invalid pension" were paid 8.10 crowns an hour or 1,500 crowns a month (75 percent of the minimum wage), and the disabled eligible for full invalid pension received only 50 percent of the minimum wage. The level is proportionally adjusted for the length of the work week. A lower minimum wage of 8.10 Kcs an hour or 1,500 Kcs a month (75 percent of the basic minimum wage) was set for workers under sixteen years of age. Moreover, younger workers are not allowed to work more than 33 hours a week.

In January of 1992 the basic minimum wage was raised to 2,200 Kcs a month (for a 42.5-hour work week) or 12 Kcs an hour. Disabled workers continued to earn 75 percent and 50 percent of the basic wage, depending on whether they were earning full or partial pension, as indicated above. A new lower minimum wage of 75 percent of the basic wage was put into

Table 3-5. Wages in the Czech Republic by Ownership of Firms, 1991:1–1993:1

Category	1991				1992							
	Q1	Q2	Q3	Q4	Q1	92:1/ 91:1	Q2	92:2/ 91:2	Q3	92:3/ 91:3	Q4	92:4/ 91:4
Total	3,341	3,692	3,792	4,563	4,059	121.5	4,607	124.8	4,628	122.0	5,461	119.7
State-owned organizations	3,378	3,720	3,832	4,643	4,098	121.3	4,625	124.3	4,639	121.1	5,523	119.0
State enterprises	3,342	3,673	3,725	4,395	4,150	120.9	4,581	124.7	4,470	120.0	5,325	121.2
Budgetary-financed organization	2,871	3,347	3,601	4,752	3,536	123.2	4,271	127.6	4,632	128.6	5,518	116.1
Partly budgetary-financed organization	2,982	3,423	3,638	4,573	3,782	126.8	4,303	125.7	4,575	125.8	5,423	118.6
Others	3,701	4,144	4,093	4,852	4,515	122.0	5,054	122.0	4,830	118.0	5,723	118.0
Cooperative	2,814	3,089	3,016	3,306	3,298	117.2	3,688	119.4	3,725	123.5	4,180	126.4
Private	3,581	3,904	4,093	4,697	4,047	113.0	4,907	125.7	5,033	123.0	5,525	117.6
Juridical persons	3,604	3,910	4,125	4,720	4,093	113.6	4,928	126.0	5,071	123.0	5,558	117.6
Private entrepreneurs	3,174	2,835	3,312	3,743	3,519	110.9	3,872	136.6	4,361	131.7	4,942	132.0
Municipal ownership	2,804	2,973	3,133	3,842	3,446	122.9	3,767	126.7	3,964	126.5	4,338	112.9
Foreign firms	3,683	7,082	4,975	5,452	4,810	130.6	6,950	98.1	6,491	130.5	6,935	127.2
Joint ventures	3,244	3,702	3,487	4,342	4,029	124.2	4,497	121.5	4,334	124.3	5,504	126.8
Agriculture cooperatives	2,728	2,961	3,077	3,597	3,023	110.8	3,362	113.5	3,632	118.0	4,029	112.0

Source: Federal Statistical Office and Czech Statistical Office.

Table 3-6. Female-Male Wage Ratio in Czechoslovakia by Branches
(*percentage*)

Branch	1988					1991				
	Total	*Educational level*[a]				*Total*	*Educational level*[a]			
		1	*2*	*3*	*4*		*1*	*2*	*3*	*4*
Total	71	72	69	73	81	76	78	74	85	85
Agriculture	81	84	83	74	76	84	83	86	81	—
Industry	68	74	67	70	76	—	—	—	—	—
Mining	55	59	54	59	69	—	—	—	—	—
Metallurgy	66	70	65	69	77	73	80	—	—	—
Chemicals	69	71	70	71	77	78	87	—	—	—
Machinery	70	77	70	72	79	78	84	—	—	—
Electrotechnology	71	81	72	75	82	69	74	—	—	—
Textile	73	82	71	71	77	—	—	—	—	—
Food	71	77	71	73	79	—	—	—	—	—
Construction	69	62	68	70	74	—	—	—	—	—
Trade	76	78	80	77	80	82	83	85	89	—
Education	73	75	71	85	84	76	85	77	91	82
Health	72	73	71	85	83	65	68	81	—	78

— Not available.

a. Educational level is classified as follows:

1 - elementary (8-9 years) of education.

2 - secondary technical/apprenticeship (2-4 years) education.

3 - secondary (4-year degree) education.

4 - university graduates.

Source: CS Statistics, 15/10 198, and Czech Statistics 1992

effect for workers between the ages of sixteen to eighteen years and those under sixteen years had a reduction in their minimum wage to only 50 percent of the basic minimum wage.

The Czech government kept the minimum wage constant at 2,200 Kcs after the separation of the two republics in 1993 and early 1994. This resulted in the minimum wage falling below the official minimum living standard in the Czech Republic. The Slovaks, in contrast, raised their minimum wage to 2,450 Ks in October 1993 in order to keep it above the minimum living standard in Slovakia.

In real terms the minimum wage was about constant, perhaps declining some in 1991-92 and falling in 1993. In 1991, the minimum wage was approximately 52.0 percent of the average wage (Kcs 3,843), whereas in 1992 it was 50.9 percent of the average wage (Kcs 4,315).

In the only empirical analysis of the minimum wage, Buchtikova (1993) uses data for the fourth quarter of 1992 on a sample of 76 (large, state) firms with 89,237 employees in the Czech Republic. In this sample the average hourly wage was 31.37, hence the minimum wage was only 38.2 percent of the average wage in this sample. Buchtikova finds that only .23 percent of the workers were earning less than 12 crowns an hour and .32 percent earned 12-13 crowns an hour. It thus would appear that these enterprises were not forced or motivated to pay wages below the minimum wage level. There are, however, differences in demographic characteristics, indicating that the young and the women may be more affected.

Responses to Policies and Shocks—Employment

As mentioned earlier, a definite result of the transformation policies and external shocks was a decline in employment in the state firms and an increase in employment in the private sector. The overall effect was a decline in employment that was further accentuated through a decline in the average number of hours worked in most enterprises because of the elimination of overtime and other measures. The number of hours worked yearly by each worker remained relatively stable from 1989 to 1990 (1,859 hours and 1,817 hours, respectively); a significant decline came in 1991 when the average number of hours worked by a worker was 1,724.

Finally, despite the continuous decline in employment, it is important to note that employment has so far declined less markedly than production, indicating that state-owned enterprises have been continuing and accentuating the practice of hoarding labor. The figures on declining labor productivity, presented earlier, show that in 1991 productivity per worker fell more rapidly than employment. Estimates of labor hoarding range between 12 percent and 30 percent of total employment (see Nesporova 1991 and Svejnar 1992), and it is hence likely that the decline in employment will continue as newly privatized firms unload redundant labor.

SECTORAL STRUCTURE OF EMPLOYMENT. Using the data published by the statistical offices, one can see that the sectoral structure of employment did not change much between 1980 and 1989 (table 3-7). The share of agriculture and forestry declined from 12.5 percent to 11.3 percent in the Czech Republic and from 17.3 percent to 14.7 percent in the Slovak Republic. Trade, education, and health sectors gained in both republics and manufacturing lost a bit in the Czech lands. Other sectors more or less retained their 1980 employment shares. The sectoral stability of employment reflected the stagnation and a lack of structural change in the Czechoslovak economy over the period. Industry (manufacturing) accounted for 38 percent of total employment and by most estimates this was the sector with the most excess labor.[11]

Since 1989 there have been greater changes in the sectoral structure of employment than in the 1980s. One observes the continuation of the decline in the relative importance of agriculture and forestry in both the Czech and Slovak republics. In the Czech Republic, however, manufacturing also reduced its share while construction, transportation, and health care gained. A broadly defined service sector gained in importance in both republics and finance and insurance, transport and communications, and national administration were the leading sectors. In Slovakia the largest gains in employment were in the service sector, followed by trade and transportation. The transformation has thus contributed to a rapid rise of the service sector, an outcome that is consistent with both the neglect of this sector under the previous regime and the trend toward a service economy in the industrialized countries.

---

11. An important point worth emphasizing is that the general quality of the Czechoslovak labor force was maintained at relatively high levels during the entire post-World-War-II period. As Boeri and Keese (1992) show, the proportion of the labor force with more than basic education is comparable with that in the average member country of the Organization for Economic Cooperation and Development.

Table 3-7. Structure of Employment by Sector
(percentage)

Sector	Czech Republic						Slovak Republic					
	1980	1985	1988	1989	1990	1991	1980	1985	1988	1989	1990	1991
Agriculture and forestry	12.5	12.1	11.6	11.3	11.2	9.9	17.3	16.3	15.3	14.7	14.2	13.0
Industry (manufacturing)	39.7	39.3	39.2	39.2	37.9	38.4	33.4	33.8	33.7	33.5	33.1	33.0
Construction	8.2	8.0	8.2	8.2	8.6	9.4	10.5	10.1	10.4	10.4	10.1	10.0
Transportation	5.2	5.1	5.0	5.0	5.4	5.6	5.4	5.1	5.1	5.2	5.3	5.6
Communications	1.4	1.5	1.4	1.4	1.6	1.6	1.2	1.2	1.3	1.2	1.3	1.4
Trade	9.9	10.9	10.7	10.7	10.2	10.9	9.5	10.4	10.1	10.2	10.2	11.1
Services	11.8	11.3	11.7	11.9	12.9	12.3	10.4	10.0	10.5	10.8	11.9	17.8
Research and development	2.3	2.3	2.3	2.3	2.1	1.7	2.1	2.3	2.4	2.4	2.1	1.7
Education	5.1	5.4	5.6	5.7	5.6	5.6	6.1	6.4	6.7	6.9	7.0	7.0
Health care	3.9	4.2	4.2	4.3	4.5	4.6	4.1	4.4	4.5	4.6	4.8	5.0
Total (in thousands)	5,148	5,209	5,313	5,343	5,351	5,059	2,277	2,397	2,491	2,487	2,478	2,280
Women	—	46.2	46.1	45.8	44.3	44.3	—	45.4	45.5	45.5	44.7	44.3

— Not available.
Note: Based on average annual employment.
Source: Czechoslovak Statistical Yearbook, 1991, 1992.

EMPLOYMENT STRUCTURE BY OWNERSHIP. One of the greatest weaknesses of the work of the Czech, Slovak, and the former federal statistical offices is their inability to capture the private sector adequately. The authorities have recently tried to adjust the data in order to address this deficiency.

The best data available at this date are only for the Czech Republic (table 3-8). They indicate that in 1985 the state sector employed 99.7 percent of the working population and that this share declined to 68.6 percent in 1992. The majority of the decline occurred in 1991 and 1992, because in 1990, 93 percent of all workers were still employed in the state sector. Hence, as of the end of 1992, it is estimated that approximately one-third of the employed were working in a private enterprise.

Data from the former Federal Ministry of Labor for the whole of Czechoslovakia indicate that in 1991 only 10.6 percent of the workers were employed either in a private enterprise or self-employed. This figure is considerably lower than the 18.8 percent for the Czech Republic (in table 3-8). It is difficult to know whether this disparity implies that the proportion in Slovakia is lower than in the Czech Republic because the disparity might simply arise from different estimation techniques. Anecdotal evidence also indicates that the private sector has been growing more rapidly in the Czech Republic than in Slovakia.

Table 3-8. Share of Private vs. Public Sector Employment in the Czech Republic, 1990-92

Year	Total (abs/percent)	State (abs/percent)	Private (abs/percent)	Mixed (abs/percent)
1985	5,294,542	5,280,396	14,146	0
	100	99.7	0.3	0
1989	5,433,102	5,363,771	69,331	0
	100	98.7	1.3	0
1990	5,387,098	5,011,053	376,045	0
	100	93	7	0
1991	4,889,281	3,955,647	916,701	16,933
	100	80.9	18.8	0.3
1992	4,766,115	3,268,261	1,482,935	14,919
	100	68.6	31.3	0.3

Source: Czechoslovak Statistical Yearbook, 1993.

Unemployment and Its Dynamics

As noted earlier, unemployment started in both republics in January of 1990 with a rate of .1 percent. The rates remained at this low level until August of 1990 when they began to rise rapidly and continued to do so throughout 1991. For ten months in 1992 they fell continuously, to 2.6 percent (CR) and 10.4 percent (SR). In December 1993, 14.4 percent of the Slovak labor force was unemployed, a rate that was 4 times that of the Czech Republic (3.5 percent).

These findings lead one naturally to ask: why did unemployment in Slovakia soar above the Czech rate? At the same time, why is the general trend in the unemployment rates of the two republics so similar throughout the 1990-93 period? Perhaps a more important question is why the Czech Republic's rate so low, not only relative to Slovakia but compared with the other Central and Eastern European (CEE) countries. Boeri (1994, table 1) has shown that over the 1990-92 period the Czech unemployment rate lies below the average rate for the Organization for Economic Cooperation and Development (OECD) countries, whereas the Slovak rate is in line with the rates for Bulgaria, Hungary, and Poland.

Factors Explaining Commonality in the Unemployment Trends in Both Republics

The general pattern of rising unemployment during the 1990-92 period, falling rates in 1992, and a subsequent rise in 1993 was shared by both the CR and SR and can be largely explained by three factors common to both republics: (a) trend in output demand (domestic and international); (b) changes in the labor market policies, including the unemployment compensation scheme; and (c) the division of Czechoslovakia into two separate republics.

INTERNAL AND EXTERNAL DEMAND.   As can be seen from table 3-1, the rapid rise in unemployment in 1991 can be explained largely by the tremendous decline in output in that year (−14 percent for each republic)—the largest in any year during 1990-93. It is also clear from the table that the Slovaks suffered an earlier slowing in the demand for their products in 1989 and 1990. This pattern is corroborated with data on foreign demand as well. Total exports from Slovakia (especially to the CMEA countries) declined slightly in the 1987-90 period, whereas in the Czech Republic they rose somewhat over this period.

When the country divided in January 1993, the economy experienced another shock. The differences in the rate of decline in GDP in 1993 also helps explain the more rapid rise in unemployment in Slovakia in that year. Why is it, however, that the unemployment rate *declined* in 1992 when output declined by about 7 percent in each republic? For an answer to this question, we must look to the government's labor market policies.

LABOR MARKET POLICIES. As will be discussed in detail, the Czech and Slovak republics implemented various active employment programs in addition to the passive employment program (unemployment compensation) discussed below. It is only noted here that total expenditures on both of these programs moved in tandem in both republics: rising in 1992 by 30 percent and 70 percent in the CR and SR, respectively, and falling below the 1991 expenditures in 1993. This shows a direct negative correlation with the unemployment rate, which fell in 1992 and rose again in 1993.

UNEMPLOYMENT COMPENSATION SCHEME. The government put into place an unemployment compensation scheme almost immediately after the revolution in January 1990. The scheme entitled anyone who was laid off, who graduated from school, or who took care of a handicapped relative or a child (up to three years of age) to one year of benefits according to the following schedule:

a. First six months of unemployment: 90 percent of the individual's net average income over the previous year if the individual was laid off for organizational reasons, 65 percent of net average income (over the previous year) if laid off for other reasons, 1,000 crowns if seeking work for the first time.

b. The second six months of unemployment: 60 percent of net average income (over the previous year).

c. If in retraining, 70 percent of net average income.

The scheme was relatively favorable to the worker. Although there was a minimum benefit of 1,000 Kcs for those who had not worked before, there was no ceiling (unlike Western unemployment insurance programs). Moreover, again unlike Western systems, there was no requirement on the minimum number of months the person had to have been employed prior to receiving benefits. Moreover, many people who were out of the labor force could be eligible for benefits after some time. For example, mothers caring for children less than three years of age were eligible for unemployment benefits after one year of child care. Similarly, people were also eligible after one year of: (a) caring for handicapped children; (b) being registered as a job applicant; (c) receiving a disability or widow's pension; (d) suffering from an illness; or (e) being detained, imprisoned, or serving in the army.

In January of 1991, the compensation scheme was altered somewhat. The replacement ratio was reduced: (a) for the first six months of entitlement it was reduced to 65 percent for those laid off for organizational reasons and 60 percent for layoffs for other reasons; (b) for the second six months it was reduced to 50 percent for all. The replacement ratio for those in retraining continued to be 70 percent.

In view of the disincentives and budgetary costs inherent in the original scheme, a more restrictive scheme was introduced on January 1, 1992. Entitlement was shortened from one year to six months (except for those undergoing retraining who are covered for one year), and the replacement ratio for those laid off for redundancy was reduced to 60 percent for the first three months but kept at 50 percent for the next three months. A maximum benefit of 3,000 Kcs also went into effect.

The reduction in entitlement in January, 1992, clearly had an impact on the unemployment rate that year. The ratio of individuals receiving benefits to the total number of unemployed was 72.0 percent in the Czech Republic and 81.3 percent in Slovakia by December, 1991. When the more restrictive scheme was introduced in January 1992, these ratios immediately fell to 58.4 percent and 52.2 percent, respectively. Moreover, as more and more unemployed exhausted their entitlements but continued to be unemployed, these ratios continued to decline until they stabilized in the third quarter of 1992 at 45-47 percent in the Czech Republic and 33-36 percent in Slovakia.[12]

Some critics of the 1990-91 scheme have argued that its generosity contributed significantly to the rising unemployment rate in 1991. There is no formal published analysis supporting or rejecting this claim; nevertheless, the decline in unemployment in 1992 when there was a reduction of benefits and restrictions in eligibility is also consistent with the claim that

---

12. As we discuss in more detail later, the difference in the two ratios reflects the higher frequency of long-term unemployment in Slovakia than in the Czech lands.

the generous unemployment insurance program contributed to the increase in unemployment in 1991.[13]

There were no major changes in the scheme in 1993. The entitlement and replacement ratios were not changed in either republic. New minimums and maximums were set, in accordance with increases in the minimum (living) wages.

Disparities in the Czech and Slovak Unemployment Rates

Whereas the two republics began with the same low rate of unemployment, in only a few months the Slovak unemployment rate was double that of the Czech Republic. The gap has expanded over the years: in January 1992 the ratio between the Slovak and Czech republics' unemployment rates was 3:1 and as of October 1993 it was 4.3:1. What explains the differences in the Slovak and Czech unemployment rates? Can any of these explanations help our understanding of unemployment dynamics in the other CEE countries?

We begin by examining the flows into and out of unemployment and proceed to examine differences in the demand for and supply of labor in these two republics, as well as differences in the implementation and impact of government labor market programs.

INFLOWS AND OUTFLOWS FROM UNEMPLOYMENT. The differences in inflows into unemployment and outflows from unemployment help us to understand the differences in the two republics' unemployment rates. Using 1992 and 1993 quarterly data on average monthly inflows into unemployment relative to the labor force and average monthly outflows from unemployment relative to the annual number of unemployed, it can be seen in table 3-9, columns (1) and (4), that the Czech Republic has lower inflows (.5 percent to .8 percent) than Slovakia (.9 percent to 1.5 percent) and significantly higher outflows (19 percent to 30 percent vs. 8 percent to 12 percent). Clearly there are more layoffs and/or more people entering from out of the labor force into unemployment. As columns (7) and (9) indicate, inflow rates in Slovakia were between 1.5 and 2.25 times the Czech rates, whereas outflow rates were less than half in all but one quarter. Clearly then, the pool of unemployed in Slovakia is growing

---

13. To examine this conjecture more rigorously, it is of course necessary to analyze microeconomic data.

more rapidly than the pool in the Czech Republic because of a worse situation in *both* inflows and outflows.

Boeri (1994) points out that the inflows of the two republics are actually low when compared with OECD rates in 1992. By contrast, the outflow of the Czech Republic is near the upper tail of the OECD countries, while that of Slovakia is near the bottom. Hence, what seems to explain the high unemployment rate in the CEE countries relative to the OECD countries is their lower outflow rate.

What table 3-9 is indicating is that turnover is higher in the pool of unemployed in the Czech than in the Slovak Republic. It can be seen from columns (2) and (3) that about one-fifth of the unemployed are flowing in or out in a given month in the Czech Republic, whereas only one-tenth of the unemployed are entering or exiting in Slovakia (columns [5] and [6]). Hence we can expect duration of unemployment to be higher in the Slovak Republic. And indeed, data from the district labor offices indicate Slovakia has always had a larger proportion of their unemployed in long-term unemployment and that this proportion has been rising more rapidly over time. Since the second quarter of 1992, the proportion has stabilized and approximately one-third of the unemployed in Slovakia have been experiencing spells of longer than one year, whereas less than one-fifth (17 percent) of the unemployed in the Czech Republic are experiencing long-term unemployment.[14]

DEMAND FACTORS.   The question that naturally arises is what underlying forces have brought about these patterns in inflows and outflows? A major demand-side reason for disparity in the unemployment rates is the differing impact of the fall of the CMEA market on each of the two republics. Because the industrialization of Slovakia occurred mainly during the communist period, much of its industrial production was aimed at the CMEA market. In 1991, after Slovak exports to the former CMEA had already fallen to 72 percent of 1989 levels, the Slovak Republic still depended on this market for 42 percent of its exports, while the former CMEA market constituted only 29 percent of the Czech Republic's exports (Vavro 1992). Although the full effects of the drop in production

14. The Slovaks are at least better off than the Poles. From the middle of 1992 to the first quarter of 1993, between 40 percent and 45 percent of the unemployed in a given month have been in that state for one year or longer. (See chapter 2 in this volume.)

Table 3-9. Inflows and Outflows from Unemployment

Quarter	Czech Republic			Slovak Republic			SR/CR		
	In/LF (1)	In/ Unem (2)	Out/ Unem (3)	In/LF (4)	In/ Unem (5)	Out/ Unem (6)	In/LF (7)	In/ Unem (8)	Out/ Unem (9)
1Q92	0.7%	17.3%	21.5%	0.9%	8.3%	7.7%	1.36	0.48	0.36
2Q92	0.5%	18.3%	29.9%	0.8%	7.7%	10.6%	1.50	0.42	0.35
3Q92	0.6%	24.7%	25.9%	0.9%	9.0%	10.9%	1.36	0.36	0.42
4Q92	0.5%	22.5%	23.0%	1.0%	10.8%	11.6%	1.83	0.48	0.50
1Q93	0.7%	24.7%	21.1%	1.4%	13.1%	8.0%	1.95	0.53	0.38
2Q93	0.5%	21.1%	24.2%	1.1%	10.3%	9.0%	2.06	0.49	0.37
3Q93	0.7%	25.4%	19.4%	1.3%	10.9%	7.8%	1.75	0.43	0.40
4Q93	0.7%	20.1%	16.6%	1.0%	8.4%	8.0%	1.57	0.42	0.48

Note: The data are monthly average values in a given quarter.

resulting from the decline of the CMEA market have yet to be revealed, the higher inflows and lower outflows (and hence higher levels of unemployment) in Slovakia can be at least partially attributed to this factor.

It is also argued that official data are not adequately capturing changes in demand because they are unable to accurately measure the growth of the private sector, especially small firms. It is generally thought that there is much faster growth of employment in small enterprises (with less than 100 employees) in the Czech Republic than in Slovakia. A study presented in 1992 by the Slovak Deputy Prime Minister Vavro (1992, p. 3), for instance, claims that the number of Czech employees in small firms grew by 250,000 in 1991, while the number in Slovakia was only 30,000. A study by Horalek (1993) estimates that the number of private entrepreneurs not registered in the commercial register grew by 400,000 in 1991.

Data on vacancies reported to the unemployment office support the view that demand conditions have been weaker in the Slovak Republic. In May 1993 the total number of vacancies in the Czech Republic was almost seven times as large as the corresponding number in Slovakia. Even if one allows for differences in reporting, the relative number of vacancies in the Czech lands and Slovakia greatly exceeds the 2:1 relative population (or labor force) ratio. Similarly, a comparison of the ratios of the number of unemployed to the number of vacancies in each republic shows that for the period October 1990 to October 1993 there are many more unemployed workers per vacancy in the Slovak lands than in the Czech lands, and that this gap grew (see figure 3-2). Both labor markets worsened until December 1991, when there were approximately thirty-seven unemployed workers for each vacancy in the Slovak lands as compared with only five unemployed workers per vacancy in the Czech lands (a ratio of 8:1). As with the unemployment rate and the growth in unemployment, conditions improved steadily throughout 1992. Beginning in January of 1993, however, the ratios began to climb again, especially so in Slovakia. As of October 1993, there were nearly three unemployed for every vacancy in the Czech Republic, whereas in Slovakia, there were forty-two.

Another indication that demand conditions might be stronger in one economy than another is that there are larger flows (or probabilities) of people moving from one job to another job without passing through unemployment. Data from an internal study carried out by the Federal Ministry of Labor indicate that 24 percent of all the workers laid off in the

Figure 3-2. Unemployed/Vacancy Ratio

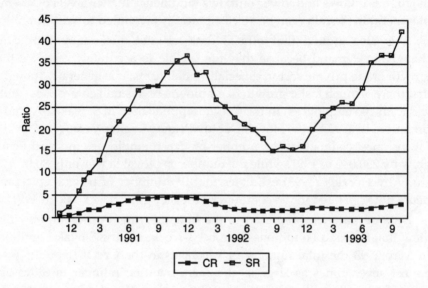

Czech Republic in 1991 found a job without being registered as unemployed. In Slovakia the proportion was only 11.3 percent.

SUPPLY-SIDE FACTORS.   Another factor that is likely to account for the higher outflow rate in the Czech Republic is the greater relative ease with which the Czechs can work in Germany and Austria because of their advantageous location. Data from the Federal Statistical Office for the entire federation suggest that foreign employment nearly doubled in 1990-91. About 60 percent of all foreign employment is in Germany and Austria, hence it is primarily affecting labor markets in the border districts.

Given the restrictions to migration imposed by the tight housing situation (and lack of housing market), we can expect that some of the unemployment phenomenon can be explained by mismatch arising from the inability of labor to move from "high-unemployment districts" to "low-unemployment districts." Some of this problem is ameliorated in the Czech Republic because of the locational factors mentioned. The data presented earlier, however, also indicate that migration flows within the Czech Republic are somewhat higher than in the Slovak Republic, and this might also help explain the relative unemployment rates.

It has been argued that there are differences in the demographic characteristics of the Czech and Slovak populations that help explain differences in their unemployment rates. According to Vavro (1992) one important factor is the higher proportion of the working age population in Slovakia accounted for by Romanies (Gypsies)—a more migrant population with a lower labor force attachment and a higher incidence of unemployment. Vavro (1992) notes that 55,400 Gypsies were unemployed in March 1992; of these, 44,700 were in Slovakia. Data from the Slovak Ministry of Labor indicates that the unemployment rate for Gypsies in Slovakia was 42.9 percent in December 1991, while the rate for the entire Slovak Republic was only 11.8 percent. It is believed that the statistics for unemployment of Gypsies collected from the district labor offices vastly underestimates the proportion of Gypsies because of self-reporting. Nevertheless, if Gypsy attachment to the labor market is low and they are a larger proportion of the Slovak population than the Czech, this is clearly a factor explaining the differences in the two republics' rates.

The differences in the age structure of the work force in the two republics may also be a factor explaining the relative unemployment rates. The work force is younger in the Slovak Republic, and since unemployment rates are higher among the younger population, this may help explain the higher overall rate.[15]

Finally, since the labor force attachment of women over their life cycle is less secure than that of men, a nation with a higher percentage of women in the labor force would most probably have a higher unemployment rate than a nation with a lower percentage. Are there more women in the labor force of the Slovak Republic? We find there are no significant differences between the two republics. From 1985 to 1991, women represented about 45 percent of the work force in each republic (with a variation of only 1 percent above or below).

Over the 1990-93 period, however, the proportion of females among the unemployed was generally larger than their share of employment in both republics. The proportion in the Czech Republic (in the 56 to 60 percent range) was still larger than in Slovakia (between 49 and 52 percent). The data on unemployment rates also confirm that since June 1991 Czech

---

15. The higher unemployment of the young seems to be a characteristic of all economies, and especially transitional economies—see the other studies in the *International Labour Review*, vol. 130, nos. 5-6, 1991. This effect was suppressed by official government policies during the central planning period prior to 1989.

women have experienced a higher incidence of unemployment than Czech men, while there is no significant difference between the unemployment rates for Slovak men and women (see Paukert 1991). Hence, the number of women in the work force and their incidence of unemployment is not a factor explaining the higher Slovak unemployment rate.

LABOR MARKET POLICIES.   Until January 1, 1993, the Czech and Slovak republics were under one federal government and had identical labor market policies. There were, however, some important differences between the two republics in the application of labor laws and regulations that also help explain their diverging experience with unemployment.

One of the more important differences in the *passive labor market policy* was that before January of 1992 district labor offices in Slovakia allowed individuals to collect severance pay and unemployment benefits concurrently. After this date, the rule was enforced that a person who is granted severance pay in his last employment can be granted unemployment benefits only after the expiration of the severance pay (usually zero to five months, since severance pay may represent up to five months' salary). In December of 1991, 82 percent of all the unemployed in Slovakia versus 74 percent of those in the Czech Republic received benefits. In January 1992, the new legislation meant that the percentage of Slovaks receiving benefits dropped to 53 percent, while that of Czechs fell to 58 percent.[16] It is hence possible that the inflow (outflow) rates were higher (lower) as a result of the more benevolent regime in 1991.

It was not until June of 1991 that each of the republics enacted legislation governing *active labor market policy.* This policy includes programs for: (a) the creation of "socially purposeful jobs" (SPJs), entrepreneurships, and long-term jobs; (b) "publicly useful jobs" (PUJs) and short-term jobs; (c) job subsidies for new graduates; and (d) retraining of the unemployed. It also appears that the district labor offices (DLOs) give subsidies to firms that introduce technological change that reduces work hours. The sub-

---

16. A job applicant becomes eligible for unemployment benefits seven days after submitting a request to the employment office. Benefits are terminated at the end of six months of benefits or sooner if the applicant: (a) did not appear in the employment office on a preset date; (b) refused a suitable job; or (c) refused retraining. If an applicant is unsuccessful in finding a job during the six-month period, he or she remains in the employment office data base. He or she may apply to the Department of Social Affairs and Health Services of the local district municipal office for social benefits (welfare).

sidy pays the difference between shorter hours of work and full-time work and hence reduces layoffs. In addition to describing these schemes, we examine the impact of the active labor policies implemented in the 1991-93 period.

SOCIALLY PURPOSEFUL JOBS.   The SPJ program consists of two different types of programs for the registered unemployed: assistance to new entrepreneurs (self-employed) and the creation of jobs with existing employers. According to the legislation, all proposals for SPJs must be for jobs that have a reasonable chance of being viable in the long run.

The decentralized nature of the administration of this program has allowed significant differences among the district offices in how the program is carried out. The local employment offices have control over the types of enterprises that are created in their district, since all proposals are first submitted to the office. The DLOs also have control over whom they place in SPJ openings. In most cases, the office tends to offer the best candidates for these jobs rather than those who might have a hard time finding a job somewhere else.

The DLO provides funding in the following three ways: (a) a subsidy; (b) an interest-free loan; and/or (c) the payment of interest on loans taken by the employer (this is done to encourage banks to lend more money and thus give to entrepreneurs access to larger amounts of capital). The unemployed person applies for one of these three options and the director of the district labor office decides which is given. The data indicate that most funding has been given through subsidies.

The maximum reimbursement per job varies in the two republics. In Slovakia it is twelve times the minimum monthly wage and in the CR it is twelve times the average monthly rate of the district's unemployment benefit.

JOBS FOR NEW GRADUATES.   There was concern in 1991 that the young people graduating from high schools and universities were not finding employment. The government then launched a special program to subsidize employment for them. This program functions exactly like the SPJ program, but it is targeted to the new graduates.

PUBLICLY USEFUL WORK.   The PUJ program offers employment for a period of up to six months. The employment is expected to be of value to the community (that is, public works). Although it is stipulated that these jobs should last for a maximum period of six months, some labor offices allow an individual to be reemployed in the same job after a brief interval of unemployment.

As in the case of SPJs, the DLO is in charge of administration of the PUJ program. The local labor office mediates between the unemployed individual and the employer and writes a contract with the employer for the provision of work that benefits the community. Although the law allows the employment office to reach agreement with any type of employer, these jobs are mainly provided by local authorities. Most jobs are for unskilled or semiskilled individuals. A large portion of these jobs are menial (for example, street cleaning). Although there is certainly no lack of other work that could be done (such as ecological work or development of local amenities), local authorities have been, for the most part, unsuccessful in creating such jobs. As a result of the nature of the job, the labor offices tend to target the most difficult to employ (such as Gypsies and alcoholics) for the PUJs, unlike the SPJs, where the most qualified individuals are selected.

Many employment offices also use PUJs as a means of testing an unemployed individual's willingness to work. If a particular job opening is deemed suitable for an unemployed individual but that person refuses the job, unemployment benefits may be suspended by the employment office.

The average contribution paid by employment offices has varied from less than 500 Kcs to nearly 3,000 Kcs a person monthly. The data in table 3-10 indicates that in the Czech Republic, the average monthly contribution was about 1,787 Kcs in 1992, and in Slovakia it was about 1,452 Ks in 1993; the average PUJ compensation is approximately equal to the minimum wage.

RETRAINING.   One of the rights to employment created by the Employment Act (Articles 10 and 11) is the right to receive retraining for a job. The labor offices have organized courses in both job-specific and general training, although the former was the more frequent form of retraining supported in 1991 in the CR (training in construction skills was the most important). A movement toward more general training was seen in 1992. The DLOs have used a wide range of providers of training who have offered courses of varying duration (from a few days to eighteen months).

At present, the data are incomplete, but there are indications that the Czech DLOs are more involved than the Slovak DLOs with their active

Table 3-10. Budget Allocation within the Active Employment Program, 1991-93
(*in thousands of crowns*)[a]

	Total	SPJ	SE	PUJ	RET	Y&SL	Hours[b]	Other[c]
Czech Republic								
1991								
Cost	772,995	330,363	166,783	78,390	39,980	47,735	79,788	29,956
Distribution	100.00%	42.7%	21.6%	10.1%	5.2%	6.2%	10.3%	3.9%
1992								
Cost	1,718,096	736,596	232,024	223,027	94,023	325,528	36,400	70,500
Distribution	100.00%	42.9%	13.5%	13.0%	5.5%	18.9%	2.1%	4.1%
1993								
Cost	749,408	170,567	159,605	159,605	73,359	245,190	4,368	49,022
Distribution	100.00%	22.8%	6.3%	21.3%	9.8%	32.7%	0.6%	6.5%
Slovak Republic								
1991								
Cost	515,259	352,375	d	108,210	54,675	—	—	—
Distribution	100.00%	68.4%	d	21.0%	10.6%	—	—	—
1992								
Cost	3,812,793	2,857,235	14,307	402,903	292,051	97,767	122,778	25,752
Distribution	100.00%	74.9%	0.4%	10.6%	7.7%	2.6%	3.2%	0.7%
1993								
Cost	1,107,216	748,047	2,445	163,932	118,280	54,232	8,029	12,250
Distribution	100.00%	67.6%	0.2%	14.8%	10.7%	4.9%	0.7%	1.1%

— Not available.

Note: Abbreviations: PUJ, publicly useful job; RET, retraining; SE, self-employed; SPJ, social purposeful jobs; Y&SL, youth and school-leaver jobs; self-employed.

a. 1993 expenditures for Slovak Republic are in Slovak crowns.

b. Subsidies to firms that implemented technical changes that led to reduction of hours worked.

c. Retired, maternity leaves, army service, imprisoned.

d. It is not clear whether allocation was zero or it was included within the SPJ jobs category.

Source: Czech and Slovak Ministry of Labor and Social Affairs.

137

employment programs. Data we have collected on a sample of approximately 6,000 individuals that became unemployed in the last quarter of 1991 and first quarter of 1992 indicate that among those who leave unemployment in a given month, the proportion of Czechs that find a job with the assistance of the DLO is higher than the proportion of Slovaks. We have tried to ascertain the validity of this finding with aggregated data from the DLOs over time. At this stage, complete data are unavailable and table 3-11 is unfinished. The sketchy data do, however, indicate that the proportion of Slovaks leaving unemployment in a given month who find a job with the DLO is lower than the proportion of Czechs. (Note that the ratio in Slovakia is calculated as a proportion of the total and the proportion in the Czech Republic is calculated as a proportion of the subtotal who found a job.)

RESOURCE ALLOCATION AND IMPACT OF ACTIVE EMPLOYMENT POLICIES. Tables 3-10 and 3-12 indicate the budget allocation to the active and passive employment programs in the two republics for 1991-93. There are several interesting observations from these statistics.

First, in 1991 and 1992, the total budget for employment policies in the Czech Republic as a percentage of GDP (.3-.4 percent) is far lower than the ratio for most other European countries in these years. The proportions of 0.9 percent to 1.9 percent found in the Slovak Republic are also below (but closer to) the European countries. Figures from the OECD *Employment Outlook* (1993, table 2.B.1) indicate that public expenditures on labor market programs as a percent of GDP were between 2.5 percent and 5.5 percent for seven European countries, with Poland on the low end and Finland on the high end. What is surprising is that the Slovaks are spending relatively more than the Czechs and are still facing higher and faster growing unemployment rates. In 1991 and 1993 the Slovaks spent approximately one-third more than the Czechs, but in 1992 they spent about three-quarters more than the Czechs.

Second, the budget for labor market programs grew in 1992 in both the CR and SR. All of this increase was in the active employment programs, which grew in nominal terms by over twofold in the CR and by over sevenfold in the SR. The amount allocated to passive programs declined somewhat. Hence, the active employment program's share of total expenditures rose in 1991-92 from 32 percent to 55 percent in the CR and from 16 percent to 69 percent in the SR. In 1993 the budget was cut back in both republics; the amount allocated to active programs in the CR

Table 3-11. Destination of People who Leave Unemployment in a Given Month, 1Q92-4Q93

Quarter	Total	Found a job Subtotal	By DLO[a]	On own	Taken off, unreliable	Other[b]
			Czech Republic			
1Q92	46,098	72.6%	—	—	—	—
2Q92	45,917	68.2%	—	—	—	—
3Q92	35,905	69.7%	—	—	—	—
4Q92	30,329	67.6%	—	—	—	—
1Q93	32,749	74.8%	35.2%	39.5%	10.4%	14.8%
2Q93	33,625	73.3%	35.8%	37.5%	10.9%	15.8%
3Q93	30,702	75.1%	35.4%	39.7%	9.1%	15.8%
4Q93	29,392	73.1%	32.8%	40.4%	10.1%	16.8%
			Slovak Republic			
1Q92	24,399	—	49.3%	—	—	—
2Q92	30,388	—	48.2%	—	—	—
3Q92	29,841	—	49.1%	—	—	—
4Q92	30,097	—	59.0%	—	—	—
1Q93	23,884	68.3%	49.7%	18.6%	8.3%	7.3%
2Q93	27,833	71.1%	41.7%	29.3%	14.1%	11.1%
3Q93	26,804	71.5%	37.7%	33.8%	15.1%	12.2%
4Q93	23,342	70.1%	37.6%	32.5%	12.5%	14.7%

— Not available.
a. Retired, deceased, imprisoned, maternity leave, army service, and so forth.
b. As a percentage of total.
Source: Czech and Slovak Ministry of Labor and Social Affairs.

was about the same as in 1991, although in the SR the budget for active programs in 1993 was double that in 1991.

Third, within the active employment program, over one-half of the resources were allocated to the SPJ program (jobs plus self-employment) in each republic, with the Slovaks allocating slightly more. In 1993 the Czech government cut back tremendously on the SPJ program, reducing its share to 29.1 percent.

The programs next in importance for the Slovaks are the PUJ and retraining programs, whereas the Czechs have emphasized the programs for the new graduates and PUJs, in order of importance. The share of the budget for the new graduates program in the CR rose from 6.2 percent in 1991, to 18.9 percent in 1992, and 32.7 percent in 1993.

Table 3-12. Budget Allocation to the Active and Passive Employment Programs, Share and Percent of GDP, 1991-93 *(in millions of crowns)[a]*

Year	Total		Active policy		Passive policy		Active share	Passive share	Share of GDP Active	Share of GDP Passive
Czech Republic										
1991	2,450.3	1.0	773.0	1.0	1,677.3	1.0	31.5%	68.5%	0.1%	0.2%
1992	3,141.4	1.3	1,718.1	2.2	1,423.4	0.8	54.7%	45.3%	0.2%	0.2%
1993	2,166.1	0.9	749.4	1.0	1,416.7	0.8	34.6%	65.4%	0.1%	0.2%
Slovak Republic										
1991	3,276.5	1.0	515.3	1.0	2,761.2	1.0	15.7%	84.3%	0.2%	1.0%
1992	5,523.7	1.7	3,812.8	7.4	1,710.9	0.6	69.0%	31.0%	1.3%	0.6%
1993	2,966.2	0.9	1,107.2	2.1	1,858.9	0.7	37.3%	62.7%	0.3%	0.6%

Note: Index relates to the expenditures of 1991.

a. In 1993 Slovak expenditures are expressed in Slovak crowns. The exchange rate between the Slovak crown and the Czech crown changed from 1:1 to about .8:1 over 1993.

Source: Czech and Slovak Ministry of Labor and Social Affairs.

Table 3-13. Average Number of People in Each Active Employment Subprogram as a Percent of Unemployed, 1Q92-4Q93

	Czech Republic				Slovak Republic				SR/CR			
Quarter	SPJ+ (1)	SE (2)	PUJ (3)	RET (4)	SPJ+ (5)	SE (6)	PUJ (7)	RET (8)	(5)/(1) (9)	(6)/(2) (10)	(7)/(3) (11)	(8)/(4) (12)
1Q92	22.7%	7.4%	3.5%	3.0%	3.4%	5.5%	3.0%	1.3%	0.15	0.74	0.86	0.43
2Q92	44.2%	13.6%	9.6%	3.0%	5.5%	8.6%	6.9%	1.6%	0.12	0.63	0.72	0.54
3Q92	57.2%	17.0%	10.3%	1.4%	8.1%	11.7%	9.3%	0.9%	0.14	0.69	0.91	0.62
4Q92	64.9%	19.4%	6.9%	3.3%	13.9%	18.2%	9.2%	2.7%	0.21	0.94	1.35	0.82
1Q93	44.8%	16.7%	3.0%	2.2%	15.4%	19.1%	3.1%	1.7%	0.34	1.14	1.03	0.78
2Q93	48.7%	18.7%	5.2%	1.7%	15.5%	17.7%	2.2%	0.9%	0.32	0.94	0.42	0.54
3Q93	40.8%	15.6%	4.6%	0.7%	14.4%	16.1%	2.0%	0.3%	0.35	1.03	0.42	0.44
4Q93	33.1%	11.9%	2.6%	1.9%	14.8%	15.7%	1.1%	0.8%	0.45	1.32	0.42	0.42

Note: SPJ+ includes FJ, Y&SL, and excludes SE. SPJ, socially purposeful jobs; SE, self-employed; PUJ, publicly useful jobs; RET, retraining; FJ, jobs at firms; Y&SL, youth and school-leaver jobs. The data are monthly average values in a given quarter.
Source: Czech and Slovak Ministry of Labor and Social Affairs.

Again, it is surprising that the substantial resources being spent on these active employment programs in Slovakia are not having a bigger impact on its unemployment rate. The relative success of the SPJ programs in the two republics is made evident by examining the proportion of the unemployed who have been given an SPJ in each republic (table 3-13). During the 1992-93 period, between 30 percent and 84 percent of the unemployed in a given month were in an SPJ in the Czech Republic, whereas the proportions for Slovakia were only between 9 percent and 34 percent.

The PUJ program has not been very important in either republic. Overall, the ratio of the publicly useful jobs to the number of unemployed has been rather low (less than 15 percent) in both republics. If one looks at the proportion of people getting a PUJ in a given month as a proportion of those leaving unemployment, it is seen that PUJs are more important as a source of outflows in Slovakia compared with the Czech Republic (see table 3-13), but they declined in importance in 1993 to account for only about 5 percent in the first three quarters. While useful as a stop-gap measure, this public works scheme has thus had a much more limited impact than its socially purposeful jobs counterpart.

The number of persons in retraining has grown by leaps and bounds from a minuscule base. The numbers grew steadily in both republics until April 1992 and have fluctuated widely since then. The program has never had a major quantitative impact, however; the number of individuals undergoing retraining ranges between 1 percent and 10 percent of all people in active employment programs in both republics and has never reached more than 3.8 percent of the unemployed in the CR and 3 percent in the SR.

Policy Options and Constraints

After the 1989 Velvet Revolution, the Czech and Slovak republics embarked on an ambitious transition path, characterized by restrictive macroeconomic policies, major microeconomic transformations centered on massive privatization, and severe external shocks. Slovakia has been harder hit and experienced a higher level of social discontent. Since 1993 it has also slowed down the course of the reform in relation to the Czech Republic.

The differences between the Czech and Slovak labor markets are an enigma. Until the separation in 1993, the decline in GDP and industrial production was very similar in the two republics. Employment declined more rapidly in Slovakia, but it cannot fully explain the much greater rise in the Slovak unemployment rate. Resources allocated to active and passive employment programs were also much greater (one-third to three-quarters) in Slovakia over the 1991-93 period. Moreover, the majority of the increase in expenditure in Slovakia has been in the active, rather than the passive, employment programs.

Potential explanations include the following: (a) data on output and employment in the Czech Republic severely underestimate the growth of the private sector and other forms of demand (such as work in Germany and Austria) and (b) resources allocated to employment programs in Slovakia may not have been spent as efficiently as in the Czech Republic. We have presented various statistics showing that demand conditions are stronger in the Czech Republic (measured by vacancy/unemployment ratios; individuals moving from job to job without experiencing a spell of unemployment; and probability of leaving unemployment in a given month). We do not have much evidence to support point (b) other than that the Slovaks allowed simultaneous payment of severance payments and unemployment benefits over 1990-91.

The challenge in both republics for the next several years is how to ensure that the reforms generate visible benefits and avoid social backlash. This means that emphasis will have to shift to engendering economic growth and a rise in living standards. On the basis of the present study, we regard the following policy issues as critical:

- Many large firms are still inefficient. The economic situation of many of these firms is more precarious than it was two or three years ago. Their indebtedness has increased, domestic investments have been postponed, and the inflow of Western capital has been limited. The management has been preoccupied with the privatization process and self-enrichment at the expense of the state. While the Czech Republic has so far been extremely successful in keeping unemployment down, this good record to date has hinged on the government's willingness to use privatization revenue to keep firms afloat through the banking system, as well as its ability to stimulate the growth of the private sector and create a large number of temporarily financed "socially purposeful jobs." An increasing number of firms are on the verge of bankruptcy, but the governments and the small number of colluding banks have so far prevented bankruptcies from occurring on a significant scale. Most large enterprises still hoard excess labor. When the rationalization of these enterprises occurs, one can expect substantial layoffs.

- Continued evaluation of the active and passive employment programs is essential given the need to use these resources as effectively as possible. One aspect of unemployment that has not been adequately dealt with by the district labor offices is the problems of the long-term unemployed. A significant proportion of the unemployed (especially in Slovakia) are long term. If the employment programs ignore this segment of the population, there is a danger that they will be marginalized and conventional duration effects will set in.

- There is also inefficiency in the mobility of labor. Housing regulations and controls have so far limited geographic mobility and created significant disparaties in regional unemployment rates.

- The tripartite system of wage setting has enabled wages to be cut severely without labor unrest because of the weakness of the post-communist trade unions and the workers' preoccupation with job security. In recent months trade unions have clashed with the government on a number of issues, including the desirability of wage controls. Since industrial peace is an important precondition for a successful transformation, the preservation of a functioning tripartite framework should be a priority for both republics.

Bibliography

Begg, David. 1991. "Economic Reform in Czechoslovakia: Should We Believe in Santa Klaus?" *Economic Policy* 13: 243-86.

Boeri, Tito. 1994. "Labor Market Flows and the Persistence of Unemployment in Central and Eastern Europe." In *Unemployment in Transition Countries*. Paris: OECD.

Boeri, Tito, and Mark Keese. 1992. *Labour Markets and the Transition in Central and Eastern Europe*. Paris: OECD.

Bound, John, and George Johnson. 1992. "Changes in the Structure of Wages in the 1980's: An Evaluation of Alternative Explanations." *American Economic Review* 82(3): 371-92.

Buchtikova, Alena. 1993. "The Empirical Analysis of the Wage Structure and the Effects of Minimum Wages in the Transition Period: The Case of the Czech Republic." Paper prepared for the International Conference on the Economic Analysis of Low Pay and the Effects of Minimum Wages, Arles, France, September 30-October 1, 1993, Institute of Economics, Czech National Bank, Prague.

Burda, Michael. 1993. "Unemployment, Labour Markets and Structural Change in Eastern Europe." *Economic Policy* 16: 101-37.

Dyba, Karel, and Jan Svejnar. 1993. "Stabilization and Transition in Czechoslovakia." In O. J. Blanchard, K. Froot, and J. Sachs, eds., *The Transition in Eastern Europe*. Chicago: University of Chicago Press.

————. 1994. "An Overview of Recent Economic Developments in the Czech Republic." Prague, CERGE/EI. Mimeo.

Employment Observatory Central and Eastern Europe, 3, 1992. Alphametrics, Belgium.

Freeman, Richard B. 1993. "What Directions for Labor Market Institutions in Eastern and Central Europe?" Paper presented at the 1992 NBER Conference on Transition in Eastern Europe. (Also in O. J. Blanchard, K. Froot, and J. Sachs, eds, *The Transition in Eastern Europe*. Chicago: University of Chicago Press.)

Horalek, Milan. 1993. "Zamestnanost a Nezamestnanost v Ceske Republice: 1991-93" (Employment and Unemployment in the Czech Republic: 1991-93). Friedrich Ebert Foundation Project, Bonn, Germany.

Nesporova, A. 1991. "Recent Labour Market and Social Policy Developments in the Czech and Slovak Republic." ILO/OECD-CCEET Conference on Labour Market and Social Policy Implications of Structural Change in Central and Eastern Europe, Paris, 11-13 September.

OECD. 1993. *Employment Outlook*. Paris.

Paukert, Liba. 1991. "The Economic Status of Women in the Transition to a Market System: The Case of Czechoslovakia." *International Labour Review* 130 (5-6): 613-33.

Svejnar, Jan. 1978. "Workers Participation in Management in Czechoslovakia." *Annals of Public and Cooperative Economy* 49(2): 177-202.

————. 1992. "Labor Market Adjustment in Transitional Economies." Part III, *Recent Developments in the Czechoslovakian Economy with Special Reference to Labor Markets in Transition*. Report to the National Council for Soviet and East European Research, Washington, D.C., November.

Svejnar, Jan, and Miroslav Singer. 1992. "The Czechoslovak Voucher Privatization: An Assessment of Results." University of Pittsburgh. Mimeo.

Swanson, Dan, and Leila Webster. 1992. "Private Sector Manufacturing in the Czech and Slovak Federal Republic: A Survey of Firms." Industry and Energy Department, The World Bank, Washington, D.C.

Terrell, Katherine. 1992. "Female-Male Wage Differentials and Occupational Structure." *International Labour Review* 133 (4-5): 387-404.

Vavro, Anton. 1992. "prícin rozdielneho vΔvoja nezamestnanosti v SR a CR" (Analysis of the Reasons for the Evolution of Different Unemployment Rates in the Slovak Republic and the Czech Republic), trans. Sharon Fisher. Bratislava: Slovak Commission for Economic Strategy, May.

Windmuller, John P. 1971. "Czechoslovakia and the Communist Union Model." *British Journal of Industrial Relations* 9(1): 35.

Yotopoulos, Pan, and Jeffrey Nugent. 1976. *Economic Development*. New York: McGraw-Hill.

4

Russia

Simon Commander, John McHale, and Ruslan Yemtsov

Since January 1992 the magnitudes of change in the Russian economy have been massive. The price level now stands over sixty times higher than at the end of 1991, sustained by large fiscal deficits in 1992 and 1993 with significant financing through money creation. Households and firms have attempted to evade the inflation tax by currency substitution so that by mid-1993 over 50 percent of broad money was nonruble; all this from a very narrow base. Beneath this monetary smokescreen, large changes in ownership, and potentially in structure, have been occurring. By mid-1993 possibly one-third of all small firms had been privatized and over 50 percent of larger units corporatized or privatized.[1]

This chapter is primarily concerned with the impact of these changes and the channels by which these changes have been transmitted. The emphasis is on labor market decisions, starting from the evident puzzle that despite large-order negative shocks to output, net changes to employment have been rather small, with unemployment yet to top 2 percent of the labor force (table 4-1). Even after including those on short-time and involuntary leave, the stability of employment—alongside significant turnover—is undeniable. Further, while we observe a more volatile short-run path for wages, there is surprising stability in relative wages.

---

1. Boycko, Schleifer, and Vishny (1993) indicate that over 20 percent of industrial employment was in privatized firms.

Table 4-1. Russia, Basic Indicators
(percentage)

Indicator	1991	1992	1993
GDP	–9	–19	–12
Consumer prices	138	2,318	840
Producer prices	236	3,275	895
Fiscal deficit (percent of GDP)	–17	–20	–8
Industrial output	–8	–19	–16
Industrial employment	–1.3	–4.5	–6.5
Unemployment rate	0.7	1.5	1.5
Real wages (cpi defl)	53.5	–50.6	–2.0
Real M2	–44.3	–46.0	–12.2[a]

a. Midyear.
Source: IMF, World Bank, Russian Goskomstat.

Drawing on both aggregate and survey-generated data, we concentrate on explaining these developments through the response of the bedrock of the system: the Russian industrial firm. We spend some time marshalling and presenting in a consistent way the available information. Net changes to employment in the state sector are shown to be small, although we observe fairly large gross flows. It is clear that there is considerable labor hoarding by firms. Later in the chapter we relate this directly to the objective function of firms dominated by insiders and think through the implications of a negative shock. Even if in an insider-dominated firm labor hoarding can be an optimum, with an adverse shock the firm will adjust employment, reducing hoarding, for a constant wage. And with adjustment costs, the path of the adjustment to steady-state values can result in an initial increase in labor hoarding. We conclude that despite the tentative emergence of conventional associations between wage claims and activity measures, the Russian labor market remains characterized by low interregional labor mobility, significant inefficiencies in labor allocation, and a large employment overhang. The elimination of these difficulties will be contingent on changes both to macroeconomic policy—particularly the flow of subsidies to the firm sector—and the behavioral rules governing firm decisions on employment and wages. The simple transfer of title to insiders, as it is occurring under the present privatization program, is unlikely in itself to force those changes. In short, the implications of these dizzying changes may be less revolutionary than they appear at first inspection.

Price Liberalization and Inflation

The cornerstone of the stabilization was the liberalization of prices. The price jump in January 1992 was enormous, far higher than projected: producer prices leapt by 382 percent and consumer prices by 245 percent over the previous month.[2] Thereafter, monthly inflation remained high, but on a declining path, albeit with considerable regional variation and instability. But, as figure 4-1 indicates, producer and consumer price changes shifted up again in the fourth quarter of the year to a monthly range of 20-25 percent, where they have remained. It also indicates that producer prices increased more than consumer prices in most months through 1991-93. Part of the explanation may continue to lie with the differential rates of liberalization of types of prices. In particular, as table 4-2 shows, consumer price changes continue to demonstrate very large regional variation, testimony to the varied and widespread presence of price controls for major items in the consumer price basket. It is notable that regional producer price changes show less dispersion on a monthly basis.[3] By late 1992 both sets of prices tend to move more closely together. Nevertheless, the wedge has been large.

We need to clarify why inflation appears, since 1992.Q3, to have reached a plateau and why product, rather than, as we might have predicted, consumer prices have led the inflation. At the heart of high inflations is generally a persistent and significant fiscal deficit, and Russia is no exception even if, partly for institutional reasons, separating out fiscal and monetary channels is difficult. The difficulty is compounded by the apparent ability of other former republics within the ruble zone to influence the money supply. But the overall picture is clear. The general government's cash deficit was around 7-8 percent of GDP in 1992 and 1993, rising in 1992 to 20 percent once unbudgeted import subsidies were included. Over 1992 and 1993.Q1, foreign financing accounted for around 65 percent of total deficit financing, while the domestic-bank-financed component of the enlarged deficit amounted to 6-7 percent of GDP, declining to under 3 percent in 1993.Q1.

The initial large contraction in credit to the economy was subsequently partially reversed, driven by lending to the firm sector and to government; this was accompanied by large order expansions in base

2. The overshoot is generally attributed to the size of the prior monetary overhang; but this is by no means obvious given the erosion already induced by accelerating inflation in the second half of 1991 (Cottarelli and Blejer 1992).
3. For example, retail milk prices exhibit far greater variance than procurement prices.

Figure 4-1. Russia, Consumer and Producer Prices, January 1991-September 1993 (monthly changes)

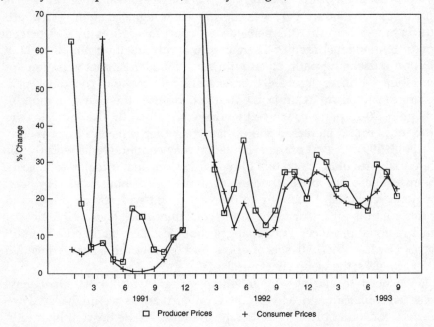

money. With the resulting acceleration in inflation giving rise to an inflation tax amounting to nearly 25 percent of monthly household income
through 1992 (Vieira da Cunha 1993), the endogenous response of households and firms was to shift rapidly out of domestic money. Dollar deposits—primarily for firms—accounted for around half of broad money by
mid-1993. At the same time, time and demand deposits dwindled to
almost nothing, as residents reduced ruble holdings to transactions minima. But given the undeveloped nature of the financial system and the
incomplete currency substitution, this still permitted the extraction of 10-
15 percent of GDP through seignorage. In short, foreign financing of the
deficit, the partial correction in early 1993, and constraints on the use of
foreign currency as liquidity may explain the high but relatively stable
nature of the inflation. There are, however, particularities of the inflation
process—notably, the behavior of producer prices—that have to be
explained.

We note that over the first half of 1992 the spikes in product prices can
generally be attributed to staggered changes to administered prices, particularly energy. In addition, intermediate and capital goods prices

Table 4-2. Changes in Prices and Wages: Regional Variations, February 1992-May 1993

Period	Inflation (percent change)	Range		Coefficient of variation	Nominal wages (percent change)	Range		Coefficient of variation
		Max	Min			Max	Min	
1992								
February	24.5	51.9	1.10	0.10	39.3	5,653	799	0.49
March	21.1	53.5	4.10	0.08	36.0	7,496	1,066	0.46
April	15.3	54.7	2.50	0.08	11.9	10,585	1,218	0.52
May	11.1	36.1	4.50	0.05	20.4	12,558	1,479	0.52
June	13.1	25.0	5.70	0.04	37.8	14,824	2,124	0.47
July	7.2	18.6	2.70	0.03	7.6	15,202	2,307	0.48
August	7.2	17.2	2.60	0.02	7.7	16,254	2,425	0.47
September	11.5	19.7	2.70	0.03	25.6	21,065	3,155	0.45
October	22.9	42.0	9.00	0.05	19.9	27,253	3,372	0.47
November	26.1	47.0	9.00	0.05	19.4	28,371	3,718	0.45
December	25.9	36.0	12.00	0.04	51.9	44,489	6,474	0.44
1993								
January	26.5	122.5	0.50	0.13	-4.5	44,858	5,537	0.48
February	25.7	49.0	12.00	0.04	24.3	54,517	7,132	0.47
March	21.4	38.2	14.10	0.04	23.5	72,777	8,958	0.50
April	24.7	95.5	13.40	0.10	29.7	88,679	11,906	0.48
May	19.3	29.5	5.80	0.04	22.7	122,084	16,102	0.50

increased more rapidly, indicating that firms selling to each other and hence accumulating interenterprise arrears were relatively indifferent to price, given the high probability of a bail-out by government at a later stage (Koen and Phillips 1993). This duly happened with the netting-out of arrears in July/August 1992. But this still leaves a need to explain the continuing asymmetry given the path of output.

Output, Product Prices, and Market Power

National income and industrial output fell by around 20 percent in 1992; the decline stabilized over the first half of 1993. Industrial branch data indicate a generalized recession in the state sector (table 4-3). Aggregate shocks appear to dominate, both through the fall in household wealth and income arising from the price liberalization, as also on the supply side. A possible indicator of the former has been the sharp increase in industrial finished goods inventory in relation to other inventory over the first half of 1992. Thereafter, finished goods stocks shift downward. In the case of supply shocks, the extra-large decline in light industry, for example, can be attributed to shortfalls in inputs delivery and inefficiencies in the payments system arising from the collapse of the CMEA and intra-CIS trade regimes. Indeed, supply constraints were cited as a secondary but major factor behind output losses for almost all industrial branches into 1993. Similarly, the sharp shift in relative energy prices drove up production costs and is likely to have had aggregate effects given the low dispersion in the ex ante ratio of energy to total costs across branches. Reallocation shocks associated with changes in relative prices driving differentiated sectoral outcomes appear, by contrast, to be a weaker explanatory factor, and figure 4-2 provides no tight link between output and relative price changes.[4] In short, aggregate shocks dominate structural shocks.[5]

The size of the negative shocks to output are indisputably large, while any offsetting growth in the private sector is impossible to quantify. Yet aggregate data suggest that gross profits of the firm sector in 1992 were around 35 percent of GDP (Vieira da Cunha 1993). Gross profits and

---

4.   If relative price increases reflect market power, this could, of course, lead to a negative correlation between relative prices and output.

5.   There is no association between output changes and a summary competitiveness measure, such as the short-run shadow profit rates calculated by Senik-Leygonie and Hughes 1992.

Figure 4-2. Output/Relative Price Changes,
March 1993/January 1991

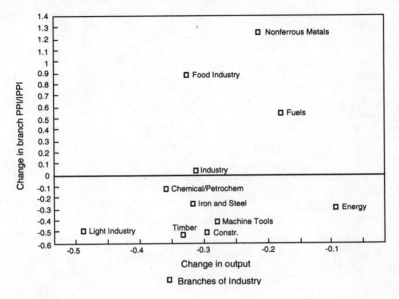

Change in output

□ Branches of Industry

Table 4-3. Industrial Branches: Output, Employment, Consumer Wages,
Relative Price, and Wage Changes, 1992/91

Branch	Output	Employment	Relative price	Relative wage	Consumer wage
Energy	−6.9	9.7	−3.4	25.5	−24.7
Fuels	−10.0	−11.4	86.2	48.7	−9.2
Iron & steel	−17.6	2.2	27.5	27.5	−23.9
Nonferrous metallurgy	−12.2	2.8	126.7	38.9	−21.4
Chemicals	−19.9	−0.3	31.9	10.8	−33.0
Machine building	−16.9	−7.2	−31.1	−15.3	−48.8
Timber	−16.5	−4.2	−33.8	23.4	−34.9
Construction materials	−18.9	−3.0	−36.2	−7.6	−45.0
Light	−31.3	−3.2	−61.9	−15.4	−51.4
Food	−23.4	−1.1	−16.8	−2.8	−48.8

Figure 4-3. Russia, Change in Output and Markup for Industry and Branches: 1992/91

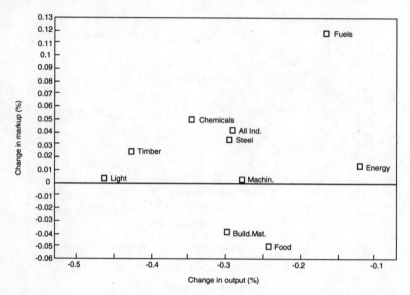

markups over total costs at the industrial branch level indicate between 8.5 percent and 4 percent increases, respectively, in 1992, with some further upward drift in the first quarter of 1993. Figure 4-3 relates the change in output to the change in branch-level markup over total costs. The results are quite striking—they show that, despite large across-the-board decreases in output, the majority of branches experience *increases* in their markup in 1992. This also appears to hold through 1993 (see Commander and Yemtsov 1994). The fact that the largest increase is for fuels may indicate one of the propagation mechanisms, although it does not, of course, explain the simultaneous increase in the markup across the majority of branches. Downstream branches with higher exposure to household demand—light, food, and construction—show negative or small positive changes to their markups, pointing to the possible role of different budget constraints in driving the pricing decision. But overall, the association between output and markup changes is weak and suggests a role for market power, arising from concentration and effective segmentation in product markets (Brown, Ickes, and Ryterman 1993), with both effects compounded by the breakup of the Soviet Union and amplified by the weakness of the distribution system.

Figure 4-4. Output and Profit Changes, Firms with Market Power

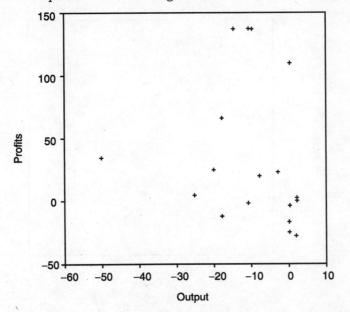

Firm-level survey results confirm the general buoyancy of profits in 1992 but drive home the point that market power has been an important determinant of the profit profile (for an extended discussion, see Commander and others 1993b). Figures 4-4 and 4-5 show clearly divergent movements in real gross profits for competitive as against firms with market power, with only the former having an unambiguous negative shock to gross profits over 1992. For a significant share of firms with market power, negative shocks to output have been associated with positive changes to gross profits.

The financial side of the picture would be quite incomplete without bringing in the large flows of subsidies and transfers to the firm sector, either explicitly through the budget or through directed and other credits. In 1992 firms were net recipients of around 7.5 percent of GDP through these channels.

Employment

The most striking asymmetry is the response of employment to output. Total state sector employment fell by around 3 percent in both 1991 and 1992, when over the full period GDP declined by around 30 percent. For

Figure 4-5. Output and Profit Changes, Competitive Firms

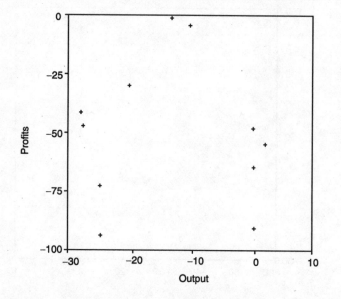

industry, employment contracted by between 3 and 5 percent in both years.[6] For 1993, employment in the state sector stabilized but it declined more rapidly in industry in the second half of the year (table 4-1 and figure 4-6). A scatter of industrial output against employment changes shows a positive correlation, but with vast asymmetry in the changes. Further, over 80 percent of gross job losses were accounted for by changes in the machine-building branch, and nearly half the branches actually registered net increases to employment over the year.

But this tells only one part of the story. While net job destruction has been very restrained, leading to large falls in labor productivity, adjustment in hours has been significant, weakening the productivity decline.[7] Between 20 and 33 percent of firms, particularly larger enterprises with more than a thousand employees, have significant shares of their work force on short time and involuntary leave. This appears to have been the dominant response of state firms since mid-1992. Goskomstat data indicate that in August 1992 nearly 8 percent of those in industrial employ-

6.   Job contraction in industry preceded the current period with total industrial employment in 1991 roughly 8 percent lower than at the peak in 1986.
7.   As regards adjustment costs, note that the employment law requires at least three months severance pay, aside from possible within-firm opposition.

Figure 4-6. Russia, Industrial Employment and Output,
January 1991-March 1993

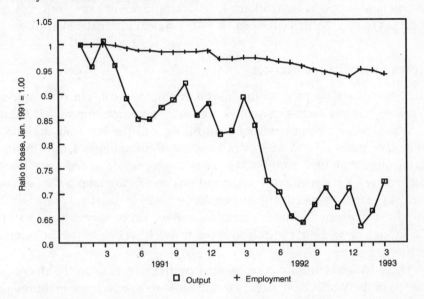

ment were on involuntary leave or short-time work. By June 1993, 11
percent of industrial workers had an involuntary leave spell and 4 percent were on reduced hours, with the proportion declining to 5 percent by
March 1993. Survey data confirm these magnitudes in mid-1993.[8] Treat-
ing this as a crude measure of the current employment overhang, we can
see that releasing the marginally employed into unemployment would
have raised the unemployment rate by at least 300 percent.

The important point is that a common response of firms has been to
continue to retain labor even in the face of large negative shocks to output. This might be interpreted as an expectation to the future, and hence
that capacity utilization would increase. But it also reflects that firms have
a broader social function that induces benevolent behavior.[9] And the

---

8.   These figures are from the VCIOM regional survey, which also shows that for
75 percent of those on involuntary leave, the spell ranged between one and four
weeks in the quarter.
9.   In the World Bank survey, over a third of the surveyed firms reported excess
employment in 1992.Q3/4. When asked why they had not laid off the excess, nearly 50 percent considered that there would be future output expansion, while nearly
25 percent cited lack of a financial burden. Legal obstacles and worker opposition
were the other cited constraints.

decision to enforce severance may further be complicated because in a large number of cases firms are the source of a broad range of benefits and income supports for workers. Loss of employment likely implies loss of access to such benefits, frequently with no clear alternative suppliers.

Flows in the Labor Market

The aggregate data pick up the inertia in employment, but this camouflages apparently large gross flows, as can be seen from figure 4-7. Aside from indicating strong persistence in hiring and the low and declining weight of mass layoffs in separations, the figure suggests that in any given month of 1992 and 1993.Q1 roughly 4 percent of the state labor force made a job transition. The separations and hiring rates at 27 percent and 24 percent, respectively, are certainly high, at least in comparison with other Eastern European countries, and would be surprising if a simple model of worker control, leading to attrition, were the dominant features.

These magnitudes are corroborated by the results from the first two rounds of the World Bank survey in the Moscow region (a more thorough presentation of results is found in Commander and others 1993b). The data relate to the third and fourth quarters of 1992 and confirm that gross

Figure 4-7. Russia, Gross Flows, 1992

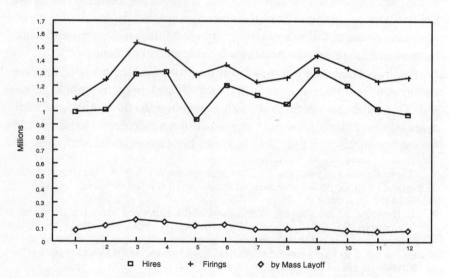

Table 4-4. Separation, Hiring, and Vacancy Rates, 1992.Q3 and 1992.Q4
(percent of labor force)

	FS1		FS2		FS3		FS4		FS5	
Item	*3Q*	*4Q*	*3Q*	*4Q*	*3Q*	*4Q*	*3Q*	*4Q*	*3Q*	*4Q*
Separations	10.5	7.8	10.0	11.0	9.5	7.2	5.7	4.8	7.8	9.0
Hires	7.2	5.8	3.7	5.2	4.8	2.1	2.5	1.9	9.9	4.9
Net separations	3.7	2.0	7.0	5.8	5.2	5.0	3.3	2.9	−2.2	4.0
Expected separa- tions, 92.4 & 93.1	2.4	0.4	2.4	0	2.3	0.9	0.5	0.6	0.5	1.7
Vacancies	1.5	2.6	3.1	3.0	1.0	0.5	2.2	0.4	1.9	—
Posted vacancies	0.1	0	1.0	0	0.7	0.4	0.9	0	1.1	—

— Not available.
Note: Firm size (FS) categories: 1=80-350; 2=351-700; 3=701-900; 4=901-1,500; 5=>1,501 employees.
Source: World Bank survey.

flows are rather large; in one quarter alone between 8 and 10 percent of the labor force changes employment in our sample. As striking is the relative buoyancy of hires. Consequently, net separation rates across the firm-size classes are quite small and actually decline in the final quarter of 1992 (table 4-4). While vacancies—particularly those posted at the labor offices—have fallen to almost zero, the general picture is one of considerable churning in the labor market, with large numbers of voluntary job transitions.

Table 4-5 pins this down more acutely. The role of quits in labor turnover dominates, while employment reductions—explicit decisions on involuntary separations—in general account for far smaller shares of total separations. Over the whole sample, quits account for more than 60 percent of all separations and staff reduction for less than 30 percent in 1992.Q3 and 1992.Q4. Of further interest are the respective weights of skills in the types of separations. While production workers account for over 70 percent of quits, over 50 percent of involuntary separations have been concentrated on technical (ITR) or clerical staff. On the hiring side, around 80 percent of hires were accounted for by production workers.

The story seems clear; quits and hires are largely accounted for by production workers. Net job losses have been concentrated among clerical and other staff. There also appear to be signs of discrimination—female full-time workers have had the largest net job losses, the ana-

Table 4-5. Job Separations by Type, 1992.Q3 and 1992.Q4
(shares)

	FS1		FS2		FS3		FS4		FS5	
Item	*3Q*	*4Q*	*3Q*	*4Q*	*3Q*	*4Q*	*3Q*	*4Q*	*3Q*	*4Q*
Quits	62.2	90.1	52.3	50.9	52.9	60.5	43.4	59.8	52.7	66.7
Disciplinary reasons	8.5	2.6	3.2	3.1	3.4	3.3	7.7	10.2	4.7	4.9
Employment reductions	10.4	2.0	31.3	45.4	10.7	34.3	37.1	14.8	3.1	6.8
Other	19.9	5.3	13.2	0.6	33.0	1.9	11.8	15.2	39.5	21.6

Note: Firm size (FS) categories: 1=80-350; 2=351-700; 3=701-900; 4=901-1,500; 5=>1,501 employees.
Source: World Bank survey.

logue of which has been the high share of females in total unemployment.[10]

Combining the aggregate and survey data provides us with a reasonable basis for breaking down the distribution over separations. First, mass layoffs account for a rather small share of separations, no more than 8 percent over 1992. Assuming that the survey results are representative, this likely implies that no more than 25 percent of separations were involuntary. Between 50 and 60 percent were quits; the residual, we assume, left the labor force. Matching this up with the unemployment data, and assuming that all involuntary separations go straight to unemployment, this would be consistent with no more than 15-20 percent of separations being layoffs. At least 60 percent would have gone straight into work in the state or private sector. We are not yet able to distinguish flows over these sectors.

Changes to employment thus have largely been driven by attrition and by quits. How can we explain this process? It seems that short-run changes to relative wages across firms are what matter, at least in local labor markets of the kind captured in surveys.[11] This is somewhat paradoxical because over periods longer than two quarters, changes to rela-

---

10. The survey shows that the male full-time labor force declined by under 7 percent between December 1991 and 1992; the equivalent female labor force was cut by nearly 16 percent.
11. In mid-1991 wages were the principal factor in explaining quits in only 25 percent of cases; by mid-1993 this share had doubled.

tive wages have been more muted than we have expected, at least in the firm sector (see section, "Outside Opportunities"). Nevertheless, these figures probably understate the magnitude of the relative wage effects, partly because they contain no information on side-earnings and private activities, which have expanded fairly rapidly, as we indicate below. Although we do find a significant private sector wage premium, most of the evidence supports the overwhelming dominance of state-to-state-sector job transitions. Sharp relative wage shifts in the state sector can generally be traced to nontrivial short-run divergences in the liquidity of state firms, arising from differential access to, and timing of, credits from the banking system and budget. Relative wage movements appear to have induced transitions over jobs by workers sensitive to wage increases and who have perceived no effect on their individual hazard rates for employment. This would have been facilitated by the dissociation of the major nonmonetary benefits or components of labor income—particularly housing—designed to attach workers to firms, from employment in a given firm (see Commander and Jackman 1993). And it is revealing to observe that in mid-1993 roughly 50 percent of those who quit did so without any clear job offer, a response consistent with the sharply decelerating rate of unemployment increase and expansion in posted vacancies.[12]

The second issue that has to be explained is why firms actively seek to replace workers and do not simply let attrition do the work of generating employment reductions, with a consequent shift up the labor demand curve with higher wages for a given membership. This obviously goes beyond tolerance of labor hoarding and is difficult to explain without reference to technology. The simplest way to do this is to represent technology in fixed factors, or Leontief technology. This appears warranted from both earlier studies indicating the presence of a fairly mechanical association of plant to human capital, as well as from growth regressions.[13] In this context, we can assume that some workers are genuinely essential and hence need to be maintained in employment for others to be productive. In effect, the employment decision is determined by technology,

---

12. Sixteen percent of respondents indicated that they were likely to quit in the near term, with that number rising to 45 percent in the private sector. The source is the VCIOM survey, but the numbers are consistent with the aggregate data.
13. Elasticities of substitution have normally been found to be no larger than 0.1/0.2 (see Easterly and Fischer 1993).

which delivers a core membership of the firm. Clearly the technology argument rather assumes that, in the case of the Moscow labor market cited above, we observe "thick" markets for production worker skills, perhaps by virtue of relative concentration among firms demanding those skills. Even so, it seems likely that from the viewpoint of the firm, turnover may reduce the stock of firm-specific skills and this may provide part of the explanation for the evident slowdown in productivity. We return in part to these questions more formally in "A Model of Labor Hoarding," below, and in the appendix.

Job Creation: The Growth of a Private Sector

The share of the private and semiprivate sectors in total employment has apparently risen dramatically; official data show a jump to nearly 32 percent in 1992 (tables 4-6 and 4-7). But the numbers are not necessarily reliable. In addition, we need to distinguish over changes to title—now occurring on a large scale—and new starts or innovations. Here, the evidence can only be drawn from surveys, but the results are quite startling. A fairly large survey administered between March and May 1993 with wide regional coverage indicates that around 22 percent of the sample worked as their principal job in semiprivate entitities—mainly firms in the process of privatization—with 10 percent in private firms. The bulk were outside of the farm sector, but included elements of an "old" private sector—the cooperatives—and new starts.[14]

What are the principal characteristics of the private sector? The high share of industrial firms is striking, but is largely accounted for by con-

Table 4-6. Employment Shares: State, Semi-State, and Private

Category	1990	1991	1992	1993
State	82.7	75.5	68.4	67.0
Private/mixed	11.3	13.5	31.7	—
Semiprivate	—	—	—	22.4
Private	—	—	—	10.4

Source: 1990-92, Russian Goskomstat; 1993, VCIOM survey; 1993.Q2.

14. The VCIOM survey was carried out in 1993.Q2 and was divided into several parts, variously sampling between 2,000 and 4,000 individuals over 24-28 oblasts.

Table 4-7. Sectoral Distribution of Employment: State, Semi-State, and Private, 1993.Q2

Category	State	Private	Semi-State
Industry and construction	43.5	29.9	51.9
Agriculture	10.6	16.5	22.6
Trade and services	8.9	36.6	18.0
Education and health	26.2	5.7	1.9
Public administration/finance	10.6	6.2	4.8

Source: VCIOM survey.

struction and by transformed entities. For new starts, it is evident that the bulk are in services, gap-filling small firms primarily financed outside of the banking system (de Melo and Ofer 1993). Aside from their limited capitalization and small-scale employment, many of the jobs are either part time or secondary, with workers retaining state jobs, where feasible, as basic insurance. The bulk of the jobs generated are precarious, with high rates of firm and labor turnover. Imminent and perceived prospects for being laid off in mid-1993 were actually higher in the private than in the state sector.[15] As might be expected, the largest share of respondents viewed state sector or joint venture employment as preferable to private sector work. The clear impression is thus of a rapidly expanding sector dominated for the most part by precarious jobs, often of a secondary nature.

What of the characteristics of the transformed and transforming firms? Here, the evidence is difficult to sort, because incentives under the mass privatization program (MPP) are not strictly compatible with any predictable or efficient sorting. Firms with below-average or bad prospects are unlikely to have been penalized relative to good firms by opting for privatization. Indeed, if we hypothesize that bad firms are likely to have shorter horizons, then insider buyouts (through the most commonly chosen 51 percent inside-share option) would facilitate rather than impede the short-run appropriation of quasi-rents, particularly given that share prices have been set as a small markup on book values. In short, the procedure is likely to have screened out only major loss-makers or those with

---

15. Twenty-one percent of private respondents were about to be laid off and only 39 percent felt their jobs to be secure; 13 percent and 60 percent, respectively, in the state sector.

large and preferential claims on public money—military and science sector firms, for example.

The occupational structure of transformed and transforming firms suggests that the process has been associated with some labor rationalization. There are clear reductions of the order of 5-10 percent in technical (ITR) and clerical personnel relative to comparable state firms. But preliminary information on layoffs over 1993 does not reveal any significantly higher level of involuntary separations for the transformed sector (results from a sample of transformed firms are discussed in Commander and Yemtsov 1994).

Wage Path and Relative Wages: State Sector

Wage comparisons over time are particularly difficult given shortages. Even so, real statistical wages were clipped back by around 55 percent through the initial price jump, which was followed by some upward drift over the next year (figure 4-8). Wage arrears in the first half of 1992, driven by liquidity constraints, further reduced take-home pay.[16] Wage controls have, in principle, been maintained throughout, with the wage bill constrained not to exceed four times the minimum wage. But given the low level of the latter and its infrequent adjustments, actual wages consistently and substantially exceeded norm wages (see figure 4-9), boosting the excess wage tax to at least 2 percent of GDP in 1992. The wage rule clearly did not bind on firms. Even so, by May 1993 real wages for both the state and the industrial sector were only about 5-10 percent higher than at the start of 1992 and roughly 20 percent below the level in the first half of 1991. Wage and price changes increasingly move together, but there is still limited explicit indexation, even though wage setters in the larger urban settings increasingly target consumer price changes and, in small parts of the private sector, set dollar wages.

We would expect significant changes in the wage distribution, given further decentralization of wage decisions and the ex ante structure of relativities.[17] And it is true that the continuing large variation in regional wage levels can partly be attributed to divergent nominal wage claims, rather than purely being driven by the variance in regional price changes.

---

16. In mid-1992 wage arrears were nearly equivalent to one-third of the industrial wage bill.

17. In particular, the low returns to skills and the consistent bias in favor of manual workers' wages.

Figure 4-8. Russia, Real State and Industrial Wages,
January 1991-September 1993 (Dec. 1990 prices)

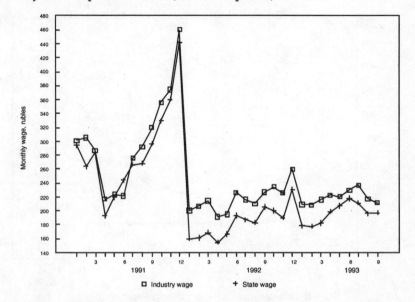

□ Industry wage   + State wage

But we also find that regional wage rankings remain largely unchanged. We find consistently high values for Spearman's rank correlation coefficient—0.78 for May 1993/1991—with the tightness of the correlation actually rising over time. Putting these two features together, it is evident that most of the change in wage variance is an amplification of the prior regional wage structure.

At a sectoral level, despite sharp across-month variation, we find limited major departures from the structure of sectoral relativities pre-1992, with the exception of the financial sector and science. The former is in effect an innovation, the latter's relative decline a function of its close integration with defense and its current weak bargaining power compared with other parts of the administrative sector, such as education. This indicates the power of institutional features in the wage setting that have tended to dominate the redistributive effects transmitted through high inflation and decentralization in wage setting.[18] At an aggregate level, we find that the ratio of the top

18.   Note that the tariff system still explicitly applies to roughly 25 percent of the labor force; the regional wage coefficients still apply while trade unions are centralized and even privatized firms form branch associations for greater coordination in wage setting.

Figure 4-9. Russia: Industry Wage Bill and Norm,
January 1992-February 1993

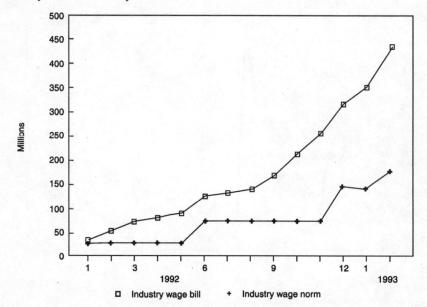

to bottom decile of per capita income has jumped from 3.5 in 1990 to 5.6 in May 1993; using the Smirnov-Kolmogorov procedure for calculating the Gini coefficient shows little change in the inequality measure.[19]

The relative stability of wages disaggregated by skill also emerges from the World Bank survey results. Between 1991.Q3 and 1992.Q4 we find convergence in changes to nominal wages across the main skill categories (table 4-8). This surely is related to the over 80 percent of cases of wages remaining administratively set rather than bargained. We may also be missing important components of labor income arising from nondivulgence, particularly by managers for whom side deals are an increasingly important part of income, but despite some widening of differentials toward the top end of the wage structure, the overall picture is more of convergence. The general conclusion appears to be that the dispersion in wages over sectors and skills that increased sharply in 1991 was, if anything, dampened in 1992.

---

19.   The Gini was 0.25 in 1991, 0.29 in January 1992, and 0.29 in March 1993. Note that underreporting of income is likely to lead to underestimation of inequality, because income increasingly acquires larger nonwage components.

Table 4-8. Real Statistical Wages by Skill: 1992.Q3 and 1992.Q4
(1991.Q3=100)

Category	FS1		FS2		FS3		FS4		FS5	
	3Q	4Q	3Q	4Q	3Q	4Q	3Q	4Q	3Q	4Q
Vice director	63	90	57	69	71	59	73	49	100	63
ITR/ professional	53	53	39	61	64	66	63	50	76	—
Production worker	56	47	54	68	68	54	73	75	85	—
Unskilled worker	69	75	55	38	56	56	77	106	89	—

Note: Firm size categories: 1=80-350; 2=351-700; 3=701-900; 4=901-1,500; 5=>1,501 employees.
Source: World Bank survey.

To what extent have wages been driven by branch performance and relative prices? For industry, branches with lower than average levels of output decline have generally had higher than average wage expansion over 1992. Figure 4-10 relates output changes to those for the real consumption wage for the major branches of industry. There is clear evidence that larger downward adjustments to output and employment have been associated with lower real wage claims. This may signal the appearance of a weak, emerging association of wage behavior and the level of employment. We can also see that relative wages have generally been positively correlated with changes to relative branch producer prices. Branches with positive relative price shocks have fairly systematically translated them into positive relative wage effects. Further, by regressing changes to the wage bill on changes to profits for 1992 using regional data, we derive figure 4-11, which shows profit and wage changes to be strongly positively correlated.

Finally, we return to the importance, particularly through to 1992.Q3 and again at the end of 1993 and early 1994, of firms borrowing from workers through large-order wage arrears. This phenomenon can generally be traced to tight liquidity constraints on firms, arising from a combination of monetary policy—particularly the large cut to credit to the economy in early 1992—and particularities of the financial system, especially the distinction over cash and noncash rubles that remained important in 1992. Given what we know about output, it is by no means sure

Figure 4-10. Output/Consumer Wage Changes, 1993.Q1/1991.Q1

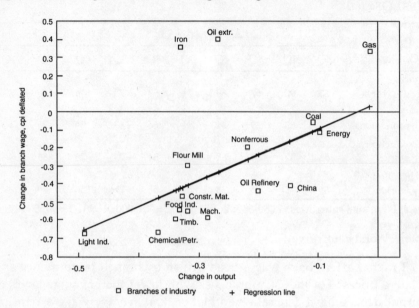

Figure 4-11. Wage Bill and Profit Changes, Russia, 1992/91 (first dif. in log)

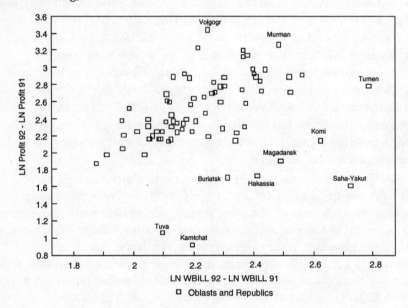

that forced borrowing was only to permit the generation of liquidity for paying wages. Rather, preferring to stabilize employment, firms ran up interfirm arrears and used these, along with wage arrears, as a bargaining chip with government. In due course, this resulted in relaxation of monetary policy and a sharp external boost to firm liquidity.

Outside Opportunities

For state sector workers, private wages and unemployment benefits summarize outside opportunities. In the case of the latter, while eligibility criteria are generous, notional benefits levels are low and in addition have generally collapsed for the majority of recipients to a minimum level with the floor given by the minimum wage.[20] Consequently, the replacement ratio has been very low, particularly if unemployment implies loss of access to some nonmonetary benefits. As already indicated, this reduces the incentive to register and probably acts as an implicit brake on firms releasing labor.

The picture with private wages is more difficult to capture. For new starts—primarily in services—the working assumption must be that incomes have been fairly volatile, driven by arbitrage and episodic windfall rents, with greater emphasis on maximizing short-run returns.[21] The secondary or parallel nature of many of these jobs further complicates comparison. But drawing again on survey data, for the 20 percent of those with secondary private jobs, the latter's wage was generally larger than the primary wage.

Table 4-9 summarizes the available information on relative wages and indicates significant monetary wage premiums offered by semiprivate and private firms. Correcting for hours reduces the premium by at least 10 percent.[22] A consistently higher share of wage payments is conditioned on individual or small group performance here than in the state sector. This suggests that title transformation is commonly linked to an

20. Benefits are calculated on an earnings-related basis, ranging between 60 and 75 percent of an individual's average wage the previous year for the first six months. The ratio falls to 45 percent for the next four months, with benefits cut off after one year. But most, in effect, get only the minimum wage, which was in all months between 1992.Q1 and 1993.Q1 no more than 10-15 percent of the average industrial wage. See World Bank 1993.
21. A feature picked up in the VCIOM survey.
22. In March 1993 state sector average hours per week was about forty, rising to forty-five for the private sector.

upward adjustment to the wage level, partly through exemption from the excess wage tax.[23] It is also clear that inequalities in the wage distribution, as measured by the Gini coefficient, are larger the greater the degree of private control (table 4-10). Further, the wage distribution is clearly more unequal in firms whose sectoral and size characteristics—primarily small trade firms—more closely correspond to semiprivate and private sectors. These numbers do not include nonmonetary wage benefits, which in state firms commonly comprise 35-40 percent of effective labor income, the absence of which would dilute the wage premium (Commander and others 1993b). But the evidence suggests that many private firms offer at least an equal range of benefits, but with greater differentiation in coverage for their workers. Access to services, such as medical help and housing, are generally egalitarian, but benefits with a more evident income component—subsidized food, material assistance, and so on—are targeted toward higher-level employees. This clearly skews the wage distribution still further in relation to state firms.

In short, title transformation appears to be associated systematically with shifts in the wage level alongside explicit use of performance-related pay arrangements. As already indicated, there are indications that the employment structure has also been changed, but the numbers—let alone the unemployment data—do not suggest that the restructuring has as yet been that radical.

Table 4-9. Relative Wages: Private/State Wage Ratios, 1992 and 1993

Item	1992.Q4	1993.Q1
Private/state	1.6	1.8
Semiprivate/state		1.3
Private/state (by skill)		
Vice director	1.9	1.8
Technical (ITR)	1.5	1.6
Production worker	1.5	0.9
Unskilled worker	1.6	1.2

Source: 1992.Q4 and 93.Q1, World Bank survey; 1993.Q1, private/state and semiprivate/state, VCIOM.

23. The VCIOM survey reports that transformation is almost invariably associated with higher wage levels, but also greater job insecurity.

Table 4-10. Mean Wages and Wage Inequality, 1993.Q1

Category	Mean (rubles)	Gini
Property form		
State	19,564	0.39
Semi-State	24,657	0.43
Private	35,402	0.51
Sector		
Industry and construction	22,199	0.38
Agriculture	16,254	0.39
Trade	29,214	0.48
Education and health	14,886	0.37
Public administration	25,653	0.41
Firm Size (employees)		
<200	20,184	0.43
201-999	23,447	0.41
>1,000	21,825	0.38

Unemployment

Contrary to initial expectations, unemployment remains not only low, but declining. After a sharp acceleration in the first half of 1992, the rate of increase decelerated and was subsequently reversed in 1993.Q2-4. At the latter point, the broad measure—total registered jobseekers—amounted to no more than 1.5 percent of the labor force, and only 0.7 percent of the labor force received benefits. This is a significant underestimate, given the limited incentives for the unemployed to remain registered.[24] Survey data suggested an unemployment level of between 5 and 6 percent by mid-1993.[25] There remains small dispersion in regional unemployment rates, whether using official or survey information. Perhaps more signifi-

24. Aside from benefits falling below a subsistence minimum, job finds through labor offices are low. Survey data indicate 60 percent registration in the first month, falling away to under 20 percent by the third month.
25. VCIOM data. Popkin and others (1992), using a household data set, provided a 3 percent estimate for 1992.Q3.

cant, there has been relatively little dispersion in growth rates of unemployment across regions. The variation is reduced yet further when the jobseekers measure is augmented with information on marginal employment. Factoring in all the marginally employed, the augmented rate jumps to just over 6 percent of the labor force in 1993.Q2. The coefficient of variation over oblasts for this measure is smaller than for the jobseekers measure alone, suggesting that the differences over oblasts can be explained largely by varying tolerances of open unemployment rather than different underlying processes.

Figure 4-12 plots the path of several unemployment measures, as well as the movement on the supply side of the labor market, vacancies. Several features stand out. First, there is a clear inverse movement of vacancies and unemployment, suggesting the presence of aggregate shocks. The deceleration in the growth rate for unemployment can be traced to 1992.Q3 and primarily attributed to the relaxation of credit constraints on the firm sector. More difficult to explain is the subsequent fall in the unemployment level and increase in vacancies in mid-1993, given the apparent decline in government subsidies and transfers to firms in relation to 1992.

Figure 4-12. Russia, Unemployment and Vacancies, December 1991-September 1993

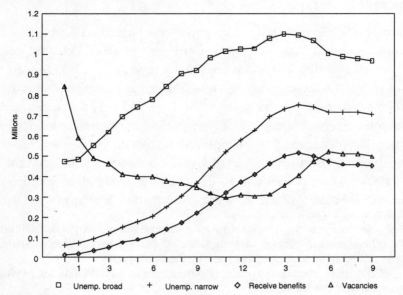

Figure 4-13. Russia, Unemployment Inflow and Outflow,
January 1992-September 1993

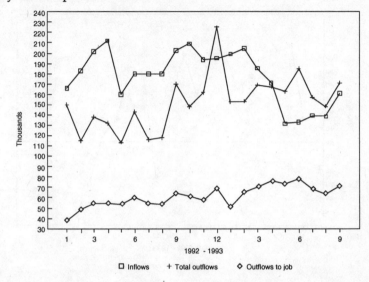

Figures 4-13 and 4-14 on flows to and from unemployment show a clear shift upward in the outflow rate after 1992.Q3. The exit rate at around 20 percent a month has been high and in sharp contrast with Eastern European experience.[26] The exit rate to jobs at over 8 percent a month has also been high, implying that around 40 percent of exits from unemployment have been to jobs. This share remained stable through 1992. The slowdown in the rate of increase in unemployment since 1992.Q3 has been driven primarily by a lower inflow rate.

Flows out of unemployment by sector are difficult to capture precisely. Data on job finds, however, show not only that the great majority—85 percent—of transitions to jobs from unemployment were to the state sector, but that there was considerable regional variation in flows to private firms or collectives, rising to as much as 25-30 percent in several regions (for more detail, see Commander, Liberman, and Yemtsov 1993c). Further, the efficiency of job finds can be identified. Over a third of job finds were achieved within an unemployment spell of less than one month, and nearly 80 percent were achieved with a spell of less than four months duration. This was also true for new entrants and youth unemployed.

---

26. For example, in Poland in 1992-93 the exit rate was just over 4 percent and the exit rate to jobs 2.2 percent.

Figure 4-14. Russia, Net Monthly Flows to Unemployment, January 1992-September 1993

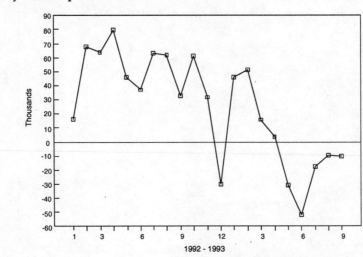

□   Net flows to unemployment

As regards unemployment durations, at the start of 1993, nearly 11 percent of the current unemployed were in a spell exceeding a year and the variance across regions was fairly small. This is a clear underestimate, given the scale of deregistration by the unemployed over time, and survey evidence for mid-1993 places nearly a third of respondents in a current spell of over eight months. Despite the high weight of females in aggregate unemployment, only 20 percent of the long-run unemployed were women, while three-quarters of the long-run unemployed were located in rural areas. This probably indicates that women tend to drop out of the labor force, or at least do not continue to register. It is not clear whether weak incentives for continuing to register contribute to explaining the very low numbers of long-run unemployed in urban areas.

What of the characteristics of the unemployment that has been generated thus far? While just under 10 percent of the stock of unemployed in early 1993 were new entrants, far more striking is that over 70 percent of registered unemployed were women, and this share has remained broadly stable through 1992-93. This matches up fairly well with what we know about changes in employment and the weight of females in total separations, particularly in involuntary separations. Figure 4-15 provides a scatter relating the share of female unemployment in total unemploy-

Figure 4-15. Russia, Women's Unemployment, 1993

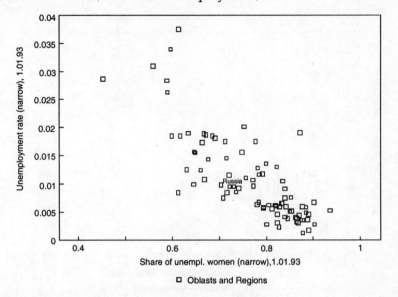

Share of unempl. women (narrow),1.01.93

□ Oblasts and Regions

ment by oblast to the oblast unemployment rate. As is readily seen, both the unemployment rate and the share of females are heavily bunched, but there is also a clear inverse association between the rate of unemployment and the female share. Oblasts with higher aggregate unemployment have notably lower female shares, suggesting that any further movement toward higher open unemployment will be associated with further compositional shifts, affecting male labor, and most likely production workers, more powerfully.

Finally, while there is no apparent association between the rate of change in wages and the unemployment level—hardly surprising given the low and fairly common level of unemployment—we do appear, as already indicated, to see some emerging link between real wage behavior and employment at the level of the industrial branch. Further, viewing oblasts as equivalent to distinct or segmented labor markets—a generally reasonable assumption given the limited internal migration that is observed—and relating wage changes to our augmented measure of labor market slack—open unemployment plus marginal employment, defined as workers on involuntary leave and short-time work—we do indeed observe a more conventional association of wage and activity variables.

Figure 4-16. Unemployment/Wage Inflation, 1992/91

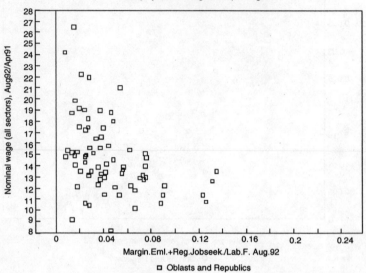

Figures 4-16 and 4-17 relate this augmented measure of slack to the change in nominal wages for the seventy-seven oblasts or republics for two consistent data points, August 1992 and March 1993. Aside from indicating increasing convergence in the augmented rate across oblasts, we can discern a weak inverse association, so that higher levels of slack are associated with lower changes to wages.

Wage and Employment Decisions: Institutional Setting

As a first approximation, we can think about the Russian firm as dominated by a coalition of workers and managers, following the collapse of the previous ministry oversight. How wages and employment are set is obviously critical given the apparently large weight attached to insiders in firm decisions and the decision to co-opt insiders by granting dominant share rights in any privatization. How well does current evidence match up to a depiction of Russian firms as dominated by inside coalitions of managers and workers, with the former having relatively small bargaining power? Here, the evidence is mostly anecdotal, but it does suggest that most Russian firms do *not* completely conform to this characterization. The World Bank and VCIOM surveys are informative. For

Figure 4-17. Unemployment/Wage Inflation, 1993/91

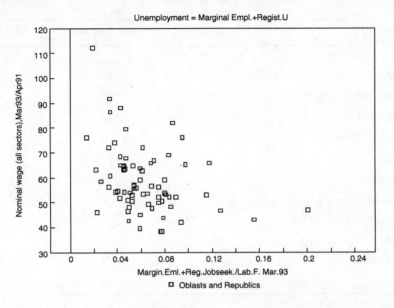

wage bargaining, in over 80 percent of cases, wages were set by the administration; in only 17 percent of cases was there any form of explicit bargaining, and these were predominantly small units with bargaining over individual wage contracts. Further, the weight of firm management in wage decisions appears to have increased.[27] Table 4-11 not only shows the weak formal presence of workers' bargaining agents but also their progressive reduction in semistate and, particularly, among private firms.

In sum, we may assume that the threat point of the managers has increased over time (and is probably likely to increase further with privatization).[28] Wages subsequently appear to have been primarily constrained by firm revenues (and subsidies) and to a much lesser extent by the tax regime. As to employment decisions, in nearly nine out of ten cases, decisions over firing workers were made exclusively by either the director of the firm or the administration. Constraints on firings from

---

27. For 1992.Q4 nearly a quarter of sampled firms reported a change in the wage setting rule and 80 percent indicated that this involved an unambiguous increase in the role and power of the firm's administration to set wages.

28. Of course, as intermediaries between state and workers preprivatization, high de facto managerial discretion does not necessarily imply greater attention to the interests of the (absentee) owner, the state.

Table 4-11. Bargaining Institutions: 1993.Q1
(percent)

Category	Significant	Insignificant	Absent
Trade union(s)			
State	19	55	9
Semi-State	15	49	12
Private	19	20	37
Workers' council			
State	7	18	47
Semi-State	8	17	41
Private	2	6	74
Strike committee			
State	0.5	2	76
Semi-State	0.4	1	76
Private	0	1	81

Note: Residual is for no replies.
Source: VCIOM survey.

worker opposition were generally absent, and the main obstacle arose from the legal system (table 4-12). Nevertheless, one should not discount the "moral" authority of workers' councils regarding these decisions or the more informal channels by which their voice is taken into account. Indeed, responses by workers to survey questions regarding the perceived gains from privatization indicate that workers expect wage increases as the price for their passivity in the privatization process.

In short, managers appear to have high discretionary powers with respect to wages and employment, but they evidently choose *not* to exert them to enforce large employment separations or restructuring; the majority of managers appear to respond to changes in the environment passively or by placing workers on short-time work.[29] But this still leaves us with the problem of explaining the sluggish adjustment of employment to negative shocks. We now sketch out a simple model of labor hoarding. A more detailed presentation is provided in the appendix.

---

29. This is supported by the VCIOM survey, but conflicts with the conclusions from a far smaller sample of firms in Fan and Schaffer 1993.

Table 4-12. Firm Decisions on Wages and Employment,
1992.Q3 & 1992.Q4

Item	Percentage
Wages	
Set by administration	83
Bargained	17
Wage benchmarks[a]	
Branch wages	27
Regional wage	15
Consumer prices	56
Available resources	93
Maximum permitted	20
Constraints on wages[a]	
Tax rules	34
Firm revenues	78
Regulation	3
Other	5
Number of wage increases per quarter (1992.Q4)	
None	11
Once	50
Twice	32
Other	7
Employment	
Source of firing decisions	
Director	69
Administration	20
Administration and TUs/or council	8
Workers' council	3
Opposition to firings	
Legal system	54
Workers' council	15
No opposition	31
Firms with excess employment	34
Reasons for not laying off[a]	
No financial burden	20
Output recovery expected	41
Legal impediments	10
Trade union pressure	7
Fear of worker discontent	7

a. Multiple responses to question.
Source: World Bank survey.

A Model of Labor Hoarding

We take as our setting a firm dominated by a coalition of insiders where the objective is to maximize the expected utility of the representative worker in the coalition, considering both the employment and wage implications of their decisions.[30] The environment of this worker-controlled firm (WCF) is given by a constant returns Leontief technology, a downward sloping demand curve for its output—reflecting market power—and a given price for material inputs. All value added is appropriated by the coalition. Given this environment, value added is maximized at some employment level L^* (appendix equation 4). The assumption regarding Leontief technology is that certain nonlabor variable inputs are required to make a worker productive. These material inputs are not costless and it is possible that more value can be generated by leaving a worker idle than by purchasing necessary inputs to make that worker productive. The issue that arises is whether labor hoarding will occur even when a worker cannot be employed productively.

In the appendix, we show that while the firm will never produce beyond L^*, as this would reduce value added, it might choose to retain more workers than L^*. This is because the possibility of labor hoarding expands the choice set available to the WCF. Whether or not the firm chooses the hoarding option depends on its indifference map. This is shown in figure 4-18 by the V^*/L curve (where V^* is the maximum possible level of value added) lying above the V/L curve at employment levels beyond L^*. If the highest indifference curve is tangent to the V^*/L curve, then labor hoarding is an optimum for the firm (figure 4-19a). By contrast, if the highest indifference is tangent to the V/L curve below L^*, then the firm will produce less than the maximum value added, and no labor hoarding will take place (figure 4-19b). Labor hoarding is thus shown to be possible, depending on the preferences of the WCF. The essence of the model is that there is a potential dichotomy between the size of the work force that maximizes value added and the size of the work force that maximizes the objective function of the employment-sensitive WCF.

We also do some comparative static experiments in the appendix to see what happens when the firm suffers an adverse shock. Assuming that labor hoarding is an optimum, the steady-state result is that hoarding will

---

30. As in Commander, Coricelli, and Staehr 1992. Note that a high degree of managerial discretion does not necessarily imply a low level of de facto worker participation in decisions.

Figure 4-18. The Opportunity Set for a WCF

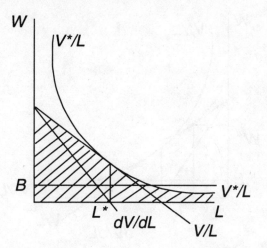

Figure 4-19A. Labor-Hoarding Regime

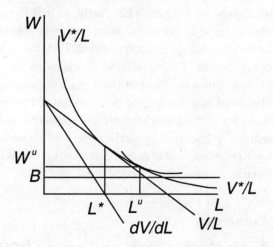

fall. But introducing adjustment costs results in employment not going immediately to its steady-state level. Instead, labor hoarding initially rises, before declining over time to its new steady-state level.

Finally, it is clear that labor hoarding and hiring can occur together in a steady state. As some workers quit, this requires—given the technology—that replacements be hired to maintain the optimal employment

Figure 4-19B. Non-Labor-Hoarding Regime

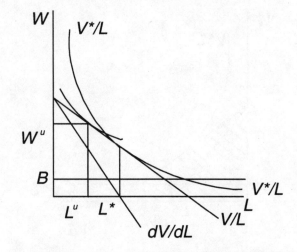

level. With regard to the possibility of simultaneous hoarding and hiring along a transition path to a steady state with a lower employment level, we assume that layoffs are prohibitively costly, so that the only option for shrinking the labor force is attrition. With homogeneous labor, no new workers will be hired during such a transition. But this is another matter if labor is heterogeneous. Taking skilled workers as an input (akin to material inputs) that must be hired at their market price, enough skilled workers must be hired to produce the optimal output level. Because outside opportunities for skilled workers are good relative to other types of workers in the firm, quits arise, requiring the firm to seek replacements even when the firm is simultaneously attempting to reduce the less-skilled work force to its new steady-state level.

Concluding Comments

Two years and more after the initial price jump and failed stabilization, the Russian experience bears only a passing resemblance to its Eastern European counterparts. That output has fallen, and by significant magnitudes is, of course, a common feature. But in employment the overall picture is of large flows in and out of state employment, with the bulk of flows out, straight to other jobs. Until early 1993, these transitions were massively dominated by state-to-state flows. Flows into and out of the private sector remain something of a black box. About 20 percent of flows out of state employment have gone to unemployment. For unemployment, we observe a high and stable outflow to jobs rate. Average unemployment spells remain low. Since end-1992 the deceleration in the growth of unemployment can be explained primarily by a fall in the inflow rate. In short, the picture is quite different from Eastern Europe. Layoffs have been limited and there is a high exit rate to jobs from unemployment, with no large stagnant pool of unemployed.

Changes in title and in the apparent bargaining power of incumbent managers with respect to workers do not as yet appear to have induced a structural break. This can be traced to a number of factors. As we indicate in our simple model, with fixed-factors technology, it can be shown that labor hoarding is a feasible choice for the firm. Introducing adjustment costs may further account for the employment path that we observe. But there are likely other factors involved. We observe a significant redistribution in favor of profits, in part the result of market power. Labor income in the state sector, sharply cut by the price jump, has yet to recover. As benefits are reduced, the already low wage levels have been further eroded. Rather than definitively signal that employment changes can translate into wage increases, firms continue to hoard, using the *threat* of unemployment to restrict wage claims.[31] Further, while managers may have increasing discretion over employment and wage decisions, it is likely that managers and workers still cooperate with respect to government, testing the latter's aversion to unemployment and using employment as a means for extracting subsidies and transfers. As such, the transfer of title may be insufficient to induce restructuring if firms believe that government's implicit aversion to employment losses remains sufficiently high. Finally, we should not ignore the wider role in local communities commonly played by enterprises. These reference points continue to restrict the freedom of action of managers and ensure that firms continue to display behavior that appears, at least partly, to be benevolent.

---

31. Nearly half the respondents to the VCIOM survey attached a high probability to losing their jobs in the near future.

Appendix
A Model of Labor Hoarding in a Worker-Controlled Firm

Optimal Labor Hoarding in a WCF

We provide a simple model of labor hoarding in a worker-controlled firm (WCF). The firm is assumed to face constant returns-to-scale Leontief technology and to have market power. The WCF cares about both wages and employment (the objective function will be made explicit later). The production and inverse demand functions are specified as follows:

(4-1) $$Y = \min(M, L)$$

(4-2) $$P = a - bY$$

where Y is output, M is material input, L is labor input, P is the price of output, and a and b are parameters. The fixed-coefficient form of the production function is crucial to the results that follow; a linear inverse demand function is not essential, however, and is adopted for convenience.[32] From equations 4-1 and 4-2, the expression for value added is:

(4-3) $$V = (a - p^m)Y - bY^2$$

where V is value added and p^m is the price of material input. If we assume for the moment that the objective is to maximize value added, we get the following expressions for optimal output, price, and value added:

(4-4) $$Y^* = (a - p^m)/2b$$

(4-5) $$P^* = (a + p^m)/2$$

(4-6) $$V^* = [(a - p^m)^2]/4b.$$

Value added is maximized at Y^*, which we know from equation 4-1 will equal both L^* and M^*. Y^* sets an upper limit on the output level of the WCF. A higher output level than Y^* would reduce the size of the surplus available for distribution to workers. It is possible that, given its concern with the employment level, the firm will choose to spread the maximum surplus, V^*, among more workers than it takes to produce it, so that the firm might choose to hold excess labor. It is also possible that the firm will choose to produce less than Y^* and to distribute the smaller value added among a smaller group of workers. The choice will depend on the precise

---

32. The same qualitative conclusions can be obtained with a constant-elasticity demand function.

form of the WCF's optimization problem and on its emphasis on employment relative to the wage.

Figure 4-18 shows the opportunity set of the firm in wage-employment space. We denote the wage as w. Value added per worker, V/L, declines linearly (given the linear demand curve) until L^*. Once L^* has been reached, V stays at V^* no matter how many more workers are "employed"; the WCF will not produce beyond L^* because to do so would reduce value added. From L^* on, V^*/L declines only because a fixed surplus is being divided among a larger group of workers. This is shown in figure 4-18 by the flattening slope of the V^*/L curve beyond L^*. Beyond L^*, value added per worker is greater if the extra workers are not productively employed than if they are. At L^*, the slopes of both the V/L and V^*/L curves are equal to $-b$, which is the slope of the inverse demand curve. Beyond L^*, the slope of V^*/L is less than the slope of V/L, which remains constant at $-b$. The slope of the V^*/L curve can be written as

(4-7) $$d(V^*/L)/dL = -\{[(a - p^m)^2]/4b\}L^2,$$

which equals $-b$ when evaluated at L^*, and is greater than $-b$ when L is greater than L^*. The important point is that the possibility of labor hoarding expands the opportunity set of the WCF.[33] In essence, beyond a certain point, a larger surplus per worker is generated if some workers are left idle; it is better to leave workers idle than to purchase enough inputs to make them all productive.

The objective function we attribute to the WCF is taken from the literature on labor unions (see McDonald and Solow 1981). It remains to be shown under what conditions the WCF will hoard labor. Figure 4-19a shows that this depends on the indifference map of the WCF. The WCF is assumed to care about both the wage and employment.[34] The indifference curves are convex and asymptotic to the outside wage-benefit line; the outside wage is denoted as B. If the highest indifference curve is tangent to the V^*/L segment, then the firm will choose to employ excess labor.

To determine the exact conditions under which hoarding will occur, it is convenient to consider two separate maximization problems. In the first, the WCF maximizes its objective function subject to the constraint

---

33. The region between the V^*/L and the V/L curves beyond L^* in figure 4-19 is the expanded portion of the opportunity set.
34. See Commander, Coricelli, and Staehr 1992 for arguments about the applicability of this objective function to the transitional economy.

that all value added goes to labor, but where there is no possibility of labor hoarding. The firm is essentially maximizing its objective function subject to the $w = V/L$ constraint. We can write this problem as:

(4-8) $\max\limits_{\{w,L\}} U = L[u(w) - u(B)]$; subject to $V = wL$.

In the second, the WCF maximizes the same utility function, but this time subject to the constraints that $V^* = wL$ and that L is greater than or equal to L^*:

(4-8′) $\max\limits_{\{w,L\}} U = L[u(w) - u(B)]$; subject to $V^* = wL$ and $L \geq L^*$.

Denoting the constrained maximum values of the objective functions from the first equation (4-8) and second equation (4-8′) problems as U^0 and U^1 respectively, the WCF will choose the wage and employment combination that yields higher utility. We denote these values of the wage and employment as w^u and L^u respectively. If U^1 is greater than U^0, then the firm is in a labor-hoarding regime; because our interest is in labor hoarding, we will assume that this condition holds.

A feature of the McDonald-Solow efficient bargaining model is that when the revenue function displays constant elasticity with respect to labor, the wage will be constant in the face of shocks to the revenue function. A similar relationship holds here: the wage is constant in the face of shocks to V^*. To see this, we differentiate the objective function with respect to labor input (according to the constraint that L is greater than or equal to L^*). This yields the first-order condition:

(4-9) $[u(w) - u(B)]/u'(w) = V^*/L^u$.

An interpretation of this condition is that the slope of the indifference curve and the V^*/L function are equal at an optimum. Substituting for V^*/L^u we obtain

(4-10) $[u(w) - u(B)]/u'(w) = w$.

The optimal wage does not depend on V^*.[35] Moreover, from $V^* = w^u L^u$ we can see that $dL^u/dV^* = 1/w$.

35. This condition seems to counterintuitive. Note, however, that the slope of the $w = V^*/L$ curve is equal to w/L, so that the wage elasticity of employment is equal to unity. A constant elasticity of labor demand also produces a constant wage result in the monopoly union model (Oswald 1985).

Comparative Statics: Adverse Shocks and Labor Hoarding

How does the level of labor hoarding respond to a product market or a material input price shock? First, how do Y^* and V^* change in response to the shock? Second, how does L^u change in response to the change in V^*? Provided that U^1 remains greater than U^0, we know that a one unit change in V^* will lead to a $1/w$ unit change in L^u. To answer the first question, we differentiate the expressions for optimal output and optimal value added with respect to p^m. The derivatives with respect to the price of material input of the expressions for optimal output and optimal value added are:

(4-11) $$dY^*/dp^m = -(1/2b)$$

(4-12) $$dV^*/dp^m = -(a - p^m)/2b.$$

It is convenient to write the effect of a change in p^m on L^u as the product of two effects:

(4-13) $$dL^u/dp^m = (dV^*/dp^m)(dL^u/dv^*) = -(a - 2b)/2bw.$$

Furthermore, after some manipulation, we can write the ratio of the percentage change in Y^* to the percentage change in L^u as

(4-14) $$[(dY^*/dp^m)/(dL^u/dp^m)](L^u/Y^*) = 1/2.$$

This means that an input price increase leads to a percentage fall in L^u that is twice as high as the percentage fall in Y^*. Moreover, if we measure excess labor as a percentage of total labor, $1 - (Y^*/L^u)$, equation 4-14 implies that labor hoarding decreases in response to an input price shock.[36] It is worth pointing out that value added per worker does not increase in the aftermath of an adverse shock; V^*/L is equal to the constant w (again assuming that a shift to a non-labor-hoarding regime does not take place). Thus the volume of output per worker, but not the value added per worker, increases as a result of an adverse shock.

In short, an increase in the input price leads to a decrease in output and value added. The decrease in value added leads to a decrease in employment but no change in the wage. Because the decrease in employment is greater than the decrease in output, labor hoarding falls.

---

36. If the inverse demand function takes the constant elasticity form, $p = (1/e)Y^{-e}$, with $e < 1$, the elasticity of Y^* with respect to L^u is $1/(1 - e)$. The same qualitative conclusion emerges: labor hoarding decreases in response to an increase in the price of material inputs.

Introducing Adjustment Costs

In this section we make a simple assumption about the costs of adjusting the size of the work force. Hiring is costless, and firing is prohibitively costly. The only way to reduce the work force is through attrition, with the number of workers lost by this means denoted by A. Assume now that A is a constant fraction, k, of the work force each period. If the WCF is attempting to reduce its work force, it will set hires, H, at zero (it is assumed that all workers are the same). This allows us to write the following first-order linear homogenous differential equation:

(4-15) $$dL/dt + kL = 0$$

where t represents time. This equation has the solution

(4-16) $$L(t) = L^u(0)e^{-kt}$$

where $L^u(0)$ is the steady-state labor force before the adverse shock. Solving for the time, t', that it takes to get to the new steady state, L^u, we obtain

(4-17) $$t' = (1/k)(\ln L^u(0) - \ln L^u)$$

where $\ln (.)$ denotes natural logarithms. To see what is happening to labor hoarding over this path, recall that between two steady states, the percentage change in Y^* is equal to half the percentage change in L^u. Therefore, at a time that $L(t) = (1/2)[L^u(0) + L^u]$, the percentage change in the labor force is equal to the percentage change in output, so that there is no change in hoarding. We denote this point in time as t''. Between $t(0)$ and t'', labor hoarding is above its preshock level; between t'' and t', below its preshock level. And at t', labor hoarding reaches its new steady-state value. The expression for t'' is:

(4-18) $$t'' = (1/k)\{\ln L^u(0) - \ln [(L^u(0) - L^u)/2)]\}.$$

An adverse movement in the price of material inputs leads initially to an increase in labor hoarding, but eventually to a decrease.

Positive Hiring in the Steady State and Along the Transition Path

We now turn to the issue of hiring both in the steady state and along the transition path. In the simplest case, if in a steady state with labor hoarding there is a certain amount of attrition each period, then the WCF will want to hire new workers. Hoarding and hiring are not mutually exclusive, even in a model with homogeneous labor and without adjustment costs.

To make this more explicit, let H represent the number who are hired each period. Thus,

(4-19) $$dL^u/dt = H - A.$$

This expression equals zero in a steady state. Provided that A is positive in a steady state (a state that, as we have shown, can involve labor hoarding), H will also be nonzero. Therefore, hoarding and hiring can occur together.

Given our assumptions, we would not expect to see new hires along the transition path to a lower employment steady state. Are there circumstances under which firms will continue to hire even though they are already employing too many workers? One possibility is when there are qualitative differences between workers and high gross flows of those workers in high demand. We assume that, ex ante, unskilled workers received more, and skilled workers received less, than they would have in a competitive market. The reforms generate an active market for both types of labor. The WCF must pay at least the relevant market wage if it is to attract and retain a worker. We make the further assumption that it is not a problem for the WCF to attract unskilled workers—the wage for less-skilled workers is above the market wage—but that skilled workers must now be offered a wage above their prereform wage. Furthermore, we assume that skilled workers do not receive *more* than their market wage; all rents go to unskilled workers. In effect, the enterprise is now being run in the interests of the unskilled workers, those workers whose opportunities in the market are not particularly favorable. Skilled labor, by contrast, is treated as an input to be purchased at the going market rate and can now be treated in a similar fashion to M in the opening paragraph.

The new production function is written as

(4-1') $$Y = \min(M, L^s, L^{us})$$

where L^s is skilled labor and L^{us} is unskilled labor. In the transition to a steady state with a smaller labor force, the firm is slowly shedding unskilled labor through attrition. By contrast, the optimal output level is held constant at Y^* over the transition path. This requires that L^s is also held constant.[37] If some of the skilled workers needed to produce Y^* leave, then they must be replaced. New hires *are* possible during the transition to a steady state with a lower labor force.

---

37. A certain quantity of skilled labor is essential to producing Y^*, and unskilled labor is not a substitute (given the Leontief technology).

Bibliography

Boycko, M., Andrei Schleifer, and Robert Vishny. 1993. "Privatizing Russia." *Brookings Papers on Economic Activity* 2.

Brown, Annette, Barry Ickes, and Randi Ryterman. 1993. "The Myth of Monopoly: A New View of Industrial Structure in Russia." World Bank, Washington, D.C. Mimeo.

Commander, Simon, Fabrizio Coricelli, and Karsten Staehr. 1992. "Wages and Employment in the Transition to a Market Economy." In G. Winckler, ed., *Central and Eastern Europe: Roads to Growth*. Washington, D.C.: IMF and Austrian National Bank.

Commander, Simon, Leonid Liberman, and Ruslan Yemtsov. 1993a. "Wage and Employment Decisions in the Russian Economy. An Analysis of Developments in 1992." Working Paper 1205, World Bank, Washington, D.C.

Commander, Simon, Leonid Liberman, Cecilia Ugaz, and Ruslan Yemtsov. 1993b. "The Behavior of Russian Firms in 1991 and 1992: Evidence from a Survey." Working Paper 1166, World Bank, Washington, D.C.

Commander, Simon, Leonid Liberman, and Ruslan Yemtsov. 1993c. "Unemployment and Labor Market Dynamics in Russia." Working Paper 1167, World Bank, Washington, D.C.

Commander, Simon, and Richard Jackman. 1993. "Firms and Government in the Provision of Benefits in Russia." Working Paper 1184, World Bank, Washington, D.C.

Commander, Simon, and Ruslan Yemtsov. 1994. "Privatization in Russia: Does it Matter? Some Early Evidence on the Behavior of Privatized and Private Firms." World Bank, Washington, D.C. Mimeo.

Cottarelli, Carlo, and Mario Blejer. 1992. "Forced Saving and Repressed Inflation in the Soviet Union, 1986-1990." *IMF Staff Papers* 39(2):256-86.

de Melo, Martha, and Gur Ofer. 1993. "Private Sector Firms in a Transitional Economy: Findings of a Survey in St. Petersburg." Studies of Economies in Transformation, No. 11, World Bank, Washington, D.C.

Easterly, William, and Stanley Fischer. 1993. "Explaining the Collapse of the Soviet Union." World Bank and MIT. Mimeo.

Fan, Qimiao, and Mark Schaffer. 1993. "Government Financial Transfers and Enterprise Adjustments in Russia." World Bank and London School of Economics. Mimeo.

Ickes, Barry, and Randi Ryterman. 1992. "Inter-enterprise Arrears in Russia." IMF and World Bank. Mimeo.

IMF. 1993. *Russian Federation: Economic Review*. Washington, D.C.

Koen, Vincent, and Steven Phillips. 1993. *Price Liberalization in Russia: The Early Record*. Occasional Paper, IMF, Washington, D.C.

McDonald, Ian, and Robert Solow. 1981. "Wage Bargaining and Employment." *American Economic Review* 71:896-908.

Oswald, Andrew. 1985. "The Economic Theory of Trade Unions: An Introduction." *Scandinavian Journal of Economics* 87:160-93.

Pinto, Brian, Marek Belka, and Stefan Krajewski. 1992. "Transforming State Enterprises in Poland: Microeconomic Evidence on Adjustment." Working Paper 1101, World Bank, Washington, D.C.

Popkin, Barry M., Marina Mozhina, and Alexander K. Bafurin. 1992. "The Development of a Subsistence Income Level in the Russian Federation." University of North Carolina at Chapel Hill. Mimeo.

Senik-Leygonie, Claudia, and Gordon Hughes. 1992. "Industrial Profitability and Trade Among the Former Soviet Republics." *Economic Policy* 15:353-86.

Standing, Guy. 1992. "Employment Dynamics of Russian Industry." Paper presented to ILO Conference on Employment Restructuring in Russian Industry. Mimeo.

Vieira da Cunha, Paulo, ed. 1993. "Enterprise Reform in Russia." World Bank, Washington, D.C. Mimeo.

World Bank. 1992. *Russian Economic Reform: Crossing the Threshold of Structural Change.* Washington, D.C.

———. 1993a. *Russia: Intergovernmental Fiscal Relations.* Washington, D.C.

———. 1993b. *Russia: Social Protection during Transition and Beyond.* Washington, D.C.

5

Bulgaria

Iskra Beleva, Richard Jackman, and Mariela Nenova-Amar

Of the Eastern European countries, Bulgaria was perhaps one of the most cut off from developments in the West both because of its geographical position and its historical ties with the Soviet Union. In consequence, the economic dislocation following the reform program of February 1991 and the collapse of CMEA trade has been greater in Bulgaria than elsewhere in the region. The decline in output, employment, and real wages has been abnormally large, and there has been a very sharp rise in unemployment. On the financial front, following an enormous price jump at the time of liberalization, inflation has been stabilized, although it continues at a rather rapid rate (about 80 percent a year).

This chapter first describes these developments and then discusses the responses of the state-owned enterprises to the reforms and to the shocks hitting the economy. It then describes the evolution of the labor market and the growth of the private sector, and describes the emerging unemployment problem, paying particular attention to the job prospects of unemployed people. The final section offers some general conclusions and suggestions for policy.

One point must be stressed at the outset. Although there is an enormous amount of data on the labor market in Bulgaria, there are also many gaps, often in the areas most crucial to understanding the economic transition. For example, for much of the period, information on private businesses and households has been poor or nonexistent.

193

The Labor Market in Bulgaria

Prereform Labor Market

The labor market of prereform Bulgaria in the late 1980s was very much in the Soviet mold, without the moves toward decentralization and privatization already apparent in Hungary and Poland. Almost all enterprises belonged to the state, and 93.5 percent of workers were employed in the state sector. The industrial structure of employment in 1989, typical for a planned economy, was heavily biased toward industry (47.5 percent of employment), with 17.8 percent in agriculture and only 34.7 percent employed in services.

Wages were regulated centrally according to a Soviet-style tariff system, so that the amount each worker was paid was determined rigidly on the basis of the worker's skill, experience, and educational qualifications as well as the industry where he or she was employed. The dispersion of relative wages under this regime was low, although nonwage benefits constituted an important part of the remuneration package, as in other centrally planned economies. This type of compensation provided for greater variation than did cash wages.

Labor turnover in Bulgaria, as elsewhere in Central and Eastern Europe, was high, although it fell slightly from 30 percent in 1980 to 26 percent in 1988. Since the industrial structure of employment displayed considerable stability, however, these high turnover rates can best be regarded as a form of churning of workers, perhaps in response to changes in the nonwage benefits offered by different firms, rather than indicative of a high degree of labor market flexibility.

Reform Program

The reform program introduced in February 1991 was in its way as radical and as comprehensive as the Polish "big bang" package of the previous year. The prices of (almost) all goods and services were freed, controls on foreign trade were abolished, and the foreign exchange market unified with a free-floating exchange rate. Subsidies were reduced or eliminated and state enterprises gained autonomy with regard to pricing, employment, and investment decisions (although wages initially remained subject to central control). Although there was no immediate large-scale privatization program, there were provisions to privatize property, to restitute land to its former owners, and to permit new private enterprises to be set up.

These liberalization measures were accompanied by an IMF-backed stabilization program, which relied on: a reduction in the budget deficit; quantitative ceilings on credit expansion; high nominal (and, it was hoped, positive real) interest rates; and a tax-based incomes policy to restrain the growth of nominal wages. The details of the liberalization and stabilization measures are given in box 5-1.

Labor Market Developments: Wages and Employment

The immediate impact of liberalization was an enormous jump in prices. While exact numbers are difficult to pin down, it is clear that prices increased by at least 100 percent in February and by a further 50 percent in March, so that by the end of March prices were three times as high as in January. The exceptional magnitude of this initial jump in prices, in the face of restrictive fiscal and monetary policies (table 5-1), can be attributed largely to the profligacy of economic policy during 1990. In the period between the fall of Zhivkov in November 1989 and the stabilization package of February 1991, the budget deficit was allowed to run out of control, and money stocks accumulated alongside continued price controls and widespread shortages of goods.

Despite the immense increase in prices, the growth of money wages following liberalization was held to an increase of about 45 percent in the first quarter (figure 5-1). This led to a very sharp initial fall in the real wage (figure 5-2), but perhaps more important, it prevented the emergence of a wage-price spiral. As a result, inflation fell to 3-4 percent a month for the remainder of the year (figure 5-1).

Table 5-1 sets out the main macroeconomic developments in Bulgaria in the two years following price liberalization. Most striking is the very sharp fall in GDP (26 percent decline from 1989 to 1992), and even sharper (37 percent) fall in industrial output.

In terms of expenditure components, the sharpest falls have been in fixed capital formation (nearly 40 percent down in 1988) and in exports (63 percent down), although the latter has been matched by an equally large (60 percent) fall in imports. Both private and government consumption rose in the 1990 interregnum, and although falling quite sharply in 1991, stabilized in 1992 at about 7.5 percent below their 1989 levels. There was, however, a very sharp fall in inventory accumulation in 1992 (see table 5-1).

Box 5-1. Reform and Stabilization Program

The February 1991 reforms entailed the liberalization of prices, opening the economy to external trade, the restitution of land, and the ending of state monopolies together with a stabilization program involving a unified free-floating exchange rate, restrictive fiscal and monetary policies, and a tax-based incomes policy.

Exchange Rate

From February 1991, the foreign exchange market has been unified, and the exchange rate allowed to float. The Central Bank sets an official rate that is determined on the basis of trading the previous day in the interbank market. At the time of the reforms, Bulgaria had virtually no hard currency reserves, and the exchange rate fell very sharply, but during 1991 and 1992 the real exchange rate appreciated and the Central Bank built up foreign exchange reserves.

Fiscal Policy

The stabilization program prescribed an objective of reducing the budget deficit from 9.2 percent of GDP in 1990 to 0.1 percent in 1991, primarily by means of cuts in subsidies, which were projected to fall from 16 percent of GDP in 1990 to only 3 percent of GDP in 1991, but also through cuts in current outlays and capital expenditure. While the prescribed cuts in expenditure were achieved, with budget expenditures declining by 46 percent in real terms, revenues fell short of projected levels because of the sharp fall in output. As a result, the 1991 budget deficit of 3.7 percent of GDP was worse than projected, but there is no doubt that fiscal policy in this period was highly deflationary.

Monetary Policy

Interest rates were raised from 4.5 percent to 45 percent a year (3.75 percent a month) and then to 54 percent a year (4.5 percent a month). Bank lending rates were 10-15 percent higher, with the result that after the initial postliberalization surge of inflation, real interest rates were positive from the second half of 1991.

At the same time, ceilings were imposed on the growth of bank credit. These were calculated on the basis of the nominal stock of credit

The introduction of the Bulgarian reform package coincided with the disintegration of the CMEA. Consequently, the internal shocks resulting from liberalization and the end of the domestic excess demand regime paralleled the termination of privileged trading arrangements with the former Soviet Union. The CMEA collapse was particularly serious for Bulgaria. As much as 76 percent of its exports were to CMEA markets, as

outstanding at the end of 1990, with the increase in credit limited to 102 percent of the base for the first quarter of 1991, 112 percent for the second quarter, 132 percent for the third quarter, and 152 percent for the fourth quarter. In the first quarter of 1992 the growth of credit was limited to a 7 percent increase over the end-1991 credit ceiling. Since October 1992, the commercial banks have been allowed to trade credit ceiling allocations.

The growth of credit has been contained within the prescribed ceilings, but it is not clear how much this was influenced by borrowing being discouraged by high interest rates compared with the effectiveness of the credit ceilings themselves.

Prices

Central to the stabilization package of February 1991 was the liberalization of all producer and consumer goods prices. Four groups of goods remained subject to some form of price control:

a) Electricity, coal, and central heating prices are fixed by the government, but were increased in June 1991, May 1992, and in February and September 1993.

b) The prices of various selected foods and now also medicine are regulated by means of a ceiling on the permitted profit margin (originally 6-8 percent, now 12 percent for foods and 20 percent for medicines).

c) The domestic price of oil and other liquid fuels is set equal to the world price, calculated as the world trading price in Italy multiplied by the lev/dollar exchange rate.

d) There are support prices for six agricultural products.

It is noteworthy that these exemptions are limited to the energy and food sectors, and there are no controls of any sort on the prices of any manufactured goods or services.

Wages

Maximum permitted ceilings on the growth of the wage bill in each enterprise were prescribed by a tripartite commission. Wage payments in excess of the ceiling were subject to an excess wage tax (see box 5-2).

compared with 45 percent for Poland and Czechoslovakia, 40 percent for Hungary, and only 24 percent for Romania (figures for 1989). The industrial sectors that experienced the biggest drops in output (electronics and chemicals) were those geared toward the Soviet market prior to the reforms.

As shown in table 5-2, exports to Western countries, in particular to the EC, started to grow, and in volume they approximately doubled (from

Table 5-1. Bulgaria: Key Economic Indicators

Indicator	Nominal (Lv mln)				Real growth rates (percent)		
	1989	1990	1991	1992	1990	1991	1992
Gross domestic product	39,579.2	45,389.8	131,058.0	195,000.0	−9.1	−11.7	−7.0
Agriculture and forestry	4,330.7	8,054.6	20,139.0	20,200.0	−3.7	7.7	−7.0
Industry	23,507.0	23,273.6	62,843.0	90,800.0	−12.5	−18.6	−1.0
Services	11,741.5	14,061.6	48,076.0	84,000.0	−4.3	−11.3	−3.0
Total consumption	27,998.7	33,584.6	99,305.0	164,170.0	0.3	−8.7	0.0
Investment in fixed assets	10,328.2	9,651.9	24,777.0	39,310.0	−18.5	−19.9	−1.0
Inventories	2,776.3	4,148.4	11,834.0	6,000.0	−49.7	−5.7	−83.0
	Numbers				Growth rates (percent)		
Employment	4,365,034.0	4,096,848.0	3,564,037.0	3,112,900.0	−6.1	−13.0	−12.0
Agriculture and forestry	814,246.0	757,527.0	696,454.0	558,900.0	−7.0	−8.1	−19.8
Industry	2,032,306.0	1,864,013.0	1,510,133.0	1,288,300.0	−8.3	−19.0	−14.0
Services	1,518,482.0	1,475,305.0	1,357,450.0	1,265,700.0	−2.8	−8.0	−6.8
Consumer price index (annual average, percent)	101.1	123.8	438.5	179.4			
Unemployment rate (end of year, percent)	0.0	1.7	11.1	15.3			

Monetary accounts

Broad money (end of year)	43,250.0	50,204.0	111,608.0	159,842.0	1.2	−18.8	−3.7
M2/GDP ratio (percent)	109.3	110.6	85.2	82.0			
M1 (end of year)	21,900.0	21,656.0	26,890.0	37,833.0	−13.8	−54.7	−5.4
M1/GDP ratio (percent)	55.3	47.7	20.5	19.4			
Quasi-money (end of year)	21,350.0	27,902.0	81,542.0	126,866.0	13.9	6.7	4.6
QM/GDP ratio (percent)	53.9	61.5	62.2	65.1			
Domestic credit to firms (end of year)	41,809.0	44,743.0	114,277.0	151,206.0	−6.7	−6.7	−11.1
Share of private sector	0.0	1.7	11.4	11.8			
Interest on new credits (simple annual, percent)	4.7	5.6	50.7	58.3			
Interest on time deposits (simple annual, percent)	0.0	0.0	36.6	45.3			
Consolidated budget deficit (percent to GDP)	−0.01	−8.5	−4.3[a]	−5.7[a]			
Subsidies (percent to GDP)	15.5	14.9	4.2	1.9			

Note: Figures for 1992 are preliminary. Sectors are classified according to the existing system in Bulgaria. Industry here includes: industry, construction, and the so-called "other material production." Services include: transport, communications, trade, and the nonmaterial sphere. They include the imputed rent of owner-occupied homes, evaluated at market prices since 1991. Private consumption includes the imputed rent of owner-occupied homes. Corrected to GDP growth and GDP deflator.
a. Preliminary.
Source: Statistical Handbook 1993, NSI; "The Bulgarian Economy, 1992," NSI; "Annual Report of the Bulgarian National Bank, 1992," BNB; Monthly Bulletin of the National Labor Office.

Figure 5-1. Bulgaria, Monthly Wage and Price Inflation

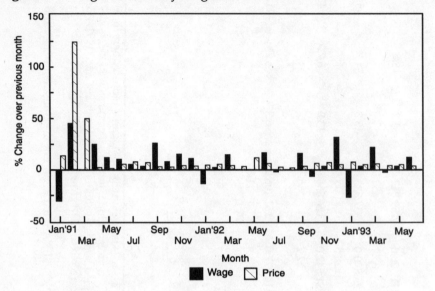

Figure 5-2. Bulgaria, Real Wage Index: December 1990-June 1993 (monthly)

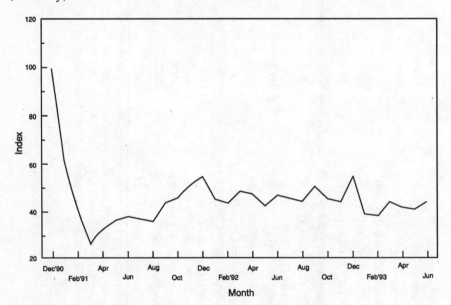

Table 5-2. Bulgaria: Foreign Trade

Item	1990	1991	1992[a]
Exchange rate (Lv/US$)	0.786	16.713	23.335
Foreign trade			
Exports (million leva)	10,559.5	57,368.3	81,644.8
Real growth (percent change)	—	−74.5	1.9
Eastern European countries (percent)	80.2	57.7	41.9
EC (percent)	5.0	15.7	30.8
Imports (million leva)	10,314.9	45,132.4	80,595.7
Real growth (percent change)	—	−79.4	27.9
Eastern European countries (percent)	75.9	49.1	37.2
EC (percent)	9.6	20.7	32.6
Trade balance (million leva)	244.6	12,235.9	1,049.1
Eastern European countries (percent)	642.0	11,239.2	4,208.5
EC (percent)	−467.9	−341.3	−1,073.3
Share of exports in total receipts			
Sales (percent)		26.6[a]	24.4[a]
Industry (percent)		17.0[a]	19.9[a]

a. Preliminary
Source: Statistical Handbook 1993, published by the NSI.

a low base) between 1991 and 1992. In 1993, however, exports fell back sharply, in large part because of United Nations sanctions against Serbia and disruptions to trade routes. Arguably these obstacles to the growth of a Western export market have been the most important factor preventing an economic recovery in Bulgaria similar to that in other Eastern European countries.

The collapse of external trade affected production on both the supply and demand sides. Like others in Eastern Europe, Bulgarian producers had depended on artificially cheap Russian oil supplies. Following the collapse of the CMEA system, imports of fuel and raw materials became available only for hard currency. Imports of oil and other raw material inputs fell by almost 30 percent. In early 1991, many state enterprises had to cut back production because of shortages of raw materials or electricity.

The fall in domestic spending, in particular consumer expenditure, was less severe than the fall in export demand. There has been a vigorous development of new private firms in areas neglected under the previous regime, such as retailing, catering, consumer and business services, and the like (see below).

Employment fell as rapidly as output, both in the economy as a whole and in industry (table 5-1). Although the 6.1 percent employment decline in 1990 lagged a little behind the decline in output in that year (9.1 percent), the subsequent employment falls of 13.0 percent in 1991 and 12.7 percent in 1992 have created a cumulative fall of nearly 29 percent since 1989, which is even bigger than the cumulative fall in output. Employment in industry also initially fell slightly more slowly than output, but the cumulative fall by 1992 (37 percent) was the same as the cumulative fall in output. Of the transition economies, Bulgaria stands out for the magnitude of the fall in state sector employment, both in absolute terms and relative to the fall in output.

Emergence of Unemployment

Given the magnitude of the decrease in employment, it is not surprising that unemployment emerged at a rapid rate. From zero in 1989, the unemployment rate reached 1.7 percent of the labor force (employed plus unemployed) by the end of 1990, then escalated to 11.1 percent by December 1991 and to 15.3 percent by December 1992 (figure 5-3). Although large, these rates of unemployment represent only about half the fall in employment over the period.

During 1990 reductions in unemployment were achieved mainly through voluntary separations, such as early retirements. Therefore, those leaving employment did not enter unemployment. In 1991 the rate of job loss accelerated, and, despite a large increase in retirements (110,000 versus 63,000 in 1990), there was a sharp rise in involuntary separations, most of whom entered unemployment (table 5-3). The slower growth of unemployment in 1992 partially reflects the slower rate of job separations, but also shows the disappearance of many of the long-term unemployed from the register. In addition, some of those leaving employment may have emigrated or found unrecorded work in the private sector.

Unemployment affected all sectors of the labor force. Reflecting the external shocks of 1991, most of the unemployed were in industry or construction (just over 50 percent at the end of 1991). But in 1992, the number of agricultural workers becoming unemployed rose sharply (to 32.0 percent of the unemployed as against only 8.7 percent in 1991) because of the

Figure 5-3. Unemployment and Vacancies in Bulgaria

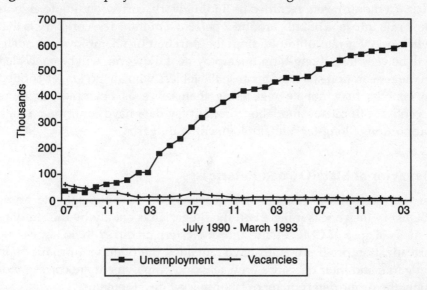

restitution of property rights and the liquidation of the agricultural coop-eratives.

Even though the overall level of unemployment in Bulgaria is excep-tionally high, its sectoral distribution is, if anything, more balanced than in other transitional economies. Male and female unemployment rates are very similar. Although youth unemployment rates are high, as a multiple of the national average, they are no higher than in other transitional—or indeed, than in many market—economies. Regional unemployment dis-parities, although marked, are smaller than in other transitional econo-mies and similar to those seen in market economies (OECD 1992). Occupational and educational differences appear qualitatively similar to those seen elsewhere, but exact comparisons are not possible because of the different classification procedures among countries.

Data on labor market flows have been collected only since February 1992. During 1992, inflows to unemployment averaged about 60,000 workers (about 2 percent of employment) a month, while outflows have averaged about 30,000 a month. About half of the inflows arise from redundancies or enterprise closures. The remainder are either voluntary quits or school leavers. More significantly, the outflow consists mainly of people exhausting their benefit entitlement and not continuing to register as unemployed. Less than a third of the people leaving unemployment (5-10,000 a month) were recorded as finding work, corresponding to an outflow rate into jobs of only around 2 percent a month. The corollary is that with so low a rate of job finding, the duration of unemployment spells will be very long. Long-term unemployment, however, will be concealed in the registration statistics because the jobless who are no longer entitled to benefits may not be registering themselves as unemployed. More recently, both census and labor force survey data have confirmed a high proportion of long-term unemployment in Bulgaria.

Behavior of State-Owned Enterprises

In this section we examine the response of state-owned enterprises (SOEs) to the shocks inflicted on the Bulgarian economy by the simultaneous collapse of CMEA trade and of Western credit. With no large-scale privatization program, SOEs have remained the dominant producers in Bulgaria, and their decisions on wages and employment are correspondingly the prime determinant of labor market developments.

Prior to the reforms, managers of state enterprises were essentially agents of government economic ministries. Their objective was to implement the plan. Wages, prices, investment, and the like were determined by the state. Following the reforms, managers were made legally responsible to government departments, through the branch minister, to determine their obligations and the criteria for assessing performance. The legislation also prescribed the remuneration of managers, whose maximum pay was linked to the average gross wage and the profitability of the enterprise.

Following widespread labor unrest and a wave of strikes during the 1990 "interregnum," the succession of minority governments without a clear political mandate, as well as the trade unions, have been able to effectively take control in many sectors. After the decentralization of wage bargaining in the second half of 1991, the threat of strikes remains a potent influence on wage setting. In the budget sector, attempts by the government to hold down wages led to nationwide strikes in 1991, 1992, and 1993.

The reforms of February 1991 allowed firms to set their prices, employment, and investment, but not their wages. Initially, wages were determined on the basis of the previous regime's centralized tariff system. In product markets, therewas an attempt to introduce a degree of compe-

Table 5-3. Bulgaria, the State Sector: A Balance of Employees

Item	1990	1991	1992	1993 (first half)
Number at the beginning of period		3,678,163	2,999,795	2,445,233
Inflows		472,525	372,285	211,872
New entrants		26,739	—	10,536
Outflows		1,158,341	926,847	357,050
Layoffs		347,848	263,151	133,706
Voluntary leave		810,493	663,696	223,344
Number at the end of period		2,999,795	2,445,233	2,303,259
Labor mobility in the state sector (percent)				
Average number of quits	13.7	17.4	14.1	7.4
Average number of layoffs	1.5	5.2	4.8	2.8
Average number of entrants	9.5	7.1	4.6	4.4
Total turnover	23.2	24.4	18.7	11.8

Source: NSI.

tition. Efforts to achieve this by splitting up enterprises and opening the economy to international trade were both unsuccessful. The efficacy of foreign trade as a source of product market competition was limited because the sharp depreciation of the exchange rate reduced import penetration. It follows that most SOEs initially had the benefit of monopolistic or imperfectly competitive conditions in domestic product markets.

State enterprises nonetheless soon found themselves in acute financial difficulties, partly because of sharp increases in taxes and nominal interest payments and partly from the depressed state of demand. In the early part of 1991, the finances of the SOEs were rescued by the very low level of real wages, but as wages recovered, financial problems became the dominant concern.

Thus, in a sense, firms went through two stages. In the first part of 1991, firms' finances were in a satisfactory state, but their input supplies were dislocated.[1] But by the first quarter of 1992, this ordering was reversed. Three times as many firms reported demand rather than supply as the constraint on their production.

Supply Shocks

A simple framework to analyze the effects of input supply shocks, set out formally in the appendix, is a fixed coefficients technology in which each unit of output requires a given number of units of energy or raw material input. Then, if the amount of inputs available to the firm is cut, the enterprise must reduce its output proportionally. Value added then falls in the same ratio and, for given factor shares, the wage bill must also fall in the same proportion.

In these circumstances, and still taking factor shares as given, the decisionmakers in the enterprise (unions) can only choose between wage cuts and employment reductions as the means of achieving the exogenously imposed wage bill reduction. (We return to the determination of factor shares shortly.) If the union's main concern is with the wages of its members (or if, as standard theory assumes, it is utilitarian or rent-maximizing), the enterprise will cut back employment in proportion to the fall in inputs and output.

By contrast, if the union is mainly concerned with protecting its members' jobs, then it will have to accept wage cuts in proportion to the fall in inputs and output. In this latter case, the union would nonetheless welcome voluntary quits, since these permit higher wages for the workers who remain. We have already noted the surge of early retirements in 1991 and the emergence of high rates of youth unemployment. Table 5-3 records the rates of quits, layoffs, and new entrants in the state sector between 1990 and 1992.

In reality, the unions' ability to achieve their objectives was circumscribed. In the first half of 1991, wage controls clearly would have forced unions to accept a far sharper cut in real wages than they would otherwise have wished. Incomes policy subsequently entailed a norm for the growth of the wage bill, and thus might appear neutral. In practice, however, employment levels were adjusted for layoffs so firms could not

---

1.   At this time, 70 percent of state enterprises in a survey reported problems with production arising from shortages of raw materials and electricity, as against around 10 percent reporting "problems with markets."

achieve higher wages within the norm by involuntary separations. We thus turn to a more detailed examination of the excess wage tax.

Wage Setting and the Excess Wage Tax

Following liberalization and in a sheltered market environment, prices rose by about 225 percent in the first quarter of 1991 instead of the forecasted increase of 100 percent. As a result, real wages fell by an average of 68 percent during the first quarter. Because the inflation compensation had been set in absolute rather than proportional terms, there was also a significant compression of the wage distribution. The fall in the mininum wage in real terms was "only" 33 percent during the first quarter.

The immediate outcome was therefore a fall in the measured ("statistical") real wage of no less than 68 percent in the first quarter. This drop is so much larger than the fall in GDP per employee at this time that it seems that one of the figures must be wrong. It is most likely that the official preform price index enormously underestimated the true cost of acquiring consumer goods. (Statistically, real wages had risen by about 20 percent during 1990, reflecting an increase in money wages at a time of price controls. With output falling during 1990, the measured real wage at the end of 1990 was unsustainably high.)

In July 1991, with the incomes policy and the excess wage tax in place, a new system of decentralized wage bargaining was introduced, and it had spread to cover the whole state sector by November of that year. Thus, from mid-1991, the only operative restraint on wages in the state sector was the excess wage tax. (Private firms were not subject to the excess wage tax.) The form of this tax, however, was substantially reformed in July 1991 (see box 5-2). The basic principle was that the permitted growth in the wage bill would be equal to the rate of retail price inflation *plus* any increase in output per employee in the enterprise (adjusted to exclude layoffs). The unit coefficient on inflation meant that the policy was neutral with regard to inflation, while the productivity term would hold constant the share of labor in value added in enterprises where productivity was growing. (In practice, at this time output per employee was falling in most enterprises, so the provision for productivity growth was inoperative.) At the same time, the rates of tax levied on firms were eased somewhat, albeit from initially punitive levels of up to 800 percent (see box 5-2).

With wage setting decentralized, many enterprises set wages in excess of the level permitted under the incomes policy. By the fourth quarter of 1991, the average level of settlements for the economy as a whole significantly exceeded the policy ceiling, and during this period the average real wage recovered much of its lost ground (see figure 5-2).

This wage pressure appears to have been absorbed in part by a sustainable increase in real wages and also to have fed through into higher inflation. It may be noted that the form of the incomes policy at this time was concerned only with wage growth and not with the level of wages, so that "excessive" wage increases in one period simply raise the base for permitted wage increases for the following period. Thus the 1992 wage ceilings adjusted fully to accommodate the higher real wages, and, by virtue of the 100 percent indexation provision, the higher inflation rate resulting from the decentralized wage settlements at the end of 1991 (figure 5-4).

During the second half of the year, the scheme for calculating the wage ceiling was changed from 100 percent *ex post* indexation on prices to a predetermined nominal ceiling based on the projected rate of inflation. As the actual rate of inflation fell below the projection, the scheme allowed some space for real wage growth. Even so, real wages overall were approximately static in 1992, at just over 70 percent of their 1990 level. This average conceals quite significant sectoral variation (see below).

In 1992 nominal wages displayed a very marked quarterly pattern, rising sharply at the end of each quarter, reflecting the quarterly timing of the adjustment of the wage bill ceilings to inflation. The timing of wage increases, and also the timing of layoffs, which are similarly bunched at the end of each quarter, seems to suggest that at this stage the excess wage tax was a major influence on the timing of firms' decisions. Over a longer time horizon, it is not as clear that the incomes policy was an effective constraint on wage setting, not only because the policy itself was rather permissive (particularly in 1992), but also because even where excess wage tax was due only a minority of firms (27 percent in 1992, 33 percent in 1993) appear to have paid it.

The main conclusions appear to be:

- During the first part of 1991, wages were held down in accordance with the incomes policy, but the crucial mechanism was the retention of the central tariff system rather than the excess wage tax.

Figure 5-4. Wage Bill Ceilings and Actual Wage Bill

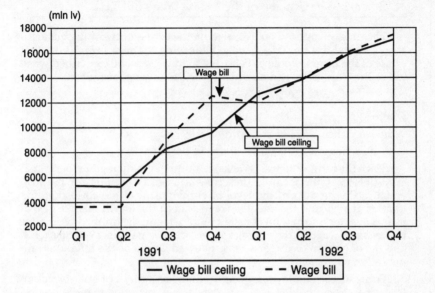

Note: Calculated aposteriori.

- The ending of the central tariff system in the second half of 1991 led to large increases in nominal wages, and by the end of the year much of the fall in real wages had been recovered (figure 5-2). The average level of nominal wages in the fourth quarter was significantly above that permitted by the incomes policy.
- In 1992 inflation remained relatively stable, possibly because of the excess wage tax. An additional factor may have been the depressed labor market. It is not clear to what extent this was also affecting wage settlements. The relationship of nominal wages to the ceiling up to the end of 1992 is shown in figure 5-4.

Financial Problems of the State Sector

Given the degree of wage restraint, nearly all enterprises were able to make positive operating profits in 1991 and 1992. For most sectors, though, operating profits in 1992 were only one-half to one-third their level in 1991 (table 5-4). Their financial difficulties arose from the treatment of debt and credit. Interest rates rose enormously (from 4.5 percent a

Box 5-2. The Scheme of the Excess Wage Bill Tax

The excess wage bill tax is levied on the excess of the wage bill actually paid and the prescribed wage bill ceiling for each firm. In the first phase of the incomes policy (February to June 1991) the prescribed wage bill ceiling was calculated according to the following formula:

$$WB_{max}(91{:}s) = WB(90{:}s) * \{W(90{:}4) \, / \, W(90{:}s)\}$$

where

$WB(90{:}s)$ is the wage bill of the firm in 1990 quarter s

$W(90{:}s)$ is the average monthly wage in 1990 quarter s.

Since the ratio $WB(90{:}s)/W(90{:}s)$ is simply employment in the firm in 1990 quarter s, the formula prescribes a wage bill ceiling for the firm equal to the product of the level of employment in the corresponding quarter of 1990 and the average wage paid in the fourth quarter of that year. Thus, for a firm with constant employment, the implied ceiling for the average wage is the average wage actually paid in 1990 quarter 4, and the only form of wage increase allowed would be the inflation compensation payments.

Firms whose employment was declining as a result of quits or voluntary separations could increase average wages, provided that the proportional increase in average wages relative to 1990 quarter 4 was no greater than the proportional decline in employment measured relative to the corresponding quarter of the previous year. Where there are involuntary layoffs, however, the wage bill of the previous year is recalculated to remove layoffs from the employment base, so that a firm reducing employment by means of layoffs is not permitted to increase its average wage.

The second phase of the policy entailed several adjustments to the formula to incorporate explicit 100 percent indexation to retail prices and to allow wages to reflect productivity growth. The formula was:

$$WB_{max}(t{:}s) = WB(t{-}1{:}s)*\{W(t{:}s{-}1)/$$
$$W(t{-}1{:}s)\}*\{P(t{:}s)/P(t{:}s{-}1)\}*\{R(t{:}s)/R(t{:}s{-}1)\}$$

where

$P(t{:}s)$ is the retail price index in year t quarter s

$R(t{:}s)$ is output per employee (productivity) in the firm in year t quarter s.

Under this new system, prescribed wage bill ceilings became the product of employment in the same quarter of the previous year, and the average wage paid in the previous quarter, but now automatically revised to incorporate inflation and productivity growth during the quarter. In practice, firms would have to set wages in relation to wage bill ceilings based on inflation forecasts, but the excess wage tax was levied *ex post* on the excess of the wage bill over the ceiling calculated on the basis of actual inflation during the quarter. Thus the system provided 100 percent *ex post* indexation, and workers' real wages were fully protected from inflation. The adjustment for productivity was less welcome in that during 1991 output per employee was falling in most enterprises, thus reducing permitted wage growth. In November 1991 it was agreed that if productivity were falling, the productivity term in the formula would be set equal to one.

The main innovation of the third phase of the policy introduced in July 1992 was to set the wage norm on the basis of forecast inflation rather than allowing it to adjust *ex post* to actual inflation. Incomes policy in this period turned out to be exceptionally permissive, both because the inflation forecasts turned out to be much too high, thereby allowing significant real wage growth within the ceiling, and because the rates of excess wage tax (see below) were reduced at this stage.

The fourth phase, introduced in 1993, involved two modifications. First, the adjustment to inflation was to be based on partial compensation for past inflation rather than 100 percent compensation for current (actual or forecast) inflation. The partial compensation was calculated in relation to the previous twelve months' price increases and took the form of full adjustment for the first nine months *plus* 85 percent of the price increase over the final three months. Second, the adjustment for productivity was reduced from 100 percent to 30 percent of the increase (or decrease) in output per head. The rates of excess wage tax were, for the first time, increased in 1993.

The tax rates (in percentages) were as follows:

	Tax rate			
Excess wage bill	Feb. '91–June '91	July '91–June '92	July '92–Dec. '92	Jan. '93–Dec. '93
up to 1	100	0	0	0
1 - 2	200	50	0	0
2 - 3	400	100	0	50
3 - 4		200	50	200
4 - 5			100	600
5 - 6	800	400	200	800
above 6			400	800

year before the reform to 4.5 percent a month, equivalent to an annual rate of 55 percent) as part of the stabilization package. Although on average about half the debt of any individual enterprise took the form of liabilities to other enterprises, the production sector as a whole was a net debtor to the banking sector and to the government. Hence, the rise in interest rates required a substantial increase in the net cash flow from enterprises to the banks and to the government.

The burden of interest payments was made even greater because they are only partially deductible (to the extent of 25 percent in 1991 and 50 percent in 1992) from operating profits for tax purposes. Enterprises were subject to a 50 percent tax rate on their taxable profits. Thus a firm with a positive operating profit might easily be in a position where its interest and tax liabilities could add up to more than 100 percent of that profit. In 1991 profit after interest and tax was still positive, but in 1992, although operating profit was positive, profit remaining after interest and tax had turned negative.

In 1992 many enterprises were unable to meet their interest and tax liabilities. In 1991 the ratio of interest paid to interest due was 85.9 percent, but in 1992 this ratio fell to 55.4 percent. The ratio of taxes paid to taxes due fell from 87.8 percent to 72.1 percent. The nonpayment of interest and taxes was simply added to the firms' indebtedness. In 1992 a selected group of enterprises had their debts canceled, with government bonds issued in their place. This precedent, together with the expectation of further debt write-offs linked to the privatization program, has created a situation in which state enterprises have little incentive to care about their indebtedness. There seems little doubt, however, that the acute financial pressures confronting SOEs, attributable to the costs of restructuring in conditions of depressed demand and aggravated by inappropriate policies for inflation accounting and dealing with bad debts, have been the proximate cause of the exceptionally sharp falls in output and employment.

The Emergence of a Labor Market

Wages

In sharp contrast to the low variation across sectors under the Socialist regime, the dispersion of relative wages increased markedly after the start of the reforms. Even before the advent of decentralized collective

Table 5-4. Key Financial Indicators for Industry
(*nominal values, bln.lv.*)

Indicator	1991		1992			
	Q1-3	Q4	Q1	Q2	Q3	Q4
Operating profit	15.8	18.6	4.1	6.5	4.2	-1.5
Financial expenditures[a] (net)	6.8	12.5	4.5	6.8	11.7	0.5
Extra expenditures	1.2	2.3	0.8	1.2	1.7	2.2
Profit–fin exp–extra exp	7.8	3.8	-1.3	-1.5	-9.2	-4.2
Liabilities	26.2	11.2	40.2	9.2	10.3	-0.2
Suppliers	17.0	2.1	16.8	6.5	5.2	-0.2
Employees	1.2	0.9	1.9	0.5	0.3	0.0
Claims	19.3	-1.2	18.1	4.6	4.9	0.6
On sales	12.9	-2.7	11.1	4.5	3.6	-0.4
Net claims	-6.9	-12.4	-22.2	-4.6	-5.4	0.8
Profit + net claims	0.9	-8.6	-22.6	-4.9	-12.8	-1.2
Wage bill + SSC[b] + Unemployment contributions	10.6	11.2	6.6	8.4	9.9	10.9
Receipts from sales (indirect taxes excluded)	114.9	88.6	46.0	49.6	57.0	69.6
Average quarterly wage (leva)	7,165.0	4,791.4	5,146.2	6,150.9	7,135.1	8,172.5
Separations (thousands)	344.9	78.8	61.8	62.8	56.8	56.5
Layoffs (thousands)	104.3	28.1	21.7	21.3	18.3	17.7

a. Financial expenditures net cover the relations with the banking system.
b. SSC: social security contributions. The average rate in 1991 for the state sector was 38 percent.

bargaining in the second half of 1991, there appear to have been quite sharp changes in relative wages. With the widespread adoption of decentralized wage bargaining, relative wages became much more unequal. The coefficient of variation of relative wages increased from an average of 16-17 percent during the 1980s to 35-40 percent at the end of 1991.

As regards the sectoral pattern of wage growth, taking 1990 as the base, the average real wage in industry in 1992 was 0.73, but among industrial branches the range was from about 1.1 in electricity and thermal power to only just over 0.4 in "other industrial." These changes in relative wages were caused in part by the different patterns of output decline and price increase across sectors reflecting the differential sectoral influence of the various supply and demand shocks, but also continuing monopoly power in the product market and the relative power and the objectives of the trade unions in wage setting.

To what extent do movements in relative wages reflect the different economic circumstances of the sectors, as measured by their output, employment, or product prices? Summary statistics measuring the variation and covariation of the annual movements of these variables across the eighteen industrial branches are given in tables 5-5 and 5-6.

Table 5-5 shows the coefficient of variation of the year-on-year changes of output, prices, and the like across the eighteen industrial branches. Conspicuous are the big increases in the variance of prices in 1991 and of relative wages in 1992. Table 5-6 shows the covariation of these year-to-year changes. The first block, marked 1990, shows that between 1989 and 1990 there was virtually no statistically significant correlation because at this stage enterprises were still subject to central direction, and wages and prices were controlled. The effects of liberalization show up in much larger correlation coefficients, in particular between wages and employment (in both years), and between output and employment in 1992. Significantly, however, the correlation of prices and output was negative if insignificant in both years, suggesting that both supply and demand shocks are affecting relative industry performance, with supply-side factors perhaps the more important. The strong positive correlation between wages and employment then suggests that relative wages are responsive to relative labor demand (employment) and that differential wage shocks are not themselves an important exogenous element in accounting for the different experiences of the sectors.

A perhaps more impressive indication of the extent to which wage setting is becoming responsive to labor market conditions is provided by the relationship between wages and unemployment across municipalities.

Table 5-5. Bulgaria: Coefficients of Variation of the Annual Indexes
across 18-th Industrial Branches
(percent)

Item	1990	1991	1992
Real output	14.3	18.4	16.2
Producer prices	7.4	42.8	15.1
Employment	8.0	9.1	11.6
Productivity	12.9	17.0	10.7
Wage rate	5.7	10.4	10.9
Real product wage	11.0	39.5	20.0
Relative wages	21.5	26.6	36.7
Share of wage bill to output[a]	16.0	30.9	20.4

a. The annual index of the ratio wage bill/output.

Figure 5-5 shows the relationship between relative wages (adjusted for
size of municipality) and the unemployment rate across 118 municipalities for 1991. There is a clear impression of an inverse relationship, and
this is confirmed by regression analysis ($t = 7.2$). The adjustment for
municipality size is needed because there is a pronounced tendency for
wages to be higher in bigger municipalities.

Figure 5-6 shows the equivalent relationship for the twenty-eight big
regional centers for 1992. In this figure relative wages are without adjustment for municipality size (all the municipalities are big), but the unemployment rate is not available and the ratio of layoffs to the sum of
employees plus layoffs is used instead. Again, the figure shows a clear
inverse relationship, which is again confirmed by regression analysis
($t = 6.7$).

Although none of the findings reported in this section could be
regarded as definitive, taken together they are clearly suggestive of a
market in which, at least to some extent, movements in relative wages are
responsive to the state of demand.

The Private Sector

Despite the absence of a formal privatization program in Bulgaria, the
growth of the private sector has been a very conspicuous feature of the
reform process. New private enterprises have started up in every sector

Figure 5-5. Relative Wages and Unemployment Rate by 118 Municipalities

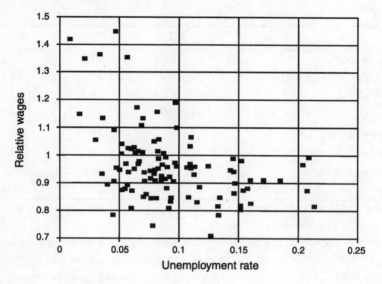

Figure 5-6. Relative Wages and Unemployment Rate by Twenty-Eight Municipal Centers

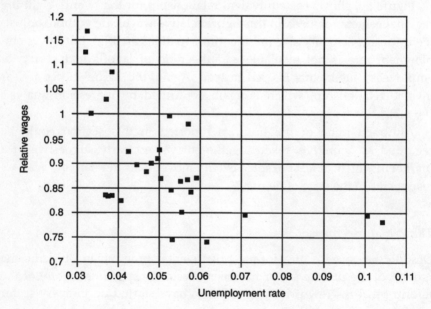

Table 5-6. Bulgaria: Correlation Coefficients between Indexes, Cross-Section of 18-th Industrial Branches

Item	Employment	Real output	Producer price	Average wage
1990				
Employment	1.00	0.41	−0.32	0.23
Real ouput	0.41	1.00	−0.01	0.32
Producer price	−0.32	−0.40	1.00	−0.15
Average price	0.23	0.32	−0.15	1.00
1991				
Employment	1.00	0.34	0.58	0.62
Real ouput	0.34	1.00	−0.18	0.34
Producer price	0.58	−0.18	1.00	0.47
Average price	0.62	0.34	0.47	1.00
1992				
Employment	1.00	0.68	0.17	0.66
Real ouput	0.68	1.00	−0.40	0.41
Producer price	0.17	−0.04	1.00	−0.19
Average price	0.66	0.41	−0.19	1.00

Source: Agency for Economic Coordination and Development, Sofia.

of the economy, but particularly in those sectors most neglected under the socialist system, such as retail trade and services. Many of these activities fall outside the traditional scope of the official statistics, so that there is little official data on the growth of the private sector. One exception is the census of December 1992, which asked people whether their employer was a state enterprise or private firm. The census established that at that time about 14 percent of workers were employed in the private sector, which was estimated to be producing 15.6 percent of GDP.

As part of this project, we carried out a survey of 200 private firms in the two major cities of Bulgaria (Sofia and Plovdiv) in January 1993.[2] The

2.   The selection of firms was based on earlier commercial surveys of the private sector, and was broadly representative of the types of firms currently operating within the private sector, without being a strict statistical sample. Within the sample, as might have been expected, a large proportion (42.9 percent) of the firms were in trade, but there were significant numbers in other sectors, including industry (15.2 percent), construction (7.3 percent), business services (6.3 percent), and media/publishing (6.3 percent).

survey confirms the presumption that the private sector is attracting the more highly skilled of the work force. No less than 80.1 percent of managers have university degrees, as do 25 percent of the workers, with a further 37 percent of workers having vocational qualifications. This parallels a finding of the 1992 survey of state firms, which noted strong complaints from enterprise managers about the lack of well-qualified professionals. Clearly the private sector has been recruiting primarily the more skilled and better qualified people.

Most of the firms in the survey were quite small, with an average level of employment of ten workers. They are, however, growing rapidly, with the average firm having increased its employment by about 80 percent between January 1992 and January 1993.

It is also notable that the great majority both of managers (72 percent) and workers were previously employed in state firms. Relatively few had previously been unemployed (and even some of those registered as unemployed may also have been working in a private firm). When asked about recruitment, firms said they relied mainly on personal contacts and recommendations, and only five said they looked for workers at the unemployment bureaus.

A complementary finding is that most unemployed people would prefer to work in the public rather than the private sector. The December 1992 census found that just over 50 percent of unemployed people would rather work in a state enterprise as against about 15 percent who would rather either set up a private firm or take work in one (the remaining 35 percent having no preference). Of the unemployed with higher education the preference for the public sector was even higher, the margin being 60 percent as against 8 percent. These findings are consistent with an earlier survey carried out by the National Institute for Youth Research in December 1991, which found a strong preference among unemployed people, and particularly among the elderly and youths, for returning to work in the public sector. All this casts some doubt on the idea that unemployment is necessary (or even helpful) for labor mobility.

Given the dominating position of trade unions in the state sector it is surprising to find an almost complete absence of unions in the private sector. Only six of the firms (3 percent) recognized a trade union (although, by contrast, nearly a quarter of the owners are members of business associations). With no trade unions, firms felt free to fire workers when they wished, and at least half had fired one or more workers during the course of 1992. The reasons given for firing workers were poor performance or bad discipline; notably, during a period of severe recession, virtually no firms had found it necessary to fire workers for reasons of depressed demand.

There was a lower response rate, and some of the responses seem of lower quality, to questions on wages and other financial variables. It seems, however, a reasonable generalization that private firms tend to pay higher wages, but this is to some extent offset by lower bonuses and more limited provision of nonwage benefits.

Overall the impression is one of an aggressive new private sector, dominated by small, although rapidly growing firms prepared to pay good wages for the right skills but not offering their workers much job security, nonwage benefits, or union recognition. From the perspective of a labor market in transition, it is striking that these firms are not recruiting unemployed people, and that the unemployed have no wish to go and work in them.

Unemployment

We have described the very rapid decline in state sector employment and the consequent rise in registered unemployment. This section looks in a little more detail at the experience of unemployed people, and in particular at their prospects of finding work. Unfortunately, the major source of unemployment statistics in Bulgaria—registrations at employment exchanges—not only provides incomplete information but also gives a seriously distorted picture of flows and durations. More recently, additional information on unemployment has been provided by the population census of December 1992, and by the Labor Force Survey of autumn 1993.

Registered unemployment statistics show unemployment rates in Bulgaria among the highest of any of the economies in transition. Both the census and the Labor Force Survey (LFS), which come closer to measuring unemployment on the international standardized definition, report unemployment rates higher, and in the case of the LFS substantially higher, than the data on registrations. Thus the census data give an unemployment rate of 17.9 percent for December 1992 as against 15.6 percent for registrations. According to the LFS, the unemployment rate in Bulgaria in autumn 1993 reached 21.4 percent; the register data give a rate of 15.7 percent at the same time.

Of equal importance in the context of economic transition are the magnitude of flows into and out of unemployment and the duration of unemployment spells. Here statistics on labor market flows based on the registrations data have been published since early 1992, but they are seriously misleading. The main component of the outflow from unemployment is people being struck off the register for failing to present themselves at an employment exchange (usually because they have exhausted their entitlement to unemployment benefits). Thus the main element of the outflow is, in the first instance, a flow from recorded to unrecorded unemployment, rather than a flow from unemployment to a job or out of the labor force.

Inflows into Unemployment

Since February 1992 monthly data for inflows into registered unemployment have been available in total and by age, sex, skill, industry, and benefit status. The structural composition of the inflow by age, sex, and skill group reflects that of the unemployment stock, with about half being women, about half youths, and a decreasing proportion skilled workers ("specialists"). By industrial classification, the main source of the inflow was manufacturing industry, followed by trade, construction, and the sciences. It is not possible to compare this with the pattern of employment decline across industrial sectors because the statistics are collected on a different basis. (See tables 5-7 and 5-8 for summaries of unemployment by group and region.)

The proportion of the inflow receiving unemployment benefits has been increasing (from 36.3 percent in February 1992 to 56.4 percent in March 1993), with a peak (71 percent) in September 1992, probably because of school-leavers registering as unemployed at the end of the summer vacation.

The high proportion of people not entitled to benefit in the inflow arises in part because some new entrants to unemployment are not entitled to benefits (for example, those who quit their job voluntarily, or temporary or seasonal workers with an insufficient contributions record; see box 5-3) and in part because some of the unemployed, on reaching the point at which their benefit expires, reregister themselves after having allowed their registration to lapse. Thus, outflows from unemployment by reason of benefit exhaustion are transformed into inflows of people not entitled to benefit, but with a lag of several months. The monthly

Table 5-7. Unemployment Structure

	December 1990	December 1991	December 1992
Unemployment			
Thousands	65.1	419.1	576.9
Rate (percent)	1.7	11.1	15.3
Women			
Thousands	42.4	228.4	302.4
Percent of total	65.2	54.5	52.4
Youths			
Thousands	30.4	203.8	258.4
Percent of total	46.8	48.6	44.8
Occupation (percent of total)			
Workers	50.6	68.3	74.9
Specialists	38.3	24.1	17.7
Managers	5.6	2.9	2.5
Auxiliary	5.5	4.7	4.9
Education (percent of total)			
Elementary	21.9	34.5	45.3
Secondary	30.8	33.0	31.0
Specialist	27.7	21.4	15.4
Higher	19.6	11.0	8.2

Source: National Labor Office.

number of benefit expirations has varied from about 13,000 (May, June, December 1992) up to 30,000 (January 1993). It is not known what proportion of benefit expirees reregister themselves as unemployed, but this proportion may be falling because people are losing confidence in employment exchanges as a means of job search and thus do not register.

According to the census data, 57.7 percent of the unemployed were dismissed after staff reduction or enterprise closure; 17.6 percent had quit employment of their own wish; and 15.9 percent became unemployed after finishing secondary school, 2.4 percent after finishing higher education, and 6.5 percent after being discharged from the national military service. It will be noted that the census uses the standard definition of unemployment, and hence those who leave recorded for unrecorded unemployment when their benefits expire, and then reregister as unemployed, will not be counted as entering unemployment on the second occasion.

Table 5-8. Regional Unemployment

District	Unemployment rates[a]				
	1990	1991	1992	1992[b]	1993[c]
Total	1.7	13.7	19.8	15.7	21.4
Sofia (capital)	1.4	10.2	11.7	9.1	16.1
Burgas	1.9	13.4	19.7	14.5	25.2
Varna	1.1	12.9	14.9	10.5	21.9
Lovech	1.1	11.7	15.5	15.5	16.6
Montana	1.7	16.1	27.3	23.1	25.2
Plovdiv	2.7	18.6	27.2	17.5	28.0
Russe	1.4	13.7	17.7	17.1	20.2
Sofia region	2.4	13.8	25.5	16.8	28.3
Haskovo	1.4	13.7	23.3	21.1	18.5

a. Registered unemployment.
b. 1992 census. Calculated as a percentage of the economically active population.
c. Labour Force Survey data.

Outflows from the Unemployment Register

Data on outflows from the unemployment register have been available since January 1992. The data classify outflows into the following categories: hires to work, voluntary deregistrations, and struck-off by failure to meet legal requirements. People are struck off mainly for not reregistering themselves in labor offices at the required time (twice a month until November 1992, and once a month since that time) or for rejecting job offers.

It is notable that the bulk of those leaving the register (about 70-80 percent) are struck off for not meeting legal requirements (figure 5-7). The increase in the number struck off may be largely the result of the increase in the number of unemployed people ineligible for benefits, such as the long-term unemployed. It may also reflect changes in the legal framework (constraints on unemployment eligibility) and the stronger control that has been implemented in this field.

Hires into work have on average constituted only around 15 percent of the outflow from the register, although the absolute number of hires has been on a rising trend, reaching about 7,000 a month toward the end of the period. The proportion of women among the hires was high, and

Figure 5-7. Unemployment Outflows

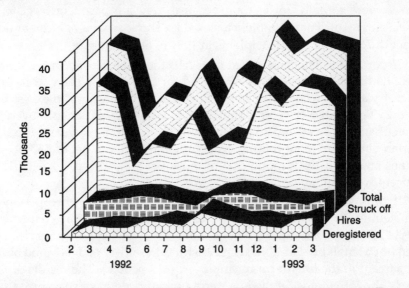

increasing (from 51 percent in February 1992 to 61.5 percent in December). The share of specialists was also increasing (up to 46.0 percent in September), as well as that of youths (43.0 percent in October).

Unemployment outflows through voluntary deregistration (about 10 percent of total outflow) have also been increasing. The very sharp increase noted in September 1992 is largely attributable to a jump in youth deregistration (4,369 in September as against only about 400 in February), which may reflect a return to school or training courses. Survey data suggest that most deregistrations are likely to be unrecorded flows into employment rather than people leaving the labor force.

Register data on inflows and outflows are somewhat misleading since they include a substantial proportion of spurious flows between registered and unrecorded unemployment. The "true" outflow rate is perhaps better represented as the sum of the outflow into jobs and of voluntary deregistrations. This is—at maximum—around 4 percent a month, implying in the steady state an average duration of unemployment spells of twenty-five months.

Long-Term Unemployment

In many of the transitional economies, outflow rates from unemployment have been low, and the duration of unemployment spells correspondingly high. Data on unemployment durations in Bulgaria, like those on flows, were initially misleading because they are based on registered unemployment. For example, survey data show an average unemployment duration of benefit recipients in 1991 of about six months.

According to the census, just over half the unemployed in December 1992 had at that time been unemployed for over a year. The LFS records as many as 54 percent of the unemployed having durations in excess of a year by September 1993, of whom 31.2 percent had been unemployed for more than two years and 13.9 percent for more than three years. The Bulgarian Unemployment Survey, which interviewed a panel of 550 people (Jones and Kato 1993) found that of those unemployed in April 1991, 60 percent were still unemployed in March 1992.

It thus seems clear that the scale of the long-term unemployment problem in Bulgaria is very severe. Less is known about the characteristics of long-term unemployed people, but the National Labor Service carried out a small pilot study in three districts in mid-1992. It covered about 30 percent of the long-term unemployed (419 people). The results of this study show that most of the long-term unemployed have specialized secondary education; they have no additional skills; they are workers, dismissed from industry; no suitable job has been offered to them; they did not finish any retraining course; and most of them registered themselves as unemployed in the second month of unemployment. The most common conclusions drawn from the results of this study are that, on the one hand, long-term unemployed people have a great desire to be in employment again and are ready to accept courses, retraining, jobs that are not in their speciality, and so forth; on the other hand, they do not do anything to achieve their goal and behave passively.

Active Labor Market Policies

In OECD countries, active labor market policies are now generally recommended as a means of counteracting structural unemployment, and it is often argued that they may have an equally important role to play in the economic restructuring process of economies in transition. But, as we have already noted, unemployment in Bulgaria has thus far been aggregative rather than structural in nature, and in such circumstances one might expect active policies to be less useful.

Active labor market policies are of three kinds. The first kind of activity is concerned with "job brokering," that is, running employment exchanges and the provision of advice and information on job vacancies. Second, there are measures to facilitate labor mobility—for example, relocation grants or finance for training schemes. Third, there are direct job creation schemes, including self-employment and start-up grants. At times of high unemployment across the labor market as a whole, one might expect the return to job brokering services and to improved labor mobility to be rather low, but at the same time the value of direct job creation activities, particularly in sectors with many displaced workers, to be high.

JOB BROKERING.   Bulgaria has a system of local labor offices, managed by the National Labor Service, that administer the payment of benefits in addition to a labor market placement service. The offices employ approximately 3,000 staff, less than one for every 100 unemployed people, a far worse ratio than in most OECD economies. As a result, the offices are not able to take an active part in seeking out vacancies (although formally employers are required to notify of vacancies, in practice they do not do so), and most unemployed people rely on personal contacts and advertisements rather than the employment exchanges as a means of job search.

POLICIES TO ASSIST LABOR MOBILITY.   Some measures for encouraging internal migration have been introduced. An unemployed person who would like to move to another locality can have his or her travel expenses paid by the Unemployment Fund. But this opportunity has not been much used; travel expenses paid by the fund have amounted to only 0.1 percent of its budget. People are reluctant to move, in part because of the inheritance of centrally planned economic management with restrictions on mobility (now mostly removed) and because the housing market is undeveloped and there is still a serious housing shortage, but mainly because of the lack of jobs everywhere in the country.

The number of unemployed people in training and retraining courses is very low compared with the number of unemployed. The proportion of unemployed in retraining in September 1992 was just over 2 percent, and the share of training in the expenditures of the Unemployment Fund was around 1.5 percent. Survey evidence (Jones and Kato 1993) suggests, however, a strongly positive effect of training on the prospects of finding a job.

JOB CREATION MEASURES

Employment subsidies. Firms have been encouraged to hire unemployed people by tax relief and direct financial support, but the willingness of firms to ask for such support and to hire unemployed people has

Box 5-3. The Unemployment Benefit System

Legislative regulations for the unemployment benefit system introduced since 1990 define: (a) eligibility for unemployment support; (b) the level of the benefits paid; (c) the duration of payment; and (d) the administration of the system.

The legal framework has been constructed in a situation of rapidly rising unemployment and severe economic crisis. Changes in the system also reflect the three changes of government since the start of the reforms.

There are two kinds of unemployment benefits: allowance and assistance. The type of benefit payable is related to the cause of unemployment and the individual to be assisted. The two kinds of benefits differ in both the amount and the duration of payment.

Eligibility

Unemployment allowance was initially payable only to redundant workers (those who became unemployed because of staff reductions or full or partial closure of their place of employment) who had been in work for at least eight months out of the last twelve or, in the case of new entrants with less than eight months service, who had been in work for seventy-five days.

Unemployment assistance was payable to youths entering the labor force with educational qualifications. Two groups of young people could qualify—those who had completed higher education (called "young specialists") and those who had completed secondary specialized education (called "qualified workers").

The rapid rate of increase of unemployment led to a broadening of eligibility criteria. Workers with fixed-term contracts that were not renewed became entitled to unemployment allowances, while young specialists and qualified workers discharged from military service became entitled to unemployment assistance.

Level of Benefits Paid

The basis for calculating benefits and allowances has been changed on a number of occasions. According to current regulations (as from July 1992), the unemployment benefit for previously full-time workers is set at 60 percent of the previous average monthly wage (on the basis of which insurance contributions were paid) over the past six months. The benefit, however, cannot be lower than 90 percent or higher than 140 percent of the minimum wage. For those previously in part-time work, the benefit is calculated proportionally to contracted working hours. When an individual entitled to unemployment benefit starts part-time work he is entitled to 50 percent of the unemployment benefit if his remuneration does not exceed the minimum wage. Assistance is paid at the minimum-wage level.

The benefit as a proportion of the average wage for full-time workers has varied enormously. The system in force up until September 1991 provided an effective replacement ratio of about 80 percent, but a more stringent formula was then implemented, according to which the benefit was set equal to the minimum wage plus 20 percent of the excess of the individual's average wage over the minimum wage, which reduced the average replacement ratio to about 40 percent. The current rules have led to an even lower replacement ratio, which has averaged around 30-35 percent since July 1992, because the minimum wage is much lower than the average wage, and the ceiling of 140 percent of the minimum wage will be binding for most workers.

Duration of Payment of Unemployment Benefits

Since June 1991, the duration for which benefits have been paid has been determined by the length of service and age of the unemployed person. The scheme is:

Length of service (years)	Age (years)	Duration of benefit payment (months)
up to 5	—	6
over 5	up to 40	7
over 5	40 & over	8
over 10	45 & over	9
over 20	51 & over, males	10
	51 & over, females	12
over 25	56 & over	12

Assistance for young specialists has a duration of six months, while assistance for qualified workers who have not signed a labor contract in advance lasts for only three months.

Administration and Finance

To receive payment of benefits, individuals are required to register at an employment exchange within seven days of their discharge from work, and thereafter report every two weeks (now once a month) to the employment exchange.

Unemployment benefits are financed from a specially established fund, financed by contributions from firms and other organizations, as well as state budget allocations. The initial level of contributions was 0.5 percent, but it has since been increased in several steps, and is now 7 percent. All contributions are currently paid by the employer, although the Ministry of Labor and Social Welfare has proposed a division of the 7 percent contributions—5 percent for employers and 2 percent for employees. The budget of the fund has been in surplus:

	1990	1991	1992	1993 (first half)
Contributions (million leva)	82	1,090	3,200	3,500
Expenditures (million leva)	—	796	1,500	1,250
Unemployment benefits (million leva)	26	720	1,429	1,092

The budget transfers to the fund in 1990 were 427 million leva and 45 million leva in 1991. The state budgets for 1992 and 1993 do not project any transfers to the fund.

been quite low. Less than 1 percent of payments from the Unemployment Fund in 1992 were for this purpose. Firms clearly may be reluctant to take on new workers, even with financial support, in conditions of depressed demand.

Temporary employment schemes and public works. There are several programs already in operation to combat the regional effects of industrial decline, and more are planned. Only two of these programs—the temporary employment scheme for the long-term unemployed and the regional employment program for areas with mining closures—have thus far been of any quantitative significance.

The temporary employment scheme provides for jobs for up to five months, in activities of benefit to the community, for long-term unemployed people rather along the lines of the "Community Programme" during the 1980s in the United Kingdom. The placements are financed from the Unemployment Fund, and there are currently around 7,000-8,000 working places, although there is an intention to increase the number of places to about 25,000. The scheme thus assists about 2 percent of the long-term unemployed.

The regional programs have mainly been targeted at the areas worst hit by mining closures and have had the objective of creating new jobs by encouraging new developments and by public works in construction and infrastructure. It is estimated that in total about 8,000 new jobs have been created on the basis of funds provided by this program, with about the same number placed in retraining schemes.

Both these schemes are targeted at sectors of the economy where unemployment is most severe, but clearly their scale of operation is at present too small to play an important role in reducing unemployment.

Conclusions

Our discussion suggests that the main factor behind the exceptionally sharp decline in output and employment in Bulgaria has been the exceptional severity of the initial shocks. Bulgaria had made virtually no moves toward domestic liberalization and had relatively little trade with the West prior to 1989. Its inheritance also included enormous hard currency debts, accelerating inflation, and macroeconomic instability.

The recovery from this disastrous starting point would clearly have been difficult under any circumstances. Without the "big bang" reforms of February 1991, the Bulgarian economy might well have gone down the same route as that of the Ukraine, with spiraling inflation, a collapse of output, and widespread shortages. The progress of economic reform has nonetheless been disappointing, and Bulgaria has lagged behind other transitional economies. The main reason is that exports to the West, which have been an important engine of growth for many countries, have not grown comparably in Bulgaria because of its location and the disruption of trade routes caused by war in the former Yugoslavia.

The key constraint on economic expansion in Bulgaria is thus the balance of payments. An improvement in Bulgaria's trading position depends largely on events outside its borders, both to the West (Serbia) and to the East (the Ukraine and Russia). In the meantime Western countries and international organizations can alleviate the problem by reducing tariff and quota barriers more rapidly, by rescheduling debt, and by extending foreign currency loans.

Turning to domestic policies, it seems likely that these must operate against a constraint of depressed domestic economic activity as a result of the international trading position. It is notable that despite the depressed state of demand, the economy remains vulnerable to inflationary pressure. State firms remain union-dominated and in the face of adverse shocks have made employment rather than wages bear the brunt of the adjustment. The incomes policy appears to have exhausted its effectiveness, and this points to the need for more rapid privatization as a longer-term means of achieving wage restraint. As in other economies in transition, this in turn entails developing bankruptcy laws and provisions for writing off bad debts. The incomes policy does not, however, appear to have prevented adjustments of relative wages across sectors.

Unemployment has affected all sectors of the economy, and in these circumstances policies to encourage labor mobility are unlikely to yield a high return. Bulgaria has a restrictive unemployment benefits regime and the replacement rate itself is low. This policy has the effect of encouraging job search and maintaining downward pressure on wages. It also prevents the emergence of "benefit dependency," but it leaves a low or nonexistent standard of support for the long-term unemployed. Despite ambitious plans to deal with these groups through targeted active labor market measures, at present the scale of these programs is very small indeed. Clearly, these conditions risk permitting the emergence of serious and large-scale poverty. They may also be conducive to the development of an informal sector.

At the margin, the most effective way of mitigating these problems would be through an expansion of targeted labor market policies such as the temporary employment scheme and the regional employment programs. But such schemes are inevitably costly, and with the resources available can do no more than scratch the surface of the problem. A sustained recovery of employment in Bulgaria depends on a recovery of export growth and on more determined domestic policies to accelerate privatization.

Appendix
A Model of Supply Shocks

This appendix develops a simple model to examine the response of a worker-controlled, state-owned enterprise (SOE) to an aggregate supply shock. The supply shock takes the form of a reduction in the quantity of the input available to the enterprise.

The Model

For analytical simplicity the economy is assumed to consist of a large number of identical firms, each producing output (Q) using labor (L) and raw materials/energy (M). Technology is Leontief (fixed coefficients in production), so that the production relationship is described by

$$(5\text{-}1) \qquad\qquad Q = \min[aL, bM].$$

The firms are assumed subject to a budget requirement (pricing rule) of the form

$$(5\text{-}2) \qquad\qquad pQ = (1 + k)wL + p_M M$$

where p is the output price, p_M the price of the input, w is the wage, and k is the markup of value added on labor costs. Taking k as given, equation 5-2 can be rewritten as an expression for the wage

$$(5\text{-}3) \qquad\qquad w = (pQ - p_M M)/(1 + k)L$$

or

$$w/p = (Q - rM)/(1 + k)L$$

where w/p is the real product wage and r ($= p_M/p$) is the relative price of energy or raw materials.

We next examine the choice over wages and employment of a worker-controlled SOE subject to the budget constraint equation 5-3. We consider two possible objectives for the union. The first is the standard utilitarian or rent-maximizing assumption $V = L((w/p) - A)$, where A is the worker's expected income outside the firm (which includes but does not consist exclusively of, unemployment benefits). The second is where the union gives greater weight to protecting jobs, which in the present context may be represented as an objective of maximizing w/p subject to a constraint $L > L_{-1}(1 - s)$, where s is the voluntary separation rate.

RENT-MAXIMIZING UNION.   Formally the union objective is to maximize

$$V = L((w/p) - A)$$

subject to the budget constraint equation 5-3 and the inequalities

$$Q < (or =)aL \text{ and } Q < (or =) bM.$$

A reduction in raw material or energy supplies can be represented by the imposition of a further constraint $M < (or =)M^*$.

Using the value of the real wage from equation 5-3 in the expression for V gives

(5-4) $$V = (Q - rM)/(1 + k) - AL.$$

Maximization of equation 5-4 subject to the inequalities set out above yields a solution in which all the inequalities are binding:

$$Q = aL = bM \text{ and } M = M^*.$$

The intuition is that if workers have raw materials and energy to work with, their contribution to the gross income of union members if they are in work is (w/p), as against an outside income of A. But if they have no raw materials or energy to work with, their contribution to gross income if they are in work is zero, while the outside income is still A. With $w/p > A > 0$, the union will want to employ people only insofar as they have other inputs available. Hence output and employment will vary in exact proportion with input supplies.

If the objective is to maintain employment, it follows that, with employment given, the real wage must also fall in the same proportion. It is easy to check from equation 5-3 that, with the technological coefficient b, the relative material price r, the markup k, and the labor force L all assumed fixed, it follows directly that the real wage is proportional to the volume of material inputs. More generally, if employment falls as a result of attrition or the detachment of secondary workers, the wage will fall by the extent to which the fall in material inputs exceeds the fall in employment (equation 5-3).

Under either assumption, the impact on labor productivity is the same as the effect on the real wage. Productivity, Q/L, is equal to bM/L, and hence varies as (M/L) varies as, in this case, does the real wage.

CASE (II): INCREASE IN RELATIVE PRICE. In the second case there is assumed to be an increase in the relative price (r) of the input, but the input is available in unlimited amounts at the higher price.

If the objective is to maintain employment, the firm will maintain its previous level of material input, and hence also its output, provided only that value added in the enterprise remains positive $(b > r)$. (Each unit produced contributes to net revenue and hence to the wage bill, so that with a given number of workers it increases the wage per worker.) If value added becomes negative, the firm will stop producing anything.

In the rent-maximizing case, the firm will again either continue its existing level of production or close down altogether. Since material inputs can be adjusted along with the level of employment, the real wage is constant independent of employment, so that as long as the real wage is greater than the outside income, employment will be maintained.

Bibliography

Jones, D. C., and T. Kato. 1993. "The Nature and Determinants of Labor Market Transitions in Former Socialist Economies: Evidence from Bulgaria." Working Paper 93/5, Department of Economics, Hamilton College, New York.

OECD. 1992. *Employment Outlook*. Paris.

6

Romania

John S. Earle and Gheorghe Oprescu

The purpose of this chapter is to describe and try to account for major developments in the aggregate Romanian labor market since the transition began in early 1990. We are concerned with the behavior of the levels and dynamics of aggregate labor market variables—such as wages, employment, and unemployment—and with the impact of external shocks and of macroeconomic, structural, and labor market policies upon them. Disentangling the effects of these many influences is difficult, not only because the changes are so large and so diverse, but also because new institutions are only gradually taking shape, and the behavior of both firms and individuals is still heavily conditioned by the hypercentralized management of the economy in the past. Our goal is to assess the

We thank the World Bank and the Central European University Privatization Project for financial and logistical support. John Earle was supported by a grant from the National Council for Soviet and East European Research. Cooperation was extended by the Romanian Ministry of Labor and Social Protection, particularly Minister Dan Mircea Popescu, Constantin Alecu, and Laurentiu Ungureanu. Participants in World Bank conferences in Stirin, the Czech Republic, and Washington, D.C., especially our discussants Simon Commander and Alan Gelb, made detailed and valuable comments on early drafts. For dedicated assistance with data-gathering and computations, we thank Sorana Baciu, Tatiana Nemeth, Catalin Pauna, Doina Rachita, Nicusor Ruiu, Dana Sapatoru, Ioan Stefan, Irina Vantu, and especially Simona Spiridon. We bear responsibility for any errors.

degree to which genuine restructuring has begun to take place in the Romanian economy and to provide some evaluation of the policies and institutions that are critical to the adjustment process.

In some ways, labor market behavior in Romania has many similarities with that of other transition economies. State sector employment, particularly in industry, has declined significantly, while both private sector employment and unemployment have risen. The adjustments are much smaller than the sharp plunge in output, so output per worker has also plummeted. Prices have risen more than nominal wages, so real earnings are down.

Yet there are also a number of unusual features. Unemployment has risen more than employment has fallen, so the labor force participation rate has risen, rather than falling as in most of the rest of the region. The adjustments in average hours of work have been nearly as great as those in employment, which also implies that the reported plunges in productivity and real wages are exaggerated. Consumer prices rose less than producer prices over most of the period, so the real consumption wage fell less than the real product wage. Although the labor force has increased, most of the unemployed are experienced workers who have suffered from mass layoffs, and relatively few are new or reentrants to the labor force. The private sector grows moderately and even the state sector engages in gross hiring, yet it is puzzling that posted vacancies have remained consistently negligible.

The aggregate behavior, moreover, conceals substantial variation at a more disaggregated level, consideration of which is both intrinsically interesting and useful for understanding the aggregate patterns. We characterize the state sector as divided into two parts: a "sheltered," or "favored," sector and an "exposed," or "disfavored," sector. Our hypothesis is that the favored sector receives preferential treatment from the state in a wide variety of forms: essentially, budget constraints are still soft in this sector. Meanwhile, the disfavored sector faces hard budget constraints and heavy taxation, both directly and through inflation. The line between the two types of firms is often not cleanly drawn in the data, but we use a number of partial proxies for it, such as property form, branch of industry, subsidies and credits (insofar as we can measure them), violation of the wage policy, and so forth. We find this approach useful in explaining the variations in employment and wage behavior and some of the dynamics of the macroeconomy. We conclude, for instance, that patterns of layoffs across branches may be associated more closely with variations in the softness of budget constraints than with the size of external shocks. Our framework also yields predictions about the future course of Romanian unemployment.

The "Aggregate Labor Market Developments" section documents the important stylized facts of the aggregate Romanian labor market in transition, which together constitute the *explicandum* of this chapter. Subsequent sections then consider the factors that may account for these developments, and also examine them in more detail and at more disaggregated levels. The first of these sections, "Exogenous Factors," briefly discusses factors external to the labor market—the communist legacy and the macroeconomic and structural developments of the past few years—that could have had significant impacts upon them. Our most important finding is that large-scale labor reallocation appears to be necessary, yet the current structural policies seem to be ineffectual in bringing this about.

The next section focuses on wage determination, trying to explain the magnitude and composition of wage adjustments in the state sector, including their interrelation with price movements. We find that the divergent behavior of producer and consumer prices in 1990-92 allowed the Romanian economy to avoid both large falls in real consumption wages (living standards) and large rises in real product wages (labor costs), thus averting the otherwise necessary tradeoffs among wages, profits, and employment. In 1993 the situation reversed, and Romania currently faces a very difficult set of choices. After briefly surveying the ever-changing wage policies and the still-developing collective bargaining institutions, we examine the interindustry variation in wages and some of their determinants.

Employment adjustment and labor mobility is the topic of the section that follows. We provide a detailed analysis of mobility into and out of the state sector, demonstrating that the nature of the adjustment has changed over time, from reducing employment through attrition to active laying off of workers. There are sizable interindustry differences in the extent of labor adjustment; we estimate the importance of various determinants for a sample of disaggregated subbranches of industry. This section also presents the available evidence on employment in the private sector and our evaluation of the "push" and "pull" factors in the labor reallocation process.

The sixth section is concerned with unemployment and its dynamics. Unemployment in Romania is a low-turnover, long-duration phenomenon, but with a great deal of heterogeneity. An analysis of the results of a 1 percent sample survey of the registered unemployed (SRU) conducted by the CEU Privatization Project extends our understanding of the intersectoral differences in the restructuring process in Romania. We evaluate the determinants of unemployment duration with a cross-section analysis by local labor office, which allows the relevance of the office caseload and a number of other variables to be tested. The statistically significant result that higher duration is negatively associated with labor office staffing, holding constant a number of other variables likely to affect duration, provides some evidence for the claim that more resources could be productively invested in active labor market policies. The final section contains concluding remarks about policy design, as well as our conjectures about the future course of wages, employment, and unemployment in Romania.

Aggregate Labor Market Developments

Figure 6-1 summarizes the changing labor force status of the Romanian working-age population from 1989 to the end of 1992. The labor force participation rate (LFPR) has risen quite significantly, from 80.4 percent in 1989 to 85.2 in 1992, both because of an increase in the labor force and because the population declined over this period.[1] Most of the increase was accounted for by women, whose LFPR rose dramatically from 76.2 to 85.2, the same rate as that for men.

The increase occurred despite a temporary reduction in the retirement age during a six-month period in 1990, the amount depending on years of experience. As shown on the figure, the average number of retired persons increased by about 450,000 in 1991 over 1990. But data on labor force participation by age group are available only from the population census in 1992 and do not exist as time series. Thus it is not possible to assess fully the degree to which the 1990 policy affected participation.

The figure distinguishes three categories of employment—state, cooperative, and private—to capture the development of the economic restructuring process fundamental to the transition: the decline of the

---

1.   Working-age population is defined as ages 16-59 for men and ages 16-54 for women, plus the subsequent 5 years for members of either sex working in agriculture. By this definition, population fell from 13.61 million in 1989 to 13.36 million in 1992.

Figure 6-1. Labor Force Status, End of Year, 1989-92

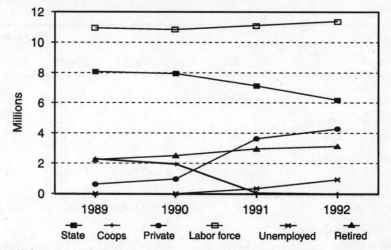

Note: All data are end-of-year, except retired, which are average over each year.
Source: CNS.

state and "pseudocooperatives" and the rise of the private sector. State sector employment has declined by about 25 percent, cooperatives have practically disappeared from the statistics, and the private sector has grown almost commensurately. The most important, although far from the only, factor in explaining these developments is the breakup of cooperatives in agriculture. Besides the privatization of about 40 percent of state trade, ownership changes in other sectors have so far been nugatory. These developments are discussed below, together with the other process of large-scale restructuring, the interindustry movement of workers.

Finally, the figure shows the rise in registered unemployment, which was particularly rapid in 1992. By the end of 1993, which is not shown on the figure because of the unavailability of the other series, the unemployment rate had just topped 10 percent. Posted vacancies are also not shown, in this case because they would be indistinguishable from zero on the scale of the figure. The unemployment-vacancy ratio has hovered in the range of 150-200 to one, despite the large movements of workers among sectors and the legal requirement for vacancy posting.

The movements of employment have been large, but the decline in the number of workers in the state sector has significantly lagged the drop in output. Table 6-1 displays the time path of industrial production and employment from 1989 to 1992. Output fell by 54 percent over this period,

Table 6-1. Measuring Productivity Decline in Romanian Industry, 1989-92

Indicator	1989	1990	1991	1992	Percent change 1989-92
Industrial production index	100.0	76.3	58.9	44.6	−54.0
Average number of workers (thd.)	3,339.3	3,387.4	3,161.3	2,763.1	−17.3
Total hours worked (mln.)	6,970.2	5,891.2	5,048.1	4,176.0	−40.1
Average annual hours of work	2,087.3	1,739.2	1,596.8	1,511.4	−27.6
Industrial production per worker	100.0	75.2	62.2	55.6	−44.4
Industrial production per hour worked	100.0	90.3	81.3	76.8	−23.2

Note: Employment and hours data refer only to workers in the state and cooperative sectors because consistent estimates for private sector employment are unavailable. The industrial production index, however, is an estimate of total output, including production originating in the private sector.
Source: CNS and authors' calculations.

while employment fell by only 17 percent, although the rate of decrease in employment is increasing (in absolute value).[2] Nevertheless, average hours of work have declined quite precipitously, from 2,087 in 1989 to 1,511 in 1992 on an annual basis. Most of this 28 percent decline occurred in 1990, when Saturday work was abolished in most enterprises, but the decline continued in 1991 and 1992.

---

2. The industrial production series used here is the "unadjusted" measure from the National Commission for Statistics (CNS). The more commonly employed index "adjusts" measured output for changes in working time. But such changes, as we will see below, have been quite significant and should be explicitly taken into account. The industrial production series includes the small contribution of the private sector, while the employment estimates do not (since private sector employment estimates by branch are available only end-of-year, rather than average over the year), but this implies a still greater discrepancy between the big drop in output and the smaller decline in employment.

The consequence is that the measurement of productivity decline is quite sensitive to the definition of labor input that is employed: output per worker fell 44 percent, but output per hour of work fell by only 23 percent. Adjustments have taken place along a dimension of labor input (amount of time) other than that which tends to receive most attention (number of workers).

Taking into account hours of work also has consequences for the measurement of the evolution of wage rates. Published wage rates in Romania, as throughout Eastern Europe, pertain to monthly wages, but if working time has changed then the path of hourly wages may diverge significantly. Figure 6-2 shows real monthly wages (MW/C and MW/P) and real hourly wages (HW/C and HW/P), defined separately from the point of view of worker and firm for the consumer price index (C) and the producer price index (P), respectively. We have constructed indexes for 1989 to 1993:III, thus capturing the changes during 1990 that are excluded from the official statistics and omitted from most commentaries.[3]

The series display widely varying behavior. Real monthly consumption wages fell by about 30 percent, but real hourly consumption wages actually rose by about 15 percent. The producer price index (PPI) had risen significantly more than the consumer price index (CPI), so the product wage is down much more than the consumption wage. Although the series are too short to permit precise statements, it is interesting that all of them display some cyclicality, with troughs around the beginning of each year and peaks somewhere in the middle. We suggest explanations for these phenomena in the following sections.

Exogenous Factors

Structural Features and Policies

Romania entered the "transition" with particularly disadvantageous initial conditions, which have been extensively explored elsewhere (see World Bank 1992; Montias 1991; Earle and Sapatoru 1993; and OECD

---

3. Unfortunately, hours of work data are unavailable for 1993, so we are able to calculate the hourly series only through the end of 1992. We thank Farid Dhanji and Alan Gelb for the suggestion to look more closely at wage changes during the year 1990. Because the official "real wage index" starts in October 1990, we have pieced together earlier wage and price series to construct a new index.

Figure 6-2. Real Consumption and Product Wages, 1990:I to 1993:III (1989=100)

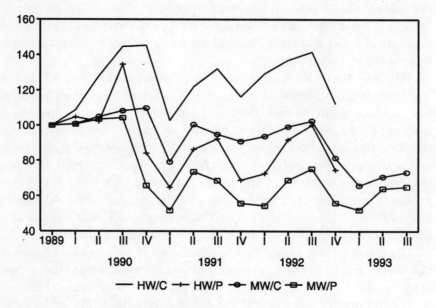

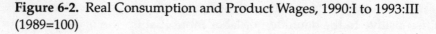

Source: CNS and authors' calculations.

1993). Probably most important among all of these is the profound magnitude of the misallocation of all resources, including labor. Three quantifiable dimensions of this misallocation make the situation plain.

First, the state dominated the economy to an extreme extent, even by Eastern European standards. Virtually all capital was state-owned. By 1985 the share of industrial output of state-owned enterprises reached 95 percent, state and collective farms owned and operated over 80 percent of all agricultural land, and approximately 90 percent of all investment was channeled to the state sector. The economy was administered vertically, from the State Planning Committee (SPC), to ministries, then "centrale" enterprises, and, finally, individual production units. Although a campaign for "bottom-up" planning was launched in the 1980s, allocation of resources was nonetheless arbitrarily dictated from the SPC down the hierarchy. Unlike other Eastern European countries, where financial planning gradually supplanted physical targets during the 1960s and 1970s, Romanian plans continued and were even increasingly elaborated in minute detail, and usually specified units of physical output.[4] Second, the general obsession of socialist countries with industrialization was still more pronounced in Romania, particularly after Ceausescu's accession to power in 1965. From a predominantly agrarian economy between 1950 and 1989, the percent of all fixed assets that were employed in industry rose two-and-a-half times, from 19.5 to 47.5, respectively, while those in services fell by half, from 34.6 to 17.1 percent. Output of light industry steadily declined during the communist period, reflecting the low priority assigned to consumption. A marked devaluation of consumption relative to investment is also apparent from their relative shares in GDP: in 1983, the shares of consumption and investment were 56 percent and 34, respectively. Meanwhile, net exports rose to close to 10 percent of GDP in the late 1980s.[5]

And even within goods production, the bias toward heavy industry was particularly strong, as is demonstrated by table 6-2.[6]

Finally, the Romanian economy was also characterized by an enormous degree of horizontal and vertical integration, and had perhaps the largest average enterprise size in all of Eastern Europe. Table 6-3 shows the remarkable dominance of larger enterprises: firms with more than 2,000 employees accounted for nearly two-thirds of the total number of employees and two-thirds of total industrial production. Less than 1 percent of workers were employed by enterprises with fewer than 200 employees.

---

4.   Most other administratively planned economies employed a much higher proportion of revenue or sales targets, allowing production units a slightly greater degree of flexibility. In Romania, the use of physical output indicators, already unusually common (even for highly centralized socialist regimes), became even more widespread during times of severe shortage.

5.   The low percentage of consumption is probably upwardly biased in the official estimates. The actual share of consumption in GDP may have been as low as 30-35 percent.

6.   The fuel and raw material intensity of Romanian production also increased enormously. One measure is the use of electricity per worker: in industry as a whole, the number of kilowatt hours increased by a factor of almost four from 1960 to 1989 (Comisia Nationala pentru Statistica). "Heavy industry" includes fuels, ferrous and nonferrous metallurgy, machine building, chemicals, and mining of nonferrous ores and abrasives. "Materials" represents building materials, forestry and woodworking, and pulp and paper; while "light industry" includes glass, china, textiles, clothing, leather goods, furs, footwear, food, cosmetics, and other miscellaneous branches.

Table 6-2. Subbranch Structure of Industrial Production in Romania, 1938-89
(percent)

Industrial production by subbranch group	1938	1950	1960	1970	1980	1985	1989
Electric and thermic power	1.1	1.9	2.5	3.2	1.8	3.5	3.9
Heavy industry	36.5	35.3	47.9	52.4	59.3	60.7	59.3
Materials	11.9	13.6	11.7	11.2	8.9	8.4	8.7
Light industry	50.5	49.2	37.9	33.2	30.0	27.4	28.1
Total	100	100	100	100	100	100	100

Source: CNS and Earle and Sapatoru 1993.

We argue that the legacy of this misallocation is a critical factor in the difficulties Romania faces in the transition, including the need to reallocate labor across sectors, branches, occupations, and regions. That in Romania there is a larger stock adjustment to be made might seem to militate in favor of the presumption that initial growth should be rapid, and the new private sector has indeed grown rapidly, particularly in trade; but the reallocation problem is obviously much more difficult in the capital-intensive sectors.

Given the severe structural problems that the Romanian transition must overcome, it is worthwhile analyzing the implications of the most important kind of structural policy—privatization. Although few results have been achieved so far, the Romanian large privatization program, at least as delineated in the Privatization Law, seems to promise rapid ownership transfer of a large part of the capital stock. The large privatization program involves two main components: a "free distribution" of 30 percent of the shares in all the enterprises scheduled to be privatized and the "subsequent sale of shares" of the remaining 70 percent held by the state in the form of a State Ownership Fund (SOF). The 30 percent in each company is distributed to one of five Private Ownership Funds (POFs), state-created intermediaries technically owned by all adult Romanian citizens to whom the state issued special certificates of ownership. In the process of corporatization, the number of enterprises has been nearly tripled, implying that the problem of excessive concentration may be on the way to being solved.

Table 6-3. Size Distribution of Industrial Enterprises in Romania, 1990

Size of enterprise (number of employees)	Enterprises		Employees		Production (percent share)
	Number	Percent share	Number	Percent share	
Less than 200	169	7.6	24,288	0.7	1.9
201-500	456	20.3	162,505	4.4	5.2
501-1,000	538	24.0	391,386	10.6	10.7
1,001-2,000	515	23.0	723,116	19.5	18.9
2,001-3,000	245	10.9	592,538	16.0	14.3
3,001-5,000	197	8.8	768,760	20.8	20.6
Over 5,000	121	5.4	1,039,263	28.0	28.4
Total	2,241	100	3,701,856	100.0	100.0

Source: CNS and Earle and Sapatoru 1993.

Nonetheless, the program faces several difficult problems, a few of which we may briefly summarize here (see Earle and Sapatoru 1993, 1994 for a detailed analysis of the Romanian program). First, despite its mass character (transfers to the POFs), it relies heavily on the success of future sales (by the SOF). Yet nowhere have sales been successful as a method for rapid privatization, and Romania's experience so far has proven no exception.[7] Second, since the 70 percent stake remains in the hands of the State Ownership Fund, control rights over the companies will have been privatized only when most of those shares have been sold. In a sense,

7.   Although the SOF was supposed to sell at least 10 percent of its holdings every year, it did not succeed in selling any shares at all in the first year of its existence, except for the management and employee buyout program for small companies. The principal large privatization transactions in Romania are to be found in the so-called "early privatization program," wherein only twenty-two companies were privatized, a disappointing result. The program was initially viewed as a potential vehicle for a privatization of a much larger number of companies, and it was expected that many different methods of privatization would be explored. In the event, fifteen of the twenty-two companies were privatized entirely, and four partially, through insider buyouts; five companies were privatized partially or completely through sales to foreigners; and two were partly privatized by public offerings. As in the other countries of the region, privatization sales to foreigners account for only a small portion of total foreign investment. And even this small number of sales has been subject to extensive criticism, in one case leading to the recent cancellation of one of the largest foreign investments in Romania.

even the POF shares are not really privatized, given the limited control rights of the citizen-holders of certificates of ownership.[8] Third, the program leaves a large proportion of the economy, around 45 percent of the capital stock according to some rough estimates, in the hands of the state. These *regii autonome* include many (although by no means all) of the wasteful dinosaurs of heavy industry. Thus, the Romanian privatization program does not seem likely to lead to rapid restructuring.

Finally, although evidence is scant (we present some later), there is reason to believe that hard budget constraints have yet to be imposed on all enterprises; we believe this observation applies particularly (although hardly exclusively) to the *regii autonome*. The forms of support may be several: direct subsidies of various types, overvalued exchange rates, soft credits, negative real interest rates, periodic clearing of enterprise arrears, centralized allocation of some inputs,[9] and other special preferences of an uncountable number and type. What is interesting for our analysis is that the pattern of favoritism displayed toward particular branches and particular enterprises is not entirely dissimilar to that of the communist years, if perhaps motivated by somewhat different reasons. Under Ceausescu, heavy industry was an integral part of the peculiar ideology of development, and it was supposed to bring prestige and export earnings. Now, the reasons seem to be purely political: the priority sectors of the past have become the powerful vested interests of the present.

Macroeconomic Policies and Developments

Romania entered 1990 with a large monetary overhang and a recession that was already at least two years old. During 1990 the decline may have been partly the result of the dismantling of the central planning coordination and the collapse of the political order of the old authoritarian regime.

The drive to reduce foreign debt and the pursuit of several prestige "investment" projects resulted in a significant reduction in the Romanian standard of living during the 1980s, and several populist measures—such as reduction of the work week, state-financed imports of consumer

---

8. The particular problems of the corporate governance and the roles to be played by the POFs are analyzed in Earle and Sapatoru 1994.
9. The Ministry of Industry still maintains "material balances" and establishes some quotas for power sources.

Table 6-4. Main Macroeconomic Indicators

Indicator	1989	1990	1991	1992	November 1993
GDP					
Current prices (lei bln)	800.0	857.9	2,198.9	5,982.3	—
Real GNP	100	92.6	79.9	67.9	—
Unemployment					
Total (thousands)	—	—	265.9	929.0	1,132.7
Rate (percent)	—	—	3.0	8.4	9.9
Industrial production	100	76.3	58.9	46.0	48.6
CPI	100	130.6	274.4	851.7	4,009.2[a]
PPI	100	126.5	450.1	1,313.1	4,196.6[b]
Trade balance ($ mln)	+2,519.6	−1,720.4	−1,345.0	−938.0	−662.6[c]
Exports	5,990.1	3,502.7	3,519.8	4,018.6	4,077.9
Imports	3,470.5	5,223.1	4,864.8	4,956.6	4,740.5
Broad money (lei bln)	547.8	612.3	1,024.7	1,856.1	3,624.7[d]
Foreign debt ($ mln, end of year)	174	230	1,143	2,354	2,994[e]
IMF credits	0	0	809	1,032	1,047

a. September 1993.
b. September 1993. Beginning January 1993, PPI covers production for export as well as for domestic consumption.
c. January-November 1993.
d. October 1993.
e. June 1993.
Source: National Commission of Statistics and National Bank of Romania.

goods, and the allocation of more energy to the population and away from industry—were implemented in 1990.

The continuing output fall after 1990 probably has several causes, among them both aggregate and sector-specific shocks. OECD (1993) places major emphasis on the energy price shock resulting from the breakup of the CMEA and the move to world prices, combined with a decline in domestic production and the continued administrative allocation by the Ministry of Industry of these scarce inputs. Other shocks included import competition—especially in wood, textiles, and food—the Gulf War, and the embargo of Yugoslavia. Our calculation of the variation of output changes across twenty-five industrial sectors indicates that the decline has been remarkably uniform: the standard deviation was 9.8 in 1990, falling to 9.0 in 1991, and rising to 11.7 in 1992.[10] Furthermore, there has been little correlation with price movements: in all three years the coefficient is small and insignificant, and it was negative in 1991. Although industrial output stabilized, at least temporarily, in 1993, it is questionable whether this represents "recovery" in the sense of growth, or merely a soft budget constraint policy that runs counter to the structural reform, and therefore to long-run growth (elaborated in Earle 1993b).

Meanwhile, inflation has skyrocketed. By September 1993, the CPI was more than 40 times above its 1989 level, with the fastest rise in food items. As noted in the previous section, the PPI increased much more than the CPI in 1990-92, and it stood at forty-two times its 1989 level in September 1993. The CPI largely caught up in mid-1993, and the future course is difficult to predict. The relationship between the two series may be partially explained by the price liberalization policy, whereby consumer prices were held down and subsidized and only freed in stages. Many producer prices, however, were also not free for most of the period, and most of them were frozen from March to September 1992.

Together with a fairly loose fiscal policy,[11] the step-by-step pattern of liberalization probably contributed to inflation through the buildup of inflationary expectations. Monetary policy, by contrast, was successful in reducing the monetary aggregates targeted by IMF agreements. Nonetheless, it was inconsistent, generally tight in the first half of each year, while much looser toward the end. The exchange rate policy, which has changed stance repeatedly, has also contributed to the deterioration of the credibility of the leu. Finally, it is our judgment that labor market factors play a role in Romania's inflation—moreover, one that is likely to increase, as we explain below.

---

10. Borensztein, Demekas, and Ostry (1993) also find little evidence of structural change, in examining data for Romania in 1990 and 1991.

11. Although the official budget deficit was only 1 percent of GDP in 1992, the World Bank (1993) finds that including a number of off-budget items and adjusting the accounts for inflation yields a "real deficit" of 21.6 percent.

Wage Determination

Aggregate Wage Behavior

As shown in figure 6-2, above, there are three important stylized facts about the course of real wages in Romania since 1989. First, average real hourly earnings behave quite differently from average real monthly earnings because of the large changes in hours of work. Second, the divergence of the CPI from the PPI implies that the evolution of real wages has appeared quite differently from the perspective of the worker compared with that of the firm. Third, all the series exhibit substantial and regular fluctuations, increasing early each year and declining toward the end. This section investigates these empirical regularities more closely and examines the effects that changes in policies and institutions concerning wage determination may have had on the observed wage behavior.

Figure 6-3 decomposes the real wage into separate series for nominal monthly and hourly wages (*MW* and *HW*, respectively), and for consumer and producer prices (CPI and PPI, respectively). Evidently the annual cycle in the real wage series may be attributed to larger increases in wages relative to prices ("*w>p*" in the figure) early in the year, and larger increases in prices relative to wages ("*p>w*" in the figure) later in the year. The causality of the relationship is undoubtedly difficult to establish, the time series are far too short to allow precise statements, and the timing of price policies certainly also plays an important role, but it seems clear that wage inflation and price inflation are feeding into each other in an inflationary spiral.

Furthermore, it is interesting, and easily seen from the figure, that wage inflation has been significantly more volatile than price inflation. Aside from the big jump of the PPI at the end of 1990, both price indexes have increased rather smoothly, at least in comparison with the volatility of nominal wages. The standard deviation of quarterly changes in *MW* is 23.3, for *HW* it is 21.1, but for the CPI it is only 16.6, and for the PPI (excluding 1990:IV) it is 19.4.

Information about the contribution of labor market factors to inflation from the cost side is contained in table 6-5, which reports the change in real unit labor cost (ULC), defined as the ratio of the hourly product wage to hourly productivity, as well as its decomposition into all of its compo-

Figure 6-3. Quarterly Wage and Price Inflation, 1990:I to 1993:III
(percent change over previous quarter)

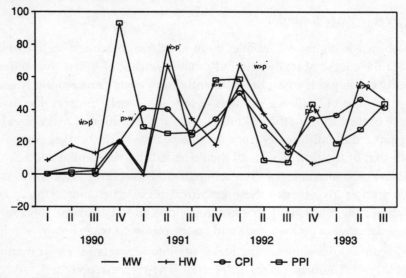

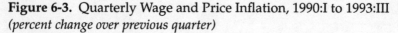

Source: CNS and authors' calculations.

nents.[12] The ULC rose 17 percent in 1990, fell 11 percent in 1991, and again rose 8 percent in 1992 and 16 percent in 1993 (to the month of September).

The components of the ULC are displayed with the arithmetic sign of their contribution to changes in the unit labor cost. Thus, the real hourly consumption wage and the ratio of consumer to producer prices enter positively, while the change in productivity enters negatively. In 1990 the factors pushing up the ULC were the 25 percent rise in real hourly wages and the 23 percent fall in output, while factors reducing the increase were the 17 percent greater rise of the PPI over the CPI and the 17 percent reduction in average hours of work. In 1991 the situation was quite different, primarily because of the 6 percent fall in the real hourly consumption wage and fewer adjustments in hours of work, with the result that the ULC fell 11 percent. In 1992 real hourly earnings were up again,

---

12. We thank Simon Commander for the suggestion to perform a decomposition of unit labor costs. A similar decomposition, but not taking into account changes in hours of work, is done for Poland in Berg and Blanchard (1994), and for Bulgaria, Czechoslovakia, Hungary, and Poland in Blanchard, Commander, and Coricelli, in this volume.

Table 6-5. Decomposition of Unit Labor Cost in Industry

Item	1990	1991	1992	September 1993
Percent change in unit labor cost	17	–11	8	16
Percent change in real hourly consumption wage	25	–6	5	–17
+ Percent change in CPI/PPI	–17	–15	–3	40
– Percent change in labor productivity	9	10	6	–7
Percent change in industrial output	23	23	22	–2
Percent change in hours worked	–15	–14	–17	—
Percent change in number of workers	2	–6	–12	–4
Percent change in average hours of work	–17	–8	–5	—

Note: Each component is measured as its contribution to the change in the ULC. For example, industrial production fell in all three of these years, thus its contribution to the ULC was positive. Starting January 1993, the PPI includes production for exports as well as the domestic market. Hours of work data are unavailable in 1993, so we have calculated the 1992-September 1993 changes in wages on a monthly basis, and those in productivity on a per-worker basis.
Source: CNS and authors' calculations.

although only by 5 percent, and the CPI increased nearly as fast as the PPI, resulting in an 8 percent rise in the ULC.

The year 1993 witnessed a completely new scenario. The ULC rose sharply by 16 percent, but this occurred in spite of two countervailing developments: a significant fall in the consumption wage and a rise in productivity associated with an increase in output and decrease in employment. These factors, which by themselves would have decreased the ULC, were more than fully offset by a 40 percent increase in the CPI relative to the PPI, close to eliminating the gap in the two indexes that had built up over three years.

This analysis may also help to explain the low proportion of wages in value added. For both 1991 and 1992, the total wage bill of industrial enterprises was about 41 percent of their gross value added. Profits, meanwhile, were about 19 percent. Unfortunately, no reliable disaggregations are available. But it seems clear that the faster rise of the PPI compared with the CPI may have been an important factor in the ability of Romanian producers to hold up profits. If profits fell in 1993, this would be evidence for our hypothesis, but unfortunately these data are not yet available. This has the further implication that profits taxes—one of the primary sources of revenue in the state budget—may likely disappear, now that the PPI is falling relative to the CPI.[13]

It is our judgment, therefore, that wage push represented a major shock to producers only in 1990, when workers managed to have their real hourly earnings pushed up by 25 percent. The ability of firms to raise their output prices more than consumer prices in 1990 and 1991, and to some extent in 1992, meant that real wages to workers could be prevented from falling at the same time as real labor costs to producers could be prevented from rising, thus averting the usual tradeoff among wages, profits, and employment. It seems unlikely, however, that such a wedge between changes in consumption and product wages could be long maintained, and we believe that the more rapid rise of the CPI than the PPI in 1993 bodes ill. The battle over a shrinking pie, postponed for several years in Romania, may be now just beginning.[14]

Developments in Policies and Institutions of Wage Determination

Controlling wages was one of the state's top priorities under communism, and the Romanian regime centralized wage determination to an extreme extent.

Many of the characteristics of the communist wage and employment system were abolished in early 1990. Wage rates were raised, pay was no longer tied to performance, restrictions were lifted on eligibility for promotions and bonuses and on internal and external migration, and performance bonds were discontinued. Hours of work were reduced from 46 to 40 a week, with no reduction in monthly wages. The boom in wages and decline in productivity following the partial liberalization of wages and reduction of hours led the government to reimpose controls partially in

---

13. Much of the profits of Romanian enterprises may be illusory anyway, primarily due to FIFO inventory accounting in an inflationary environment. See OECD 1993.

14. Our earlier papers (Earle and Oprescu 1993a,b) contain much more detail about both prereform wage and employment determination and subsequent institutional changes.

April 1990. In the meantime, enterprises had become more bold in evading it; the lack of success in containing wage growth, however, led to a general wage freeze for the latter part of the year.

The new Wage Law 14/1991, passed in February 1991, formally decentralized wage determination, granting all state and privately owned commercial companies, as well as most *regie autonome*, the right to determine their wage structure autonomously through collective or individual negotiations between employees and employers. In addition, the law establishes the government's right to impose wage regulations on state-owned companies, *regie autonome*, and budget-financed institutions, anticipating the possibility that, given complete freedom, they might begin paying employees irresponsibly high wages. Yet at the same time, the new law includes provisions allowing the government to pass indexation and "compensation" regulations, designed to recompense wage earners for the expected decline in real wages because of inflation. In the rest of this section, we discuss the new institutions for collective bargaining, the minimum wage agreement, the government's wage compensation techniques, and the three different incomes policies of 1991, 1992, and 1993.

Unionization is certainly quite high in Romania, although this cannot necessarily be inferred from the claims made by unions concerning the numbers of their members, since the sum of all individual confederation claims substantially exceeds Romania's total active population! But, according to estimates based on an incomplete census carried out in January 1991, the rate was situated around 60 percent of all employees. Collective bargaining coverage is still more widespread than union membership, as shown in table 6-6. The CNS asked all state enterprises in October 1992 whether a "collective contract applies to their employees." More than 90 percent said "yes." Unions are largely nonexistent in the private sector, however, and both unemployment and privatization are expected to affect unionization, although by how much is difficult to forecast. Membership is reportedly decreasing, especially in branches and sectors such as engineering and the chemical and metallurgical industries.

The degree of centralization in the new bargaining institutions is difficult to judge, and is continually evolving. According to the unions, the low minimum membership requirements set in 1991 stimulated the formation of thousands of workers' organizations. Some confederations, however, have been able to significantly consolidate their positions. Of

Table 6-6. Collective Bargaining Coverage, October 1992, Employees of State Enterprises with Collective Contracts

Branch	Employees	Percentage covered
Agriculture	532,281	95.08
Total industry	2,949,294	96.07
Mining	303,421	99.99
Coal	121,488	100.00
Crude petroleum and natural gas	83,378	100.00
Radioactive minerals	7,510	100.00
Metals	65,735	100.00
Nonmetals	25,310	99.90
Manufacturing	2,645,873	95.62
Food, beverages, and tobacco	254,964	97.72
Textiles and apparel	521,351	88.11
Footwear	93,824	94.60
Wood	79,491	98.80
Paper and allied products	51,547	93.49
Coal, oil, and nuclear fuel products	22,586	100.00
Chemical products	159,621	99.00
Rubber and plastic products	58,973	96.00
Glass, pottery, china, etc.	141,757	98.00
Metallurgy	184,405	99.90
Fabricated metal products	142,802	97.50
Machinery and equipment	413,168	97.50
Electrical and optical equipment	144,533	94.11
Transportation equipment	223,810	99.84
Other manufacturing (furniture, etc.)	153,041	94.15
Construction	429,708	95.40
Trade	398,880	92.53
Transportation	441,519	97.32
Telecommunications	92,669	97.50
Education and research	486,878	74.05
Health	303,163	68.30
Administration	128,543	24.70
Total economy	6,174,150	90.80

Source: CNS.

the approximately 20 active union confederations that now exist, uniting over 150 branch organizations, 4 of the largest have emerged as possible leaders in the movement (with the following claimed memberships, respectively): CNSLR (Confederatia Nationala a Sindicatelor Libre din Romania), 2.5 million; Cartel Alfa, 1.2 million; Fratia, 1 million; and BNS (Confederatia Blocul National Sindical), 0.8 million. Two of these, CNSLR and Fratia, merged in May 1993 to form a "superconfederation" that includes sixty-five branch confederations and an announced membership of over 3.7 million, supposedly the largest in southeastern Europe. Although national-level bargaining takes place in a tripartite setting among the confederations of unions, the confederations of employers (a rather weak and ill-defined group), and the government, negotiations are subsequently conducted at the branch and individual firm levels.

While clearly capable of enlisting a relatively large fraction of the work force, unions seem to have been much less successful in mobilizing their members to action. Repeated calls for nationwide strikes—in June of 1991, February of 1992, and, most recently, in May of 1993—ended with only scattered demonstrations. It is therefore difficult to assess the strength of union bargaining power.

Nonetheless, we think that the time pattern of union negotiations provides some explanation for the regularities in wage and price inflation discussed earlier and shown in figure 6-3, in addition to the patterns in the price policies. The national collective contract negotiations are held early each year and the agreement then takes some time to trickle down to the company level, where wage increases are finally realized.[15] It is therefore consistent that we find large increases in nominal wages in the middle of each year. Wage growth is always faster than price growth in the second quarter of each year, and this is also usually true in the third quarter. The contracts are then set for one year; during the time to the next negotiation, prices continue to rise, and they even accelerate in the fourth quarter of each year, perhaps "surprising" the workers. This annual end-of-year inflation bout may arise from a lagged response of prices to the wage increase, it could be the result of the relaxation in monetary policy that has generally occurred at this time of year, or, most likely, the two are related—the wage claims are sanctioned through

15. This pattern has actually differed somewhat each year. The details of this process, and its history, are contained in our earlier paper, (Earle and Oprescu 1993b).

expanded credits. As real wages decline, the "surprised" unions prepare greater demands for the next year, and the process continues.

But nominal wages also continued to rise for most of the year. To explain this phenomenon and to understand better the forces moving wages in Romania, we turn to a brief account of government policies concerning wages.[16]

The rapid price increases in Romania have necessitated indexation of wages to prevent real wages from falling to nothing. At the same time, the indexation feeds back into price inflation. Rather than following a consistent indexation policy, wage indexation coefficients are sporadically calculated, providing supplementary compensation for state employees. Indexation decisions "suggest" that companies index wages "according to their financial resources," using the government's calculations as an upper limit. Automatic and full indexation occurs only in budget-financed institutions and some *regie autonome*, where wages are set by the government.

In addition to the indexation of wages, the government also occasionally "suggests" that state employers add permanent fixed-sum "compensation" to all employee wages.[17] These payments are usually supposed to reimburse 100 percent of the increased cost of staple consumer goods resulting from the withdrawal of production subsidies and are scheduled to correspond with each phase of subsidy withdrawal. They are financed entirely from company budgets and are to be distributed equally to all employees, regardless of wage level.

Table 6-7 lists each individual indexation and compensation regulation. The table does not show the cumulative effects of these measures, but only the additional amount of each increase.

We may summarize the wage policies very briefly as consisting, essentially, of three separate policies in 1991, 1992, and 1993.[18] Each was revised periodically over the course of the year, according to the decisions listed in table 6-7. The 1991 policy established ceilings on the individual wage

---

16. Concerning the minimum wage, no legal minimum has existed in Romania. The minimum wage reached at the national negotiations represents only a kind of indicative floor, and it is possible to pay less.

17. The government also pays compensation to pensioners out of a social security fund to which companies contribute.

18. This discussion ignores many aspects of the policies. Again, we refer the interested reader to our earlier paper, Earle and Oprescu 1993b, Croitoru 1992, or Fox and Bogetic 1993.

received by each worker based on an itemized list of job categories much like the ones employed under the communist wage determination system. Any wage paid to any individual above the ceiling was subject to a tax, calculated according to fixed rates (between 40 and 60 percent) applied to the difference between the ceiling "norms" and the actual amounts paid.

Table 6-7. Compensation and Indexation of Wages, 1990 to December 1993

Date	Compensation (lump sum)	Indexation (lump sum)	Indexation (percent increase)
11/90	975		
4/91	1,300	1,525	
4/91			60[a]
9/91			13.43
11/91			12.5
1/92			25%*RWB[b]
3/92			26%*RWB
3/92			40.5%*RWB[c]
5/92	1,790		7.8[d]
5/92			20[a]
9/92	1,100	2,650	
11/92		5,250	
1/93		3,450[a]	3,450/AW[e,f]
3/93		2,500[a]	2,500/AW[f]
5/93	10,160		6.8[a]
			3,000/AW[f]
6/93		2,800[a]	2,800/AW[f]
8/93			24[a]
			13,200/AW[f]
9/93		16,245[f]	22.2[a]
12/93		4,800[f]	6.5[a]

a. Only for budgetary institutions, individual wages.
b. Reference Wage Bill, October 1991.
c. End of March.
d. Total: 65%*RWB.
e. AW = average wage.
f. For commercial companies.
Source: Government decrees 1109/1990, 219/1991, 579/1991, 780/1991, 120/1992, 149/1992, 218/1992, 774/1992, 94/1993, 124/1993, 177/1993, 299/1993.

In 1992 the individual wage ceilings were replaced with a ceiling on the wage bill of each company. The calculation of the ceiling was quite complex and also revised upward periodically. Companies expanding their production were allowed to increase their wage bill in proportion to the number of new workers they hired, thus turning the policy into an average wage rather than wage bill policy for these companies on the upside. Other exceptions were also allowed, and they were vague enough to make one question the degree to which the policy could be enforced. The penalty taxes were more stringent (varying up to 500 percent, for increasing the wage bill more than 20 percent above the norm), although not necessarily more rigorously enforced, than those in 1991. It was also possible to save up "unused norms," which could be exercised later.

In early 1993 no wage policy was in effect, and unions negotiated large increases. The policy established in May 1993 was essentially an average wage policy, because the norms were calculated by dividing the wage bill by the number of employees. Taxes, however, are assessed on excessive increases in the wage bill according to the same rate schedule as in 1992. The norm could again be increased according to several indicators, for the most part concerned with increasing profits or efficiency.

Has the wage policy been enforced? The response from the Ministry of Finance is a firm assent, but also a refusal to provide any data on the amount of penalty taxes actually paid. Such data are available from the National Commission of Statistics, but the reported amounts are rather trivial on average. According to these data, *regii autonome* in industry paid 3.6 percent of the wage bill in the first half of 1991 and 0.8 percent in the second, while state-owned commercial companies paid 1.1 and 0.5 percent, respectively. In the first half of 1992, a somewhat different breakdown is available, from which we may glean that 0.8 percent of the total wage bill was paid in penalty taxes by *regii autonome*, and 0.1 percent by commercial companies, while 0.3 percent was paid both in industry and in agriculture. In the second half of the year, yet another breakdown is available, containing none of the aggregates, but allowing some comparisons for individual branches. The branch of processing of coal, oil, and nuclear fuel chemical products paid a penalty representing 31.7 percent of their total wage bill during the second semester of 1992, but only 3.2 percent during the first semester. This might be attributed to the implicit subsidization of exported goods produced from imports because of the "freezing" of the exchange rate at a grossly overvalued level during the second half of 1992. Also, for the same period, crude petroleum and natural gas extraction paid 14 percent of the wage bill as penalties, as compared with a significant, but lower, 6.3 percent in the first semester; the reason could be the determination of the authorities to build up the reserves for winter using subsidized credit. In any case, the amounts are generally quite small.

The low tax revenues suggest that the ceilings were perhaps not binding on wage behavior. In the next section, we examine some data on actual wages paid in 1991—by branch, property form, and occupation—which allows us to evaluate the extent to which the policy was binding and the degree to which it was enforced.[19]

Interindustry Differences in Wage Behavior

Table 6-8 displays the evolution of relative wages from October 1990 to September 1993. This breakdown is, unfortunately, the most detailed available over this period. It is incompatible with our analysis of employment and production, as well as with much of our other information about industry characteristics. Nonetheless, it makes some of the empirical regularities plain.

Wages are highest in several heavy industry branches—mining, metallurgy, and chemical manufacturing—and in utilities (mostly electricity generation) and transportation. These "wage leaders" were not only better off in 1990, they have since widened the wage gap. By contrast, services and light industry have remained poorly paid. The standard deviation of interindustry wage differentials has more than doubled, from 15.8 to 33.6, over the three-year period, but the rank order of industries has remained nearly the same.

Because of the inconsistency between the wage data classification system and that in most of the rest of our data, we offer only some impressionistic words here to account for the interindustry differences. First, it is evident that the branches that were favored under communism have continued to receive relatively high wages during the "transition," even widening the gap with the others. Second, the branches with the highest

19. Our earlier paper, Earle and Oprescu 1993b, and Spiridon 1993a,b examined changes in the composition of labor compensation, and concluded that the composition shifted to types of payment that are either untaxed or taxed at lower rates; thus, the wage policy was evaded in this way as well.

Table 6-8. Evolution of Wage Differentials, by Branches and Subbranches, 1990-93

Branch	October 1990	Average 1991	Average 1992	September 1993
All-branch average	100	100	100	100
Industry	95	99	99	102
Extractive	129	148	161	170
Coal mining	132	162	164	169
Crude petroleum and natural gas	120	132	153	192
Manufacturing	93	94	93	91
Machinery and equipment	97	96	95	97
Metallurgy	108	113	115	123
Chemical	99	112	119	110
Building materials	92	98	99	93
Wood	82	87	87	81
Light	84	81	71	69
Food, beverage, and tobacco	88	99	99	90
Utilities	114	136	152	153
Agriculture	104	89	83	80
Construction	112	107	106	106
Transportation	117	119	127	113
Trade	77	91	87	73
Hotels and restaurants	78	77	71	77
Education	89	99	92	75
Health	92	106	97	89
Public administration	119	115	103	93
Standard deviation across branches	15.81	20.57	26.40	33.59

Source: CNS and authors' calculations.

levels and rates of growth of wages tend to be those with a significant concentration of *regii autonome*. Mining industries, utilities, and transportation all have well-known *regii*. We were able to obtain some separate information on average wages for state-owned commercial companies

Table 6-9. Average Wages by Property Form, 1991 and 1992

Category	Net average wage, Oct. 1991 (lei)	Net average wage, Sept. 1992 (lei)	Index of real wage, Oct. 91/Sept. 92 (percent)
Romania	9,824	23,306	88.54
Regii autonome	13,382	34,204	95.41
Commercial companies	10,472	21,722	77.42
Budgetary institutions	9,829	22,401	85.07

Note: CPI in September 1992 over October 1990 = 267.9 percent.
Source: Ministry of Labor and Social Protection.

compared with *regii*, as shown in table 6-9. The *regii* have been much more successful than the commercial companies in preventing a drop in real wages.[20]

Third, the levels and growth rates of wages seem to be correlated with union strength; this is difficult to prove in practice, however, because union density data (in table 6-6) show almost uniformly high collective bargaining coverage, but it does not measure the amount of union bargaining power. In this connection, it is important to recognize that, although the "employers" are the putative opponents of the unions at the bargaining table, and many "employers' associations" have formed, in practice they are very weak, and the unions find their true adversary (or partner, as the case may be) in the government. This may seem natural, insofar as the government is the ultimate owner. The government is also not subject to a hard budget constraint, however, and is moreover able to exercise a fair amount of discretion over its treatment of unions in various sectors of the economy, certainly much more so than would an owner interested in the maximization of profits. We believe it possible that the government has exercised just that sort of discretion, and that this would explain much of what one can observe about Romania's labor market and macroeconomic performance.

---

20. It is also unclear to us why the economywide average wage in 1991 should be lower than that for commercial companies. We take these figures as illustrative of the gap, without placing too much emphasis on the exact magnitudes. It is important to note, in addition, that many *regii* pay very high fringe benefits, which further aggravates the wage gap.

Finally, earnings data from September 1991 show that the wage ceilings were exceeded for a large proportion of workers: for instance, 51 percent of unskilled workers received wages above the ceiling. The number of workers in various ranges of earnings is available by occupation, branch, and legal form. In table 6-10, we have tabulated by legal form the percentage of workers in each occupational group specified in the 1991 wage policy whose wages exceeded the ceiling. According to these data over half the unskilled workers' and foremen's wages exceeded the ceilings, while it was close to half for most others (sub-engineers and university graduates, for whom the percentage was around 30, being the chief exceptions). *Regii autonome* and particular sectors of industry—coal mining, chemicals, metallurgy, and energy—as well as railways paid most workers well above their ceilings. Excessive wage payments on such a scale were supposed to be heavily penalized, but we saw earlier that none of these sectors paid more than a few percentage points of their wage bill in penalty taxes.

The implication of this is not only that the wage policy, at least in 1991, was poorly enforced, but that the degree of the enforcement seems to have been uneven, allowing certain favored sectors to advance. The pattern that seems to have developed is one where the wage leaders achieve some sizable increase, which is followed with a lag by price increases and somewhat smaller wage increases in the other branches. It is particularly interesting that the wage leaders seem to be engaging in the least restructuring, as measured by the degree to which they have adjusted employment to changes in output. We turn to this in the next section.

Employment Adjustment and Labor Mobility

Since 1989 we observe significant movements of labor; these changes are disaggregated in table 6-11. Clearly the composition of employment, both by ownership category and by economic branch, has changed: it appears that the decline of the state, "pseudocooperatives," and industry is well under way, while the private sector and the trade and services branches are on the rise. It is also interesting to note the reagrarianization: the proportion of employment in agriculture fell from 74.3 percent in 1950 to 27.9 percent in 1989, but rose again to 33.0 percent in 1992.[21] Nonethe-

---

21. An examination of hours of work would likely reveal an even greater swing toward agriculture. Rose and Haerpfer (1992) found that 61 percent of Romanians report that they, or someone in their household, spend some time each week growing food.

Table 6-10. Proportion of Employees Receiving Wages
above the Ceilings, September 1991
(percent)

Occupation categories[a]	State-owned enterprises			Total economy
	Regii autonome	*Commercial companies*	*Budgetary institutions*	*Total economy*
Workers				
Skilled	50	26	17	31
Unskilled	64	48	30	51
Executives				
University graduates	40	19	20	28
Lycee and other graduates				
Professionals	38	30	22	32
Administrative personnel	42	42	30	42
Sub-engineers	50	26	19	30
Foremen	73	58	31	61
Managers				
Company level	54	49	37	41
Departmental level	50	38	34	49

a. According to G.D. 127/1991.
Source: CNS and authors' calculations.

less, nearly half of employment in trade is still state, and private sector
growth has been modest in most sectors. Thus, although an economywide restructuring process is evidently under way, it has a long way to
go. This section explores the ways in which labor is moving out of (as
well as into) the state sector, estimates the determinants of employment
adjustment for a sample of twenty-five subbranches of industry, and presents the available data on the composition of employment in the private
sector.

Labor Mobility

Probably the single number best testifying to the existence of genuine
restructuring in Romania is the 936,000 (23.6 percent) decline in employment in state industry from 1989 to 1992. This major net reallocation of

labor, however, has coexisted with considerable gross flows into and out of state industry. In table 6-12 we have converted the data on flows into turnover rates of several different kinds and summarized their evolution in aggregate state-owned industry from 1987 to 1992.[22] Several conclusions may be drawn.

First, Romania in the late 1980s was not a particularly low-turnover economy. Annual accession and separation rates varied within the 15 to 17 percent range, of which less than 5 percentage points involved flows out of the labor force. Layoff rates were quite low, but not entirely negligible, and both disciplinary separations and voluntary job-to-job quits were significant. Second, 1990 was the big year for job changing, because hiring jumped to about 130 percent of the average of the past three years; quits, both to new jobs and to out of the labor force, more than doubled. Third, turnover in 1991 and 1992 fell back to pre-"revolutionary" levels: for several categories, including overall separations, 1991 and 1992 look much more like 1987 to 1989 than 1990. The hiring rate collapsed, however, and the little change in total separations masks a rising rate of dismissals and a falling quit rate, especially to other jobs.

These data may be taken as indicators of the beginnings of restructuring in Romanian state-owned industry: the form of labor shedding follows the pattern seen in a number of other countries (see Boeri 1994 and Blanchard, Commander, and Coricelli, this volume), although the evidence is still clearer in the Romanian data. Initially, state enterprises reduce their hiring, allow employment to fall through attrition, and make cuts in hours of work (as we saw earlier). Later, the disemployment policy becomes more active, and layoffs are enacted.

But we would like to offer two additional reasons for the accelerated employment decline in 1992. The first is the effect of the price scissors we discussed earlier; in 1992 the rate of opening of the wedge between the increase of producer compared with consumer prices already had started to slow.[23] In the context of declining real sales, firms and workers started to face the tradeoff between wages and employment. The second is the

---

22. The data in table 6-12 pertain only to "workers" (in BLS terminology, "production workers") rather than all employees, and the total number employed is therefore smaller than the numbers in table 6-11.

23. The reduced PPI inflation was partly the result of the freeze on most producer prices from March to September 1992, but even with the big PPI jump at the end of the year, when producer prices were once again liberalized, PPI inflation slowed considerably in relation to CPI inflation for the year 1992.

Table 6-11. Employment by Ownership Category and Economic Branches, End of Year, 1989-92

	1989				1990				1991				1992			
	Total	State	Coop-erative	Private	Total	State	Coop-erative	Private	Total	State	Coop-erative	Private	Total	State	Coop-erative	Private
Total	10,945.7	8,059.6	2,269.6	616.5	10,839.5	7,937.7	1,941.7	960.1	10,785.8	7,111.0	54.0	3,620.8	10,458.0	6,174.2	0.0	4,283.8
Industry	4,169.0	3,973.1	155.6	40.3	4,015.1	3,847.2	115.5	52.4	3,817.4	3,586.2	5.5	225.7	3,300.9	3,037.3	0.0	263.6
Construction	766.7	709.7	41.0	16.0	653.1	604.4	26.0	22.7	462.7	437.9	1.6	23.2	579.2	405.2	0.0	174.0
Agriculture and forestry	3,056.3	525.1	2,067.0	464.2	3,096.9	567.6	1,794.6	734.7	3,094.7	507.3	43.0	2,582.8	3,448.8	511.4	0.0	2,937.4
Transport and communications	757.1	705.6	0.2	51.3	752.3	706.6	0.2	45.5	680.9	646.1	0.2	34.6	648.6	587.4	0.0	61.2
Trade	648.9	643.0	3.9	2.0	678.5	636.0	4.2	38.3	871.9	518.6	2.7	350.6	929.2	400.4	0.0	528.8
Education and culture	372.8	366.4	0.0	6.4	452.2	443.2	0.0	9.0	467.9	456.9	0.0	11.0	490.3	474.5	0.0	15.8
Health and social assistance	292.3	292.3	0.0	0.0	303.9	303.9	0.0	0.0	297.8	297.4	0.0	0.4	306.6	302.8	0.0	3.8
Finance, banking, and insurance	35.3	35.3	0.0	0.0	43.8	43.8	0.0	0.0	49.1	49.1	0.0	0.0	57.1	51.3	0.0	5.8
Public administration	53.8	50.2	0.0	3.6	67.9	64.5	0.0	3.4	83.2	79.3	0.0	3.9	112.7	108.6	0.0	4.1

Note: Certain sectors have been omitted because consistency across time could not be ensured. Starting 1992, the cooperative sector in industry and trade is included in the state sector.
Source: CNS.

263

Table 6-12. Labor Mobility of Workers in State-owned Industry, 1982 and 1987-92

Definition	1982	1987	1988	1989	1990	1991	1992
Total separations	481,488	474,313	410,480	399,535	688,531	495,282	484,461
Separation rate	17.95	17.09	15.16	14.50	24.30	17.60	18.39
Dismissal rate	5.82	5.33	5.00	4.17	4.55	6.67	7.77
Layoff rate	1.62	1.62	1.16	0.75	0.80	3.74	—
Disciplinary dismissal rate	4.20	3.71	3.84	3.42	3.75	2.93	—
Quit rate	9.95	9.99	8.62	8.85	17.95	9.54	6.90
Job-to-job quit rate	3.62	3.52	2.88	2.71	6.40	4.42	1.57
Out of LF quit rate	4.09	4.93	4.43	4.87	10.07	4.10	4.71
Other quit rate	2.24	1.54	1.31	1.27	1.47	1.01	0.62
Other reasons rate	2.18	1.77	1.54	1.47	1.81	1.39	3.72
Total accessions	507,603	427,778	459,501	467,984	595,110	252,282	141,852
Accession rate	15.42	15.42	16.97	16.98	21.01	8.96	5.38
Employment (January 1)	2,683,226	2,775,004	2,707,163	2,756,079	2,832,881	2,814,511	2,634,468

Note: The end-of-year figures for employment (equal to January 1 employment plus accessions minus separations) differ from January 1 employment for the subsequent year, probably because of reclassification of enterprises in and out of industry. Layoffs were not reported separately from disciplinary dismissals in 1992, but were included together in a category called "contract canceled at the initiative of the firm," and possibly in the "other reasons" category.
Source: CNS and Earle 1993b.

wage policy of 1992, which placed a ceiling on the growth of the wage bill. Such a policy increases incentives for labor shedding in order to protect or increase the wages of remaining workers (see, for instance, Commander, Coricelli, and Staehr 1992).

As shown in table 6-13, turnover behavior differed substantially across industries, with especially large employment declines in textiles, radioactive minerals, nonmetallic mining, fabricated metals, machine building, and electrical equipment. In some subbranches—such as oil and gas, metallic minerals, food, chemicals, transportation equipment, and railways—employment fell comparatively little. It actually rose in coal mining, where there was great turnover: both accession and separation rates were close to 20 percent. Most of the variation in employment declines arises from differences across subbranches in dismissal rates, with textiles showing the greatest active restructuring: nearly 12 percent of textile employees were dismissed in 1992.

Explaining Interindustry Differences in Employment Adjustment

Why should different branches exhibit such large differences in their employment behavior? One obvious hypothesis is that some have been hit with larger output shocks than others. Although the variance of output declines was relatively small, they may nonetheless account for some of the differences in employment decline. To investigate this possibility, we relate output changes and employment changes in table 6-14. Output change is defined over the period 1989 to 1992, while, because of lack of consistent data for 1989 and the likelihood that the employment adjustment is lagged, employment change is defined for 1990 to end-of-1992. We have defined the "Labor Adjustment Coefficient" (LAC) as the ratio of the change in employment to the change in output.

Clearly, the extent of labor adjustment differs widely across industries. Large adjustments (defined as an LAC over 50 percent) have occurred in textiles, machinery, equipment, instruments, and furniture manufacturing. But some industries have adjusted very little: for coal mining, petroleum and natural gas, and utilities, the LAC is negative! Thus, it is clear that output changes fail to account for much of the variation in employment, and we consider other possible determinants.

The size of the energy shock could be an important factor. As is well known, Romanian industry has been extraordinarily energy-intensive, with a reported ratio of primary energy consumption to GDP five times higher than in Western Europe and more than twice that in other Eastern

Table 6-13. Labor Mobility of All Employees, by Selected Subbranches, 1992

Branch	Employees on January 1	Change in employment (percent)	Accession rate (percent)	Separation rate (percent)	Dismissal[b] rate (percent)	Quit rate (percent)	Job-to-job quit rate (percent)	Out of LF quit rate (percent)	Other quit rate (percent)	Other reasons rate (percent)
Total industry[a]	3,027,478	-12.51	5.18	17.69	7.27	6.83	1.66	4.57	0.60	3.59
Mining	279,024	-3.18	13.17	16.35	5.14	6.33	1.17	4.83	0.34	4.88
Coal mining	105,328	1.48	20.52	19.05	6.58	7.12	1.40	5.41	0.31	5.35
Crude petroleum and natural gas extraction	77,002	-1.20	8.89	10.09	4.41	3.94	0.53	3.32	0.09	1.74
Radioactive minerals extraction and products	3,124	-15.56	2.40	17.96	8.07	7.30	1.12	5.31	0.86	2.59
Metallic mining	61,739	-4.12	10.43	14.55	2.60	6.65	1.27	4.95	0.43	5.30
Nonmetallic mining and quarrying	31,831	-20.33	5.56	25.89	6.79	8.79	1.77	6.23	0.78	10.31
Manufacturing	2,748,454	-13.46	4.37	17.83	7.49	6.88	1.71	4.55	0.62	3.46
Food, beverage, and tobacco	220,322	-6.77	8.74	15.51	5.39	5.92	1.60	3.70	0.62	4.20
Textile, knit, wearing apparel, and leather	521,485	-19.21	4.27	23.47	11.83	6.53	1.69	4.03	0.81	5.11
Footwear	96,111	-13.06	3.53	16.58	6.24	6.26	1.22	4.27	0.78	4.08
Wood	83,599	-10.27	6.53	16.81	3.59	10.34	1.99	7.19	1.16	2.88
Paper and allied products	51,786	-13.02	3.14	16.16	5.92	8.05	1.66	5.58	0.81	2.19

Coal, oil, and nuclear fuel chemical products	29,696	−0.23	5.18	5.40	1.88	3.20	0.63	2.45	0.12	0.32
Chemical products	157,751	−6.24	4.28	10.51	3.76	5.39	1.78	3.22	0.39	1.36
Rubber and plastic products	64,808	−13.58	3.65	17.23	6.43	6.82	1.42	4.93	0.47	3.99
Glass, pottery, china, etc.	136,585	−12.08	5.67	17.75	7.00	7.90	1.39	5.88	0.62	2.86
Metallurgy	204,669	−10.32	4.27	14.58	6.03	6.44	1.07	4.96	0.41	2.11
Fabricated metal products	171,941	−19.68	3.66	23.34	9.76	8.72	2.88	5.23	0.61	4.86
Machinery and equipment	443,984	−15.44	3.02	18.46	7.68	7.71	1.84	5.37	0.50	3.07
Electrical and optical equipment and supplies	146,192	−17.78	1.94	19.73	9.55	6.18	1.82	3.90	0.47	3.99
Transportation equipment	204,219	−7.53	4.45	11.98	4.53	5.28	1.23	3.68	0.37	2.18
Other (including furniture)	215,306	−12.50	4.32	16.82	6.27	7.56	2.14	4.44	0.98	2.99
Construction	385,337	−13.31	13.16	26.47	7.21	11.45	4.37	5.46	1.62	7.80
Railroad transportation	193,957	−6.10	3.97	10.07	1.43	7.29	1.10	5.97	0.22	1.34
Highway transportation	151,726	−11.08	4.86	15.94	3.61	9.37	3.71	4.80	0.86	2.97

a. The figures for "total industry" in this table differ from those in the preceding one because all employees, rather than workers, are included here.
b. Layoffs were not reported separately from disciplinary dismissals in 1992, but were included together in a category called "contract canceled at the initiative of the firm," and possibly in the "other reasons" category.
Source: CNS and Earle 1994.

European countries (OECD 1993). The move to world prices for imported energy has increased real energy costs dramatically.

Table 6-14. Labor Adjustment in Subbranches of Industry, 1990-92

Subbranch	Output change (1992 as percent of 1989)	Employment change[a] (end-1992 as percent of 1990)	Labor adjustment coefficient
Total industry	46.0	78.2	40.4
Mining	55.7	95.5	10.0
Coal mining	57.0	102.3	−5.4
Crude petroleum and natural gas extraction	72.2	106.9	−24.8
Metallic mining	48.0	88.3	22.6
Other extractive activities	45.5	72.4	50.6
Manufacturing	42.6	78.5	37.4
Food and beverage	53.6	91.6	18.1
Tobacco	75.0	98.9	4.5
Textiles, apparel, and leather	44.8	75.6	44.1
Fabrics, fur, and leather goods	45.5	84.1	29.1
Footwear	47.8	77.9	42.3
Wood	45.7	80.7	35.5
Paper and allied products	35.8	80.4	30.5
Coal, oil, and nuclear fuel chemical products	43.7	94.0	10.6
Chemical products	43.7	87.1	22.8
Rubber and plastic products	36.5	76.8	36.5
Glass, pottery, china, etc.	39.0	82.6	28.5
Metallurgy	36.2	80.9	30.0
Fabricated metal products	36.2	70.2	46.7
Machinery and equipment	45.4	71.2	52.8
Computers and associated equipment	32.8	61.4	57.5
Electric machines and appliances	47.1	71.9	53.2
Equipment and communication apparatus	38.4	76.2	38.7
Medical, optical, and watch instruments	39.3	64.5	58.5
Road transportation equipment	39.7	81.2	31.1
Other transportation equipment	44.9	78.4	39.2
Other (including furniture)	67.0	83.9	48.8
Electricity and utilities	59.2	104.2	−10.3
Standard deviation	10.87	11.49	

a. Employment change is calculated from 1990 because the classification in this table is unavailable in 1989.
Note: The labor adjustment coefficient is defined as the ratio of change in employment from 1990 to the change in output from 1989 to 1992, in percent.
Source: CNS.

We also hypothesize that the state may be aiding certain firms to stay afloat, keep up wages, and avoid large-scale layoffs. To capture this possibility, we measure the following variables for each subbranch: the proportion of sales accounted for by *regii autonome* (RA), the ratio of total subsidies to the value of output (SUBS), and the proportion of unskilled workers receiving wages higher than the ceilings imposed in 1991 (EXWU). These data were all calculated from the balance sheets of approximately 1,700 state-owned companies in industry. Although they have many problems and omissions, for the time being they are the best available.

The following OLS regression was estimated to try to account for interindustry differences:

$$\Delta L = -10.90 + .46\Delta X + .039EI + .053RA + .038SUBS + .269EXWU$$
$$(9.70) \quad (.146) \quad (.141) \quad (.036) \quad (.029) \quad (.082)$$

$$R^2 = .82 \quad F = 23.05 \quad N = 25.$$

where

ΔL	=	percentage change in employment (1990 to end 1992)
ΔX	=	percentage change in output (1989 to 1992)
EI	=	energy intensity ratio, calculated as ratio between the energy consumption (in terajouli) and the industrial production (mln. lei, 1992) in the subbranch
RA	=	the percentage of sales accounted for by *regii autonome* in total sales in the subbranch
SUBS	=	the ratio (in percent) between total subsidies and total output in each subbranch, where total subsidies are calculated as the sum of subsidies for covering price differences and subsidies to cover losses from sales
EXWU	=	proportion of workers receiving wages above their respective ceilings in 1991

Standard errors are shown in parentheses.

The results suggest that the government policy variables play important roles in influencing the employment behavior of firms. Industries receiving subsidies and those in which *regii autonome* are more important are likely to adjust less (thus their coefficients are positive, since more adjustment means a larger negative movement of employment) than other industries, controlling for output and energy price shocks. The statistically most significant variable, the extent of violation of the wage ceilings in 1991, we take to be measuring the degree of favoritism shown the sector, thus allowing excessive wage increases in 1991 and preventing employment from falling over the whole period. Energy intensity, in contrast, appears to have little effect on employment adjustment.

An alternative specification, with the labor adjustment coefficient as the dependent variable, yielded the following results (standard errors in parentheses):

$$LAC = 67.301 + .110EI - .251RA - .050SUBS - .551EXWU$$
$$(7.791) \quad (.283) \quad (.072) \quad (.068) \quad (.173)$$

$$R^2 = .695 \qquad F = 14.665 \qquad N = 25.$$

In this specification, the effect of *regii autonome* is statistically significant and negative (implying that RA is negatively associated with the degree of adjustment). EXWU also exerts a strong negative effect, while SUBS and EI are insignificant. We interpret this result as further evidence that a pattern of favoritism in some unmeasurable dimensions (because SUBS captures very little) is responsible for interindustry differences in the degree of employment adjustment.

The Private Sector and Dynamics of Reallocation

As shown in table 6-11, the private sector accounted for about 41 percent of employment by the end of 1992. Slightly over two-thirds were in agriculture, primarily the result of the breakup of the agricultural cooperatives; thus employment in the nonagricultural private sector was 19 percent of total nonagricultural employment. Private employment in trade grew from nil in 1989 to over half a million by the end of 1992, partly because of the sale of assets program, but mostly as a result of the growth of new private ventures. Private employment also grew significantly in industry and construction.

Table 6-15 shows some estimates of "privatized employment"—the private nonagricultural employment resulting from title changes. The three privatization programs that have had some results so far are shown. "MEBO" refers to the program for management and employee buyouts for small companies; unfortunately, no other breakdowns of employment are available from the State Ownership Fund for these companies. Second, "sale of assets" refers to the auctions of parts of enterprises, generally shops or service establishments. Finally, the National Agency for Privatization's "early privatization" program sold twenty-two large com-

Table 6-15. Employment in the Privatized Sector, September 1993

Privatization method	Number of employees
MEBO, total workers	16,200
Shareholders	12,954
Sale of assets	12,108
Early privatization, total	19,167
Industry	14,811
Construction	3,934
Commerce	72
Services	350
Total	47,475

Source: National Agency for Privatization and State Ownership Fund.

panies, mostly engaged in manufacturing activities. Other than the total of about 50,000 workers in this table, the growth in the nonagricultural private sector represents new private sector growth.

A small amount of additional information on private sector employment is available from local chambers of labor, where employees register their labor booklets and arrange for social security. Registration is extremely incomplete, both because agricultural workers and the self-employed do not register and because there is probably a fair amount of evasion of wage taxes and social security contributions. Nonetheless, it is the only available source on the composition of private sector employment. Figure 6-4 presents information about the evolution of the composition according to educational attainment. According to these data, an overwhelming number of employees in the private sector have only basic education; that is, they are qualified only for low-skilled jobs. It is notable that the gap-filling of the private sector should be so biased toward these occupations.

There is a complete lack of official information about private sector wages in Romania. This is unfortunate, for no doubt the methods by which private firms attract and motivate workers constitute a critical aspect of overall wage, employment, and unemployment dynamics. Nevertheless, we hazard several conclusions. We believe that, aside from wholly foreign-owned firms and perhaps some joint ventures, the private sector does not pay significantly higher wages than the state sector, per-

Figure 6-4. Employment in the Private Sector by Education, August 1992 to December 1993

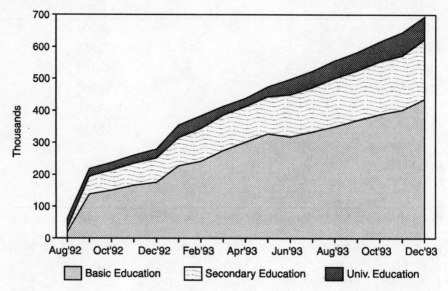

Note: The numbers in this chart pertain only to employees registered with local chambers of labor. Unregistered individuals, including self-employed, are excluded.
Source: MLSP.

haps especially so after adjusting for fringe benefits. If this is true, then the push mechanism is dominating over pull in the Romanian transition: reallocation involves involuntary movement—layoffs—rather than voluntary quits to new jobs. On the one hand, the private sector is not constrained by high labor costs, but on the other, workers have few incentives to move—both are symptoms of low labor demand in the private sector.

Some circumstantial evidence concerning this comes from the Survey of Registered Unemployed, discussed in the next section. First, nearly 70 percent of the registered unemployed are job losers, although this is partly an artifact of benefits eligibility rules. Second, nearly 75 percent of the unemployed would prefer to find a job in the state sector, and only 20 percent prefer the private sector. Third, less than half of those preferring the private sector cite as a reason that they believe it pays a higher wage than the state sector. Fourth, unemployed workers evidently value most highly what they perceive to be the relative security of jobs in the state sector, implying that any private sector wage premium may represent a compensating differential for the higher risk of layoff.[24]

Unemployment and Its Dynamics

Unemployment[25] has followed a more gradual, if no less inexorable, course than in most neighboring countries. Figure 6-5 shows the growth of registered unemployment from February 1991 (when recordkeeping began) to December 1993.[26] Total registered unemployed ("registered" on the diagram) rose particularly rapidly from November 1991 to February 1992, from July 1992 to November 1992, and again at the end of 1993. The concentration of the increase during the year 1992 is probably explained by the combination of four policies: first, the use of the wage bill as the norm in the 1992 wage policy; second, the reduced rate of producer price in relation to consumer price inflation (possibly because of the temporary freeze on producer prices for the middle part of that year); third, the extension of unemployment benefits from six to nine months in late 1991; and fourth, the beginning of a new extended benefit program, the support allowance, in August 1992.

Figure 6-5 displays the evolution in the three types of benefit-recipiency status: "UB recipient" represents those receiving unemployment benefits, "SA recipient" represents those receiving the support allowance, and "nonrecipient" represents those who register in hopes of receiving help from the labor office in finding work, but who receive no benefits. The rate of growth of UB recipients slowed in 1992, and even fell in the first half of 1993, as benefits were exhausted; to some degree, this was off-

---

24. It is interesting that the unemployed do not appear to believe that private sector employers demand higher effort: 2.7 percent of those respondents preferring the state sector cited low effort as a criterion, while the comparable number was 5.8 percent for the private sector.

25. This section draws heavily on Earle 1993a, although the sample analyzed here is larger. More detailed analysis of the survey results can be found in those papers. Codin and Zecheriu 1992; Pert 1992; and Pauna 1993 also discuss Romanian unemployment.

26. A labor force survey is currently being tested in Romania, but results are not yet available. Thus, all official data on Romanian unemployment concern registered unemployed.

Figure 6-5. Unemployment Benefit Recipients, February 1991 to December 1993

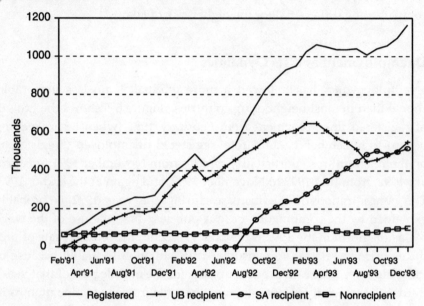

Source: MLSP.

set by increased numbers receiving SA, but the offset was not complete, since not all UB exhaustees are eligible for SA.

Further understanding of the dynamics of unemployment can be obtained from an analysis of the gross flows into and out of unemployment, our rough calculations for which are shown in figure 6-6. It is not easy to calculate gross unemployment flows from the figures reported by the MLSP in Romania. Prior to August 1992, when the support allowance was introduced, as described below, unemployed individuals who exhausted their eligibility for benefits and did not reregister as nonrecipients were neither counted as part of "deregistrations," nor were they enumerated separately. Deregistrations are reported for job finders and suspensions (for no longer complying with the conditions for benefit eligibility) separately, but exhaustees simply disappear. But some conclusions may still be drawn, if one takes into account the pattern of benefit durations (see figure 6-7 for summary of duration of unemployment) in the context of the Romanian program: we know in which months benefit exhaustion occurred and therefore when to avoid spurious calculations.

Figure 6-6. Unemployment Gross Flows, February 1991
to December 1993

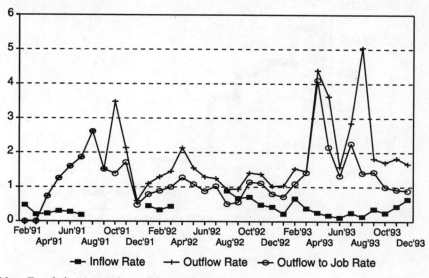

Note: For definitions of variables, see text.
Source: MLSP and authors' calculations.

In the first six months (February to August 1991), there was no benefit exhaustion, nor, after benefits were extended to nine months, was there from January to March 1992 as former exhaustees returned for three months to the rolls. Finally, beginning August 1992, benefits exhaustees were automatically transferred into the support allowance category, so that they remained counted. Only starting January 1994 will SA recipients begin to exhaust their eighteen months of support, but it is hoped that by that time the ministry will be ready to start counting them.

Operating under these constraints, figure 6-6 shows the total outflows from unemployment, outflows to jobs, inflows to unemployment, and the corresponding rates for all the months in which these flows may be precisely calculated. Both the inflow rates (calculated as a percent of the population aged fifteen to fifty-nine) and the outflow rates (calculated as a percent of total employment) are quite low. In general, it seems that Romania is similar to many other transition economies, the Czech Republic being the notable exception, in having unemployment characterized by very low turnover. Indeed, with an approximately 2 percent monthly

Figure 6-7. Distribution of Unemployment Duration, August 1993

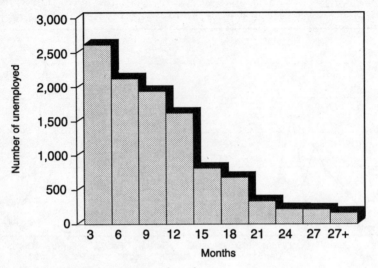

Source: Survey of Registered Unemployed.

outflow rate, the average expected unemployment duration would be more than four years!

Nevertheless, it appears that fluctuations in inflows are much more important than outflow fluctuations in explaining the time-series evolution of the unemployment rate. Monthly inflows vary from 15,000 to 123,000, while outflows vary only within a range of about 10,000 to 50,000 after mid-1992. Unemployment appears to be a low-inflow, long-duration phenomenon in Romania, but fluctuations in the rate are given predominantly by changes in inflows.[27]

Reliable unemployment data on a disaggregated basis are still more difficult to come by. The ministry reports regularly only the total number of unemployed and the number in a few basic categories: sex, age groups, counties (*judet*), broad educational ("socio-professional") groups, and disaggregated occupations. But many other characteristics, particularly those involving origins and reasons, are also critical for a full assessment

27. This conclusion applies to aggregate unemployment behavior and also seems to hold for most groups of the unemployed (defined by sex, age, and the like). But there are some systematic exceptions, which we analyze below. The mean duration of unemployment differs significantly across some groups, suggesting that some may be characterized by high turnover, others by long-term unemployment.

of unemployment. Moreover, registration data concern only absolute numbers and the composition of unemployment, but allow no evaluation of incidence. Yet it is crucial to know not only who accounts for most of unemployment, but also in which groups unemployment is particularly concentrated.

For these reasons, we draw upon a 1 percent (11,500 persons), geographically representative sample survey of the unemployed: the Survey of Registered Unemployed (SRU) provides much more detailed characteristics of unemployed individuals and allows an explicit examination of the origins and causes of unemployment.[28] We also combine figures on the number unemployed from both the SRU and MLSP with employment and labor force figures from a wide variety of sources within the CNS to generate rates of unemployment for many demographic and economic categories.

One of the most important kinds of information concerning Romanian unemployment that has been unavailable is the distribution by reason; the calculations from the SRU are shown in table 6-16. Job losers are divided into four categories: those losing their jobs in a "mass layoff" (defined as involving more than ten employees), those from a "group layoff" (defined as two to ten employees), those laid off individually, and those losing their jobs as a result of a plant closing. Quits, new entrants, and reentrants are defined conventionally, while "out of LF" (out of the labor force) represents individuals whom we judged not to be truly unemployed (generally because they were unavailable for work) as defined in a standard Western labor force survey. "Others" were unclassifiable, mostly because of lack of response to this question.

Job losers altogether account for over 60 percent of the registered unemployed, with the only other substantial group being new entrants, at 34 percent of the total. More than two-thirds of the job losers, and thus over 40 percent of the unemployed, lost their jobs through a plant closing or a mass layoff, evidence of some serious restructuring. These individuals also have the longest mean duration of unemployment, 9.2 months for both, compared with a sample mean of 8.6. People who voluntarily quit (technically, who leave without the "approval" of the enterprise) are not

28. For further information about the SRU, see Earle 1993a. We thank the CEU Privatization Project for funding for this undertaking and Catalin Pauna for research assistance and substantive contributions to the design and organization of the survey.

Table 6-16. Unemployment by Reason, August 1993

Reason	Count	Percentage	Mean duration
Mass layoff (>10 employees)	3,974	35.9	9.2
Group layoff (2-10 employees)	1,466	13.2	8.3
Individual layoff	662	6.0	7.9
Plant closure	625	5.6	9.2
Quit	95	0.9	8.3
New entrant	3,788	34.2	8.1
Reentrant	325	2.9	8.0
Out of LF	55	0.5	7.5
Other	93	0.8	8.5

Note: "Count" indicates the number of unemployed in the sample of the SRU in the given category. "Percentage" refers to the composition of the unemployment pool. "Mean duration" is the measure, in months, of the average duration of unemployment for the indicated group.
Source: SRU.

eligible for benefits, nor are most reentrants, which accounts for their low numbers among the registered unemployed.

As in many other transition countries, women have a much higher incidence of unemployment than do men: they account for 62 percent of unemployed and have an unemployment rate of 11.4 percent, nearly double the 6.5 rate of men. But, as we have just seen, this cannot be caused by a higher rate of reentrants among women; rather, the differential is the result of higher layoff and new entrant rates. Women account for 57 percent of mass layoffs, 61 percent of job losses related to plant closings, and 68 percent of new entrants. New entrants are, naturally, young people: 90 percent were under age twenty-five. A wage subsidy program for new graduates had helped a total of 21,558 new entrants to find jobs, as of the end of 1993. Interestingly, 88 percent of those jobs were in the state sector.

The important implication of this analysis of unemployment incidence is that the rise in the labor force participation rate is not from reentrants or older new entrants coming into unemployment; they account for very few of the unemployed, thus they must instead have found jobs. Unemployment comes predominantly from people who were already employed or from young new entrants, who presumably would have joined the labor force in any case. Perhaps the job losers were displaced by the newcomers, or perhaps the newcomers joined growing sectors; but in either case, it seems that neither flows from employment to out of the labor force nor flows from out of the labor force into unemployment were very important.

Several features of the cross-sectional variation in unemployment rates and duration are suggestive for evaluating the past and future course of the restructuring process in Romania. Concerning education, the unemployment rate of high school and vocational school graduates is much higher, at 15.8 percent, than that of university graduates, at 6.1 percent, and workers with only basic education, at 7.5 percent. The duration is also highest for the first group: the three averages are 9.0, 7.9, and 8.3 months, respectively. A possible explanation of this phenomenon is the high degree of specific training of medium-skilled workers, slowing their ability to adjust to changing labor market conditions.

Concerning occupation, the unemployment rate is highest among unskilled workers, at 21.3 percent, with average duration of 8.9 months, followed by skilled workers, with a rate of 15.3 and average duration of 8.8 months. Technicians have a relatively low unemployment rate but high duration: 7.5 percent and 8.9 months, respectively. Administrative personnel and professionals have higher rates—13.8 and 9.0—but lower mean duration—8.0 and 6.6 months, respectively. The implication of this is that there is some reason to believe that groups of the unemployed differ systematically in the ease with which they find new jobs, and therefore in their durations; furthermore, there seems to be a negative correlation between the incidence and duration of unemployment across different groups.

More evidence on these issues and the nature of the restructuring process appears in table 6-17 on the incidence of unemployment by "legal form" of former employer. The highest rates of experienced unemployment are in privatized firms, which seem to be laying off large proportions of their work forces. Close behind come the nonagricultural cooperatives, which have nearly disappeared. Among state-owned enterprises, the commercial companies have a much higher unemployment rate than do the *regii autonomes*. Although the latter include many of the dinosaurs of Romanian industry, it appears that commercial companies are engaging in significantly more restructuring. At the same time, the pattern of average duration looks rather different: the unemployed laid off from *regii* have been unemployed an average of 10.3 months, while the average duration for commercial companies is 8.7 months.

Table 6-17. Unemployment by Legal Form, August 1993

Legal form	Count	Percentage	Unemployment rate	Mean duration
Budgetary institutions	310	4.2	4.98	8.9
Regii autonome	343	4.7	4.21	10.3
Commercial companies	5,301	72.2	16.93	8.7
Cooperatives, nonagricultural	739	10.1	23.99	8.8
Private firms	204	2.8	6.68	6.4
Privatized firms	121	1.6	26.63	9.4
Joint venture	24	0.3	2.35	10.4

Source: SRU and CNS.

These issues are approached from a different dimension in figure 6-8, which shows the behavior of unemployment by branch. On one scale, we have plotted the mean duration by branch, on the other the "inflow rate," obtained by dividing the unemployment rate by the mean duration for each branch.[29] It is interesting that the inflow rates are negatively associated with average duration by subbranch: the correlation coefficient is –0.52. The inflow and the unemployment rate is often higher, but duration lower, for branches that are, according to our earlier criteria, "disfavored." We hypothesize that the favored branches have been forced to undertake little restructuring, but the workers who do lose their jobs from those branches have more difficulty finding new jobs because of the heavy weight of specific skills in their human capital.

Geographic patterns in unemployment follow a similar pattern. Unemployment rates are highly variable across *judet*, with a high of 22.1 percent in Vaslui (Moldova) to a low of 3.7 percent in Gorj. Mean unemployment duration also has a high variance: the range is from 4.2 to 12.4. The implied inflow rates vary from .45 to 3.31. Finally, there is again a negative and statistically significant correlation between the inflow rate and average duration across judet of –.40.

---

29. This inflow rate is defined as a percentage of the relevant labor force, unlike those in figure 6-6, above, where they are a percentage of the relevant population. The implied national average is just over 1 percent of the labor force entering unemployment each month. Strictly speaking, this procedure of calculating inflows is correct only in a steady state. If unemployment is increasing (and duration lengthening), then these inflows represent maxima on the size of the true inflows.

Figure 6-8. Unemployment: Inflow and Duration by Branch, August 1993

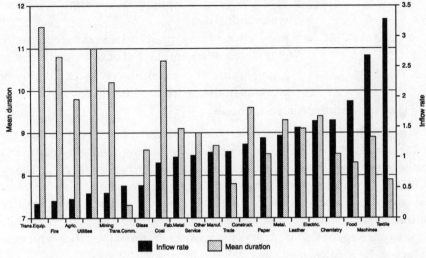

Source: SRU and CNS.

The SRU was conducted at the level of local labor offices, which provides even finer disaggregation of unemployment behavior. Across these offices, average duration varies from .3 to 18.1 months. We have tried to account for this variation in a simple regression framework (these results are elaborated in Earle 1993a):

$$\text{Log(DUR)} = -5.617 + .370 \, \text{SEX} + .875 \, \text{Log(AGE)} + 1.297 \, \text{Log(EDUC)} - 1.204 \, \text{UR}$$
$$(2.500) \; (.249) \qquad (.388) \qquad\qquad (.594) \qquad\qquad (.762)$$

$$+ .128 \, \text{HEAVIND} + .326 \, \text{MASSLAYOFF} + .204 \, \text{Log(CASELOAD)}$$
$$(.087) \qquad\qquad (.198) \qquad\qquad\quad (.069)$$

$$R^2 = .104 \qquad F = 3.660 \qquad N = 163$$

where

DUR	=	average unemployment duration in the local labor office
SEX	=	proportion female
AGE	=	average age
EDUC	=	average years of education
UR	=	unemployment rate in the relevant judet

HEAVIND   =   proportion of unemployed previously em-
                   ployed in chemistry, metallurgy, metal products,
                   machinery and equipment, energy, gas, and
                   water industries

MASSLAYOFF =   proportion of unemployed laid off together with
                   at least ten other employees or in a plant closing

CASELOAD   =   ratio of number of unemployed to the number of
                   workers in the district office.

Standard errors are in parentheses.

The results suggest that, *ceteris paribus*, women, older people, and the better educated may have greater difficulty finding reemployment, and furthermore, that a greater predominance of former workers in heavy industry and of those losing their jobs through a mass layoff or plant closing are also associated with longer average duration. The positive (although with a significance level of only .14) coefficient on HEAVIND implies once again that it may be the workers in these branches who may be facing the greatest obstacles.

Probably the most interesting result is the significantly positive association of the local labor office caseload with duration. The results suggest that a 1 percent decrease in the number of unemployed persons for each office worker could lead to a .2 percent decrease in duration for each unemployed person there. Or, since the average caseload is 668 (with a range from 242 to 3,454), and a total of 1,552 people work in the local labor offices, we estimate that increasing the number of personnel by 1,500 nationwide could lead to a reduction in average duration of 10 percent, or .86 months, and therefore a reduction in the unemployment rate from 10 to 9 percent. In the steady state, there could be about 100,000 fewer people unemployed at any one time.

We do not want to exaggerate the significance of our simple regression results, but the implication of this analysis is that there may be much potential for more effective active labor market policies in Romania. Passive policies provide a bare income maintenance, with fairly low mean and median replacement rates: .38 and .45, respectively.[30] We also already

---

30. We excluded from this analysis the outliers reporting former wages implying replacement rates over 2, probably the result of misreporting. The 75th percentile of the distribution of replacement rates was .59 and the 90th percentile was 1.14. For more information about the legal organization and number of beneficiaries of the unemployment benefit and support allowance program, see Earle 1993a.

mentioned the existence of the wage subsidy program for new graduates. The necessity for massive reallocation, however, implies that many workers should be retrained, and the Ministry of Labor indeed has had such a program under way. The results of the program are shown in table 6-18.

It is somewhat surprising that only 159,694 had participated in training courses, and only 115,132, about 10 percent of the total unemployed, had completed courses by the end of 1993. The table also shows that only the courses organized by firms (with obvious interest, as well as obligation, to hire subsequently) were very successful in getting jobs for the unemployed participants (85 percent), but these courses involved only about 7 percent of trainees. By contrast, most courses were organized at the initiative of local labor offices, but only about 17 percent of trainees were placed in jobs thereafter, a rather dismal record. The "courses for entrepreneurs" fared no better: again, only 16 percent actually started a business after the course.

Table 6-18. Retraining Programs for the Unemployed, September 1991 to September 1993

Participants	September to December 1991	1992	1993	Total
Total number of participants	12,064	45,640	101,990	159,694
Total number of trainees[a]	3,458	31,665	80,009	115,132
Company requested	688	2,498	5,069	8,255
Trainees hired	622	2,107	4,286	7,015
Percent	90.4	84.4	84.6	85.0
Labor Office initiative	2,191	28,327	71,859	102,377
Trainees hired	350	5,209	11,462	17,021
Percent	16.0	18.4	16.0	16.63
Entrepreneurs	579	840	3,081	4,500
Started a business	104	181	432	717
Percent	18.0	21.6	14.0	15.9

a. Those who completed the training programs.
Source: MLSP.

The small scale and low participation of retraining may have several explanations. First, according to some observers, the unemployed are not interested in retraining, preferring to remain dependent on the state.[31] The Survey of Registered Unemployed, however, found that a large proportion of the unemployed believe they must change occupations in order to find a new job; thus, they must have some recognition of the need for retraining. A second possible explanation is that labor offices may be offering courses that correspond only poorly with the structure of growth in labor demand. This is difficult to evaluate, but many service occupations are included in the course offerings. Third, the local labor offices may be too poorly staffed to match retrained individuals with new jobs. The regression results above lend some support to this.

Conclusions

The restructuring of transition economies involves the massive reallocation of labor across many dimensions, including ownership sectors, economic branches, geographic regions, occupations, firms, particular jobs, and a wide variety of activities. In Romania, we have seen that the scale of the distortions left from the communist era implies that the reallocation process is particularly daunting. Nonetheless, our evaluation is that the process is going forward, if also marching to a somewhat different drumbeat than other countries in the region.

Because of the much better quality and availability of data on the state-owned industrial sector and on unemployment than for the private sector or other branches, the ways in which the decline of employment in industry and under state ownership is occurring have been the focus of our analysis. Complete information even about this topic is unavailable, but our evaluation of the evidence suggests certain conclusions.

To start, the dominant method for the reduction of employment in state industry is through a large drop in hiring, at least until mid-1992. After the jump in retirements in 1990, the quit rate to out-of-the-labor-force has resumed its normal level. But employment reduction is increasingly active, and the second most important method is involuntary layoffs of workers. Job-to-job quits have fallen greatly, thus voluntary

---

31. Interview with Iulian Oneasca, reporting some unpublished results of an unemployment survey concerned with these questions.

movement from state industry to the private sector and to growing branches seems relatively inconsequential.

Next, that the private sector and unemployment together have grown more than the state sector has declined (so that labor force participation has increased) may seem to imply that increases in unemployment are largely accounted for by movements from out of the labor force. But we find that most unemployed are experienced workers, coming from all ownership sectors: state, cooperative, new private, and privatized. Because the rate of gross hiring in state industry is low, the flow of former nonparticipants through the state sector and into unemployment and the private sector must be low. Finally, combined with the very low exit rate from unemployment, this implies that private sector growth has been largely fed by former nonparticipants.

To summarize, the dominant transition routes in the restructuring of the aggregate Romanian labor market are from both state and private sectors into unemployment and from out of the labor force into the private sector. Only a small proportion of state sector workers seem to move voluntarily, thus we surmise they must undergo an intervening period of unemployment before becoming reemployed with either the state or a private firm. Thus, the forces "pushing" workers out of the state sector are clearly stronger than those "pulling" them (at least from the state, if not from nonparticipation), although both forces seem quite weak. Aside from agriculture, title transfers so far play little role in the aggregate restructuring process.

Our analysis of wage developments was, for reasons of data availability, almost exclusively concerned with the state sector. But it may help explain why the forces of reallocation are weak, although not negligible, in Romania. The development of real consumption wages for most of the period since 1989 has diverged quite significantly from that of real product wages: although both were extremely volatile, the former was generally well above the latter. The result of this pattern was that workers' wages remained relatively high, particularly on an hourly basis, while firms' labor costs remained relatively low. If workers' wages had declined more, they would have had more incentive to move; while if firms' labor costs had risen more, they would have laid more workers off. Of late, however, the price scissors between the CPI and PPI has rapidly closed, leading to a reversal of real wage behavior: now, the consumption wage is falling and the product wage is rising dramatically. Clearly, the tradeoff between wages and employment in the state sector will be much more starkly posed, and both the push and the pull forces of reallocation are likely to be greatly strengthened.

Our disaggregated analysis of employment behavior and of unemployment also carries implications for the future course of the aggregate restructuring process. We have presented evidence for the hypothesis that there is a nontransparent "industrial policy" in Romania, one that systematically favors particular sectors and firms in a wide variety of ways, most of which we can measure only quite imperfectly. As a result, the pattern of restructuring is systematically biased against the disfavored firms and sectors, and we think there may be a danger that they (as well as the private sector) are crowded out through high inflation and tax rates to the point that an "over-shooting" of the downsizing process occurs. It is, of course, difficult to evaluate the precise amount of labor shedding necessary to reach a competitive position in a market environment, but some subbranches of industry that might have great potential (textiles and furniture) are losing large numbers of their workers.

Furthermore, we have found what appears to be a systematically negative correlation between the inflow to unemployment and the duration of unemployment. This relationship holds across occupational, industrial, and geographic classifications of the data, and it is striking, given that we usually expect that there are decreasing returns to unemployment in the job-matching function. If we interpret the inflow rate as representing one possible measure of the extent of restructuring, then the implication is that those sectors (areas, occupations) where restructuring has proceeded the least tend to be those with the highest average duration of joblessness of their laid-off workers. Thus, at the same time as our analysis suggests that active labor market policies may have considerable scope for improving the reemployment prospects of laid-off workers, the beginnings of restructuring in the heavy industry sectors, impelled by the rise in unit labor costs, seem likely to greatly swell unemployment.

Bibliography

Berg, A., and O. Blanchard. 1994. "Stabilization and Transition: Poland, 1990-91." In O. T. Blanchard, K. Frost, and J. Sachs, eds., *Transformation in Eastern Europe*. University of Chicago Press.

Boeri, Tito. 1994. "Labor Market Flows and the Persistence of Unemployment in Central and Eastern Europe." In *Unemployment in Transition Countries*. Paris: OECD.

Borensztein, E. R., D. Demekas, and J. Ostry. 1993. "Output Decline in the Aftermath of Reform: The Cases of Bulgaria, Czechoslovakia, and Romania." In M. Blejev and others, eds., *Eastern Europe in Transition: From Recession to Growth?* World Bank Discussion Paper 196, Washington, D.C.

Codin, M., and M. Zecheriu. 1992. "Unemployment and the Behavior of Unemployed Workers" (in Romanian). Institute for Research on the Quality of Life, Bucharest.

Comisia Nationala pentru Statistica. 1991, 1992. *Statistical Yearbooks of Romania, 1990.* Bucharest.

Commander, S., F. Coricelli, and K. Staehr. 1992. "Wages and Employment in the Transition to a Market Economy." In G. Winckler, ed., *Central and Eastern Europe: Roads to Growth.* Washington D.C.: IMF and Austrian National Bank.

Croitoru, L. 1992. "Incomes Policy in Romania." *Romanian Economic Review* 2.

Earle, J. 1993a. "Unemployment and Policies in Romania." In T. Boeri, ed., *Unemployment in Eastern Europe: Transient or Persistent?* Paris: OECD.

————. 1993b. "Output Decline and Labor Market Responses in Romanian Industry." Paper presented to the Conference on Output Decline in Eastern Europe—Prospects for Recovery, IIASA, Laxenburg.

Earle, J., and G. Oprescu. 1993a. "Romanian Labor Markets in Transition: A Preliminary Exploration of Issues and Institutions." Paper presented at the Workshop on Labor Markets in Transitional Socialist Economies, Stirin, Czech Republic, April.

————. 1993b. "Employment and Wage Determination, Unemployment, and Labor Policies in Romania." Paper presented at the World Bank Conference on Unemployment Restructuring and the Labor Market in East Europe and Russia, Washington, D.C., October.

Earle, J., and D. Sapatoru. 1993. "Privatization in a Hypercentralized Economy: The Case of Romania." In J. Earle, R. Frydman, and A. Rapaczynski, eds., *Privatization in the Transition to a Market Economy.* London and New York: Pinter and St. Martin's.

————. 1994. "Incentive Contracts, Corporate Governance, and Privatization Funds in Romania." *Atlantic Economic Journal* 22(2).

Fox, L., and Z. Bogetic. 1993. "Incomes Policy During Stabilization: A Review and Lessons from Bulgaria and Romania." World Bank Internal Discussion Paper, Report No. IDP-123, Washington, D.C.

Montias, J. M. 1991. "The Romanian Economy: A Survey of Current Problems." *European Economy*, Special Edition (2): 177-98.

OECD. 1993. *OECD Economic Surveys: Romania.* Paris.

Pauna, C. 1993. "Patterns of Unemployment in Romania." Central European University Department of Economics, Prague.

Pert, S. 1992. "Persistent Unemployment—A New Phenomenon: Dimensions, Characteristics, Trends" (in Romanian). National Institute for Economic Research, Bucharest.

Rose, R. 1992. "Who Needs Social Protection in Eastern Europe? A Constrained Empirical Analysis of Romania." Studies in Public Policy No. 202, Strathclyde University, Glasgow.

Rose, R., and C. Haerpfer. 1992. "New Democracies between State and Market." Studies in Public Policy No. 204, Strathclyde University, Glasgow.

Spiridon, S. 1993a. "The Wage Subsidy Program in Romania." Central European University Department of Economics, Prague.

———. 1993b. "Comparative Analysis of the Compensation Package under the Communist Regime and during the Transition Period in Romania." Central European University Department of Economics, Prague.

World Bank. 1992. *Romania: Human Resources and the Transition to a Market Economy.* Washington, D.C.

———. 1993. *Romania: Fiscal Policy in the Transition.* Washington, D.C.

7

Unemployment and Restructuring in Eastern Europe and Russia

Olivier Blanchard, Simon Commander, and Fabrizio Coricelli

The recent evolution of unemployment in Eastern Europe is given in figure 7-1. The figure has several striking features. The first is the general increase in unemployment rates since 1990. The second is the heterogeneity of experiences. While the bulk of the countries in our sample now display unemployment rates in the range of 10-15 percent, the Czech Republic and Russia have rates that are extremely low.

The set of questions raised by figure 7-1 is obvious. Why have rates increased, and why do they differ? Is unemployment a stagnant pool, or a way station between jobs? Will unemployment rates increase further or can one take comfort from the current leveling off one observes in most countries? What labor market policies should governments adopt? Should they keep their policy of terminating unemployment benefits after six months or a year? These are some of the questions that shape this chapter. In it we put the pieces together, based on the information from the country studies. We first lay out a framework for our thinking before presenting the main outline of the picture. In later sections we fill in the details.

We thank Michael Burda, John Flemming, and Janos Kornai for comments on an earlier draft.

Figure 7-1. Unemployment Rates in Selected Countries, Period Averages

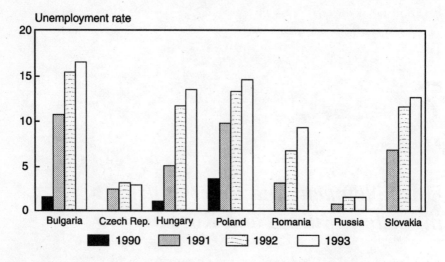

Note: The average for 1993 is mid-year, except for the Czech Republic and Romania (February).
Source: Employment Observatory and World Bank.

The Framework

The general framework one must use to think about unemployment in the transition is clear. On the one hand, a once dominant state sector is being steadily eroded. State firms are shedding labor; some are restructuring; others are closing. A new private sector is emerging and growing. Unemployment is the result of this process of reallocation.

But reallocation processes come in many shapes. Consider two extreme views. In the first, the main force is the collapse of state firms, unable to adapt to a market environment. The embryonic private sector grows, but not enough to pick up much of the slack. In that view, transition rapidly leads to high unemployment, and unemployment rapidly becomes a stagnant pool. Workers who have the misfortune to become unemployed are likely to drop out or become long-term unemployed. High unemployment represents a high economic and social cost and one that endangers reform, slowing the desired restructuring of the state sector and discrediting reforming governments. In the second view, the main force is the rapid growth of the private sector, which steals workers away from state firms, thereby inducing, as well as allowing, them to reorganize. In that view, unemployment is the result of a healthy process of reallocation. Even if the unemployment pool is large, it is a pool with high turnover and a central part of an efficient reallocation. How does one get the available data to bear on which view is right, or more likely, to divine where the truth falls between these two views?

The General Picture

The Decline in State Sector Employment

Table 7-1 provides estimates of the evolution of state employment over the period 1990-92. The broad picture is clear. There are large declines in all countries. Because of the slow progress on medium and large privatization, the numbers represent mostly true declines rather than title changes; the major exception is Russia, where reclassification explains most of the decline, and employment in state firms declined by under 4 percent in 1992.

These numbers, however, hide differences both over time and across countries. To understand these, one must think about the internal and external environment facing state firms prior to privatization. This is particularly important because privatization has proven to be a slow process.

Firms differ across and within countries both in their initial position and in the size of the shock they have experienced. Some firms have lost their entire market in the collapse of CMEA trade. And some countries, such as Bulgaria, have been affected much more than others by the initial shocks.

Firms differ across countries in their internal incentives. In most countries, decisions reflect the interests of managers and workers. The relative weight of the two, however, depends on both institutional and historical factors. The objectives of each group also vary; the horizon of privatization and the perceived stakes of each group are particularly important here, and those perceptions have changed as the transition has proceeded.

Finally, firms differ in the outside environment they face. In most countries, firms have quickly faced a hard budget constraint because subsidies and other supports have been drastically decreased and governments have so far stood firm in their commitment to let firms close.

Elsewhere, the current or prospective budget constraint is much softer, and so far firms have been able to avoid most hard choices.

How have these factors combined? In Poland, Hungary, and the Czech Republic one can see a clear evolution. At the beginning of transition, firms appeared to be in a holding pattern. The decline in employment was slower than the decline in output. Most separations were voluntary, or at least relatively painless, such as early retirements. Wages were set to appropriate most of the earlier profits without threatening employment. But as time passes, one sees increasing signs of labor shedding beyond attrition. Separations appear increasingly involuntary and more to unemployment rather than to other jobs. Firms appear to be operating under increasingly long horizons, even before privatization.

Other countries fall into two groups. On one side is Bulgaria, which has had a much larger initial shock and far smaller buffers, where the initial decrease in state output and in state employment has been unusually large. On the other is Russia and, to a lesser extent, Romania, where a softer budget constraint has so far allowed state firms to limit losses in employment much below the decline in output.

The Growth of Private Sector Employment

As is shown in table 7-1, the growth of the private sector has been strong. Further, much of this, again with the exception of Russia, can be accounted for by growth in the new—as opposed to privatized—private sector.

Thus far, this growth has reflected mostly a stock adjustment process, the filling of the gap left in trade and services under socialism. And the nature of the new private sector has been shaped both by the nature of activity in trade and services and by a number of severe constraints, from limited access to credit to lack of expertise. The private sector is composed of very small firms, internally financed, and, when account is taken of the nonwage aspects of compensation, typically paying their workers less than state firms. Gross flows of both layoffs and quits are high, suggesting high failure rates and mediocre jobs.

Some countries, such as Poland or Hungary, are at the stage where the share of trade and services is not far from that of other market economies at a roughly similar level of income. This raises the question of whether job creation in the private sector will level off. We find little evidence that

Table 7-1. Employment by Ownership Form

	In thousands			Share of total employment		
Item	1990	1991	1992	1990	1991	1992
Hungary						
Total employed	4,699.0	4,334.0	4,120.0			
State	—	2,860.4	2,645.0	—	66.0	64.2
Private	—	1,473.6	1,475.0	—	34.0	35.8
Poland						
Total employed	16,511.0	15,601.0	15,379.0			
State	10,963.3	9,313.8	8,550.7	66.4	59.7	55.6
Private	5,547.7	6,287.2	6,828.3	33.6	40.3	44.4
Czech Republic						
Total employed	5,351.0	5,059.0	4,880.0			
State	4,917.0	4,052.0	—	91.9	80.1	—
Private	434.0	1,007.0	—	8.1	19.9	—
Slovakia						
Total employed	2,478.0	2,281.0	2,160.0			
State	2,357.0	1,989.0	1,793.0	95.1	87.2	83.0
Private	121.0	292.0	367.0	4.9	12.8	17.0
Bulgaria						
Total employed	4,097.0	3,564.0	3,113.0			
State	4,097.0	3,204.0	2,673.0	100.0	89.9	85.9
Private	—	360.0	440.0	—	10.1	14.1
Romania						
Total employed	10,840.0	10,786.0	10,205.0			
State	—	10,041.8	8,980.4	—	93.1	88.0
Private	—	744.2	1,224.6	—	6.9	12.0
Russia						
Total employed	75,400	73,800	72,300			
State	66,900	60,300	53,600	88.7	81.7	74.1
Private	8,300	13,500	18,700	11.0	18.3	25.9

— Not available.
Note: Figures for Poland in 1989 are 17,600, 12,126, and 5,474, giving a state employment share of 68.9 percent and a private share of 31.1 percent.
Source: Employment Observatory, Russian Gomkomstat, and World Bank estimates.

private sector growth elsewhere—in industry, for example—can occur at the same sustained rate.

Unemployment

The evolution of unemployment follows from our characterization of state and private evolutions.

Focusing first on Hungary, Poland, and the Czech Republic, one sees a change in the nature of unemployment over time. The initial employment adjustment in the state sector was largely accommodated both by direct flows to other jobs and by movements out of the labor force through early retirements and "disabilities." For those unlucky enough to find themselves unemployed, prospects were dim. Exit rates, especially exit rates to jobs, were low. Over time, as separations have become increasingly involuntary, flows from state firms and private firms into unemployment have both increased, and so have flows out of unemployment. The majority of "job-to-job" movement now takes place through unemployment. The low unemployment rate in the Czech Republic, compared with Poland and Hungary, appears to come from both a stronger growth of the private sector—from a smaller base—and from increasingly restrictive unemployment benefit eligibility requirements.

One should not, however, overestimate the change in the nature of unemployment over time. In comparison to Western countries, unemployment remains a low turnover pool. In Poland or Hungary today, the monthly exit rate from unemployment to jobs is still less than 3 percent; for comparison, the U.S. rate in 1992 was 25 percent. And the aggregate numbers hide a large heterogeneity across regions. Unemployment rates vary greatly across regions within each country, both because of variations in the rate of state sector decline and in the rate of private sector growth. Constraints on labor mobility accentuate these regional imbalances.

Other countries fall again into two groups. In Bulgaria, high unemployment appears to come from large decreases in state employment with little compensating growth of the private sector. And a broadly similar story, although with a different time path for the flows out of the state sector, appears to hold for Slovakia. In contrast to the Czech Republic, the private sector was initially far smaller, resulting in much lower rates of transitions to jobs by those losing work in the state sector. For Romania and Russia, lower unemployment at the start of the transition is primarily the result of the smaller decline in state employment. The subsequent increase in Romania in 1992 reflects some tightening of the budget constraint, although policy changes have been frequent and unpredictable.

A Tentative Classification

Overall, we see three forms of evolution. The first is that of the three more advanced countries of Central Europe—Poland, Hungary, and the Czech Republic—where the state sector is declining and restructuring and the private sector is expanding. The issues are twofold. How much labor must be shed in state firms? And what will happen to growth in the private sector when the stock adjustment process comes to an end?

The second is that of Bulgaria and, to a lesser extent, Slovakia, where the decline of the state sector has been strong, the growth of the private sector weak, and unemployment has risen very high. The obvious issue there is whether the economic and political weight of unemployment and depression will allow reform to proceed.

The third is that of Russia and, to a lesser extent, Romania, where a soft budget constraint is allowing state firms to maintain employment at the cost of an impending hyperinflation. Unemployment is low, but reallocation is generally yet to come. And the costs associated with an inability to stabilize the economy and provide an environment for enduring structural reforms are clearly large.

The following sections look at the different parts of the picture, state employment, private employment, and unemployment in more detail. The last section speculates about the future.

Employment and Wage Decisions of State Firms: A Framework

Since the beginning of reform, state firms have been under the de facto control of their workers and managers. The formal, legal owner—the state, usually in the incarnation of the treasury, or a newly created state organization—has been largely absent. There has been no formal advocate for capital.

It does not, however, follow that the right model of the firm is the standard model of the labor-managed firm. Insider models, such as those developed for market economies, in which wages are set as high as possible subject to maintaining enough employment for the insiders, appear more appropriate (Commander, Coricelli, and Staehr 1992 and Lane and

Dinopoulos 1991 provide applications to a transition context). But they apply only with three important qualifications.

The first is that of the relative role of the workers versus managers. Institutionally, the role of workers varies sharply across countries. Case studies indicate a strong relationship between institutional arrangements and actual practice. By 1992, CSFR and Hungarian industrial workers generally had little or no decisionmaking authority, while in Poland and Romania workers were substantially more influential (Estrin, Schaffer, and Singh 1993). One may ask how managers can have any power in firms, given the absence of an ultimate owner. The answer comes partly from the form of institutions—such as the right of workers' councils in Poland to dismiss managers—and from the need of the workers for the expertise of managers in getting the firm through hard times.

An issue here is that of the relation between trade union power and workers' influence within firms. Trade union membership remains large across all countries, but militancy differs widely. Membership and militancy clearly have been higher in Bulgaria and Romania, with militancy being partly driven by "new" unions battling with the old union structures over the membership pool. Although data on strikes are not available, it is clear that strike incidence has been highest in Romania, Poland, and Bulgaria. Militancy in the former CSFR and Hungary is almost completely absent. Trade union power appears related across countries to workers' strength in firms, but one should probably see both as reflections of the same cause, the general role of workers in the transition process, rather than as causally related to each other.

The second qualification is that of the horizons of both workers and managers, which in turn depend on the process of privatization. Country approaches to privatization have varied very significantly in scale, procedure, and timing (see Frydman, Rapaczynski, and Earle 1993). In some countries such as Bulgaria and Romania, despite elaborate plans, little has been accomplished, save with small-scale, largely retail, privatization. And with the exception of Russia and the Czech Republic, large-scale privatization has been slow in implementation, with actual changes to ownership and control rights significantly lagging announced schedules.

In Russia insiders have been encouraged to take over their firms, with managers getting a disproportionate share (Boycko, Schleifer, and Vishny 1993).[1] By contrast, the Czech and Romanian mass privatizations have

1. Over 75 percent of firms have been transformed by purchase of majority shares through closed subscription by insiders.

conferred more limited rights to insiders, but the full effects have yet to work through in both instances. Poland stands somewhere in between.

In general, as time has passed, the likelihood that insiders would get substantial rights has steadily increased, largely as the political price to be paid for privatization to actually take place. This is important because it has affected the effective horizon of both managers and workers pre-privatization. When, at the beginning of reform, privatization seemed imminent, and the stakes of the current insiders postprivatization appeared small, there was little reason for either managers or workers to act with long horizons and to embark on restructuring. In some cases—such as Poland in 1991—this resulted in wage claims and associated behavior consistent with decapitalization of the firm. But delays in privatization and higher postprivatization stakes have led firms to act with a longer horizon. This appears to be the case in Poland (Pinto, Belka, and Krajewski 1993). This is a delicate equilibrium, however, and delays can be a symptom of a wider inability to forge a consensus for ownership change. In such cases—Bulgaria and Romania are perhaps the best examples—the gains from nonmyopic behavior are less obvious and effective decapitalization may proceed. While not necessarily showing up in large wage claims, low investment and absent restructuring are likely outcomes.

The third qualification is that the external environment in which state firms have operated is very different from that of firms in Western countries. Of particular relevance is the degree of softness, current and prospective, of the budget constraint. In most countries, a commitment to reform, as well as a dire fiscal situation, led quickly to a hardened budget constraint for state firms—Russia is again the obvious exception. The evolution of subsidies is given in table 7-2. The decline is large across most countries, save in Russia and Romania.[2] But the perception that the constraint was hard and would likely remain so took longer for firms to accept. Moreover, subsidies have commonly constituted only one measure of the budget constraint. In most contexts, other mechanisms, such as tax arrears, unpaid social security contributions, and cheap credit lines, have contributed to softening the budget constraint or at least blurring

---

2. The table likely underestimates subsidies to firms because it does not include subsidies through quasi-fiscal channels. A measure of the difference this can make is Romania in 1992; subsidies through the budget were no more than 3 percent of GDP; including the interest rate and other channels yields 12 percent.

Table 7-2. Subsidies to State Enterprise
(percent of GDP)

Country	1990	1991	1992
Hungary	3.2	2.6	2.1
Poland	6.2	3.1	1.4
CSFR	14.2	9.7	5.5
Slovakia	9.6	5.5	4.1
Bulgaria	8.8	3.0	3.2
Romania	3.6	2.5	2/3
Russia	—	—	28.7

— Not available.
Note: Covers only budgetary subsidies.
Source: Hungary, National Bank of Hungary; Poland, *Statistical Bulletin*; CSFR, IMF; Slovakia, IMF; Bulgaria, Ministry of Finance; Romania, World Bank; Russia, World Bank.

the financing issue. As firms' perceptions have changed, so has their setting of wages and employment.

It is in this light that one must look at the evolution of wages and employment since the beginning of the transition. What we see—and present in more detail below—corresponds to a clear pattern, with some caveats. At the outset of reforms, employment reductions were small and often came through quits and early retirements. Wages were set either below or close to the ceilings indicated by the incomes policies (Blanchard and Layard 1992; Jackman and Pages 1993). As the transition has proceeded, longer horizons and the perception of tighter budget constraints have led state firms to shed labor faster. Involuntary separations have increased. At the same time, wages have increased, but usually in relation to the performance of firms.

Employment and Wages in the State Sector

The Decline in Output

Figures 7-2 and 7-3 show the decline in both GDP and in industrial output for the countries since 1990. GDP reflects in part the evolution of the private sector, but industrial production is very much dominated by state firms.

Figure 7-2. GDP at Constant Prices

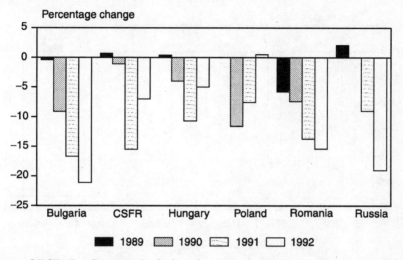

Source: OECD *Employment Outlook*, July 1992; *Employment Observatory* 4, May 1993; *Goskomstat* (various issues).

The figures indicate the very large decline in production that has affected all countries since the start of transition. The cumulated decrease in GDP since 1989 ranges from 18 percent in Poland to 40 percent in Bulgaria. The cumulated decrease in industrial production ranges from 31 percent in Hungary to 54 percent in Bulgaria. Even if we believe that official statistics overestimate the size of output loss, we are still left with large contractions, which have come on top of an earlier deceleration in growth.

A closer look shows different time patterns across countries. In the three more advanced Central European countries, the largest decline in output happened in the year in which transition started in earnest—1990 for Poland, 1991 for the other two. By mid-1992 in Poland, the decline in industrial output appears to have stabilized, with industrial output in the first half of 1993 nearly 10 percent higher than in the previous year. In Hungary and the Czech Republic the decline stabilizes in 1993, and there are now weak signs of an upturn. Bulgaria differs in that, while it also has its largest decline at the beginning of reform, the rate of decline is still very large in 1992. And in Russia and Romania the rate of decline is still increasing in 1992.

Figure 7-3. Industrial Production

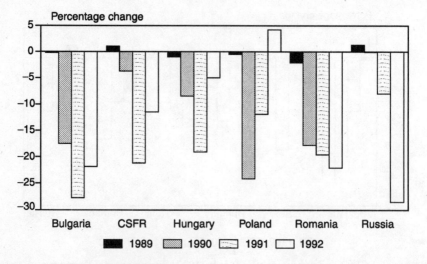

Source: OECD *Employment Outlook*, July 1992; *Employment Observatory 4*, May 1993; *Goskomstat* (various issues).

While this is not our main focus, understanding why output has declined so much is essential to our task. From the evidence gathered by others, as well as for this project, the decline in most countries appears to have two conceptually distinct causes.

The first, which dominated the beginning of transition, is an aggregate shock, a combination of depressed aggregate demand and a credit squeeze. The second, which has become increasingly important, is reallocation, shifts in relative costs, and shifts in relative demand. This interpretation is based on many clues. Among them is the small variance of relative output movements across sectors at the beginning of transition, with the variance increasing in the second and third years of transition. The evolution of those variances is shown in table 7-3. An exception to the general pattern seems to be Hungary, where structural changes played a more important role earlier, with clear asymmetric response across sectors as early as 1990. Another clue is the correlation between relative sectoral price and output changes. If relative demand shocks were dominant from the start, one would expect to see a positive correlation between the two. And, with the exception of Hungary and Bulgaria, during the first year of reform correlations are very low—in absolute value. In Poland the

Table 7-3. Variation of Output Changes in Industry
(percent, absolute value)

Country	1990	1991	1992
Hungary	62	42	33
Poland	26	68	208
Czech Republic	147	43	52
Slovak Republic	240	45	206
Bulgaria	186[a]	96	102
Romania	40	36	96

a. 1989 for Bulgaria.

correlation that was negative and insignificant in 1990 has turned positive and significant in 1991 and 1992 (Borensztein, Demekas, and Ostry 1993; Chapter 2 of this volume). Interestingly—but this may tell us more about the indicators than about Central Europe—the correlation between indicators of ex ante comparative advantage, such as domestic resource costs, and output is not significant in any of the countries.

The Adjustment of Employment

Figure 7-4 gives the movements of employment, output, and labor productivity in industry for the various countries, beginning in 1989 for Poland and 1990 for the others.

In all countries, except Russia, the employment decline since the beginning of transition exceeds 20 percent. But the figure also shows that the employment decline has lagged behind the output decline. At the start of the reforms firms commonly reaped windfall profits and this, coupled with short horizons, led firms to react to the sharp initial drop in output with only gradual reductions in employment. Bulgaria stands as one exception, perhaps because of the size of the output shock and the inability of firms to protect employment. And Russia, because of the soft budget constraint, represents the most extreme case; some sectors indeed reported increases in employment in 1992, probably reflecting an elasticity of subsidies with respect to the firm's employment close to unity.

In the general pattern, as output was declining, employment declined, but more slowly; in countries where output has stabilized, employment has kept declining. Productivity has gone down, and is now stable, or

Figure 7-4. Developments in Industry

Bulgaria, 1990.Q4–1993.Q1

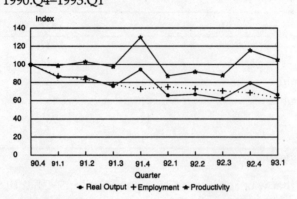

CSFR, 1990.Q1–1992.Q4

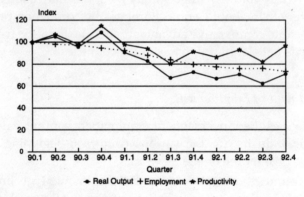

Hungary, 1990.Q1–1992.Q4

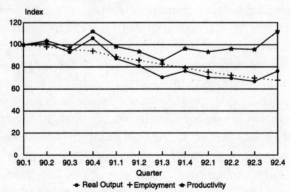

Figure 7-4. Developments in Industry *(continued)*

Poland, 1989.Q1–1993.Q1

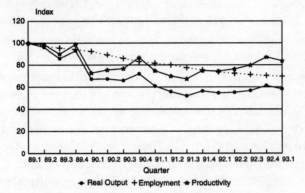

● Real Output   + Employment   ✦ Productivity

Romania, 1990.Q4–1993.Q1

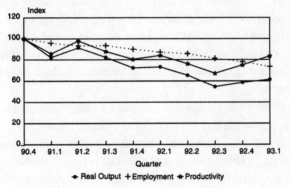

● Real Output   + Employment   ✦ Productivity

Russia, 1991.Q1–1993.Q1

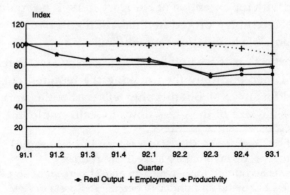

● Real Output   + Employment   ✦ Productivity

going up. Productivity in Poland stands at 85 percent of its value at the start of the transition, up from 70 percent at the trough. In what was Czechoslovakia, it stands back at 100 percent, up from 80 percent. And in Hungary, it stands at 110 percent, up from 85 percent. The outliers are Bulgaria, where the employment decline has followed closely the decline in output, and Russia, where productivity is still declining.

The evidence allows us to draw a more detailed picture, one in which separations were initially voluntary and have become increasingly involuntary. The approach of firms was first to use shorter working hours and involuntary holidays, as well as government programs that allowed for transfers to workers who left.[3] In Poland in 1990, at least 70 percent of the employment decline was through early retirements, and although elsewhere the numbers were smaller—as in Hungary, with 20 percent of the decline between 1990 and 1992 conducted by this route—the response is fairly common. Further, involuntary separations were concentrated on ancillary workers, including administrative and clerical staff. This may partly explain the high initial weight of females in total unemployment. It is revealing that it is only in Hungary, where we detect more significant structural change by 1992, that male unemployment dominates female unemployment.

Nevertheless, over time one observes a clear acceleration in involuntary separations—CSFR, Hungary, and Poland from 1991, and Romania from 1992. Even so, exits from the labor force remain important. And mass layoffs have been infrequent. This can be attributed to a combination of legal impediments, high separation costs, and, implicitly, the continuing right of workers to influence large employment decisions. The latter factor seems particularly important in Poland, Romania, and Russia.[4] Further, with the exception of Hungary in 1992, no country has had a functioning bankruptcy procedure, making the resolution of large-scale layoffs and possible liquidation more difficult.

At first inspection, these numbers suggest a state sector relying first on attrition, and then and only then making the required cuts in employment needed for survival. But this only tells part of the story. Another set of numbers—the size of the gross flows in state employment—indicates

---

3.   The most striking case is Russia, where by mid-1993 nearly 15 percent of the state work force was on involuntary leave or short time.
4.   Mass layoffs accounted for between 16 and 21 percent of employment losses in 1990 and 1991 in Poland and under 10 percent in Russia in 1992.

that this picture must be at least shaded. In the countries for which we have data, flows into state employment have been far from insignificant. In Poland in 1992, while the flow out of state employment was 20 percent of total employment, the inflow was a surprisingly high 10 percent. In Hungary, the flow out for 1992 was 22 percent, the flow in 10 percent. In Russia, the numbers were a surprising 22 percent and 19 percent, respectively. Although these inflow rates are a long way from the 35 percent observed in the U.S. labor market, they are nevertheless significant.

We think that these high numbers for hires have different causes. The high rates in Russia probably reflect a combination of factors. These include the option that firms have to increase the subsidies they receive by hiring additional workers, overoptimistic perceptions of the future path of output, and technology with Leontief properties (Commander and Jackman 1993). This, however, can hardly be the story in Hungary and Poland in 1992. Heterogeneity of workers and the need to replace some quits even in the face of declining employment may be part of the explanation. Heterogeneity of firms, with some firms expanding even in a depressed sector, may be the other. Hungarian evidence on hiring by firms over time appears to support this view, but evidence on the distribution of employment movements by firms is still fragmentary.

How much more labor shedding and restructuring is still to come is too hard a question for us to answer. The survey by Pinto, Belka, and Krajewski (1993) gives assessments by managers of firms of remaining excess employment as of mid-1992 in Poland. The median stands between 5 and 10 percent and the mean around 12 percent, with excess employment still at 10 percent in profitable firms. In Hungary, the proportion of firms reporting new hires has steadily increased, from about 10 percent in the second half of 1991 to about 25 percent in the first half of 1993. The stabilization of state employment in some countries may be an indication that under existing ownership arrangements we are seeing the end of the decline. But it may also reflect governments' reluctance to tolerate more employment losses. This may explain the recent evolution of state employment in Bulgaria, where the fiscal and political implications of further employment losses have led to de facto subsidies to firms, with consequent labor hoarding.

But this raises the issue of what happens as privatization is actually implemented. Regressions associating employment changes with actual or projected ownership change in Hungary indicate a reasonably robust, negative relationship. But, in general, there is little hard evidence that change of title or ownership has consistently proven—in employment—a measure of regime change. And in the Czech Republic, it is striking to find that despite the introduction of a bankruptcy law (April 1993) and conclusion of the first round of voucher privatization, this has not triggered any significant scale of of closures. Banks appear fearful of unleashing large secondary bankruptcies. The general pattern is thus of employment reductions being widely initiated by state firms, with title change as yet a weak measure of structural change. We have given earlier the reasons why this is the case.

The Evolution of Wages

Figure 7-5 details the evolution of consumption wages, product wages, and unit labor costs for the various countries, since 1989 in Poland and since 1990 elsewhere.

Table 7-4 summarizes the same information in a different way, by giving a decomposition of unit labor costs. Unit labor costs can be expressed as the product of the consumption wage, times the ratio of the consumption deflator to the product price, times the inverse of labor productivity. Thus, they go up if either consumption wages go up, the wedge of consumption over product prices goes up, or if labor productivity goes down. The table gives the contribution of each of the three components.

The figure and the table suggest a largely similar picture across countries. In all cases, the start of the transition was associated with a sharp decrease in consumption wages.[5] The cut in real consumption wages in the first month of stabilization ranged from 27 percent in CSFR to 57 percent in Bulgaria. By the end of the first year, consumption wages were down between 18 percent and 40 percent in Bulgaria, the former CSFR, Poland, Romania, and Russia. Only Hungary, which had a far smaller increase in the price level, had little or no real wage decline. One would have expected these wage declines to come from binding wage ceilings, associated with incomplete indexation. Indeed, this is why such ceilings were put in place. But wages were initially consistently set below

---

5.   This is the place to reiterate the often made point that measured wage declines are in part statistical artifacts because preliberalization regimes were often associated with shortages. In short, these numbers may overstate quite significantly the real wage decline, with the possible exception of CSFR, where ex ante goods market imbalances were limited.

Figure 7-5. Wage Developments

Bulgaria, 1990.Q4–1993.Q1

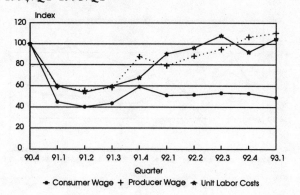

- Consumer Wage + Producer Wage ✶ Unit Labor Costs

CSFR, 1990.Q1–1992.Q4

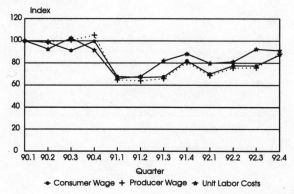

- Consumer Wage + Producer Wage ✶ Unit Labor Costs

Romania, 1990.Q4–1992.Q4

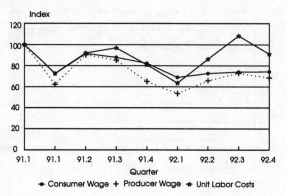

- Consumer Wage + Producer Wage ✶ Unit Labor Costs

Figure 7-5. Wage Developments *(continued)*
Poland, 1989.Q1–1993.Q1

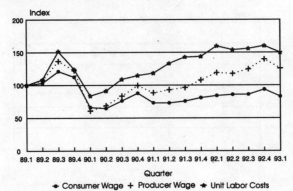

Quarter

● Consumer Wage + Producer Wage ✱ Unit Labor Costs

Russia, 1991.Q1–1993.Q1

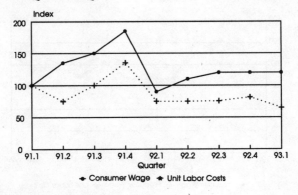

Quarter

● Consumer Wage ✱ Unit Labor Costs

Hungary, 1990.Q1–1992.Q4

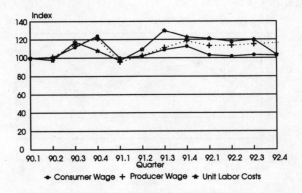

Quarter

● Consumer Wage + Producer Wage ✱ Unit Labor Costs

Table 7-4. Decomposition of Unit Labor Cost in Industry
(percentage)

Item	Bulgaria	
	1991	1992
Change in ULC	−0.39	0.31
Change in real constant wage	−0.52	−0.11
+ Change in pc/p	0.39	0.31
− Change in labor productivity	0.26	−0.12
Change in Y	−0.06	−0.17
Change in L	−0.32	−0.06

Item	CSFR		
	1990	1991	1992
Change in ULC	−0.01	−0.24	0.13
Change in real constant wage	−0.06	−0.31	0.10
+ Change in pc/p	0.05	−0.07	0.02
− Change in labor productivity	0.00	−0.14	−0.02
Change in Y	−0.03	−0.27	−0.15
Change in L	−0.03	−0.13	−0.13

Item	Hungary		
Change in ULC	0.07	0.08	0.01
Change in real constant wage	−0.02	−0.03	−0.03
+ Change in pc/p	0.06	0.01	0.10
− Change in labor productivity	−0.04	−0.10	0.06
Change in Y	−0.09	−0.24	−0.10
Change in L	−0.05	−0.14	−0.16

Item	Poland		
Change in ULC	−0.19	0.30	0.16
Change in real constant wage	−0.39	0.03	0.14
+ Change in pc/p	−0.02	0.18	0.12
− Change in labor productivity	−0.22	−0.08	0.10
Change in Y	−0.32	−0.19	0.01
Change in L	−0.10	−0.11	−0.09

Source: National statistical bulletins and World Bank.

the ceilings imposed by wage policy in all countries except Hungary. This can be attributed to a number of reasons, the most important of which were prudence in the face of uncertainty and the desire to maintain employment; both were compounded by a liquidity squeeze (Calvo and Coricelli 1993). The initial decrease in consumption wages was followed by a partial recovery. But, by the end of 1992, consumption wages were still 20 to 35 percent below their pretransition levels; the exception is again Hungary, where consumption wages have remained roughly constant.

The evolution of product wages also reflects the increasing wedge between consumption and product prices, which is brought about by the continuing process of price liberalization. Thus, after their initial decrease, product wages have increased faster than consumption wages and are now much closer to their pretransition level. While consumption wages in Bulgaria are at 50 percent of their pretransition level, product wages are higher than before the transition! Product wages are equal to 100 percent of the pretransition level in Poland, 90 percent in the former CSFR, 110 percent in Hungary, and 80 percent in Romania.

In addition, the evolution of unit labor costs reflects the decline in labor productivity. As a result, unit labor costs stand at or above pretransition levels. The converse side is that profits are very low; wage and employment behavior of firms has been such as to appropriate most of the available profit. Table 7-5 provides, with all due caveats about the reliability of profit measures, a clear view of the sharp decline in the ratio of gross profits to sales, save in the Czech Republic pre-1992. An indicator of the scale of the decline of profits in Poland is that by early 1992, over 45 percent of Polish firms would have faced liquidation if bankruptcy procedures had been implemented (Miszei 1993).

Although we do not attempt in the table the same decomposition for Russia, the rapid acceleration in producer compared with consumer prices in 1992 and the size of the consumption wage shock offset the large fall in

Table 7-5. Gross Profits/Sales, 1989-92
(percent)

Country	1989	1990	1991	1992
Hungary	5.0	3.3	−1.1	—
Poland	28.0	23.3	6.9	3.0
CSFR	9.2	9.4	9.8	—
Slovakia	—	14.4	6.1	0.8
Bulgaria	34.7	14.7	8.2	−2.4
Romania			4.2	3.7

— Not available.
Source: IMF; World Bank; GUS; National Bank of Hungary.

labor productivity. Paradoxically, we seem to be observing a shift in favor of profits, even at a time when capitalists would be difficult to identify!

Can we say more about the determination of wages, the relative weight of employment versus wages, and the effect of labor market conditions? Even if we still lack a sharp picture, we now have a number of clues.

In all cases, wages in principle have been governed by incomes policies. This seems to have dampened dispersion in changes across sectors and branches. But more disaggregated analysis, as with Hungarian branch data, pick up greater diversity and strong branch effects. Similarly, we find divergences across countries. In Russia, real wages have hardly moved from the level given by the price shock of January 1992. The clear impression is that workers have accepted small wage adjustments, trading this off against employment stability. This may also be in anticipation of privatization, because wages appear to increase noticeably after privatization. Where macroeconomic and structural policies have been inconsistent—Romania—incumbent workers have increasingly demanded higher wages for relatively constant employment.

There appears to be an emerging correlation between labor market conditions and wage changes. One view is that countries with more generous unemployment benefits have been characterized by stronger wage pressure (Burda 1993), as suggested by the difference between Hungary and the Czech Republic. One may, however, question whether this is indeed a causal relation. High replacement ratios in Hungary for some—largely unskilled—workers cannot explain unemployment persistence or the changing composition of unemployment and do not appear to be a strong factor behind duration effects. But more generally, it is clear that unemployment benefit levels are low in all countries, with sharp declines in replacement rates over the short durations normally sanctioned by the various benefits' regimes (Scarpetta, Boeri, and Reuterswand 1993).

Hungarian data indicate a reasonably robust association between regional labor market variables and wage changes, and the regional unemployment rate displays a conventional inverse association with wages. Czech and Slovak wage regressions similarly point to strong regional unemployment effects. For the major industrial branches in Russia, aggregate and firm-level data suggest that wages have been responsive to the size of the output loss, and relating regional wage changes to an augmented unemployment rate (jobseekers plus those on involuntary leave and short-time work) yields a weak inverse association; higher levels of slack translate into lower changes to wages. In Bulgaria regional data pick out a developing and conventional negative association between the behavior of regional relative wages and regional unemployment for both 1991 and 1992.

Employment and Wages in the Private Sector

Getting an accurate handle on the size and production of the private sector is difficult, because official series understate the size of the private sector, as well as its growth. In particular, information on very small firms, which account for much of the private sector's growth, is very incomplete. To address these data gaps, we rely in part in this section on survey data.

Table 7-1 has already given our best estimates of private employment by year and country. Ideally we would have wished to match this up with information on the contribution of the private sector to GDP. But this is not yet possible; estimates vary widely and are often grossly inconsistent. But the employment data give us a good approximation of the changes.

Private sector employment has increased in all countries, often aided by explicit or implicit tax incentives. In Poland and Hungary, they have increased from a high level. Private employment in both countries is above 35 percent. In Poland, this reflects that agriculture was primarily private to start. In Hungary, this reflects the earlier presence of a large, underreported second economy that is gradually coming into statistical vision.[6] In countries with little entrepreneurial tradition—such as Bulgaria, Romania, Russia, and Slovakia—the increase has been nearly from scratch, and private sector employment stands at a smaller 10-25 percent. Only in Russia does the employment increase reflect substantial medium and large firm privatization.

New versus Old Private Sector

Net numbers hide an important compositional effect—the decline of an old private sector and the development of a new one. Part of the initial private sector either took advantage of opportunities present in socialist

---

6.   In the mid-1980s the formal private sector employed over 4 percent of the labor force, but time allocation studies indicated as much as 33 percent of active time spent in the second economy; Kornai 1993.

economies or was tied tightly to state firms. This part is, not surprisingly, not doing well. In Poland, where these compositional effects can be monitored, in 1990 failures or suspensions of "old" firms dominate new starts through most of the year so that firm destruction was at around 90 percent of the firm creation level over the full year. Similarly, in Russia the decline of the cooperatives represents the failure of the "old" private sector.

In short, the majority of private sector employment growth is accounted for by new starts, with some changes arising from transformation of title. Privatization accounts for some of the growth in small-scale retail outlets. In almost all settings, the majority of designated small units was privatized through leases or a combination of insider buyouts or auctions (ECE 1993).

The Nature of New Private Sector Firms

Our survey data give a picture of a sector dominated by small, often household-based, firms with limited use of hired labor and concentrated in the trade sector. They suggest an initial phase when the "noise" generated by price liberalization and selective dismantling of trade controls facilitated above-normal profits as small-scale entrepreneurs exploited transitory rents and market niches. This commonly was combined with retention of state sector employment as individuals hedged their risk. Over time, as relative prices adjusted, temporary windfalls have withered away, leaving the bulk of services providers with much lower margins. At this point, the overall picture is of a low-wage, low-productivity sector with low levels of capitalization and very restricted access to formal financing.

Firms are usually small employers, generally having not more than five to ten employees, are nonunion, and are weakly diversified in product markets. Firms selling directly to households appear most exposed to the contractionary effects of the reforms. In general, we observe fairly high failure rates and consequent turnover of firms, even if, for institutional reasons, the numbers are underestimated. Employment growth in these firms tends to level off quite sharply within two years of founding.

The scant available information on wages confirms the impression of a trade and services sector with jobs that are, on net, less attractive than state sector jobs.

Table 7-6. Wage Ratios, Private/State Sectors, 1991-93

Country	1991	1992	1993
Hungary			
Wages	—	1.09	0.93
Hourly earnings	—	1.02	—
Poland			
Aggregate	0.93	0.92	0.86
Blue collar	0.89	0.92	—
White collar	1.04	0.99	—
CSFR	—	1.08	—
Bulgaria	—	—	1.16-1.5
Russia	—	1.61	1.82

— Not available.
Source: Hungary, 1992 figures are for March (Kollo 1993), 1993 for January (Vilagi 1993); Poland, GUS; CSFR, Federal Statistical Office; Bulgaria, World Bank survey results (Jan. 1993); Russia, World Bank survey (Dec. 1992) and VCIOM data, March 1993.

The evidence we have about relative private-state wages is given in table 7-6. In looking at those numbers, one must remember that private firms in general offer no or few benefits compared with their state counterparts, so that at equal wages, a state job is likely to be more attractive. At a maximum, nonmonetary benefits may account for 35 percent of wages, as in Russia (Commander and Jackman 1993), but elsewhere the nonmonetary component, while lower, has also been significant. Evidence from Hungary and Poland shows large differences in the incidence of benefits between the state and private sectors.

Except in Russia, the average wage is not significantly different between the two sectors. In Poland, where three years of data are available, it is striking to observe almost no movement in the aggregate private/state wage ratio during 1991, 1992, and the first half of 1993. Private wages remain around 90-95 percent of state wages, with a slightly lower ratio for industrial firms. There is little difference between the ratios for white and blue collar workers. For Hungary, we can control for individual attributes. The results suggest that wages, earnings, and income are all higher in private firms but hours are longer, so that hourly earnings are actually lower.

Wage functions using the country survey data find weak sector effects, indicating that only small parts of the difference in wages can be explained by sectoral differences in Bulgaria, Hungary, and Poland. Firm size and turnover vary in significance, with wages generally positively related to firm size in Bulgaria and Hungary, but not in Poland. There seems to be a weak but conventional association of wages to educational attributes and other skill characteristics, suggesting a clear departure in relative occupational wages from the state sector. In almost all cases wages are systematically lower for women. The surveys show that university graduates compose a higher proportion of entrepreneurs in modern services and production sectors and that this may, at least in Bulgaria and Poland, be weakly associated with higher wage levels for employees, including higher performance-related wage components. But in general, performance-related pay remains marginal.

Differences across Countries and across Time

Aside from the role of initial conditions, especially the prior size of the sector, can we explain the differences across countries? At this stage, we can hazard a number of educated guesses. "Bad" outcomes in which private sector expansion is relatively small can be traced to a number of possible environments.

One, which appears to summarize the Bulgarian experience, involves the overadjustment of the state sector early in the reforms. Large job destruction in the state sector was compounded by a large fiscal correction and fall in government spending. The recessionary effects swamped the potential for rapid growth in the private sector. A variant—Slovakia, but also regions within overall high private growth environments, such as northeast Hungary, for example—has private growth constrained by regional or locational attributes. The simplest case is when state sector job destruction is highly concentrated within a region—through, for example, the dominance of one industry—and the shock to the regional economy, amplified by labor immobility, is sufficiently large to determine low private expansion.

A second variant—Romania—has private growth constrained by the low credibility of the reform program and the perpetuation of soft budgets in the state sector. The stimulus to private job creation through either a wage effect from labor shedding and a crowding-in effect arising from reduction in state sector claims are absent. Again, a variant on this—Russia—has nonprivatized private sector growth concentrated in activities with short-run returns and maximization of rents, a function of the unstable economic and political environment.

By contrast, our overview suggests that "good" outcomes—the Czech Republic, Hungary, and Poland—arise through a combination of credible macroeconomic policies, proximity to strong neighboring markets, higher relative inflows of foreign direct investment, and good luck; that is, Prague or Budapest.

One major issue for the future is what happens when the stock adjustment process in trade and services comes to an end. Of crucial importance here is the growth of the new private sector in manufacturing. Private employment in industry remains small, and small scale. In Poland, the private industrial sector, which at the end of 1992 accounted for just over 35 percent of total private sector employment, had an average firm size less than 10 percent of state industrial firms.[7] Many of those firms remain closely linked to the state sector, either as suppliers or as dependent for inputs. This accounts for the mixed effects of the reforms on these firms. Those that prosper generally have higher export orientation and lower exposure to domestic markets. While access to financial institutions is greater than for the firms in trade and services, we nevertheless find consistent evidence of limited access to credit. Even so, there is some evidence that manufacturing firms offer more stable employment and higher wage levels than the bulk of jobs in services.

Finally, we note that the private sector's growth has been assisted by low tax burdens. In some cases, these have been by way of explicit incentives for investment but, more commonly, by tax evasion. The limited data that are available indicate that the private sector's contribution to tax revenues is much lower than the contribution to output. For Poland in 1992 the contribution to sales was 46 percent; the contribution to corporate income tax, 27 percent. And these numbers are overestimates given the scale of outright evasion.

This position will clearly change as governments try to close their fiscal gaps through higher revenue yields. But, by the same token, a more

---

7.   State firms—often behemoths—had an average work force of 650, as against 45 for private firms.

efficient tax administration and incidence is likely to choke off some of the growth in the private sector.

Unemployment

Employment and Unemployment Changes

Table 7-7 puts employment and unemployment changes together. It gives, for each country, the change in total employment, decomposed between the decline in state employment and the increase in private employment, as well as the change in unemployment since the beginning of the transition (1989 for Poland, 1990 for the other countries). All are expressed in terms of the labor force at the beginning of the transition. Finally, it gives the ratio of the change in unemployment to the absolute value of the change in employment. The motivation is simple. Under the benchmark case of no change in working-age population, and all workers going from employment to unemployment, the ratio is equal to 1. Values much below 1 indicate that much of the employment decline has translated into nonparticipation rather than unemployment.

Table 7-7. Employment and Unemployment Changes
(percent of initial labor force)

Country	Change in employment	Change in state employment	Change in private employment	Change in unemployment	Ratio
Poland	−12.6	(−20.3)	(7.7)	14.6	1.14
Hungary	−12.3	(−34.0)[a]	(21.0)[a]	13.1	1.06
Czech Republic	−7.5	(−16.0)[b]	(11.3)[b]	3.0	0.40
Slovakia	−12.4	(−22.4)	(9.6)	11.6	0.93
Bulgaria	−23.9	(−21.7)[b]	(8.7)	12.1	0.51
Romania	−5.9	(−9.8)[c]	(4.4)	6.4	1.08
Russia	−4.1	(−17.6)	(13.8)	1.3	0.31

a. Kollo 1993.
b. 1991 over 1990.
c. 1992 over 1991.
Note: Results are given as percentage of initial labor force: Poland, 1992 over 1989; others 1992 over 1990.

Consider first the three major Central European countries—Poland, Hungary, and the Czech Republic.[8] The table suggests two proximate reasons for the lower unemployment rate in the Czech Republic. The first is a larger offset of the decline in state employment by private sector growth. The decrease in state employment is similar to that of Poland, but private sector employment is higher. The second is a much lower ratio of the change in unemployment to the change in employment; tough unemployment eligibility rules clearly have led many more workers in the Czech Republic to become nonparticipants rather than unemployed. In Poland, by contrast, the ratio is greater than 1, indicating that, despite the importance of early retirements at the beginning of the transition, much of the subsequent decrease in employment has translated into unemployment rather than nonparticipation. Were the Czech Republic to have the same ratio as Poland, the unemployment rate would be close to 8 percent. Were the Czech Republic to have the same ratio as Slovakia, the rate would be close to 7 percent, compared with 11.6 percent for Slovakia. Thus, the short answer to why unemployment is lower in the Czech Republic includes both stronger private employment growth and a larger increase in nonparticipation.

In Bulgaria the primary cause of high unemployment is the combination of large losses in state employment and a struggling private sector. And a large part of the employment decline has translated into nonparticipation. Were Bulgaria to have a ratio of 1 rather than .5, its unemployment rate would be close to 30 percent.

Russia, and to a lesser extent Romania, offer yet another configuration, one in which state employment has declined less (except through reclassification from privatization), private employment has increased less (except, again, through reclassification), and unemployment is thus relatively low. In Russia, the ratio of unemployment to employment changes is again very low; were it equal to 1, the unemployment rate would stand around 4 percent. Thus, the short answer to why unemployment is low in Russia is little state employment decline and increases in nonparticipation.

---

8.   While the change in total employment for Hungary is reliable, the decomposition between changes in state and private employment is not. The number for 1990 may understate private employment. The change in private employment from 1991 to 1992, for which data exist, is small, less than 2 percent of the labor force. See table 7-1.

Table 7-8. Unemployment Inflow Rates and Outflow Rates, 1992 Averages

Country	Unemployment rate	Inflow rate	Outflow rate	Outflow rate to jobs	Long-term unemployed share
Poland	14.9	0.7	4.0	2.3	43.4
Hungary	11.7	0.5	7.0	3.0	37.3
Czech Republic	3.1	0.6	25.8	18.0	28.4
Slovakia	11.4	1.0	9.8	4.8	25.5
Bulgaria	6.0	1.8	5.5	1.1	—
Romania	8.3	—	1.2	0.9	—
Russia	1.3	0.3	18.0	7.5	—

Note: Inflow rate as a proportion of the labor force; outflow rate as a proportion of unemployment.
Source: Unemployment rates: *Employment Observatory*; flows, country papers and World Bank.

The Nature of Unemployment

We contrasted earlier two extreme views of unemployment in the transition. The first was that of a stagnant pool, with a small exit rate from unemployment to jobs; the other was of a high turnover pool, a way station between jobs. In most countries, the reality is still much closer to the first than to the second. Table 7-8 gives the inflow and outflow rates for 1992 for the different countries.

In all countries except the Czech Republic and Russia exit rates from unemployment to jobs are below 5 percent, ranging from 0.9 percent in Romania (an expected duration, conditional on exit to a job, of eight years) to 4.8 percent (an expected duration of two years) in Slovakia.

Again, the Czech Republic and Russia stand in contrast to the other countries, and, again, they do so for very different reasons. In both countries, the monthly outflow rate from unemployment to jobs is high, standing at 18 percent. Another way of thinking about the Czech Republic is to look at the outflow rate as a proportion of employment rather than unemployment; this rate is equal to .55 percent, roughly similar, for example, to .34 percent in Poland. If we add the flow from nonparticipation to employment, which, as we saw, is likely to be higher in the Czech Republic, the picture this gives is one with larger job creation, a smaller unemployment pool, and thus higher exit rates. While unemployment eligibility has been strongly tightened and expires after six months, more than two-thirds of exits from unemployment are to jobs rather than to nonparticipation. In Russia, the high outflow rate corresponds to a low ratio of outflows to employment, and the outflows reflect the high level of turnover in the state sector, which can ultimately be traced to the continuing soft budget constraint.

The increase in unemployment rates and the low exit rates have come in the face of a drastic tightening of eligibility rules for unemployment. With increasing deficits in all countries—in the range of 5-9 percent of GDP by 1992—fiscal realities, more than a desire to increase search incentives, have motivated these changes. Although benefits expenditures by 1992 rarely exceeded 2 percent of GDP, and were often much lower, this measure excludes social assistance to those ineligible for benefits and pension and other payments that, given the increase in early retirements and nonparticipation, are akin to benefits. Total social security program expenditures variously account for 8-25 percent of GDP, on a clear rising trend.[9]

As regards the incidence of unemployment by gender, age, and educational attainment, the main message from figure 7-6 is that the distribution of unemployment does not appear very different from that of Western countries at similar rates of unemployment. Unemployment rates are slightly higher for women than men, except in Hungary.[10] But the pattern is less pronounced than for France and Spain. Although one may have expected retrenchment in the state sector to lead to high unemployment among new entrants, unemployment rates for the young, while higher than for older workers, are again not out of line with those of France and Spain, and one does not see unusually low rates for skilled workers.

There is, however, one major difference, by region. Figure 7-7 shows unemployment rates across regions in various countries. There is large dispersion in regional unemployment rates. Even economies that are now experiencing growth, such as Hungary and Poland, have large regional differences. The causes are various. Some reflect long-term differences,

---

9.   See *Employment Observatory* for a full description of the various systems.
10.   The obvious exception remains Russia, where the unemployment rate is very low and where the share of women is particularly high, about 70 percent.

Figure 7-6. Characteristics of the Unemployed

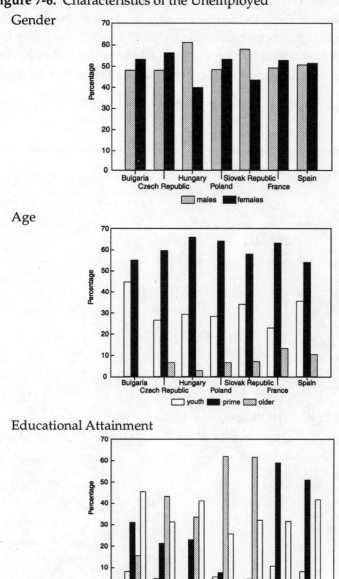

Gender

Age

Educational Attainment

Note: All data relate to 1993, second and third quarter.
Source: OECD, CCET Data base, and ILO *Bulletin of Labor Statistics.*

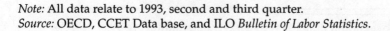

exaggerated by the earlier policy of placing heavy industry in "backward" areas. Because these industries are now in decline, the shocks to local employment have been profound. Indeed, this, writ large, is the inheritance of Slovakia and Bulgaria, and to a lesser extent of northeast Hungary.[11] Similarly, regions with dominant industries and low diversity

Figure 7-7. Regional Unemployment, 1993.Q2

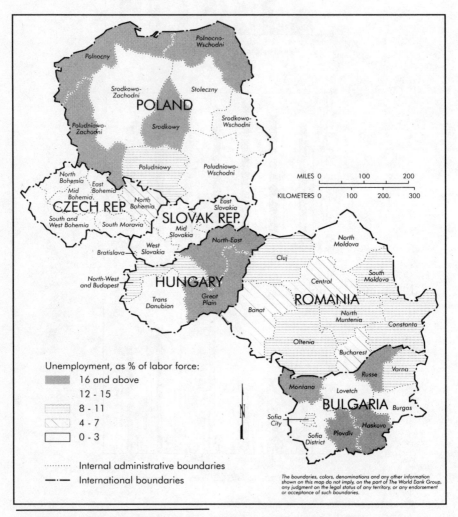

---

11. Both Slovakia and Bulgaria were largely agricultural pre-1950.

in production that have experienced large adverse shocks have offered few opportunities for compensating private sector growth.

As indicated earlier, it appears that private growth has been concentrated in the large cities and in border regions. Unemployment rates in cities are consistently and significantly below national averages across all our countries. A combination of more prior diversity in the state sector and market concentration for the emerging private sector seem to be the explanatory factors.

Looking at Gross Flows

One would want to see a full picture of the role of unemployment versus nonparticipation, decline and turnover in the state sector, and increase and turnover in the private sector. There are only two countries where such a picture can be put together, using the information from household surveys, unemployment registers, and data on the size and composition of separations and accessions by firms. These are Poland and Hungary, for 1992 over 1991.

The full set of flows for both countries is represented in figures 7-8 and 7-9.[12] But a few points need to be made in the text. The flows for Poland refer to the year 1992 and are put together from data on firms and unemployment registers. The flows for Hungary refer to changes between March 1991 and March 1992 and come mostly from the household survey. The numbers with stars are the results of computations that rely partly on guesses; the others come straight out of one of the data sources.

The flows for Poland suggest the following conclusions. The first is that state sector declines have been associated with substantial gross flows, a point made earlier. The composition of separations in 1992 is clearly different from that earlier in the transition. Layoffs dominate, accounting for 56 percent of separations (a better number is the range computed under the various assumptions, which varies from 46 percent to 56 percent). Quits account for 26 percent (with a range of 26 to 32 percent), and movements out of the labor force for 18 percent (with a range of 18 to 22 percent).

The second is that there is substantial turnover in the private sector as well. The numbers suggest a slowly growing private sector in 1992; part of the explanation is that these numbers do not reflect title changes. Lay-

---

12. The details of construction are available from the authors.

Figure 7-8. Poland, Flows

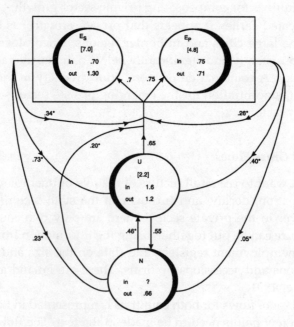

Figure 7-9. Hungary, Flows

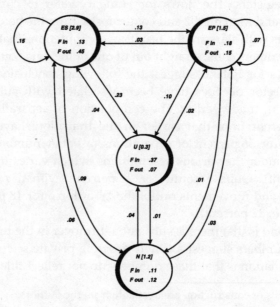

offs and quits both account for the bulk of separations. The figure assumes that layoffs account for 56 percent of separations, quits for 37 percent. The respective ranges overlap, however—34 percent to 56 percent for layoffs, 55 percent to 37 percent for quits.

The third is that flows to and from unemployment dominate those from nonparticipation. Of the flow of accessions, 40 percent come directly from other jobs, 45 percent from unemployment, and only 15 percent from out of the labor force. It is also wrong to think of unemployment as mostly composed of state workers who have lost their jobs. Of the flows into unemployment, 45 percent come from state employment, 25 percent from private employment, and 30 percent are new or reentrants. These are very close to the proportions of the stock from each of the three sources, implying that exit rates are roughly independent of where the workers come from. The figure confirms, however, that while there are flows in and out of unemployment, these flows are small compared with the stock; equivalently, the exit rate from unemployment to jobs is low, standing at 30 percent a year, or 2.4 percent at a monthly rate.

The picture from Hungary for 1991-92 is interesting for two reasons. The first is that it is another observation; the second is that it gives us a picture of an economy roughly one year after transition started in earnest, whereas transition in Poland is already in its third year. Thus, it gives us a pseudo time dimension.

Many of the features are similar to Poland. Both the private and state sectors show reasonably high turnover, with the ratio of inflows to employment of at least 5 percent in the declining state sector and at least 12 percent in the private sector. But one is different. Much more of the movement in and out of the two sectors comes from quits rather than layoffs. The ratio of quits to layoffs is equal to 1.12 compared with about .5 to .8 (depending on which values are picked in the ranges given above) in Poland. As a result, the flows from employment to employment dominate the flows from unemployment to employment. Unemployment is growing, but with a low exit rate.

This difference between Poland and Hungary fits well the evolution of the transition we have developed earlier, one where the initial adjustment is largely due to voluntary separations, and unemployment plays a minor role, and where involuntary separations and unemployment become increasingly central to the adjustment process as time passes.

Conclusions

We have tried to bind together the various transitions and to have a clear sight of the larger picture. We now flag both the labor market issues we see as central for the future of these countries and—the two are closely related—the outstanding research issues we want to focus on in the second part of our research program.

For the three major Central European countries—Poland, Hungary, and the Czech Republic—a bad scenario might proceed along the following lines. Labor shedding continues at a rapid pace in the state and privatized sectors and the process of stock adjustment that has led to high new private sector growth so far comes to an end. Unemployment further increases, endangering reform through its effect on the fiscal position and by sapping political support for reform. We do not attach a high probability to such a scenario.

Many feedback mechanisms are at work. Some are conventional. Higher unemployment and a lower rate of hiring likely make remaining employed in state firms more attractive, leading to more wage moderation and more wage concessions aimed at slowing down labor shedding. Some are more specific to this process of transition. It is clear that the speed of privatization is endogenous; privatization from below is becoming increasingly the rule and requires acceptance by insiders. Worse labor market conditions and opportunities for those who lose their jobs are likely to slow it down. Top-down privatization, imposed on firms, is of limited importance. But even there, its speed is very much affected by the political process, which in turn is very much affected by the shape of transition. The recent elections in Poland can be seen as part of this feedback mechanism. We believe that if private sector growth slows down, the result is likely to be a slowdown of restructuring in the state sector, rather than an increase in unemployment. The risk, however, is that there will be pressure on the state to help state firms in trouble through subsidies, fiscal deficits, and monetization. So far, this risk has been avoided.

The research questions associated with this argument are clear. They involve finding out how much labor shedding remains to be done in state firms, and whether, and how fast, the private sector can extend beyond trade and services. They involve finding the elasticity of labor shedding, of private sector growth to wages, and labor market conditions. They involve understanding the dynamics of privatization from below.

The picture elsewhere is sadly less bright. A bad scenario is easier to envisage for Bulgaria and, to a lesser degree, Slovakia. It is roughly a continuation of the current depression. We see what is happening there as reflecting both a larger shock and two perverse feedback mechanisms. Too large a decline in the state sector can both decrease demand so much as to make difficult any substantial growth from the private sector, and decrease fiscal revenues so as to create either a fiscal crisis or drastically reduce the range of measures the government can take to help the transition.

This brings us to a set of research questions we have alluded to in the chapter at various points, but not systematically explored—those of the interactions between the transition and fiscal policy. Appropriation of rents in state firms preprivatization has led to the disappearance of profit, and thus of profit taxation. Privatization of firms may eventually recreate a profit tax base, but labor shedding leads to higher unemployment and larger social expenditures. The growth of the private sector holds the promise of a stronger economy and a stronger tax base. But so far the private sector has been able to avoid most of the burden of taxation. New wide-based taxes, such as the VAT, have been introduced only recently. Empirical and analytical exploration of those interactions and of the overall implications of the fiscal position for government's decisions is urgently needed.

This leaves a last set of countries, Russia and Romania. In Russia, despite the progress on privatization, the process of transition from state to private employment has barely begun. State firms still operate under soft budget constraints, one consequence of which is acute macroeconomic instability. Romania now seems to be further along. The issues are clearly of whether, how, and how fast the budget constraint will be hardened. Doing this too quickly could lead to a Bulgarian outcome. At this stage it appears politically unlikely.

Bibliography

Aghion, P., and Olivier Blanchard. 1993. "On the Speed of Transition in Eastern Europe." MIT, Cambridge, Mass. Mimeo.

Blanchard, Olivier, and R. Layard. 1992. "Post Stabilization Inflation in Poland." In F. Coricelli and A. Revenga, eds., *Wage Policy during the Transition to a Market Economy, Poland 1990-1991.* Washington, D.C.: World Bank.

Borensztein, E. R., D. Demekas, and J. Ostry. 1993. "Output Decline in the Aftermath of Reform: The Cases of Bulgaria, Czechoslovakia and Romania." In

M. Blejer and others, eds., *Eastern Europe in Transition: From Recession to Growth?* World Bank Discussion Paper 196, Washington, D.C.

Boycko, M., A. Schleifer, and R. Vishny. 1993. "Privatizing Russia." *Brookings Papers on Economic Activity* 2: 139-92.

Burda, M., 1993. "Labor Markets in Eastern Europe." *Economic Policy*: 102-37.

Calvo, Guillermo, and F. Coricelli. 1993. *Credit Market Imperfections and Output Response in Previously Centrally Planned Economies.* Washington, D.C.: IMF and World Bank.

Commander, Simon, Fabrizio Coricelli, and Karsten Staehr. 1992. "Wages and Employment in the Transition to a Market Economy." In G. Winckler, ed., *Central and Eastern Europe: Roads to Growth.* Washington, D.C.: IMF and Austrian National Bank.

Commander, Simon, and Richard Jackman. 1993. *Providing Social Benefits in Russia: The Role of Firms and Government.* World Bank Working Paper 1184, Washington, D.C.

Commander, Simon, John McHale, and Ruslan Yemtsov. 1993. "Russia." Paper prepared for Conference on Unemployment and Restructuring in East Europe and Russia, World Bank, October.

ECE (Economic Commission for Europe). 1993. *Progress in Privatization 1990-1992.* Geneva.

Employment Observatory, Central and Eastern Europe: Employment Trends and Developments. Various issues. Brussels.

Estrin, Saul, A. Gelb, and I. J. Singh. 1993. *Restructuring, Viability and Privatization: A Comparative Study of Enterprise Adjustment in Transition.* Washington, D.C.: London Business School and the World Bank.

Estrin, Saul, M. Schaffer, and I. J. Singh. 1993. "Enterprise Adjustment in Transition Economies: Czechoslovakia, Hungary and Poland." In M. Blejer and others, eds., *Eastern Europe in Transition: From Recession to Growth?* World Bank Discussion Paper 196, Washington, D.C.

Frydman, Roman, A. Rapaczynski, and J. Earle. 1993. *The Privatization Process in Central Europe.* London: Central European University Press.

Jackman, Richard, and Carmen Pages. 1993. "Wage Policy and Inflation in East Europe." World Bank, Washington, D.C. Mimeo.

Johnson, Simon. 1993. "Who Creates the Good Jobs after Communism? Evidence from the Polish Private Sector." Duke University, Durham, N.C.

Kollo, Janos. 1993. "Flows of Labor, Employment and Wages in the Private Sector in Hungary." Institute of Economics, Budapest.

Kornai, Janos. 1993. "Transformational Recession: A General Phenomenon Examined through the Example of Hungary's Development." Discussion Paper 1, Collegium Budapest, Institute for Advanced Study.

Lane, Timothy D., and Elias Dinopoulos. 1991. "Fiscal Constraints on Market-Oriented Reform in a Socialist Economy." IMF Working Paper WP/91/75, Washington, D.C.

Miszei, Kalman. 1993. *Bankruptcy and the Post-Communist Economies of East Central Europe.* New York: Institute for East-West Studies.

Pinto, Brian, M. Belka, and S. Krajewski. 1993. "Transforming State Enterprises in Poland. Microeconomic Evidence on Adjustment." World Bank, Washington, D.C.

Scarpetta, Stefano, Tito Boeri, and Anders Reuterswand. 1993. "Unemployment Benefit Systems and Active Labor Market Policies in Central and Eastern Europe; An Overview." Paper presented at OECD Technical Workshop on the Persistence of Unemployment in Central and Eastern Europe, Paris, October.

8

Labor Market Institutions and the Economic Transformation of Central and Eastern Europe

Michael C. Burda

In modern advanced capitalist economies, the market mechanism allocates resources as diverse as agricultural products, complex machinery, financial assets, and contracts for future delivery of all sorts of goods and services. Yet market allocation of labor services can have socially undesirable consequences. First, the average citizen or median voter may prefer not to observe extreme inequality of income or live in a society where such disparity reigns. Second, societies may choose to exclude extreme outcomes ex ante through a "Rawlsian contract" of progressive income taxation and "social insurance" guaranteeing minimum living standards. Finally, regulation of labor markets may be justified by purely utilitarian motives; for example, to prevent a breakdown of social consensus that might be associated with their efficient functioning.

This chapter was prepared for the conference "Unemployment, Restructuring, and the Labor Market in East Europe and Russia," World Bank/EDI, Washington D.C., October 7-8, 1993. I would like to thank Simon Commander, Marek Góra, Krzyzstof Hagemejer, Janos Köllô, Alan Krueger, Pavol Ochotnicky, Gheorghe Oprescu, Mariela Nenová, and Jan Svejnar for data and useful discussions.

These issues are of particular importance to the emerging market economies of Central and Eastern Europe (CEE). Concern for "solidarity"—which has a natural Rawlsian interpretation—motivates policymakers in the area just as it does in the richest continental European countries. Yet policies aimed at increasing equity and security can be seen as a costly public good (in lost efficiency) that only richer societies may wish to have or can afford to adopt. The CEE economies thus face the difficult problem of selecting labor market institutions in the midst of radical structural change. In one sense these countries have an advantage of starting from *tabula rasa*; at the same time, their citizens have expectations of significant and rapid improvements in living standards. Recent setbacks for reform governments are a sign that the tolerance of the general public is limited and perhaps growing thin. By setting incentives in the most important of all markets, the choice of labor market institutions will be crucial to the transition.

This chapter surveys the role of these institutions in the economies of Central and Eastern Europe. The following section reviews the central purpose of such institutions and presents a framework in which they can be analyzed. In the following sections some of the usual arguments for labor market regulations are investigated and the current institutional state of affairs in Eastern Europe is reviewed and compared. On the basis of the effects of these policies in OECD countries, the prospects for a return to low unemployment rates in the medium to long term in the CEE economies will be evaluated.

What are Labor Market Institutions?

The notion of "labor market institutions" is a broad one. At a minimum, all advanced industrial economies possess a body of labor and contract law that eliminates fundamental kinds of uncertainty and establishes a minimal environment for individual or collective labor agreements. Workers generally possess the right to organize and to strike under certain conditions, and firms have the right to lock out workers or to circumscribe their influence on management decisionmaking. Some countries have gone further in regulating the employment relationship. Collective bargaining may be governed by institutional guidelines or active tripartite participation by the government (see Flanagan, Soskice, and Ullman 1983 or Bruno and Sachs 1985). Through works councils, employees may have substantial say in the day-to-day management of personnel matters, as well as detailed information on the functioning of the firm. Employers' ability to fire workers for economic or noneconomic (disciplinary) reasons may be regulated or limited by labor ministries or the courts, and minimum severance bonus payments may be legally mandated.

Interventions may be designed to prevent market clearing; the price of labor can fall in real terms when labor markets are slack or when certain types of labor are in excess supply. Minimum wages and other administered wage systems can be seen as bounding the extent to which this can occur. Some interventions go further and secure monopoly power for existing unions and employers' associations. In Germany, for example, there is no legal minimum wage, yet either explicitly or implicitly the collectively bargained wage is generally extended to all employers and employees in the industry. It has also been argued that minimum wages can counteract local monopsony power (Machin and Manning 1992) or improve the selection of workers. For those whose benefits expire or who do not qualify, systems of unemployment assistance and, more generally, the social safety net are conceived to guarantee some minimum standard of living while unemployed.

A final important role of institutions and state intervention is to ensure the orderly accumulation of human capital. Job loss is a partially insurable random event that puts existing human capital at risk. As either a substitute for or a complement to the market, the state has implemented systems of unemployment insurance that protect human capital from premature occupational, industrial, or locational change. Another well-justified intervention is linked to market failures in the provision of adequate training that results from credit market failures, moral hazard, or imperfect information. Manpower programs can be justified if training has external benefits or if the firms are reluctant to train because workers may leave. Another aspect is the role of experience in earnings, which suggests that "keeping at it" long enough is an investment, and that learning-by-doing is an important mechanism for adapting to new technologies. The exponential pace of technical progress rapidly renders knowledge and know-how obsolete. The level of human capital in the population may be a public good, justifying state intervention and more draconian administration of unemployment benefits in order to prevent its obsolescence through idleness (for evidence, see Jackman, Pissarides, and Savouri 1990).

The Importance of Institutions for Labor Market Outcomes

The benefits of policies that increase equity and reduce inequality must be balanced against the associated costs. Such interventions may interfere directly with the working of the marketplace or distort individual incentives. In so doing they affect the mechanism by which the labor market mediates adverse shocks to tastes, technology, or demand. Figure 8-1 gives a schematic representation of this interaction. An excellent example is the minimum wage, which is designed to reduce inequality at the lower end of the wage distribution. In the United States the minimum wage is roughly 20 percent of the average wage; in France and Germany it is more than 50 percent. The consequence of the drastic increase in returns to skill all over the world is that wage dispersion in the U.S. has increased the most; at the same time, Freeman (1987) finds that the degree of wage dispersion is negatively correlated with employment growth.[1]

Evidence for the importance of institutions stems from cross-country analyses of OECD countries. Bruno and Sachs (1985) were among the first to demonstrate empirically the extent to which corporatism influences macroeconomic performance. Freeman (1987) and Calmfors and Driffill (1988) adduce evidence that highly decentralized and highly centralized systems both tend to have superior labor market outcomes. In a cross-section of countries, Barro (1988) finds an association of unionization and

Figure 8-1. Labor Market Institutions and Outcomes

1.   One problem with Freeman's findings is the absence of correlation of unionization with the *level* of wages that would be expected if employment were determined along a stable demand curve. Evidence of a more structural sort has been provided by Risager (1993), who finds that wage compression can explain a great deal of the relative job loss for unskilled workers in Denmark.

lack of corporatism with the persistence of unemployment over time. Burda (1988) and Layard, Nickell, and Jackman (1991) demonstrate a positive relationship between the generosity of unemployment benefits—especially the statutory duration—and average and long-term unemployment rates in a cross-section of OECD countries; the mechanism is still hotly disputed (see Atkinson and Micklewright 1991). In a panel of OECD countries, Lazear (1990) finds a negative effect of prior notification requirements and severance benefits on employment.

A number of studies point to the role of active labor market policies (ALMP). These include retraining programs for the unemployed, wage subsidies, public works, youth apprenticeships, career counseling, and the like. Jackman, Pissarides, and Savouri (1990); Layard, Nickell, and Jackman (1991); and others demonstrate a significant negative cross-country correlation between spending on ALMPs and average unemployment rates. Although the sharp rise in unemployment has called into question the robustness of the Swedish model (see Lindbeck and others 1993), it is generally agreed that high rates of exit from unemployment achieved by such programs help maintain human capital as well as a consensus regarding the role of work in modern society.

Why Institutions Matter: A Benchmark Model

We now sketch a simple model that captures the role of several diverse institutions in a single, common framework.[2] It should be stressed at the outset that only medium to longer-run determinants of unemployment are considered, and that the model ignores short-run issues related to price and wage flexibility, indexation, and the level of aggregate demand. Although demand and its determinants are undoubtedly important, the more important issue now confronting Central and Eastern Europe concerns the reorganization of the supply side.

The longer-run equilibrium of the economy can be described as the intersection of two curves in the space of unemployment (u) and vacancy (v) rates depicted in figure 8-2. The UV locus describes a dynamic equilibrium between inflows and outflows into and out of unemployment. This locus is downward-sloping and convex to the origin. Its slope is based on the efficiency of the *matching technology* that brings workers and vacancies together, as well as the separation rate, or the rate at which employed

---

2.   For formal details, see the appendix.

Figure 8-2. A Simple Model of Equilibrium Unemployment

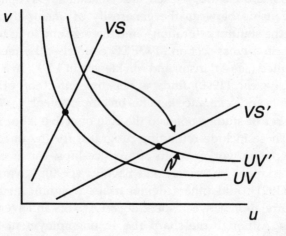

workers enter unemployment (because of layoffs, bankruptcies, and so forth). Increases in matching efficiency and decreases in the separation rate will shift the curve toward the origin. To the extent that these factors are relatively constant over time, the *UV* curve is simply the Beveridge curve, or the empirical relationship between unemployment and vacancies that exists in many countries.

The second labor market relationship, denoted as the *VS* curve, stems from the incentives for firms to offer vacancies, or create jobs. This *supply of vacancies* is more susceptible to labor market policy intervention than the *UV* curve. While the relationship can be derived from several theoretical models, it is generally upward-sloping, for two reasons. First, an increase in the unemployment rate reduces real wages and increases the incentives to employers of creating jobs. Second, increases in unemployment at given vacancies increases the probability of locating a worker, making the opening of a vacancy more attractive. In the context of the model in the appendix, increases in worker power, the cost of posting vacancies or firm-initiated search, the interest rate, unemployment benefits, income from the informal sector, and the net severance burden to firms rotate the *VS* curve clockwise. For a given *UV* curve this results in increased unemployment and a reduction of vacancies.

The model offers the following interpretation of the transformation in the CEE countries shown in figure 8-2: rising real interest rates, collapsing demand and terms of trade, an increase in effective union power, institution of severance regulations, and introduction of unemployment benefits (as opposed to the *penalties* that were associated with unemployment in the old regime) shifted the *VS* curve to *VS'*. Clearly the collapse of demand will also depress the supply of vacancies, and a model explicitly addressing nominal rigidities would capture this element as well. Because we are concerned with the longer-run evolution of labor markets, we suppress this factor. In addition, an increase in separation rates to normal Western levels shifted the *UV* curve outward to *UV'*. The outcome is a decline in vacancies and an increase in unemployment (this interpretation follows Burda 1993).

Extension: On-the-Job Search, Multiple Equilibria, and Congestion

In the benchmark model, the pool of workers for possible matching was taken to be the unemployment stock. This is unrealistic, because many employed workers search while working (see Pissarides and Wadsworth 1989). In Hungary a large fraction of turnover is attributable to employer-to-employer switches (see Chapter 2 of this volume). The model can be modified to allow for on-the-job search. We assume that some fraction of the employed participate in the matching process along with the unemployed and that this on-the-job search depends negatively on unemployment, capturing the fact that job turnover is procyclical and more generally negatively related to labor market slack (see, for example, Akerlof, Rose, and Yellen 1988).

The impact of these assumptions can be seen in figure 8-3. First, the *UV* need not be strictly convex or even downward-sloping; this is because an increase in unemployment implies lower employment, which in turn implies fewer effective searchers. Second, if on-the-job search intensity is sufficiently responsive to unemployment, the *VS* curve can be downward-sloping for some range. This is because as unemployment rises, fewer employed search, rendering vacancies less "productive" and therefore less attractive. Under such conditions, multiple equilibria are possible. Figure 8-3 depicts two possible *VS* curves, along with a *UV* curve that slopes upward at high unemployment rates. In the first (VS_1), the fraction of on-the-job searchers among the employed is constant; when the fraction of employed searchers varies, there are two equilibria (VS_2).

Figure 8-3. Equilibrium Unemployment with On-the-Job Search

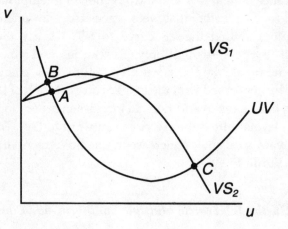

To the extent that matching is related to the dynamics of new firms and job creation, figure 8-3 holds implications for the "big bang" approach to reforming formerly planned economies. On the one hand, it modifies the conclusion that increased unemployment can accelerate restructuring by forcing individuals out of dead-end jobs and into the matching process. The shadow value of unemployment for inducing vacancy creation will be less under such conditions, since higher unemployment implies fewer on-the-job seekers and lower matching efficiency. On the other hand, the rise in unemployment leads to a lower rate of turnover, which will retard the "spontaneous transformation" of state enterprises through attrition (quits), making the closure of state enterprises more valuable.[3]

3.   In most countries the net hiring is being done by the private sector, which needs labor resources. One exception seems to be Hungary, where exits from unemployment into state enterprises are just as high as into the private sector. It cannot be ruled out, however, that the UI system is encouraging the wrong type of turnover—including temporary layoffs (Köllő, Fazekas, and Nagy 1993). The quit rate into unemployment currently appears high in Eastern Europe, and it seems to be associated with the generosity of unemployment benefits; in Poland 30.7 percent of all flows into unemployment are quits, compared with only 18.6 percent in the Czech Republic (Boeri 1993, table 6, 1992 data). This seems high compared with the United States or Britain, where the figure runs between 15 and 20 percent (see Akerlof, Rose, and Yellen 1988 or Pissarides and Wadsworth 1989).

Dangers for a Transforming Economy: Multiple Equilibria and Hysteresis

The role of institutions in the emerging labor markets of Eastern Europe is widely recognized.[4] Especially in periods of structural transformation, social minima must be established, and expectations of a social safety net must be credible and realistic. Should inequality become too excessive or the future improvement too distant, the danger exists that the frustrated will vote against economic reform (Wyplosz 1993). Yet herein lies the dilemma: a *soziale Marktwirtschaft* seems designed for stable, developed economies, not for those undergoing structural change or economic transition. While heavy industry is contracting and restructuring across Central and Eastern Europe, the services sector is expanding (Berg and Sachs 1992). Policies designed to protect human capital in mature economies from overly hasty mobility should not preclude scrapping of obsolete human capital or discourage workers from changing labor market states, occupations, or industries in periods of structural change. The signaling function of wages is extremely important in the transformation, and wage structures have indeed changed radically (see Bellmann 1993 for the case of eastern Germany). The allocative function of wages should not be distorted by extension of unrealistic "soft-budget" bargains or outdated compensation structures.

A widely recognized danger in the literature on Western labor markets is *hysteresis*. A property familiar to physicists, hysteresis is the failure of a system subjected to an external influence to return to its initial conditions after the influence has been removed (an excellent review can be found in Franz 1990). Labor markets are constantly subjected to *shocks*. For example, in the 1970s the price of oil rose in real terms by fourfold in 1973-74 and doubled again in 1979-80. Unemployment rose in the aftermath of these shocks. In the meantime, these price increases have been largely undone; the nominal price of oil has declined, while inflation has eroded the real price back to levels of the early 1970s. Yet unemployment in EC Europe—in contrast to the United States (as well as Japan)—has ratcheted upward and shows no sign of reverting to its previous mean.[5]

---

4.   See, for example, the articles in the first issue of the *ILO Central and Eastern European Newsletter* 1: 1993.

5.   This is not to say that the United States and Japan do not suffer from the same problem in a less severe form. Indeed, the "natural rate of unemployment" in those countries may have increased as well, if only moderately.

The economic cause of hysteresis, or long-term persistence, in labor markets remains controversial. In the evolving economies of Central and Eastern Europe, the danger of hysteresis is on every policymaker's mind. Several *institutional* factors worth mentioning can lead to hysteresis or hysteretic-like phenomena. Social insurance, especially unemployment insurance, can interact through the tax system to depress the demand for employment by firms in the formal economy. Unemployment can lead to the deterioration of human capital and the labeling (ranking) of the long-term unemployed. Trade unions may negotiate primarily with an eye to the well-being of current members, leading to the exclusion of "outsiders," who may be unemployed. Fixed costs associated with change of occupation, labor force status, or industry may lead to hysteresis for some range of incentives to do so.

Finally, it may be difficult to distinguish between inherently hysteretic and apparently hysteretic phenomena. In the former case, the steady state is path-dependent or determined by initial conditions. In the latter case, hysteresis in the system merely reflects our ignorance; with more information we could add the appropriate missing variables to the system and characterize their evolution over time. An alternative interpretation of hysteresis is simply the existence of multiple equilibria; unforeseen shocks simply move the economy from one equilibrium to another. Indeed, a necessary condition for hysteresis is the absence of a unique resting point of the economy.

Institutions and Multiple Equilibria: Bad Public Finance

In this section we illustrate how the interaction of the tax and funding systems of social security can influence employment outcomes. Here the problem is the difference between active and passive labor market programs. Given high rates of joblessness, unemployment benefits in CEE countries currently consume a large part of the general government budget and virtually all the employment-related spending by labor ministries.[6] The decision to fund these expenditures by taxing existing firms can lead to multiple equilibria.

---

6.   This is also true of the industrial Western economies, where the IMF recently estimated that unemployment benefits accounted for 3.5 percent of total government spending in 1991 (*Financial Times*, 23 September 1993, p. 5).

The logic is straightforward. Consider an economy without access to credit markets. Its unemployment benefits are funded on a pay-as-you-go basis by existing firms (that is, firm-worker matches). Denote the *net* tax rate on firms' output by τ, which is measured net of direct employment subsides. The period-by-period government budget constraint is $\tau y(1 - u)$ $= ub$. Imposing this budget constraint on the benchmark model will lead to two different expressions for the *VS* curve, *depending on whether b or τ is* exogenous. If b is assumed to be exogenous, taxes must respond endogenously to changing labor markets. An increase in unemployment will lead to an increase in benefit recipients and necessitate tax increases. These tax increases on the legal sector will reduce the supply of vacancies for given labor market conditions. The *VS* curve is backward-bending, as in figure 8-4. Abstracting from dynamics, it is possible in the former case to reach bad equilibria when there is feedback from unemployment to taxes. It should be stressed that this argument has nothing to do with the intensity of search or immobility of workers or with the decreasing returns in the matching function. The criticism of overloading the private sector through indirect taxes has been leveled recently at several CEE countries, especially Hungary, which has the most generous system of unemployment benefits and the most punitive system of indirect taxation on firms.[7] It is possible that the rise of the informal sector is a direct consequence of high and rising tax burdens. The model can be extended to study funding of active labor market programs, which can be "crowded out" in a similar fashion by higher unemployment benefit expenditures.

Institutions and Hysteresis: Passively Reactive Unemployment Benefits

In this section, we demonstrate a simple example of hysteresis or pure state dependence in an economy when unemployment benefits react passively to labor market conditions. The mechanism involves feedback from unemployment to the benefit. This is based on the insight that if s is separation rate and f the outflow rate from unemployment, then

$$(8\text{-}1) \qquad \dot{u} = s(1 - u) - uf = s + (s + f)u$$

---

7. Taxation of firms for funding unemployment benefits there has risen since 1990 from 1.5 percent of payroll to 7 percent in 1993. In Romania a similar problem may be emerging, where firms now face a 5 percent contribution for funding the unemployment insurance system.

Figure 8-4. Multiple Equilibria

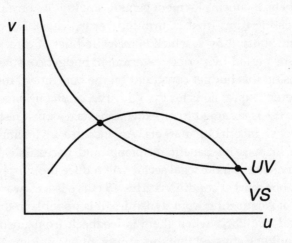

where f is a function of all the relevant labor market policy parameters. We make a further crucial assumption that the *change* in the rate of unemployment causes changes in the generosity of the benefit. The logic is that as unemployment rises, the perceived risk of belonging to the pool rises as well. As such, the median voter is more likely to vote for higher unemployment benefit levels.[8] We do not explicitly model the political economy behind such a behavioral assumption, but such considerations are evident throughout Europe as well as in the United States.[9] In order to strengthen the force of the argument, we ignore financing of unemployment pay in this section; following the arguments of the previous section, a pay-as-you-go financing constraint is likely to aggravate matters.[10]

---

8.   Arguments of this nature lie behind Wright's (1986) model of unemployment insurance.

9.   Democratic administrations in the United States have been especially prone to extending the duration of unemployment benefits in recessions. Usually these extensions are temporary, but they are plagued with time-inconsistency problems. The evidence indicates that unemployment benefit duration, coverage, and replacement rates rose through the 1970s and early 1980s in most high unemployment EC countries; see Burda 1988.

10.   Of course, there are a number of reasons why a "difference-difference" relation might arise independent of the government reaction to unemployment conditions. For example, the size of the underground economy or the human capital of workers might change in response to changes in the duration of unemployment. Both of these would lead to similar "hysteretic" properties.

Figure 8-5. Hysteresis in the Simple Model

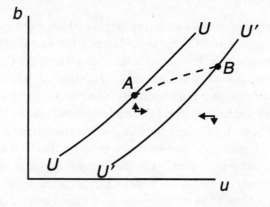

The outcome can be seen in figure 8-5, which is a phase diagram in the space of b (benefit levels) and unemployment. There are an infinity of equilibria, all lying along the curve UU. Consider the outcome of a temporary shock to worker productivity considered in the appendix. The curve shifts to $U'U'$; the dynamics of unemployment raise the benefit. The path is state-dependent, because the resting point B will depend on initial conditions relative to the new curve. When the original shock is reversed, there is no guarantee that the economy will return to point A.

Sachs (1986) has shown that optimal policy in models with hysteresis can lead to the government's acceptance of bad equilibria such as point B if costs of moving away are sufficiently high. One key institution that some reforming Eastern European countries have adopted is an aggressive active labor market policy that puts a limit on growth in passive unemployment support, replacing it with mandatory workfare, or "socially purposeful jobs" in the Czech terminology. This is equivalent to countercyclical job subsidies (they are indeed targeted to troubled regions, with Prague receiving little aid). Such a policy moves the economy in a virtuous direction in bad times. Especially in Central and Eastern Europe, where the shocks are more likely to be associated with structural change (restructuring) than a temporary decline in aggregate demand, it would seem important to counteract the tendency toward hysteresis.

Comparisons of Labor Market Institutions in Central and Eastern Europe

The last two sections stressed the importance of institutions for medium-to long-term labor market outcomes. Table 8-1, which replicates regression results available in Layard, Nickell, and Jackman (1991) and elsewhere buttress this claim (several regressions with insignificant institutional variables are not reported). The results show a robust correlation between measures of average and long-term unemployment on the one hand, and unemployment benefit generosity, corporatism, and centralization on the other. As stressed above, our objective here is to assess longer-run relationships, specifically the determinants of the natural rate of unemployment, and this section evaluates long-term prospects for average unemployment in these countries on the basis of current institutions and trends.

Unemployment Benefits in CEE

Table 8-2 shows the state of unemployment benefits programs in the CEE in mid-1992. The index shown is a crude measure that combines income replacement, duration, and coverage of unemployment benefits. It can be thought of as the present value of the package in percent of current salary gross-of-tax (income taxes on benefits are minimal in the CEE and are ignored here). The table shows wide dispersion among the CEE countries with regard to the provision of jobless benefits.

Since summer 1992 several changes in the administration of benefits have been adopted. Interestingly, not all have been in the same direction. Among the Visegrad countries, it is possible to distinguish among three groups of countries: first, those that have "held the line," keeping statutory rules roughly constant; second, those that have tightened their unemployment assistance programs in either a statutory sense or in stricter administration of existing rules; and third, those that have moved to a more accommodative (generous) stance. Earlier in this chapter a model was sketched in which reaction of the benefit to worsening economic conditions led to hysteresis, so the last category is important. The first group consists of the Czech and Slovak republics and Bulgaria. In Hungary, in contrast, eligibility conditions have been tightened. In 1993, the maximal duration was reduced from eighteen to twelve months. The first benefit tranche was reduced to three months at 75 percent income

Table 8-1. Cross-Country Regression Evidence on Labor Market Institutions

Dependent variable		UI	CORP	CENT	CENT^2	AEM	R^2
Average standardized unemployment rate, 1986-90							
	1)	0.85	0.93			−0.18	0.79
		(5.0)	(3.8)			(−2.8)	
	2)	0.95		1.03	−0.047	−0.24	0.49
		(1.9)		(1.3)	(−1.0)	(−1.9)	
	3)	0.96	1.06	−0.57	0.027	−0.20	0.81
		(3.6)	(3.6)	(−1.4)	(1.4)	(−2.6)	
	4)	1.13	1.10	−0.66	0.039		0.75
		(3.5)	(3.7)	(−1.3)	(1.4)		
Percentage of 1988 unemployed with spells longer than 12 months							
	5)	8.61	3.50			0.04	0.79
		(4.8)	(2.9)			(0.1)	
	6)	5.96		12.50	−0.62	0.09	0.83
		(2.8)		(3.7)	(−3.4)	(0.2)	
	7)	6.15	2.31	9.49	−0.48	0.29	0.89
		(3.0)	(1.9)	(2.6)	(−2.6)	(0.6)	
	8)	5.93	2.20	9.22	−0.48		0.88
		(3.2)	(2.0)	(2.6)	(−2.6)		

Note: UI=measure of unemployment benefit system generosity that considers duration, eligibility, and income replacement, following Burda (1988); CORP = Tarantelli's (1986) corporatism ranking (lower value = more corporatist); CENT=Calmfors and Driffill (1988) ordinal measure of centralization of bargaining (lower value = more centralized); AEM = spending on ALMP, measured as expenditure per unemployed as a fraction of output per employed (Jackman, Pissarides, and Savouri 1990).
Source: Burda 1993; dependent variable data from Bean 1992. Sample consists of cross-sectional observations on eighteen OECD countries.

replacement, with a cap of 18,000 HFT a month, or twice the minimum wage; the next nine months were governed by 60 percent replacement with a cap of 15,000 HFT. At the same time, the minimum benefit was raised to 8,600 HFT, which is only slightly below the minimum wage of

346 Unemployment, Restructuring, and the Labor Market in Eastern Europe and Russia

Table 8-2. Unemployment Benefits in CEE, Summer 1992

Country	Effective coverage	Eligibility rules	Replacement ratio and prospective duration	Index
Bulgaria	37%	Employed > 6 of last 12 months; job-losers only	60% of gross AW in last 6-12 months, from 90 to 140% of MW, for 6 to 12 months	671
CR/SR	38%	Employed > 12 months of last 3 years; quitters, school-leavers ineligible	3 months at 60%, 3 months at 50% (topped up if < SM)	522
Hungary	78%	Eligibility by contribution; quitters & school-leavers after 90 days unemployment	First 2/3 of *ex-ante* duration: 70% of AW over last 4 years; then 50%; duration depends on work experience, max = 18 months	3,388
Poland	73%	Employed > 180 days in last year; except school-leavers, disabled, mass layoffs	36% of last quarter's economywide AW; duration = 1 year	1,240
Romania	64%	School-leavers eligible after 60 days unemployment; means-tested: income < 50% of MW	Workers 60%, university graduates 70%, duration up to 270 days	1,286

Note: SM=statutory social minimum; AW=average wage; MW=minimum wage; SA=supplementary allowance.
Source: Burda 1993.

9,000 HFT. Under these conditions the index calculated above declines to roughly half of its level in 1992. The final group, consisting of Poland and Romania, have loosened—more accurately, extended—provision of benefits. In 1993 Poland extended its benefit duration to eighteen months in regions where the council of ministers deem "crisis" conditions to exist. Romania has also extended its benefits by an additional eighteen months' social allowance at 40 percent of the minimum wage if a means test is passed (in principle, no real estate or other family income is permitted). A similar social welfare benefit exists in Hungary: unemployed who exhaust their benefits are entitled to 80 percent of the minimum old-age pension (roughly 50 percent of the minimum wage). Poland and the CR have similar programs that begin after exhaustion of benefits.

At the same time, coverage, or insured unemployment, has fallen in all CEE countries as benefit claims expire and recipients are forced from the unemployment registry. In Bulgaria the fraction of unemployed receiving some form of unemployment benefit declined from 41 percent at year-end 1991, to 35 percent at the end of 1992, and to 30 percent in June 1993. Similar circumstances prevail in Hungary, with a large number of unemployed leaving the benefit register in recent months. In Poland there has been a dramatic decline in coverage, about 40-50 percent in 1993 compared with almost 75 percent in 1992. The divorce of the CSFR into the Czech Republic and Slovakia implies a potential divergence; in Slovakia, coverage had fallen to 33 percent by June 1993 compared with a decline to 45 percent in the Czech Republic (Ham, Svenjar, and Terrell in this volume). Yet the two systems remain almost identical, except perhaps in their administration (see below).

To summarize, the past year has been characterized by a widespread reduction in eligibility criteria in all countries, leading to reductions in effective unemployment benefits despite relatively few statutory changes. In percentage of gross income replacement in work, Eastern Europe increasingly resembles the most restrictive of OECD countries, including the United States, Japan, and Switzerland.

Corporatism and Severance Protection

The regression results of table 8-1 suggest that, for the OECD countries at least, some sort of corporatist wage bargaining system may contain important advantages. In a much larger sample, Barro (1988) finds weak evidence that unemployment rates in highly unionized economies tend to exhibit more persistence if the organization of collective bargaining is not of the "corporatist" type. The most commonly cited model explaining this is that of Calmfors and Driffill (1988) with modifications by Rowthorn (1993).

The CSFR and Hungary are potential high corporatism countries. Similarly, bargaining in Bulgaria seems to have become more corporatist and centralized in the 1993 wage and indexation bargaining rounds. Poland's unions, while concentrated, are handicapped because workers at the enterprise already have considerable power over management—rendering Poland a low corporatist country when viewed through the terms of the benchmark model (earlier in this chapter). Romania lacks any corporatist features of importance. The chapter on Romania reveals that only 12 percent of managers considered that employer's associations had any say in bargaining. They also find that bargaining occurs primarily with middle management, indicating that wage decisions remain of secondary importance to enterprises; given that privatization remains tenuous and the soft budget constraint applies, this is not surprising.

Active Labor Market Programs

There is considerable debate over which kind of active labor market programs (ALMPs) are the most appropriate in a period of radical structural change. The Swedish model, which had been praised as a solution to long-term unemployment (Jackman, Pissarides, and Savouri 1990), is now under considerable strain because of the largest aggregate demand decline since the Great Depression. It has also been called into question for fiscal reasons (Calmfors 1993), a factor of great relevance for the CEE countries. Nevertheless, ALMPs are the most relevant labor market policy in times of structural change, when human capital becomes obsolete and occupational, industrial, and regional mobility are required.

ALMPs can range from the more passive type (public works programs, job creation grants, and wage subsidies) to active (retraining by job centers, job vouchers for school-leavers or job-losers, subsidies for moving to other regions, and the like). In the context of the benchmark model, ALMPs can be thought of as measures that lower k (the cost of maintaining vacancies), lower τ through job subsidies, direct creation of vacancies through the public sector (shifting up the VS curve), or policies that act directly on the matching process. The last includes the effectiveness of the employment services and the labor market in general or the enforcement of the search requirement for benefit entitlement.

Active labor market policies can also influence labor supply. They can reduce labor supply from groups that have little chance of reemployment, or redistribute employment opportunities from one group to another by affecting the labor supply decisions of certain target groups (for example, the youth or the low-skilled). One active labor market policy that has received relatively little attention in Eastern Europe is early retirement. In eastern Germany early retirement has been a key aspect of the ALMP; since unification more than 800,000 older workers have been removed from the labor force. This makes room for school-leavers and other young people at the bottom of the seniority ladder to accumulate human capital on the job. Simple present discounted value calculations comparing unemployment benefit support with early retirement show that the latter can indeed increase GDP in present value, especially if older workers have human capital of the "clay" variety.

A simple example is instructive. Suppose that a fifty-five year-old with a life expectancy of seventy-five has (marginal) productivity of 200,000 forint a year, assumed constant until retirement at sixty-five. This is roughly twice the 1993 gross minimum wage (108,000 forint/year) and the minimum allowable benefit (103,200 forint/year). Assume that a young person aged twenty can begin work in a new enterprise with new technology at a lower initial productivity level but with real growth of 2 percent a year until retirement. For the sake of the example we suppose further that the young person loses no human capital and retains the "work ethic" while unemployed (probably unrealistic), but always begins with the same initial productivity level. For simplicity we assume (generously) that the retirement benefit for current older workers equals the unemployment benefit, and assume a real discount rate of 3 percent. If the total number of jobs is fixed—which is patently false in the medium to longer run but a good approximation in the short run—the *present value* of GDP is raised by substituting younger for older workers as long as the younger worker's productivity exceeds 120,000 HFT a year, or 60 percent of the older colleagues. At the same time, current GDP is reduced at the margin by such a policy, and the intertemporal budget of the government is worsened. This explains the success of early retirement in Germany, where resources were available to finance it. The unwillingness or inability of the state to offer an attractive package to older workers (or to force them aside) explains why these programs have met with less success in Hungary, Poland, or elsewhere.

Another aspect of labor supply policy regards the "self-selection" of low-productivity workers out of the labor force. This can only be achieved by administering jobless benefits in a way that increases the cost of labor force participation toward levels observed in OECD countries. Guaranteed employment was a vehicle for social protection in socialist countries, which is evident in their significantly higher labor force participation rates compared with OECD countries. With the introduction of profit motives and the removal of social obligations, firms have shed low-productivity staff, which to some extent may leave the labor force. This applies particularly to older workers who continued to work past statutory retirement age. The reduction in labor force participation has occurred to different degrees in the CEE countries, as can be seen from the relationship between changes in employment and unemployment. In a world with a fixed labor supply and stagnant demographics, the ratio of the two should be unity. Yet it ranges from less than 0.5 in the CR, Slovakia, and Bulgaria to greater than 1 in Hungary, Poland, and Romania (Blanchard, Commander, and Coricelli, in this volume).

The CEE countries can be classified into three groups along the ALMP dimension. The first consists of countries that have seen most of their spending "crowded out" (see Burda 1993 for details). *Bulgaria* and *Romania* belong to this group. Despite increases of active labor market expenditures from 1 million leva in 1991 to 22.2 million leva in the first half of 1993, the effort in Bulgaria remains only about 1.8 percent of total labor market expenditure, and less than 0.2 percent of GDP. In Romania programs are plagued by operational problems: entrepreneurial loans have been limited or abandoned because of malfeasance, these programs are labor-intensive and are difficult to supervise, and labor offices in Romania are poorly manned (Earle 1993).

A second group of countries have maintained high levels of spending. *The Czech Republic* and *Slovakia* belong to this group. The *Czech Republic* is the darling of ALMP proponents, because spending on ALMP increased to 53 percent of the total budget in 1992. Most of this is targeted toward young people, unskilled workers, and school-leavers, and focuses on new job creation and public works projects administered by the municipal authorities; 94,000 jobs were created in such programs in 1992 (Janácek 1993). Preventing initial long spells of unemployment among youth is a top priority; the fraction of unemployed Czechs with a duration of six months has been declining since mid-year 1992 and seems to have stabilized at about 35 percent, the envy of any European country. Advance payment of unemployment benefits as a start-up loan has been relatively successful in comparison with other CEE countries. *Slovakia* has retained these institutions; despite financial pressure, more than 100,000 jobs were created in 1992. Retraining is also significant in both republics, with roughly 2 percent of the labor force in some form of program (2.1 percent in CR, 1.8 percent in SR).

The success of the Czechs and Slovaks is evidence of multiple equilibria of the "good" type; more employment implies higher tax revenues and less burden from passive expenditure. The virtuous circle is completed as younger people develop skills and attachment to the work force; judging from the experience of Western economies, their spells of unemployment will be shorter as a result. A recent trend that may split the two countries in labor market experience is the unequal intensity of staffing between the two republics. Although there are more than three times as many unemployed in Slovakia as in the Czech Republic, Czech labor offices have more than twice as many staff and 40 percent more consultants (Uldrichova and Karpisek 1993). High and rising unemployment with fixed staff leads to reduced supervision and less effective job intermediation and assistance, and represents another potential source of multiple equilibria.

In the third group, consisting of Hungary and Poland, countries have increased active labor policy spending somewhat, but from very low levels. *Hungary* boosted spending from 4.9 billion to 13.6 billion HFT, a considerable increase in real terms. Total spending on ALMP (total expenditures from the Employment Policy Fund) represented 15.4 percent of all spending on employment programs in 1992 (Köllô, Fazekas, and Nagy 1993, pp. 28-30). The spending is concentrated on subsidization of employment at existing enterprises—for example, with a wage subsidy to firms reducing total hours by at least one-third. The obvious drawback to this development is an evident entrenchment of the status quo, with a considerable political economy dimension.[11] Furthermore, they make it more difficult for new private sector firms to enter and compete, since a wage subsidy also benefits the firm if labor supply is not perfectly inelastic at some horizon.[12] Köllô, Fazekas, and Nagy (1993) show that the ratio of training versus subsidies in 1990 was 65:35 for the OECD, compared with 18:72 for Hungary. Even in 1992, however, the extent of the program was modest (roughly 12,000 workers, compared with 97,000 in the CR and 50,000 in the SR). *Poland* is slated to increase spending on ALMP in the current year; outlays were 32 percent of the total budget in 1990, 7 percent in 1991, 5 percent in 1992, and 10 percent was planned for 1993. Increasing emphasis has been placed on training and public works at the local level, which is characteristic of the Czechoslovak ALMPs. Poland is also considering a training voucher scheme on an experimental basis. One distressing development is that subsidies for the employment of younger workers seem to be declining, from 13.6 percent in 1990 to 2.8 percent expected for 1993, a clear departure from the Czech approach.

---

11. This issue was central in the debate over east Germany (see Akerlof and others 1991 compared with Siebert 1992). In the end it appears that the naysayers were right—subsidies simply rigidify the status quo.
12. Earle (1993) argues that the same holds for Romania, where in 1992, 88 percent of subsidies for hiring new graduates went to state firms.

Conclusions

The theoretical section of this paper implies above all that the joint provision of passive unemployment income support and its counterpart, the active provision of alternative jobs and retraining, will shape the natural rate of unemployment in these countries. Among other causes, the tax system and the history of unemployment makes it likely that without active measures, the CEE countries will attain "bad" equilibria. With the exception of the Czech Republic, the CEE countries have apparently been unable to mobilize enough manpower and organization to "flip" the labor market from bad (high levels of passive policies, low levels of ALMPs) to good equilibria (the reverse). This can be achieved by fixing the benefit at a relatively restricted level (especially with respect to duration) with the provision of a viable alternative for individuals upon exhausting jobless benefits; this is possible through job subsidies or direct public works job creation. The infrastructral needs in these countries are high, and thus it seems that the binding constraint on action comes from the lack of organizational talent and manpower as much as from budget considerations. Such programs are unlikely to have an effect until they reach the magnitude of that in the Czech Republic. Given the desire to promote, or at least not hinder, structural change, public works and employment subsidies to new firms should be given preference over aid to state firms.

Early retirement should be considered more carefully, especially in countries with a relatively young demographic age structure. In Germany this was imperative, because macroeconomic policies such as a depreciation of the currency were unavailable to reduce the real wages of less productive workers. Under fairly plausible assumptions about the future productivity of the young, a more aggressive early retirement policy combined with a Czech focus on the young and unskilled will help prevent cohorts from "missing the boat" as was the case with youth unemployment in the United Kingdom, Italy, and France in the early 1980s.

Overall, it is evident that active labor market programs must be: (a) truly *active*, creating new job opportunities rather than subsidizing wait unemployment or existing inefficient firms; (b) decentralized, in order to react to the needs of communities and regions—this is especially true of public works and retraining; and (c) individually focused, labor (supervisory-staff) intensive, in order to guarantee that the objective of improving turnover in the unemployment pool has a chance of succeeding.

Appendix

We now describe the formal model behind the discussion in the text (this model is based on Pissarides 1990 with modifications by Burda 1992, 1993). We consider an economy populated by a large number of workers and firms that operate under an identical linear technology: a firm can produce output with a worker per unit period. Without a worker, output is zero. Information about the location of workers and firms is imperfect, and workers and firms are brought together by a matching process. This process is summarized by a constant returns to scale matching function x: $R^2 \rightarrow R$, which takes the stocks of unemployment u and vacancies v as arguments and returns an instantaneous flow of new matches. Initially, the pool of workers available for matching is assumed to equal the stock of unemployment and that of firms willing to hire anew is given by the stock of vacancies, or firms in the market without workers. The former assumption will be relaxed below to admit on-the-job search. Inflows into unemployment derive from job destruction and are assumed to be an exogenous proportion s of the employment stock, e. The labor force is assumed constant and is normalized to unity, so the unemployment rate evolves according to

(8-2) $$\dot{u} = s(1 - u) - x(u,v).$$

Thus one condition for equilibrium in the labor market is simply the equality of inflows into and outflows from unemployment:

(8-3) $$s(1 - u) = x(u,v).$$

The loci of (u,v) combinations satisfying equation 8-3 are given by the downward-sloping *UV* curve in figure 8-2.

Vacancies are posted by existing firms lacking a worker. The number of firms is endogenous, however, and will be determined by the profitability of entry, which in turn is driven by real wages. We begin by assuming that the real wage w is set by bargaining between workers and employers that are matched. Unemployed workers have access to underground income l as well as an unemployment benefit b. The probability of finding a job match in a given instant, f, is given by $x(u,v)/u = x(1,\theta)$ where $\theta \equiv v/u$. Let E and U be the steady-state asset values of being employed and unemployed respectively. If r is the real interest rate, it follows in the steady state that

(8-4) $$rU = b + l + f(\theta)(E - U).$$

In case of a severance, the worker is assumed to receive a lump-sum payment T, which is independent of the wage and may or may not be paid by the firm, so

(8-5) $$rE = w - s(E - U - T).$$

Combining equations 8-4 and 8-5 yields

(8-6) $$E - U = (w - b - l + sT)/(r + s + f).$$

Note that the existence of a severance benefit raises the steady-state value of having a job.

Similar logic from the firm's perspective can be used to derive the surplus value of having a worker in place J, versus that of having posted a vacancy that is currently unfilled, V. Suppose a firm must pay a flow cost k to keep a vacancy posted, which can represent advertising and interviewing costs, and the like. For producing firms, a severance results in a cost F, which may or may not equal T, the benefit received by the worker; the case $F > T$ corresponds to "red tape" costs, $F - T$ of which are not received by the worker. If we denote the hiring rate $x/v = x(\theta^{-1},1) = f\theta = h$, we have

(8-7) $$rJ = y - w - s(J - V - F)$$
(8-8) $$rV = -k + h(\theta)(J - V)$$

so we can write

(8-9) $$J - V = (y - w - sF + k)/(r + s + h).$$

We now suppose that workers and firms set the wage in Nash bargaining without taking into account the effect they have on other wage setters or on the respective fallback positions. If β denotes the weight attached to the worker's surplus, the objective is

(8-10) $$(J - V)^{1-\beta}(E - U)^{\beta}.$$

For the bargain to have positive value we require $y + k + s(T - F) > b + l$. Logarithmic differentiation (taking f and h as parametric) gives the solution for the wage[13]

(8-11) $$w = (1 - \beta)(b + l - sT) + \beta(y - sF + k).$$

---

13. Note that the wage is independent of labor market tightness, in contrast to Pissarides 1990. This is because workers and firms are assumed here to be myopic, and do not take into account effects of their actions on aggregate outcomes.

Under the assumption of free entry by firms, $V = 0$. Substitution of equation 8-11 into 8-8 and 8-9 yields an upward-sloping ray VS in (u,v) space in figure 8-2, characterized by

$$(8\text{-}12) \qquad k = \{(1 - \beta)[y - (b + l) - s(F - T)] - \beta k\}h(\theta)/(r + s).$$

The interpretation of equation 8-12 is that the flow cost of a vacancy in equilibrium is equal to its appropriately discounted expected gain. Comparative statics exercises can show the effects of changes in model parameters. In this model[14] this is particularly easy. Rewrite equation 8-12 as

$$(8\text{-}13) \qquad v = uh^{-1}(k(r + s)/\{(1 - \beta)[y - (b + l) - s(F - T)] - \beta k\}).$$

Since $h^{-1'} < 0$, it is straightforward to show that increases in worker power (β), the cost of vacancy or firm search (k), the interest rate (r), the unemployment benefit (b), income from the informal sector (l) and the severance wedge or excess burden of employer costs over the benefits received by the worker ($F - T$) will shift the VS curve down, leading to an increase in unemployment and a decline in vacancies.

On-the-Job Search, Multiple Equilibria, and Congestion

Suppose that in any instant the fraction of employed e participating in the matching process is given by $\pi(u)$, with $\pi \in (0,1)$, $\pi(0) = \underline{\pi}$, $\pi'(0) = 0$, $\pi' \leq 0$, $\pi'' < 0$. Both employed and unemployed compete on equal footing for the same stock of vacancies. We also make the simplifying assumption that the fallback positions of both unemployed and on-the-job searchers are equal.[15] Under these conditions flow market equilibrium is given by

$$(8\text{-}14) \qquad s(1 - u) = \{u/[u + \pi(1 - u)]\} x[u + \pi(1 - u),v]$$

or more compactly

$$s(1/u - 1) = x\{1,v/[u + \pi(1 - u)]\},$$

which need not be strictly convex or even downward-sloping.

---

14. This model differs from the standard one in that workers do not consider that their wage bargain affects future wages or the fallback of other workers in unemployment or employment. In Pissarides 1990 and Burda 1992, qualitatively similar results are derived by implicit differentiation of a more complicated version of equation 8-12.

15. This somewhat unrealistic assumption simplifies the analysis considerably. It implies that workers who are searching while on the job commit *ex ante* to leave their job when a match is found.

The *VS* curve with on-the-job search is similar to equation 8-12; the difference is that it is no longer a straight line emanating from the origin, but rather

(8-15) $$v = [\pi + u(1 - \pi)]\,K$$

where $K \equiv h^{-1}(k(r + s)/\{(1 - \beta)[y - (b + l) - s(F - T)] - \beta k\}).$[16] It is easy to show

$$dv/du = [1 - \pi + \pi'(1 - u)]K$$

$$d^2v/du^2 = [\pi''(1 - u)]K < 0.$$

If on-the-job search intensity is sufficiently responsive to unemployment $\pi' < -(1 - \pi)/(1 - u)$, the *VS* curve can be downward-sloping for some range. As u approaches zero, the supply of vacancies remains positive; π' tends to zero, so the *VS* curve is initially upward-sloping.

Multiple Equilibria and Hysteresis

INSTITUTIONS AND MULTIPLE EQUILIBRIA: BAD PUBLIC FINANCE. Consider the first example of an economy without access to credit markets. Its unemployment benefits are funded on a pay-as-you-go basis by existing firms (firm/worker matches). Denote the *net* tax rate on firms' output by τ, which is measured net of direct employment subsides. The period-by-period government budget constraint is $\tau y(1 - u) = ub$. Imposing this budget constraint on the benchmark model will lead to two different expressions for the *VS* curve, depending on whether b or τ is assumed exogenous. If b is fixed, then $\tau = ub/[y(1 - u)]$ and

(8-15′) $v = uh^{-1}(k(r + s)/\{(1 - \beta)[y - b/(1 - u) - l - s(F - T)] - \beta k\}).$

This case is displayed in figure 8-4 as the downward-bending *VS* curve. If, instead, b is adjusted continuously to maintain a constant tax rate, $b = \tau y(1 - u)/u$ and

(8-15″) $v = uh^{-1}(k(r + s)/\{(1 - \beta)[y - \tau/u - l - s(F - T)] - \beta k\}),$

and the *VS* curve bends upward instead.

INSTITUTIONS AND HYSTERESIS: PASSIVELY REACTIVE UNEMPLOYMENT BENEFITS. Combining equations 8-2 and 8-13, we have

(8-16) $\dot{u} = s(1 - u) - ux(1, h^{-1}(k(r + s)/\{(1 - \beta)[y - (b + l) - s(F - T)] - \beta k\})$

$\qquad = s - (s + f)u$

---

16. If π is constant π, the *VS* curve is a straight line with slope $(1 - \pi)\,K$ and intercept πK.

where $f = x(1, h^{-1}(k(r+s)/\{(1-\beta)[y-(b+l)-s(F-T)]-\beta k\})$. The *change* in the rate of unemployment causes changes in the generosity of the benefit or formally that

$$(8\text{-}17) \qquad\qquad \dot{b} = \lambda \, \dot{u}$$

with $\lambda > 0$. The outcome in figure 8-5 is a phase diagram in (b,u) space. There are an infinity of multiple equilibria, all lying along the curve UU. The roots of the dynamic system are 0 and $-(s + f + \lambda f_b)$, with the zero root implying hysteresis in the usual sense (Giavazzi and Wyplosz 1985).

Bibliography

Akerlof, G., A. Rose, and J. Yellen. 1988. "Job Switching and Job Satisfaction in the United States Labor Market." *Brookings Papers on Economic Activity* 1988 (2): 495-594.

Akerlof, G., A. Rose, J. Yellen, and H. Hessenius. 1991. "East Germany in from the Cold: The Economic Aftermath of Currency Union." *Brookings Papers on Economic Activity* 1991 (2): 1-105.

Atkinson, T., and J. Micklewright. 1991. "Unemployment Compensation and Labor Market Transitions: A Critical Review." *Journal of Economic Literature* 29: 1679-727.

Barro, R. 1988. "The Persistence of Unemployment." *American Economic Review* 78: 32-37.

Bean, C. 1992. "European Unemployment: A Survey." WP 71, Centre for Economic Performance, London School of Economics.

Bellmann, L. 1993. "Transformation der Wirtschaft und betriebliche Lohnpolitik in den neuen Bundesländern." Berlin. Mimeo.

Berg, A., and J. Sachs. 1992. "Structural Adjustment and International Trade in Eastern Europe: The Case of Poland." *Economic Policy* 12: 117-75.

Blanchard, O. J., and L. Summers. 1986. "Hysteresis and the European Unemployment Problem." *NBER Macroeconomics Annual 1986:* 15-78.

———— 1987. "Increasing Returns, Hysteresis, Real Wages, and Unemployment." *European Economic Review*: 288-95.

Boeri, T. 1993. "Labor Market Flows and the Persistence of Unemployment in Central and Eastern Europe." In *Unemployment in Transition Countries; Transient or Persistent?* Paris: OECD.

Bruno, M., and J. Sachs. 1985. *The Economics of Worldwide Stagflation.* Cambridge, Mass.: Harvard University Press.

Burda, M. 1988. "Wait Unemployment in Europe." *Economic Policy* 7: 391-426.

—— 1992. "A Note on Firing Costs and Severance Benefits in Equilibrium Unemployment." *Scandinavian Journal of Economics* 94:479-89.

—— 1993. "Unemployment, Labor Markets, and Structural Change in Eastern Europe." *Economic Policy* 16: 101-37.

Calmfors, L. 1993. "Lessons from the Macroeconomic Policy Experience of Sweden." *European Journal of Political Economy* 9: 25-72.

Calmfors, L., and J. Driffill. 1988. "Bargaining Structure, Corporatism, and Macroeconomic Perfomance." *Economic Policy* 6: 13-62.

Commission of the European Communities. 1992. *Employment Observatory: Central and Eastern Europe*, nos. 1 and 2.

Earle, J. 1993. "Unemployment and Policies in Romania" Paper presented at the OECD-CCET Technical Workshop "The Persistence of Unemployment in Central and Eastern Europe," September.

Fajth, G., and J. Lakatos. 1993. "Labor Markets Policies and Some Aspects of Long-Term Unemployment in Hungary." In *Unemployment in Transition Countries; Transient or Persistent?* Paris: OECD.

Flanagan, R., D. Soskice, and L. Ullman. 1983. *Unionism, Economic Stabilization, and Incomes Policies: The European Experience*. Washington, D.C.: The Brookings Institution.

Franz, W. 1990. "Hysteresis Effects in Economic Relationships." *Empirical Economics* 15:109-27.

Freeman, R. 1987. "Labor Market Institutions and Economic Performance." *Economic Policy* 6: 63-80.

—— 1991. "Labor Market Tightness and the Declining Economic Position of Less-Educated Male Workers in the United States." In Padoa-Schioppa, ed., *Mismatch and Labor Market Mobility*. Cambridge, U.K.: Cambridge University Press.

—— 1992. "What Direction for Labor Market Institutions in Eastern and Central Europe?" Paper presented at the NBER Conference on Transition in Eastern Europe, Cambridge, Massachusetts, February 26-29.

Giavazzi, F., and C. Wyplosz. 1985. "The Zero Root Problem: A Note on the Dynamic Determination of the Stationary Equilibrium in Linear Models." *Review of Economics and Statistics* 12: 353-57.

Jackman, R., C. Pissarides, and S. Savouri. 1990. "Labor Market Policies and Unemployment in the OECD." *Economic Policy* 10: 450-83.

Janácek, K. 1993. "Unemployment and Labor Market in Czechoslovakia (Czech Republic) 1990-1992." Working Paper, Ceska Narodni Banka Institut Ekonomie.

Köllô, J., K. Fazekas, and G. Nagy. 1993. "Background Paper on Unemployment and Unemployment-Related Expenditures." Institute of Economics, Budapest. Mimeo.

Layard, R., S. Nickell, and R. Jackman. 1991. *Unemployment*. Oxford, U.K.: Oxford University Press.

Lazear, E. 1990. "Job Security Provisions and Unemployment." *Quarterly Journal of Economics* 105: 699-726.

Lindbeck, A., P. Molander, T. Persson, O. Peterson, A. Sandmo, B. Swedenbourg, and N. Tygesen. 1993. "Options for Economic and Political Reform in Sweden." Institute for International Economic Studies, Seminar Paper 540, Stockholm.

Machin, S., and A. Manning. 1992. "Minimum Wages, Wage Dispersion, and Employment: Evidence from the U.K. Wage Councils." Discussion Paper 80, Centre for Economic Performance, London School of Economics, June.

Pissarides, C. 1985. "Short-Run Equilibrium Dynamics of Unemployment, Vacancies, and Real Wages." *American Economic Review* 75: 676-90.

———— 1990. *Equilibrium Unemployment Theory*. London: Basil Blackwell.

Pissarides, C., and J. Wadsworth. 1989. "On the Job Search: Some Empirical Evidence from Britain." Working Paper 1063, Centre for Labor Economics, London School of Economics.

Risager, Ole. 1993. "Labor Substitution in Denmark." *Oxford Bulletin of Economics and Statistics* 55: 123-35.

Rowthorn, R. E. 1993. "Corporatism, Laissez-Faire and the Rise in Unemployment." *Economic European Review* 31: 260-82.

Sachs, J. 1986. "High Unemployment in Europe: Diagnosis and Policy Implications." Working Paper 1830, National Bureau for Economic Research, Cambridge, Mass.

Scarpetta, S., and A. Reuterswand. 1993. "Unemployment Benefits Systems and Active Labor Market Policies in Central and Eastern Europe: An Overview." In *Unemployment in Transition Countries; Transient or Persistent?* Paris: OECD.

Siebert, H. 1992. "German Unification: The Economics of Transition." *Economic Policy* 13: 287-340.

Tarantelli, E. 1986. "The Regulation of Inflation and Unemployment." *Industrial Relations* 25: 1-15.

Uldrichova, V., and Z. Karpisek. 1993. "Labor Market Policy in the Former Czech and Slovak Federal Republic." In *Unemployment in Transition Countries; Transient or Persistent?* Paris: OECD.

Wright, R. 1986. "The Redistributive Roles of Unemployment Insurance and the Dynamics of Voting." *Journal of Public Economics* 31: 377-99.

Wyplosz, C. 1993. "After the Honeymoon: On the Economics and the Politics of Economic Transformation." *European Economic Review Papers and Proceedings* 37: 379-86.

9

Unemployment Dynamics and Labor Market Policies

Tito Boeri

Since the start of transition in Central and Eastern Europe, two conflicting views of the scope of the transformation process and of its social implications have emerged. On the one hand, some have advocated a faster transformation process, involving the immediate closure of many inefficient state enterprises, and hence large-scale labor shedding. High, although it is hoped short-lived, unemployment had to be welcomed according to this view because it induces wage moderation. It would thereby foster the creation of new jobs in the emerging private sector and act as a powerful "disciplining device," potentially leading to labor productivity enhancements in surviving state enterprises. On the other hand, some have argued that the transition should take place with as little unemployment as possible. According to this view, high unemployment creates strong pressures on the budget for unemployment benefits and has little impact on wage moderation and job creation. The employment performance of the private sector is deemed to rely on factors ultimately exogenous to the labor market, such as the availability of finance, the

---

The views expressed herein are those of the author and do not necessarily reflect those of the OECD.

nature and extent of trade protection, regulations on foreign direct investment, and the modernization of productive infrastructure.

Both views are based on the implicit assumption that it is possible to keep the dynamics of unemployment under control by simply increasing or reducing the pace of labor shedding in state enterprises. In particular, by accelerating or postponing the privatization process and by introducing more or less tight regulations on job security (for example, laws on collective dismissals), governments are supposed to be in a position to control the rise of unemployment. After all, the levels reached by unemployment in different transition countries have often been used—more or less explicitly—as indicators of the extent to which the restructuring process has gotten under way.

The recent experience of Central and Eastern European countries shows the fallacy of this assumption. First, unemployment can rise even when inflows are low, but those entering the unemployment pool have very little chance of being reintegrated into work. Second, flows other than those from employment to unemployment can feed the ranks of the unemployed. Especially under conditions where employment reductions are attained mainly through attrition and the freezing of new hires, inflows from out of the labor force—for example, inflows of school-leavers—into unemployment may be important.

The purpose of this chapter is to highlight the main characteristics of unemployment dynamics in Central and Eastern Europe on the basis of information that has only recently become available and to discuss their implications for the design of policies. The first section shows that in spite of the magnitude of job losses and the scope of the restructuring process, inflows into unemployment have been relatively modest and that the rise of unemployment has been associated with its rapidly increasing duration. The second section shows that large flows from employment to out-of-the-labor force involving significant declines of participation rates may account for these relatively small inflow rates. The third section analyzes the capacity of the emerging private sector to absorb unemployment and the factors that may have prevented a higher turnover of the pool. Finally, the last section evaluates the policy response to the rise of unemployment and its increasing duration.

In spite of increasingly diversified adjustment patterns, the focus will be on the features that are shared with varying intensity by all countries. The task of highlighting country-specificities has been dealt with in other chapters in this volume.

Increasing Unemployment and Increasing Duration

High unemployment has already become a basic feature of Central and Eastern European economies. The restructuring process started in most countries only toward the end of 1990 and the beginning of 1991, and yet unemployment rates for the region above OECD average levels were registered as early as at the beginning of 1992 (table 9-1). Furthermore, the gap in unemployment rates between, on the one hand, OECD countries, and, on the other hand, Central and Eastern European countries is continuously increasing. The high incidence of unemployment in transition countries is confirmed by results from the labor force surveys (LFS) introduced in most countries of the region in 1992 and in the first semester of 1993. The rates of unemployment computed on the basis of LFS results are generally remarkably close to those based on counts of the registered unemployed.[1] There is, however, a limited overlap between the two statistical sources—between 60 and 80 percent of the unemployed, according to the survey definitions, declared that they were also being registered at labor offices (see OECD-EUROSTAT 1993 and Boeri 1993 for comparisons between LFS and unemployment register data in transition countries). In other words, between 20 and 40 percent of those registered appear not to be without work, actively looking for a job, and immediately available for work, as required to meet the ILO-OECD definition of unemployment. But also between 20 and 40 percent of those without work, actively looking for a job, and immediately available for work would appear not to be registered as unemployed, possibly because they do not (or no longer) receive unemployment benefits and do not believe that registration can increase the chance to find a job.

A steep rise of unemployment in Central and Eastern Europe was generally predicted, and yet perhaps the factors underlying the growth in the number of jobseekers in transition countries were not fully understood. The common belief was that the growth of unemployment would have been driven by labor shedding in the state sector, and that workers

---

1. Only in the Czech Republic is the survey-based unemployment rate significantly higher than that computed on the basis of registration data. This is in quite striking contrast with evidence from OECD countries where "survey unemployment" is generally lower than "registered unemployment" and could suggest that the tightening of unemployment benefit schemes may have played some role in bringing down the official unemployment rate in the Czech Republic in the course of 1992.

Table 9-1. The Rise of Unemployment in Central and Eastern Europe

(percentage)

	1990				1991				1992				1993	
	IQ	IIQ	IIIQ	IVQ	IQ	IIQ	IIIQ	IVQ	IQ	IIQ	IIIQ	IVQ	IQ	IIQ
Bulgaria	—	0.5	0.9	1.6	3.1	6.2	8.8	11.1	12.2	13.1	15.1	16.4	17.2	16.7
Czech Republic	—	—	—	0.8	1.7	2.7	3.9	4.3	3.8	2.8	2.8	2.8	3.1	2.8
Slovak Republic	—	—	—	1.6	3.8	6.6	10.0	12.5	12.9	12.1	11.5	11.5	13.1	13.5
Hungary	0.6	0.8	1.1	1.5	2.7	3.5	5.5	7.8	10.0	11.4	13.1	14.0	15.1	14.3
Poland	1.5	3.1	5.1	6.1	7.2	8.5	10.6	11.5	12.3	13.1	14.2	14.3	15.1	15.4
Romania	—	—	—	—	—	1.8	2.4	3.0	4.4	5.8	7.4	8.2	9.3	9.1
CCEET average[a]	—	—	—	—	—	2.9	3.9	5.2	7.2	8.4	9.7	10.4	11.6	12.4
OECD average[a]	6.0	5.9	6.1	6.3	6.6	6.8	6.9	7.0	7.2	7.4	7.5	7.6	7.6	7.8

— Not available.

Note: Registered unemployment as a percentage of the labor force. Monthly labor force estimates are obtained by interpolating yearly labor force figures using a compound growth formula. The last benchmark is then held constant until a new benchmark is obtained. Unemployment rates are calculated using the number of registered unemployed in each month over the interpolated labor force figure. The OECD unemployment rate is the average standardized rate of the OECD countries that are found in the OECD *Quarterly Labour Force Statistics* publication.

a. Weighted by the labor force.

Source: OECD-CCEET, Labour Market Database.

released from state enterprises eventually would have been absorbed by similar large flows (although insufficient to prevent the rise of unemployment) from the unemployment ranks to the emerging private sector. In other words, shifts of workers from the state to the private sector were generally considered to be the driving force behind the rise of unemployment (see Aghion and Blanchard 1993 for a model developed along these lines). Given that employment in state enterprises was indeed rapidly falling and that employment in the private sector, however measured, was booming, a large turnover of the unemployment pool was thought to be taking place. Evidence on flows into and out of the unemployment pool has started to become available only more recently and suggests that quite a different relationship between the dynamics of employment and unemployment is at work in these countries.

One of the most striking features of unemployment in Central and Eastern Europe is the small turnover of the unemployment pool. In spite of the depth of structural change, notably of large job losses in state enterprises, inflows into unemployment are low, compared not only with those of high-unemployment OECD countries, but also with those of countries experiencing relatively low unemployment rates, such as Austria and Norway (table 9-2).[2] Nevertheless, unemployment has built up rapidly throughout the region, owing to low numbers of people leaving the unemployment pool each month. In all the countries except the Slovak Republic, it seems to involve less than .8 percent of the labor force each month compared with between 1 and 1.6 percent in the OECD countries for which data are available. Moreover, many of those leaving the unemployment registers appear to leave the labor force altogether, rather than finding a job[3] (third column).

2. The information provided by table 9-2 is drawn from unemployment register data, but the low magnitude of inflows into unemployment in transition countries is also confirmed when the focus is not on new registrations, but on the number of persons that at the time of each labor force survey had experienced unemployment spells shorter than one month. The latter is a lower bound for the total inflows into survey unemployment because some of those who become unemployed may find another job or leave the labor force (that is, they stop actively looking for a job during the reference week) within a month.

3. It should be emphasized that available data on flows from unemployment to employment are dependent on the role played by labor offices in job placement. If most vacancies are filled by private placement agencies, then the number of placements reported by labor offices may seriously underestimate actual outflows to jobs.

Table 9-2. The Turnover of the Unemployment Pool, 1992
(percentage of labor force)

Economy	Monthly inflows[a]		Monthly outflows[b]	Monthly outflows to jobs[c]	Unemployment turnover[d]
	UR	LFS			
Bulgaria	1.6	(1.7)	0.8	0.2	2.4
Czech Republic	0.6	(0.6)	0.8	0.6	1.4
Hungary[e]	0.6	(0.9)	0.6	0.3	1.2
Poland	0.7	(0.9)	0.6	0.3	1.3
Slovak Republic	1.1	(1.0)	1.3	0.6	2.3
East Germany	1.7		1.6	0.6	3.4
West Germany	1.1		1.0	0.4	2.1
Austria	1.5		1.4	0.9	2.8
France (1991)	1.4		1.3	0.5	2.6
Norway (1991)	1.6		1.6	0.8	3.3
United Kingdom (1991)	1.3		1.1	—	2.4

— Data not available.

Note: Average monthly unemployment inflows and outflows, Central and Eastern Europe and in selected OECD countries.

a. The 1992 average monthly inflows into unemployment to labor force (inflow rates estimated on the basis of LFS data are displayed in brackets; for the Czech and Slovak Republics refer to the first LFS (Q1 93); for Bulgaria they are estimated on the basis of the December 1992 population census).

b. The 1992 average monthly outflows from unemployment to the average yearly labor force.

c. The 1992 average monthly number of vacancies filled through the intermediation of the public employment service to the average yearly labor force.

d. Column 1 + column 2.

e. Administrative data on inflows and outflows refer only to unemployment benefit recipients.

The 1992 average yearly share of unemployment benefit recipients to the total unemployed was 78.25.

Source: OECD-CCEET Labour Market Database for data on Central and Eastern European countries. National sources for data on unemployment flows in OECD countries: Germany, BA; Austria, Ministry of Labor; France, ANPE; Norway, Labor Directorate. OECD, ADB for data on working age population and labor force in OECD countries.

Given the small magnitude of inflows and outflows in Central and Eastern Europe, the duration of unemployment is bound to continue to rise, even if unemployment levels were to stabilize at their current levels. The share of jobseekers having experienced unemployment spells longer than twelve months is indeed rapidly increasing throughout the region (table 9-3). In all the countries except the Czech Republic, more than 30 percent of the registered jobseekers would already appear to have been unemployed for at least twelve months, in spite of the relatively short duration of unemployment benefits and the short history of open unemployment in these countries. These figures suggest that *the rise in unemployment in Central and Eastern Europe may lead to a reduced capacity of labor markets to reintegrate a large number of jobseekers into gainful and productive employment.* The experience of OECD countries in the 1980s demonstrates that unemployment tends to be more persistent when its rise is associated with the spread of long-term unemployment.

Table 9-3. The Spread of Long-term Unemployment

Country	Period	Share (percent)	Rate
Bulgaria[a]	1992	50.4	6.1
Czech Republic	1991	3.9	0.2
	1992	17.1	0.4
	Q2 1993	18.1	0.4
Hungary	1991	13.2	1.0
	1992	24.5	3.4
	Q2 1993	32.3	3.5
Poland	1992	30.2	4.8
	Q2 1993	42.9	6.7
Slovak Republic	1991	6.1	0.7
	1992	36.3	3.7
	Q2 1993	32.8	4.1

Note: Long-term unemployment is defined as lasting for twelve months or more.
a. Data on duration are referred only to those with previous work experience.
Source: OECD-CCET Labour Market Database. Bulgaria: population census, December 1992. Czech Republic: 1991 and 1992 data come from the unemployment register; 1993 data come from the LFS. Hungary: all data come from the LFS (1991 data refer to Q1 92). Poland: all data come from the LFS. Slovak Republic: 1991 and 1992 data come from the unemployment register; 1993 data come from the LFS.

In the next two sections an attempt will be made to assess the magnitude of the fall in labor supply in these countries. The focus will be first on trends in labor force participation in the eastern countries. Then reemployment opportunities for those in the unemployment pool will be analyzed.

Declining Labor Force Participation

The disemployment process seems to have proceeded in most countries in three distinct phases. Initially, staff reductions were achieved mainly through attrition and "soft" measures, such as the freezing of new hires,[4] induced retirements, and disciplinary layoffs. The results were a rather moderate initial decline of employment (with the exception of Poland, where employment has been rapidly declining from the very beginning of transition); little rise in the number of unemployed with previous work experience (and conversely a relatively large proportion of unemployed school-leavers);[5] and a relatively large number of workers above the retirement age induced to retire.[6] The next stage included major layoffs of workers, particularly those close to retirement age, and the quite extensive use of invalidity pensions to cope with redundancies. As a result, not only unemployment, but also the number of beneficiaries of early retirements and invalidity pensions started to rise sharply. It is only in the third phase, which has just begun in most countries, that employment reductions seem to be closely associated with inflows into unemployment, rather than flows out of the labor force. Perhaps this is because a further expansion of early retirement schemes is not fiscally sustainable.

Both the hiring freeze that seems to have occurred at the beginning of the transition process (Boeri 1993) and the fact that most of those involved in staff reductions were pushed out of the labor force rather than becoming unemployed have resulted in significant drops in labor force partici-

---

4. For instance, in Poland gross hirings declined by more than 30 percent in the first year of transition (OECD 1993a).

5. The share of school-leavers in total unemployment was relatively large at the beginning of transition, and since then has been declining because of larger inflows of displaced workers and possibly also because of the effects of the tightening of eligibility criteria to unemployment benefits (OECD 1992).

6. For instance, in Hungary the number of "active earners" above the retirement age decreased by almost 200,000 in the two years from December 1990 to January 1993.

pation. As shown in table 9-4, labor force participation rates have dramatically declined in all countries of the region since the start of transition.[7] The case of Bulgaria is particularly striking: in that country not only has a tendency toward the increase in labor force participation prevailing over the 1980s (OECD 1992) been reversed, but a drop in participation of the order of 8 percentage points has also occurred within only two years. In addition, in the Czech and Slovak republics, labor force participation has dramatically decreased since the start of transition. The extensive use of retirement schemes[8] in conjunction with the tightening of the unemployment benefit system has contributed to keeping unemployment at relatively low levels.

It is frequently argued that labor force participation in Central and Eastern European countries was initially so high that a strong decline was inevitable. Gaps in participation rates between OECD countries and Central and Eastern European countries, however, had already narrowed down considerably over the 1980s (OECD 1992), owing to rising participation of women in Western countries. Unfortunately, data displayed in table 9-4 are not comparable across countries because (a) they are based on administrative data on unemployment, which are affected by the degree of tightness of benefits in the different countries, and (b) they use definitions of working-age that are dependent on country-specific definitions of compulsory schooling and retirement age. Two adjustments have therefore been made in table 9-5, partly to improve the cross-country comparability of data on participation. First, unemployment data coming from labor force surveys have been used rather than registration data. Second, a common definition of working-age population has been adopted for all countries (ages fifteen to sixty-four), in spite of significant

---

7.　It should be stressed that series on labor force participation may be affected by the limited coverage of the private sector provided by labor census statistics. A declining trend is also visible, however, when data are drawn (as in the case of Hungary and Poland) from labor force survey data, which also adopt a much broader definition of employment than standard employment series of these countries.

8.　The impact of job losses on unemployment in the Czech Republic has been reduced significantly by extensive use of early retirement (70,000 beneficiaries at the end of 1992, according to the Czech Labor Ministry) and by the dismissal of working pensioners (who accounted for about 6 percent of total employment at the end of 1991, down from more than 10 percent in 1989).

Table 9-4. The Decline of Labor Force Participation Rates
(labor force as percentage of the working-age population)

Country	Period	Total	Male	Female
Bulgaria	1990	82	77	87
	1992	74	67	80
Czech Republic	1990	86	90	74
	1992	80	87	66
Hungary	1990	83	86	80
	1992	74	77	70
	1993	71	74	67
Poland	1989	76	82	69
	1992	74	81	68
	1993	71	79	64
Slovak Republic	1990	84	91	76
	1992	73	79	66

Note: Working-age population is defined according to national definitions of retirement age: men fifteen to sixty; women fifteen to fifty-five.
Source: Bulgaria: all data come from the labor census and include the private sector. Czech Republic: all data on the labor force come from "Main Economic Indicators of the Czech Republic," Research Institute of Labor and Social Affairs (1993). Hungary: data on the labor force in 1990 come from the labor census and the unemployment register; data on 1992 and 1993 come from the LFS. Poland: data on the labor force in 1989 come from the labor census; data on 1992 and 1993 from the LFS. Slovak Republic: all data come from the labor census and include the private sector.

differences in national regulations on retirement and compulsory schooling age.[9]

Bearing the above caveats in mind, table 9-5 suggests that labor supply in relation to the size of the population may indeed already be lower in transition countries than in OECD countries.[10] Differences in participa-

---

9. The proposed definition (population between ages fifteen and sixty-four) fits the conditions of most OECD countries better than those of transition countries, where the age of retirement is notoriously low by Western standards. Yet choosing a common definition provides a better basis for assessing the capacity of economies to mobilize labor supply.

10. Only in Hungary does the proposed labor force participation measure appear to be higher than in OECD countries, but this is because for this country LFS data were available at the time of writing only for those aged between fifteen and sixty.

Table 9-5. International Comparisons of Labor Force Participation Rates *(percentage)*

Economy	Period	Total	Male	Female
Hungary[a]	1992	73.2	77.0	69.5
Poland[b]	1992	71.3	78.5	64.4
Slovak Republic[c]	Q2 1993	68.7	79.1	58.5
Czech Republic[c]	Q2 1993	69.0	72.0	65.8
OECD total	1991	71.3	82.4	60.5
OECD Europe	1991	66.6	78.3	54.0

Note: Labor force as percentage of the population between fifteen and sixty-four, LFS data.
a. Data on labor force and working-age refer only to persons between fifteen and sixty.
b. Data referred to the first published LFS (Q2 92)
c. Data on labor force come from the first LFS (Q2 93)
Source: OECD-CCET Labour Market Database for data on Central and Eastern European countries; *Employment Outlook* (1993) for data on OECD countries.

tion are less marked when comparisons are made with Western European countries (whose average participation rate was 67 percent in 1991) and when the focus is on participation among women. Regulations aimed at reducing labor supply (for example, in addition to early retirements and invalidities, measures such as tax penalties for firms employing workers above the retirement age) seem to have been a factor in reducing labor force participation among men. Discouragement from job search, especially of those close to retirement age, may have been another factor.[11]

Overall, small inflows into unemployment are, in these countries, the by-product of large flows from employment to out-of-the-labor force. Employment reductions have involved quite dramatic falls in labor force participation rates that may be very difficult to reverse. This fall in participation may be undesirable in the medium term, if not in the short run,

---

11. Data on "discouraged workers"—estimated on the basis of the quarterly LFS—point to nonnegligible numbers of persons without a job and not actively engaged in job search. According to the Hungarian LFS, for instance, in the second quarter of 1993 about one in four persons without a job was not actively engaged in job search.

especially under the conditions of these countries where the old age dependency ratio is increasing.

Are the Unemployed Reemployable?

Low outflows from unemployment, and particularly low outflows from unemployment to employment, suggest that it may be particularly difficult to absorb unemployment in these countries even in "good times." To put it another way, the growth of unemployment could by itself be a factor leading to a fall in effective labor supply. As long as the unemployed are particularly difficult to reemploy, even the buildup of a large unemployment stock may have little impact on the dynamics of wages, and hence on the job-generation process.

Because one of the salient features of economic restructuring in Central and Eastern Europe is the shift of workers from the state to the private sector, one would expect reemployment opportunities for the unemployed to be concentrated in the private sector. Available evidence suggests that gross job creation in the private sector has indeed been substantial. Figure 9-1 displays changes that have occurred in the distribution of employment between public and private sectors against the background of aggregate employment declines (all magnitudes are expressed as percentages of employment in the base year). Given the limited coverage provided by statistics in these countries of the small business sector, where most of the job creation in the private sector is concentrated, available figures are likely to underestimate employment in the private sector. Nevertheless, figure 9-1 shows that the share of employment in private enterprises has rapidly increased in all countries, and this is not simply because of a drop of employment in the state sector, but also because of the actual expansion of private sector employment.

In spite of its rapid growth, the private sector has so far played a relatively small role in absorbing unemployment. On the one hand, results from household surveys in Hungary, the Czech Republic, and Slovakia[12] suggest that most workers have moved directly from the state to the pri-

12. See Köllô 1993 and Vecernik 1993 for, respectively, a description of the main results of the Household Panel Survey in Hungary and of the Survey on Economic Expectations and Attitudes of the Population in the former CSFR. As discussed in Boeri 1993, both surveys suggest that most shifts of workers from the public to the private sector occurred without any intervening unemployment spell.

Figure 9-1. Public-Private Shifts and Employment Decline

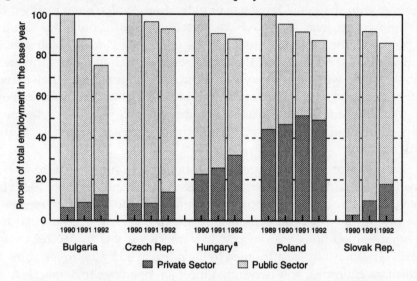

a. Estimates based on the Household Panel Surveys from 1991 and 1992.
Source: OECD-CCET Labour Market Database.

vate sector without experiencing any intervening spell of joblessness. On the other hand, microeconomic evidence indicates that while the public sector still plays a dominant role in hiring people from the unemployment ranks,[13] the private sector is often a net contributor to the unemployment pool.[14]

Why do private employers prefer hiring workers employed in the state sector, rather than recruiting them, possibly at lower cost, from the unemployment ranks? Perhaps it is because the private employers in these countries have little information regarding the characteristics of jobseekers and that those who have lost their job are often considered not to

---

13. According to the Hungarian Household Panel Survey, more than 10 percent of the unemployed found a job in the public sector over the year between March 1991 and 1992, compared with about 5 percent in the private sector.
14. As documented in OECD 1993, a large share of the unemployed in Poland come from the nonagricultural private sector. The chapter on Hungary in this book shows—based on results from the 1992 Hungarian Household Panel Survey (HHP)—that in Hungary net flows from the private sector to the unemployment pool have been negative. Preliminary results from the 1993 HHP would seem to confirm such a finding (OECD 1993a).

be "high-quality" workers. The selective nature of the disemployment process, with the initial large use of individual layoffs, often justified by disciplinary reasons, may have supported this sort of prejudice. On the supply side, the passive attitudes of the unemployed toward job search, and perhaps the belief that the state sector should and will ultimately provide them with jobs,[15] may have been a factor in reducing flows from unemployment to employment in the private sector. Additional factors are the little information available to the unemployed on employment opportunities in the private sector and the obstacles to geographical and skill mobility.

Estimates of matching functions in transition countries (Burda 1993; Boeri 1993) would also suggest that increasing demand for labor has relatively little impact on flows from unemployment to jobs. Notwithstanding problems with vacancy data in these countries, it appears that the elasticity of job finds with respect to vacancies is low by Western standards. This may also be attributed to the role played by job-to-job shifts in transition countries, and hence that most job openings may be taken by those who are searching for jobs while still employed. Inherited lax work discipline or, more important, reduced working time, may make it easier for those employed in the state sector to search for a job while keeping their posts. Another possible explanation for the small effect of vacancies on job finds is in the mismatch between the regional distribution of job-seekers and that of the unemployed. Particularly in transition countries—where there are major housing shortages and other kinds of barriers to mobility—regional mismatch may be an important factor preventing increased demand for labor from having a significant impact on flows from unemployment to employment.[16] Another factor that may have negatively affected outflows to jobs is the spread of long-term unemployment. A large pool of long-term unemployment may by itself reduce outflow rates if the increasing duration of unemployment is associated with the loss of skills (Pissarides 1992) and lower search intensity, or if employ-

---

15. The term "postsocialised" unemployment is often used in Poland to describe conditions where a significant portion of the unemployed are not actively seeking new employment opportunities and are still convinced that the public sector should provide them with a job.

16. As shown in Boeri 1993, common measures of regional mismatch in Central and Eastern Europe point to a steep increase in discrepancies between the regional dispersion of unemployment and vacancies since the start of the transition process. (See also the chapter on Poland in this volume.)

ers use the length of unemployment as a screening device (Meager and Metcalf 1987; Blanchard and Diamond 1990).

There is some evidence of negative effects of unemployment durations on job finds in Central and Eastern Europe. First, regressions of outflows to jobs against vacancies and two separate unemployment pools—the short-term unemployed and the long-term unemployed—show that an increase in the number of those unemployed for a relatively short period greatly stimulates outflows to jobs, whereas a larger number of long-term unemployed has little, if any, effect on job finds[17] (Boeri 1993). Second, longitudinal data from the quarterly Hungarian labor force surveys show that exit to job probabilities are decreasing with the length of unemployment spells, even when control is provided for basic socioeconomic characteristics of the unemployed (Boeri 1993). This points to the presence of forms of "negative duration dependence" in transitions from unemployment to employment.

In sum, despite significant job creation in the private sector, an unemployed person has relatively little chance to find a job. Thus the growth of unemployment is itself a source of decline in effective labor supply. Low exit-to-job probabilities may be caused partly by the importance of on-the-job search, and incumbents have more of a chance to find a job in the emerging private sector than those coming from the unemployment ranks, which would also explain the low elasticity of outflows to jobs to vacancies observed in Central and Eastern Europe. Another factor negatively affecting flows from unemployment to employment is regional mismatch in a context where labor mobility is often prevented by housing shortages, if not sociocultural ties.

Whatever the reason for the low flows from unemployment to employment in transition countries, matters may improve over time as

---

17. Boeri 1993 estimated a matching function of the form:

$$0 = AV^a[wU_{st}^{-\rho} + (1-w)U_{lt}^{-\rho}]^{-v/\rho}$$

where subscripts distinguish the short-term (*st*) from the long-term (*lt*) unemployed. By taking logarithms and linearizing around $\rho=0$, one obtains the estimated equation from which it is then possible to recover the underlying "distributional" parameter *w*. A value of this parameter greater than .5 suggests that outflows to jobs are more responsive to an increase in the number of short-term unemployed than to a rise in the number of long-term unemployed. The estimated values of *w* ranged from .6 in the Czech Republic, to .7 in Poland, and .9 in the Slovak Republic. In Hungary the elasticity of job finds with respect to the stock of long-term unemployed was negative, but not significant at conventional levels.

long as labor markets operate more efficiently and economic recovery gets under way. Emerging labor markets may display little turnover of the pool, but flows out of unemployment may pick up significantly as soon as new labor market institutions—for example, more flexible labor contracts—are put in place. The crucial issue is therefore: will matters improve quickly enough to prevent a further increase in the share of long-term unemployment?

Some indications on whether and how rapidly the job matching process is improving in Central and Eastern Europe can be obtained by looking at the estimated residuals of matching functions in transition countries, which should tentatively capture "technological progress" in job matching. Figure 9-2 displays the estimated coefficients of time dummies in pooled time-series and cross-section (regional-level data were available in all countries) regressions of outflows to jobs against the stocks of unemployment and vacancies in different Central and Eastern European countries.[18] As shown by the figure, an increasing trend is visible only in the case of the Czech and Slovak republics and may be attributed partly to the implementation on a large-scale of active labor market policies since 1992. In other countries, a clear trend is not emerging, although some quite marked seasonal patterns are apparent—for example, related to the effects of the entry of large cohorts of school-leavers at the beginning of the third quarter each year.

In conclusion, there are not clear signs of greater efficiency in job matching in Central and Eastern Europe that could make it easier to absorb unemployment in "good times." Meanwhile, the duration of unemployment is rapidly increasing, and this sets in motion a self-fulfilling phenomenon: the larger the share of unemployment that is long term, the lower the outflows for given levels of unemployment and vacancies.

The Policy Response

The above suggests that not only high unemployment but also high *long-term* unemployment may become permanent features of these countries. To what extent are labor market policies in these countries adequate to cope with the spread of long-term unemployment? Can they succeed in redistributing employment opportunities to reduce the risk of marginalization of a large segment of the labor force?

---

18. See Boeri 1993 for details on the data and on the estimation procedure.

Figure 9-2. Fixed-Time Effects[a]

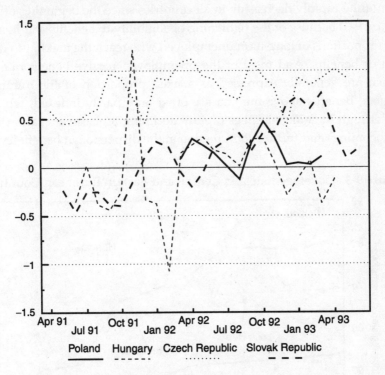

a. The estimated coefficients of time-dummies in pooled regressions of outflows to jobs on the stock of vacancies and unemployment.
Source: Boeri 1993.

Within less than three years, Central and Eastern European countries have succeeded in introducing a rich menu of policy instruments to combat unemployment (OECD 1992; Scarpetta, Boeri, and Reuterswand 1993). Not only have unemployment benefit systems been put in place that aim at improving the sharing across society at large of the costs of unemployment, but a legal basis (if not always an adequate delivery mechanism) for a diversified package of active labor market policies has also been established. Needless to say, similar developments in the OECD area have occurred over several decades.

Unemployment benefit systems in transition countries do not seem to be as generous as sometimes claimed by the literature (Jackman and Layard 1990; Layard 1990; Burda 1993). Neither do they appear to discourage job search on the part of the unemployed. The coverage of these schemes has been quite rapidly decreasing in all countries since the beginning of 1992 (figure 9-3) because of the tightening of eligibility to benefits and increasing proportions of long-term unemployed who reach the maximum duration of benefits. And most of the unemployed receive benefit minima, which are generally expressed as a fixed proportion of the minimum wage.[19] Benefits above minima are often only partly indexed, which—under high inflation—implies rapidly declining replacement rates (Boeri forthcoming) and further compression in the dispersion of benefit levels.

Figure 9-3. Coverage Rates[a] in Central and Eastern European Countries

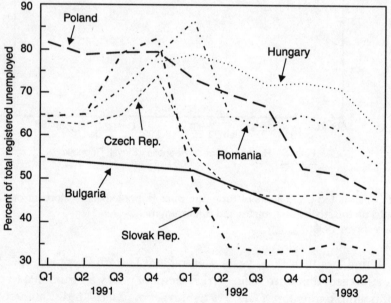

a. Share of registered unemployed receiving benefits; unemployment register data.
Source: OECD-CCET *Short-term Economic Indicators.*

---

19. In Bulgaria unemployment benefits cannot be lower than 90 percent of the minimum wage, in Hungary 96 percent, and in Romania 40 percent. In the Czech and Slovak republics there are no minima, while in Poland the flat rate system introduced at the end of 1991 sets, in practice, unemployment benefits at the level of the minimum wage.

If unemployment benefit systems do not reduce incentives to job search,[20] a problem that is becoming increasingly important is their failure to provide income support to the long-term unemployed. The maximum duration of benefits is generally lower in Eastern than in Western Europe,[21] and the transition from unemployment benefits to social assistance is neither automatic, nor does it often provide enough income support. As estimated in Scarpetta, Boeri, and Reuterswand (1993), replacement rates for the average earning group may fall to less than 20 percent in countries such as Bulgaria after the transition to social assistance.

As mentioned above, a legal basis for a wide-ranging set of *active labor market policy* instruments has been established in all Central and Eastern European countries. An adequate delivery mechanism for such policies, however, is only gradually developing. Labor offices are generally understaffed and little staff time is devoted to job placement activities and to the selection of participants for active programs. The administration of unemployment benefits takes most of the staff's time, which means that activities targeted to the long-term unemployed falling out of the benefit system are rather limited. In some cases even formal rules prevent the long-term unemployed from having access to measures aimed at reintegrating the unemployed into work.[22]

In addition to these implementation problems, which are preventing the targeting of active labor market measures to the long-term unemployed, the labor market policy mix that is prevailing in most countries is not always well-tailored to cope with the needs of those with longer unemployment duration. Figure 9-4 compares participant inflows in active labor market policies across transition countries and selected OECD countries. The comparison suggests that transition countries are devoting relatively more resources to wage subsidies to employers (gen-

---

20. Tests of stability of matching functions before and after the tightening of unemployment benefit systems do not point to changes in the relationship between, on the one hand, outflows to jobs and, on the other hand, vacancies and unemployment (Burda 1993; Boeri forthcoming).

21. After regulatory changes introduced from the end of 1991 to the beginning of 1992, the duration of unemployment benefits cannot exceed six months in the Czech Republic and in Slovakia, nine months in Romania, and twelve months in Poland, Bulgaria, and Hungary. In most OECD countries benefit duration is no shorter than one year.

22. In the case of Bulgaria, for instance, only unemployment benefit recipients are eligible to training, which clearly excludes the "exhaustees" as well as workers who have received notification of group dismissals.

erally targeted to the school-leavers) and less resources to training than OECD countries.

This concentration of efforts on job subsidy schemes may be questioned, not least because the experience of OECD countries (OECD 1993b) suggests that subsidies to regular employment in the private sector tend to generate heavy "deadweight" costs and relevant "substitution effects."[23] Furthermore, given the spread of long-term unemployment and the limited coverage offered by unemployment benefit schemes to those with long unemployment duration, it may be preferable to target labor market policies to the long-term unemployed rather than to new entrants in the labor market. Training schemes and public work programs are generally used in OECD countries to promote the reintegration into work of the long-term unemployed. In spite of earlier plans to expand the coverage of public work programs in transition countries, the expansion of such programs so far has met with many obstacles because of the administrative and resource constraints on the part of local administrations that are supposed to contribute to the organization and financing of these schemes.

Labor market policies in most transition countries are financed through payroll taxes earmarked to extra-budgetary funds. Budgetary transfers covering the deficits of these funds are also quite significant in most of these countries. The necessary fiscal restraint and the impossibility of further raising contribution rates of employers and employees[24] mean that clear priorities in the allocation of resources for active labor market policies need to be established and that improvements in the cost-effectiveness of the different policy instruments should be pursued. As mentioned above, there may be a case for targeting policies to the long-term unemployed. Deadweight costs could be reduced especially if, as

---

23. The "deadweight" element alone has been estimated in a number of microeconomic studies to exceed one-half of total participation in the programs; that is, over half of the participants would probably have obtained work regardless of the subsidies. Substitution effects, related to the displacement of other workers, were also quite significant (OECD 1993b).

24. As discussed in OECD 1993a, a more viable strategy to raise more resources for labor market policies would be to expand the tax base by introducing stricter controls of the reporting of earnings in the private sector or to shift resources across the "social sphere" at large (including education).

Figure 9-4. Participants Entering Active Labor Market Programs, Central and Eastern European Countries and Selected OECD Countries, 1992

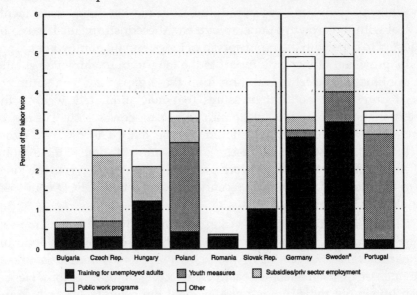

a. 1991-92.
Source: OECD Employment Outlook, 1993; national submissions.

seems to be the case, the short-term unemployed on average have a greater chance of finding work even without support.[25]

Concluding Remarks

Economic restructuring in Central and Eastern Europe has involved not only rising unemployment, but also the buildup of a large pool of long-term unemployed. Increased job creation in the private sector has not always proved capable of absorbing unemployment. Contrary to a priori expectations, most shifts of workers from the state to the private sector often take place without persons experiencing spells of joblessness. Although this may seem to be, prima facie, a rather encouraging feature of labor market adjustment in these countries, the spread of long-term unemployment, combined with rapidly decreasing labor force participa-

25. The short-term unemployed, however, may also be more job-motivated, and hence most ready to benefit from training and similar measures.

tion, may become a heavy burden facing the capacity of economies to recover from recessions.

While all countries have introduced labor market policy instruments to deal with the growth of unemployment, these instruments need to be adjusted to cope with the rapid spread of long-term unemployment. Gaps in the provision of income support to the long-term unemployed should be minimized. Hardship resulting from these gaps may be a source of social unrest and political pressures that may ultimately weaken the determination of governments to pursue reforms consistently. The mix of active labor policy measures should also be refined in order to avoid excluding the most "difficult cases." The targeting of some of the existing schemes (for example, public work programs, if not training) to the long-term unemployed, along with recent developments in OECD countries, should also be considered.

Clearly, labor market policies cannot by themselves solve the problem. They seem often to work by simply redistributing employment opportunities rather than by creating new jobs. But the spread of long-term unemployment is by itself a factor negatively affecting outflows to jobs. Hence, even by simply redistributing employment opportunities to reduce the spread of the distribution of unemployment by duration may have positive effects on the pace at which economies absorb unemployment.

Bibliography

Aghion, P., and O. Blanchard. 1993. *On the Speed of Transition in Central Europe.* EBRD Working Papers, No. 6, London.

Blanchard, O., and P. Diamond. 1990. "The Aggregate Matching Function." In P. Diamond, ed., *Productivity, Growth, Unemployment.* Cambridge, Mass.: MIT Press.

Boeri, T. 1993. "Labor Market Flows and the Persistence of Unemployment in Central and Eastern Europe." Paper presented at the OECD Workshop, "The Persistence of Unemployment in CEECs," Paris, September.

————. Forthcoming. "Transitional Unemployment." In *Economics of Transition.*

Burda, M. 1993. "Unemployment, Labor Markets and Structural Change in Eastern Europe." *Economic Policy* 16.

Jackman, R., and R. Layard 1990. "Social Policy and Unemployment." Paper presented at the OECD-World Bank Conference on "The Transition to a Market Economy in Central and Eastern Europe," Paris, November.

Köllô, J. 1993. "Unemployment and Unemployment-Related Expenditures." Report for the Blue Ribbon Commission, Budapest, May.

Layard, R. 1990. *Economic Change in Poland.* Working Paper No. 3, London School of Economics, Centre for Economic Performance.

Meager, N., and H. Metcalf. 1987. *Recruitment of the Long-term Unemployed.* Institute of Manpower Studies, Report No. 138.

OECD. 1992. *Employment Outlook.* Paris.

———. 1993a. *The Labor Market in Poland.* Paris.

———. 1993b. *Employment Outlook.* Paris.

OECD-EUROSTAT. 1993. *Employment and Unemployment in Economies in Transition: Conceptual and Measurement Issues.* Paris.

Pissarides, C. 1992. *Search Theory at Twenty-one.* Centre for Economic Performance Discussion Papers, No. 90.

Scarpetta, S., T. Boeri, and A. Reuterswand. 1993. "Unemployment Benefit Systems and Active Labor Market Policies in Central and Eastern Europe: An Overview." Paper presented at the OECD Workshop, "The Persistence of Unemployment in CEECs," Paris, September 1993.

Vecernik, J. 1993. "Czechoslovakia and the Czech Republic in 1990-93." Institute of Sociology, Academy of Sciences, Prague. Mimeo.

Index

(Page numbers in italics refer to nontext material.)